# Grand Blue Dreaming 8

**PRESENTED BY KENJI INOUE & KIMITAKE YOSHIOKA**

# The Colorful Cast of Grand Blue Dreaming

## Diving Club Peek-a-Boo (PaB)

**Iori Kitahara**
An Izu U first-year staying in a detached room at the Kotegawa Home. Can't swim.

"I'M STILL NOT AS TAINTED AS YOU THINK!"

**Kohei Imamura**
An Izu U first-year. Handsome, but a diehard otaku.

"I MIGHT NOT LOOK LIKE IT, BUT I USED TO BE A HUGE OTAKU."

"SHOULD I STEP ON HIM WHILE I'M AT IT?"

"MY ALBUM'S COVERED IN MOSAICS!"

**Aina Yoshiwara**
A first-year at Oumi U. Also known as "Cakey."

**Chisa Kotegawa**
An Izu U first-year and Iori's cousin.

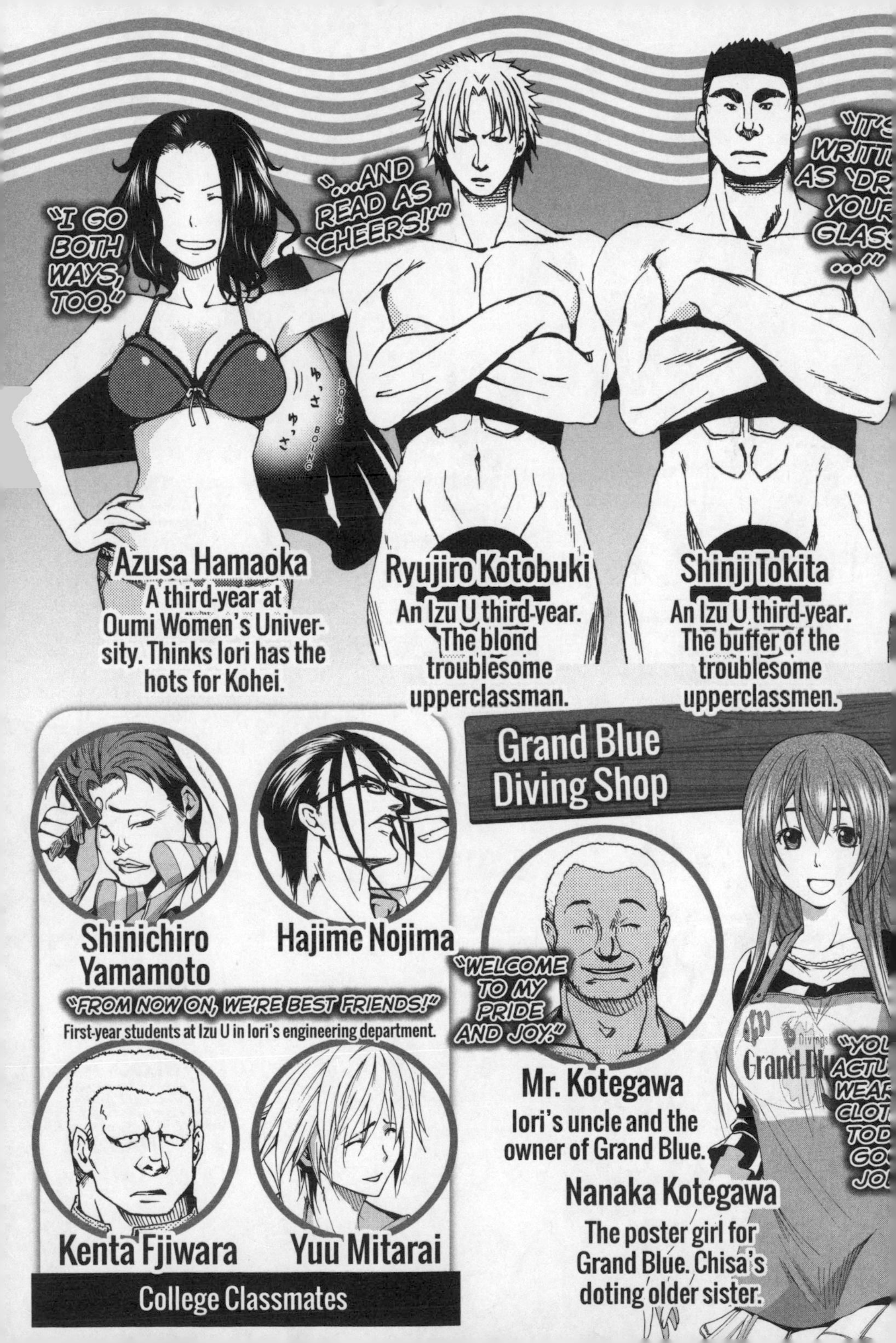

“IT'S WRITT AS ‘DR YOUR GLAS ...’”
Shinji Tokita
An Izu U third-year. The buffer of the troublesome upperclassmen.
“...AND READ AS ‘CHEERS!’”
Ryujiro Kotobuki
An Izu U third-year. The blond troublesome upperclassman.
“I GO BOTH WAYS, TOO.”
BOING BOING
Azusa Hamaoka
A third-year at Oumi Women's University. Thinks Iori has the hots for Kohei.
Grand Blue Diving Shop
“YOU ACTU WEAR CLOT TOD GO JO
Grand Blue
Nanaka Kotegawa
The poster girl for Grand Blue. Chisa's doting older sister.
“WELCOME TO MY PRIDE AND JOY.”
Mr. Kotegawa
Iori's uncle and the owner of Grand Blue.
College Classmates
Hajime Nojima
Shinichiro Yamamoto
“FROM NOW ON, WE'RE BEST FRIENDS!”
First-year students at Izu U in Iori's engineering department.
Yuu Mitarai
Kenta Fjiwara

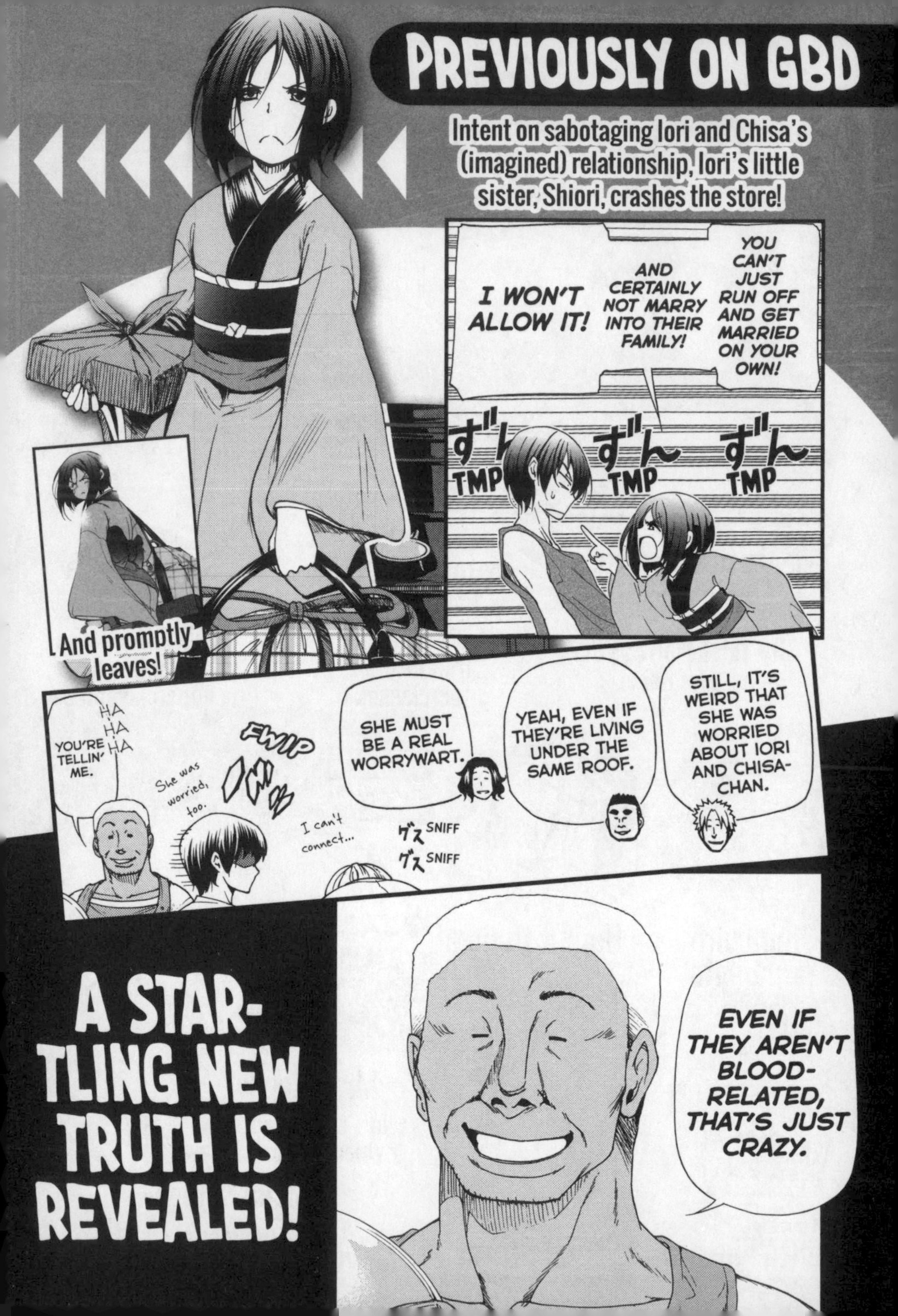
PREVIOUSLY ON GBD
Intent on sabotaging Iori and Chisa's (imagined) relationship, Iori's little sister, Shiori, crashes the store!
YOU CAN'T JUST RUN OFF AND GET MARRIED ON YOUR OWN!
AND CERTAINLY NOT MARRY INTO THEIR FAMILY!
I WON'T ALLOW IT!
ずん TMP
ずん TMP
ずん TMP
And promptly leaves!
STILL, IT'S WEIRD THAT SHE WAS WORRIED ABOUT IORI AND CHISA-CHAN.
YEAH, EVEN IF THEY'RE LIVING UNDER THE SAME ROOF.
SHE MUST BE A REAL WORRYWART.
グス SNIFF
グス SNIFF
I can't connect...
FWIP
She was worried, too.
HA HA HA
YOU'RE TELLIN' ME.
EVEN IF THEY AREN'T BLOOD-RELATED, THAT'S JUST CRAZY.
A STAR-TLING NEW TRUTH IS REVEALED!

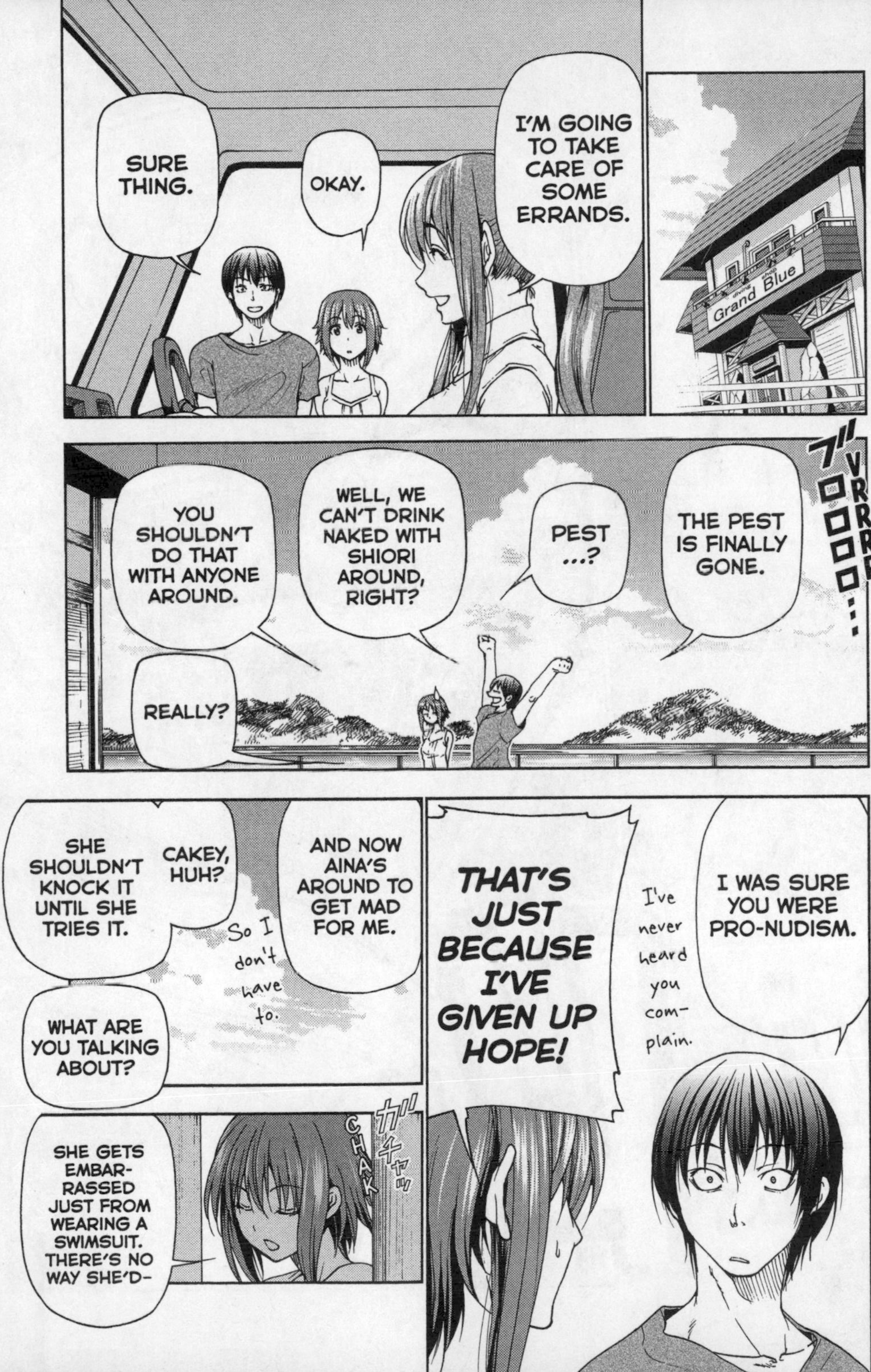
diving shop
Grand Blue
I'M GOING TO TAKE CARE OF SOME ERRANDS.
OKAY.
SURE THING.
ブロロロ…
VRRRR
THE PEST IS FINALLY GONE.
PEST...?
WELL, WE CAN'T DRINK NAKED WITH SHIORI AROUND, RIGHT?
YOU SHOULDN'T DO THAT WITH ANYONE AROUND.
REALLY?
I WAS SURE YOU WERE PRO-NUDISM.
I've never heard you com-plain.
THAT'S JUST BECAUSE I'VE GIVEN UP HOPE!
AND NOW AINA'S AROUND TO GET MAD FOR ME.
So I don't have to.
CAKEY, HUH?
SHE SHOULDN'T KNOCK IT UNTIL SHE TRIES IT.
WHAT ARE YOU TALKING ABOUT?
ガチャッ
CHAK
SHE GETS EMBAR-RASSED JUST FROM WEARING A SWIMSUIT. THERE'S NO WAY SHE'D-

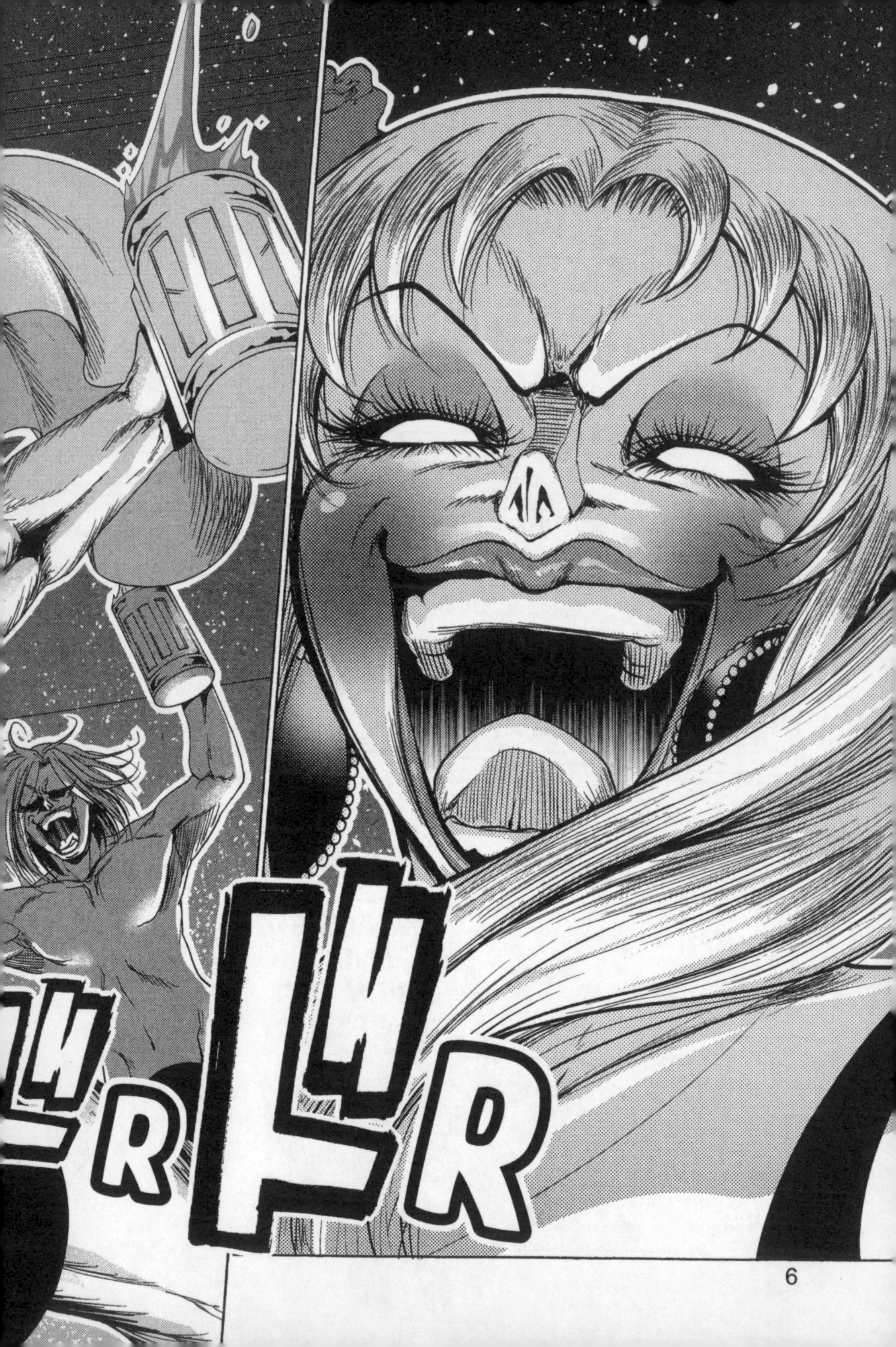
WHR
WHR

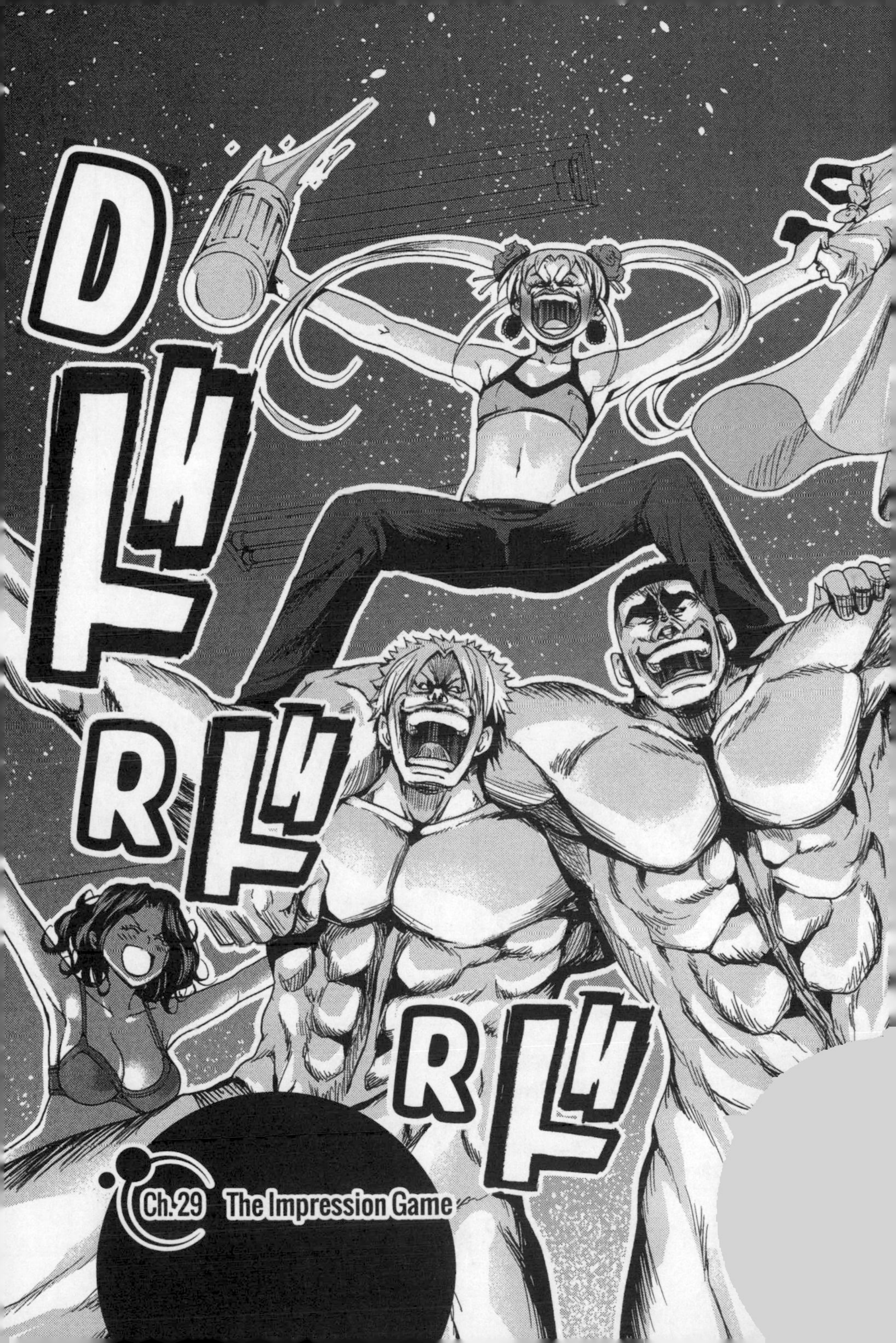
DWAAH
RWAAH
RWAAH
Ch.29 The Impression Game

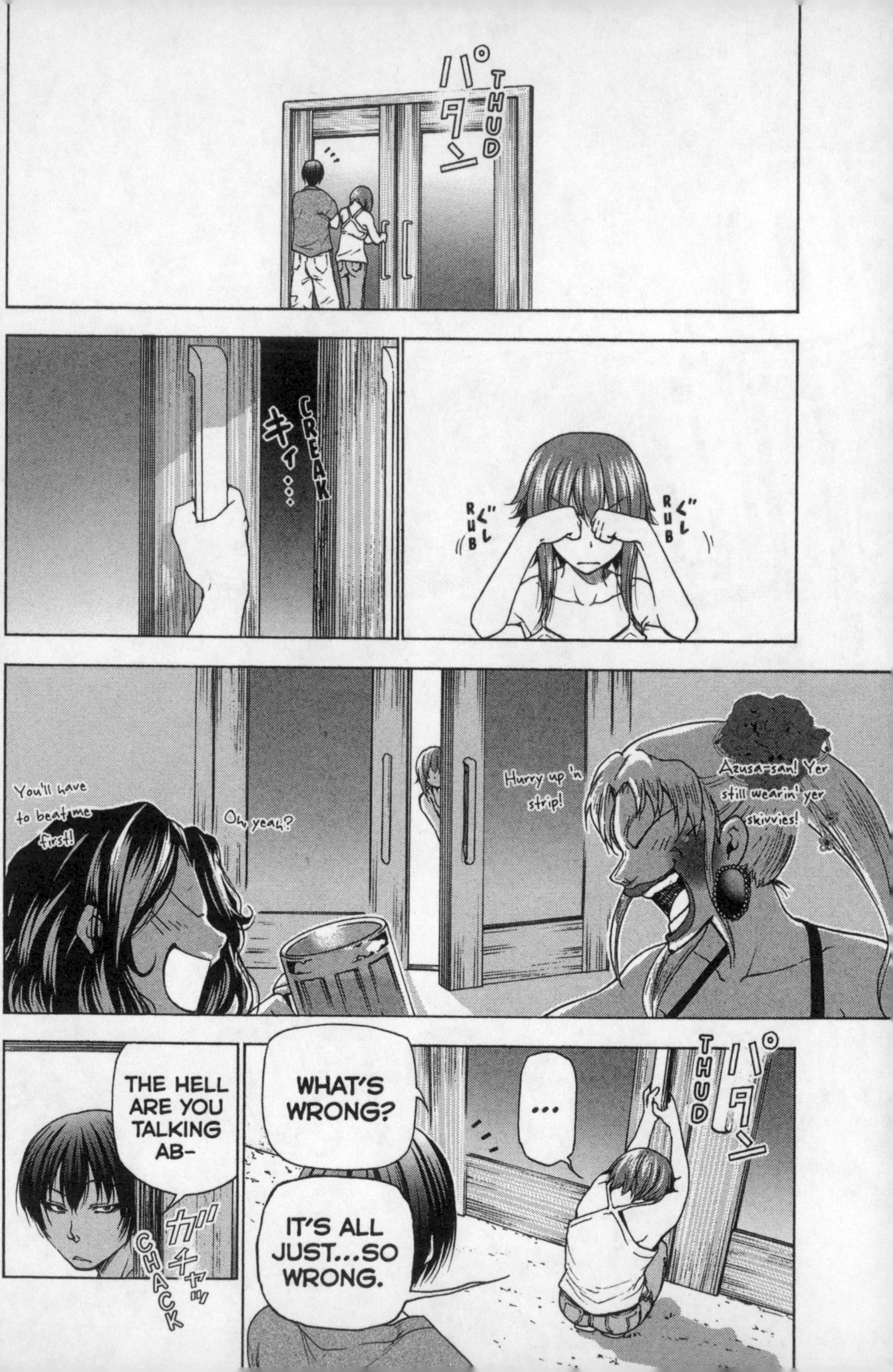

パタン
THUD
ぐし
RUB
ぐし
RUB
キィ…
CREAK
Azusa-san! Yer still wearin' yer skivvies!
Hurry up 'n strip!
Oh yeah?
You'll have to beat me first!
パタン
THUD
...
WHAT'S WRONG?
IT'S ALL JUST...SO WRONG.
THE HELL ARE YOU TALKING AB-
ガチャッ
CHACK

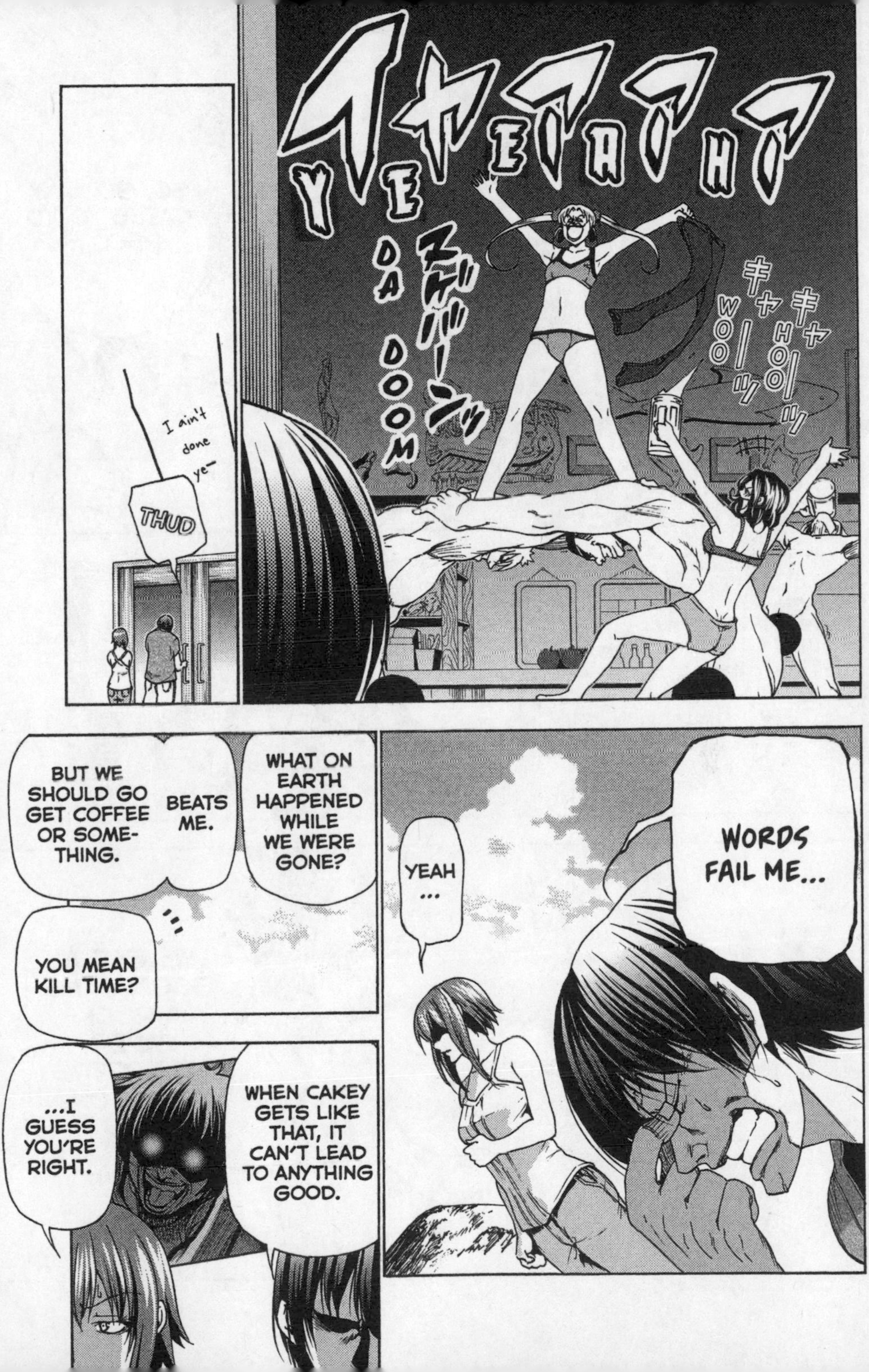

イヤアアア
YEEIAIHI
ズゲゲーンッ
DA DOOOM
キャホーーッ
HOO
キャーーッ
WOO
I ain't done ye—
THUD
WORDS FAIL ME...
YEAH ...
WHAT ON EARTH HAPPENED WHILE WE WERE GONE?
BEATS ME.
BUT WE SHOULD GO GET COFFEE OR SOME-THING.
YOU MEAN KILL TIME?
WHEN CAKEY GETS LIKE THAT, IT CAN'T LEAD TO ANYTHING GOOD.
...I GUESS YOU'RE RIGHT.

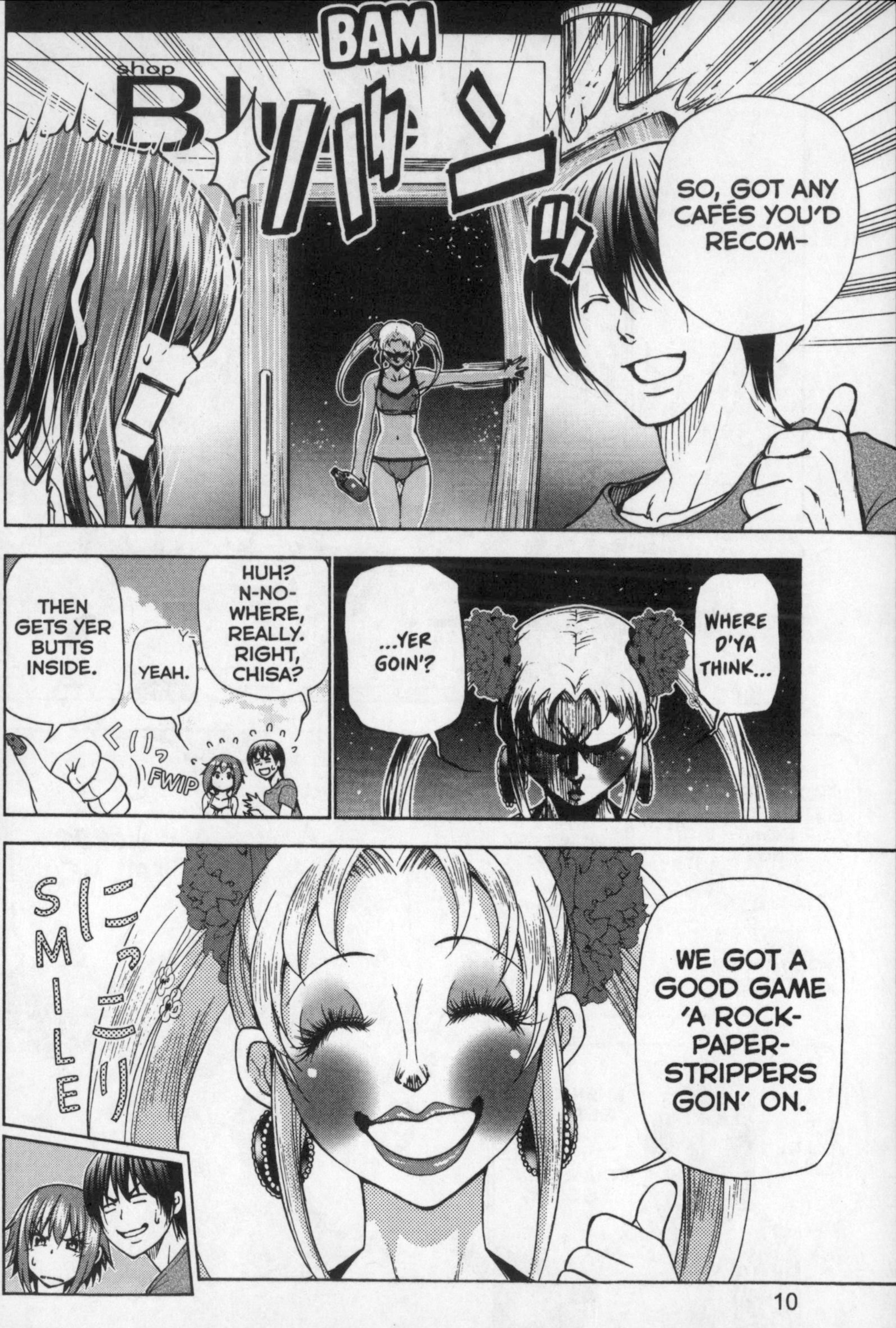
BAM
shop B
SO, GOT ANY CAFÉS YOU'D RECOM–
WHERE D'YA THINK...
...YER GOIN'?
HUH? N-NO-WHERE, REALLY. RIGHT, CHISA?
Y- YEAH.
THEN GETS YER BUTTS INSIDE.
FWIP
WE GOT A GOOD GAME 'A ROCK-PAPER-STRIPPERS GOIN' ON.
SMILE

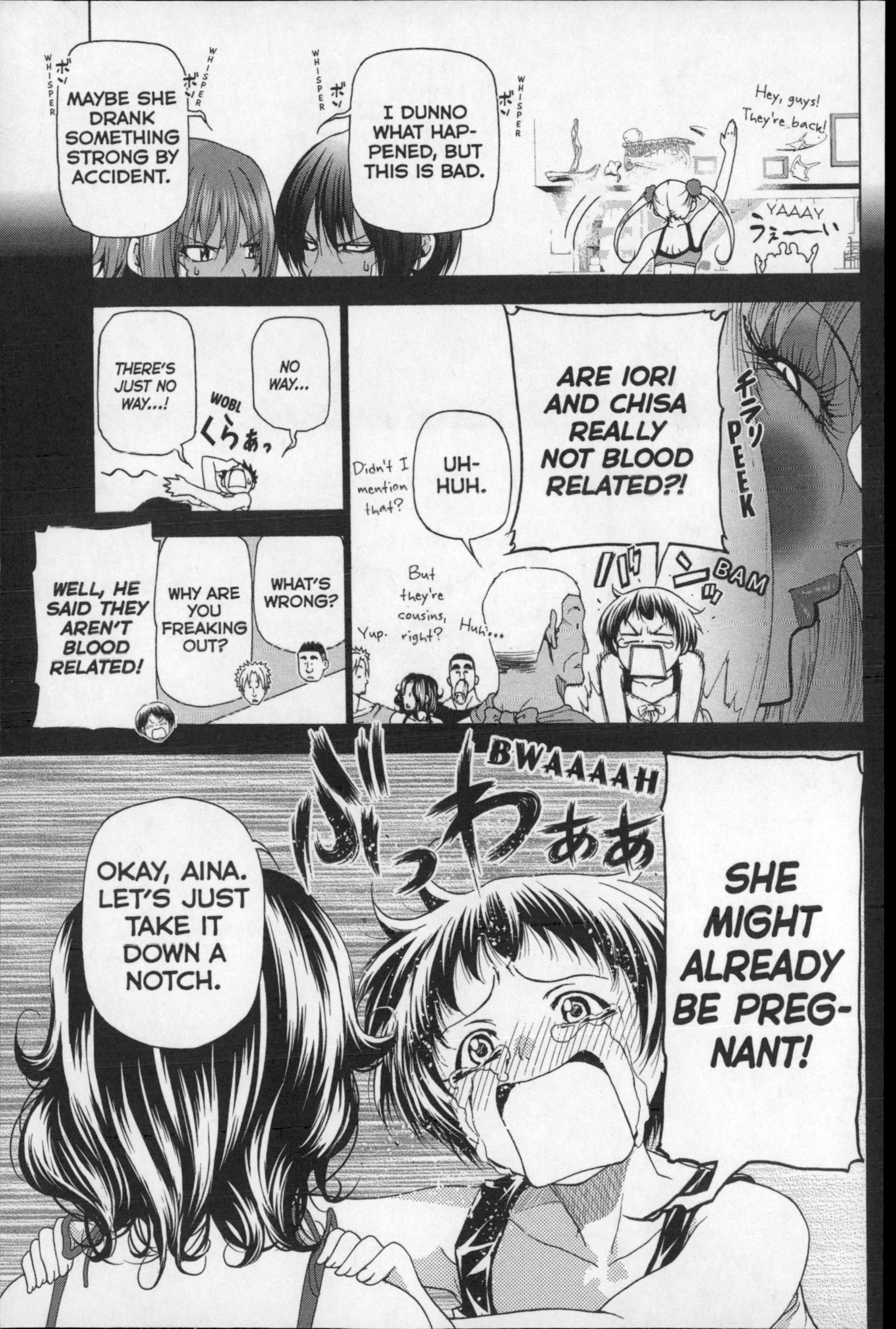
Hey, guys! They're back!
YAAAY
うぇーい
WHISPER ボソ
WHISPER ボソ
I DUNNO WHAT HAPPENED, BUT THIS IS BAD.
WHISPER ボソ
WHISPER ボソ
MAYBE SHE DRANK SOMETHING STRONG BY ACCIDENT.
チラリ PEEK
ARE IORI AND CHISA REALLY NOT BLOOD RELATED?!
バン BAM
UH-HUH.
Didn't I mention that?
But they're cousins, right?
Huh...
Yup.
NO WAY...
THERE'S JUST NO WAY...!
WOBL くらぁっ
WHAT'S WRONG?
WHY ARE YOU FREAKING OUT?
WELL, HE SAID THEY AREN'T BLOOD RELATED!
SHE MIGHT ALREADY BE PREG-NANT!
BWAAAAH
ぶっわああ
OKAY, AINA. LET'S JUST TAKE IT DOWN A NOTCH.

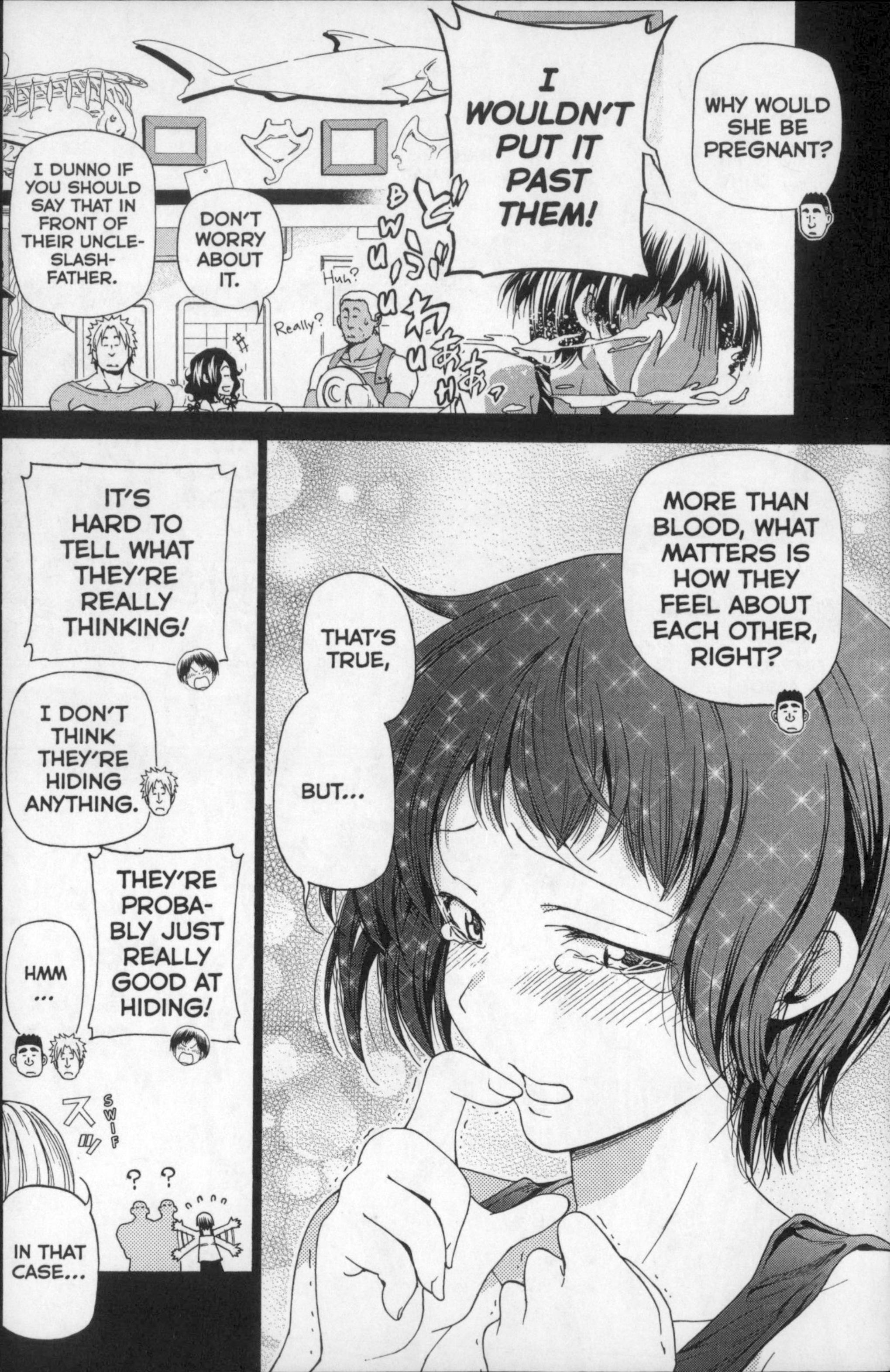

WHY WOULD SHE BE PREGNANT?
I WOULDN'T PUT IT PAST THEM!
BWUUUUH
Huh?
Really?
DON'T WORRY ABOUT IT.
I DUNNO IF YOU SHOULD SAY THAT IN FRONT OF THEIR UNCLE-SLASH-FATHER.
MORE THAN BLOOD, WHAT MATTERS IS HOW THEY FEEL ABOUT EACH OTHER, RIGHT?
THAT'S TRUE,
BUT...
IT'S HARD TO TELL WHAT THEY'RE REALLY THINKING!
I DON'T THINK THEY'RE HIDING ANYTHING.
THEY'RE PROBA-BLY JUST REALLY GOOD AT HIDING!
HMM ...
SWIF
? ?
IN THAT CASE...

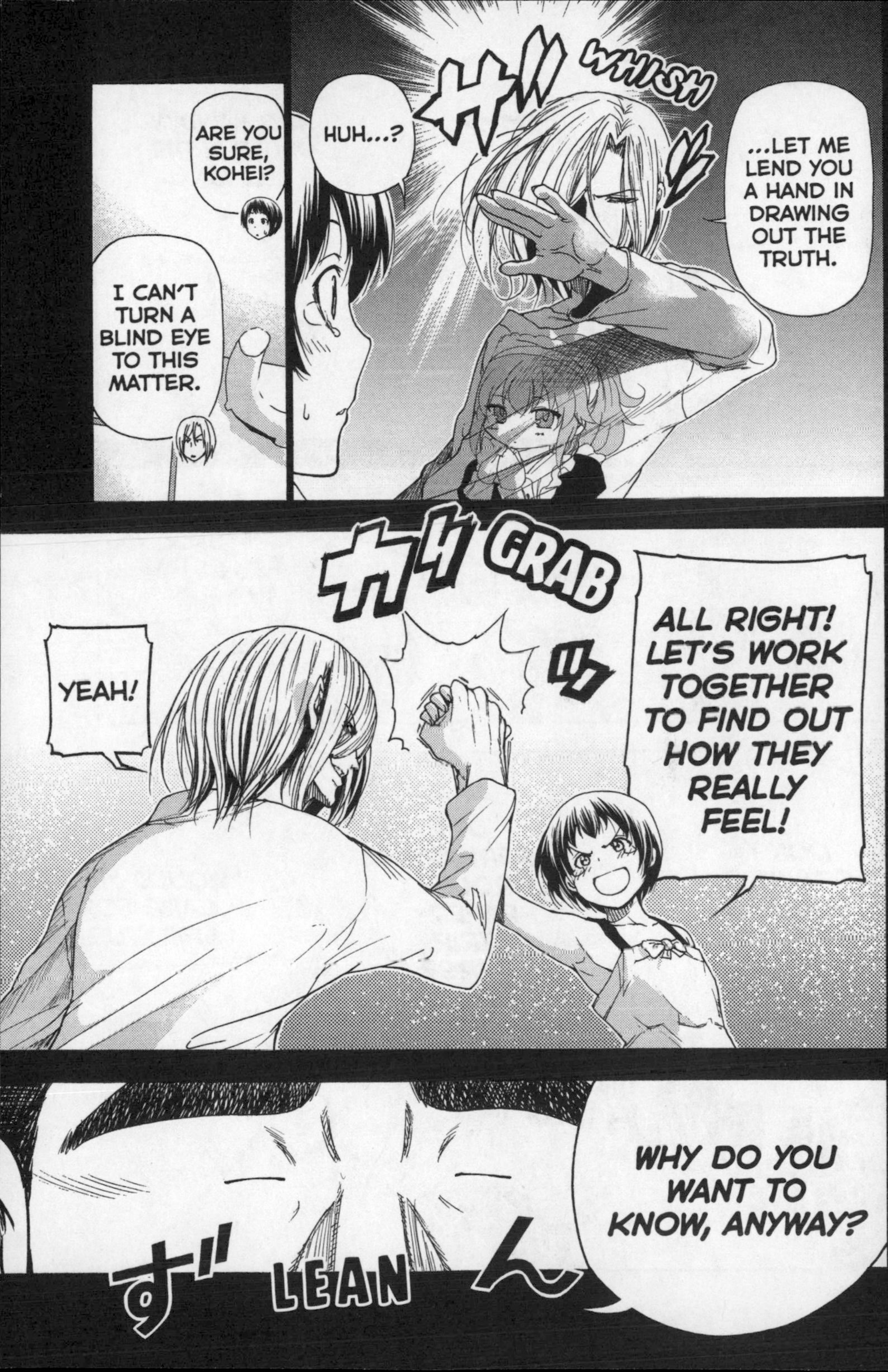
WHISH
...LET ME LEND YOU A HAND IN DRAWING OUT THE TRUTH.
HUH...?
ARE YOU SURE, KOHEI?
I CAN'T TURN A BLIND EYE TO THIS MATTER.
GRAB
ALL RIGHT! LET'S WORK TOGETHER TO FIND OUT HOW THEY REALLY FEEL!
YEAH!
WHY DO YOU WANT TO KNOW, ANYWAY?
LEAN

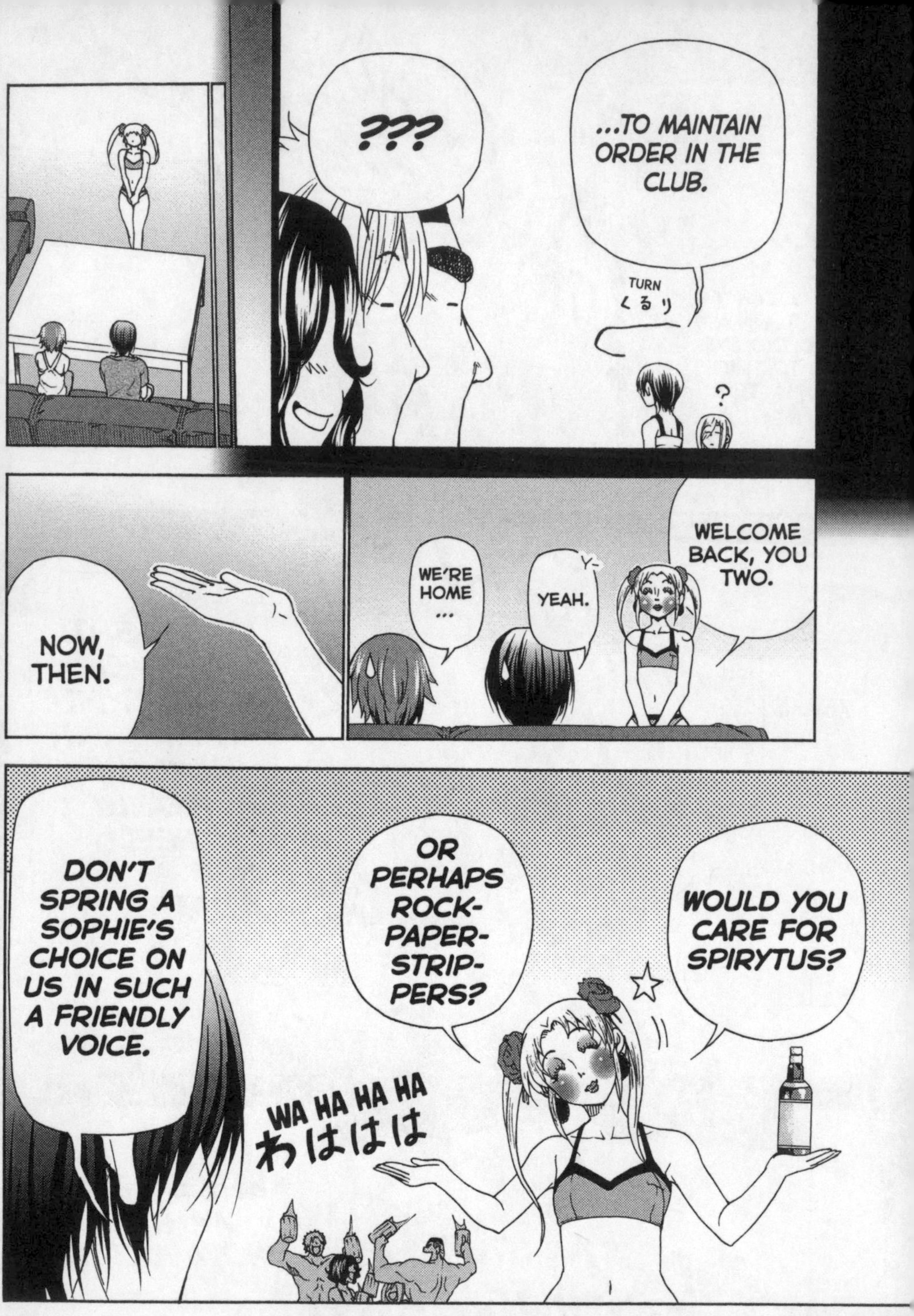
...TO MAINTAIN ORDER IN THE CLUB.
TURN
くるり
?
???
WELCOME BACK, YOU TWO.
Y-
YEAH.
WE'RE HOME ...
NOW, THEN.
WOULD YOU CARE FOR SPIRYTUS?
OR PERHAPS ROCK-PAPER-STRIP-PERS?
WA HA HA HA
わははは
DON'T SPRING A SOPHIE'S CHOICE ON US IN SUCH A FRIENDLY VOICE.

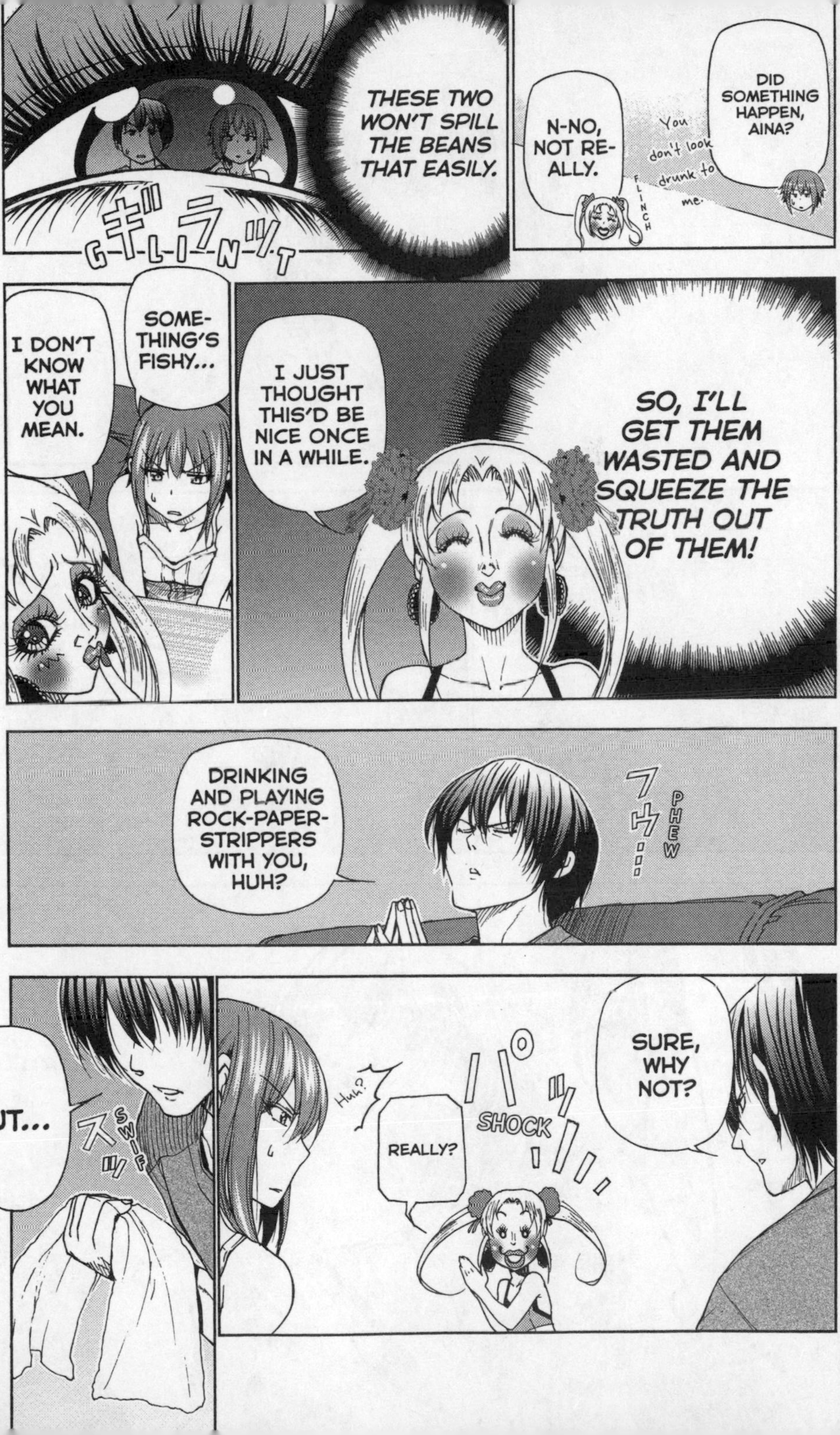
DID SOMETHING HAPPEN, AINA?
You don't look drunk to me.
N-NO, NOT RE-ALLY.
FLINCH
THESE TWO WON'T SPILL THE BEANS THAT EASILY.
G-L-I-N-T
SO, I'LL GET THEM WASTED AND SQUEEZE THE TRUTH OUT OF THEM!
I JUST THOUGHT THIS'D BE NICE ONCE IN A WHILE.
SOME-THING'S FISHY...
I DON'T KNOW WHAT YOU MEAN.
PHEW
DRINKING AND PLAYING ROCK-PAPER-STRIPPERS WITH YOU, HUH?
SURE, WHY NOT?
SHOCK
Huh?
REALLY?
SWIF
BUT...

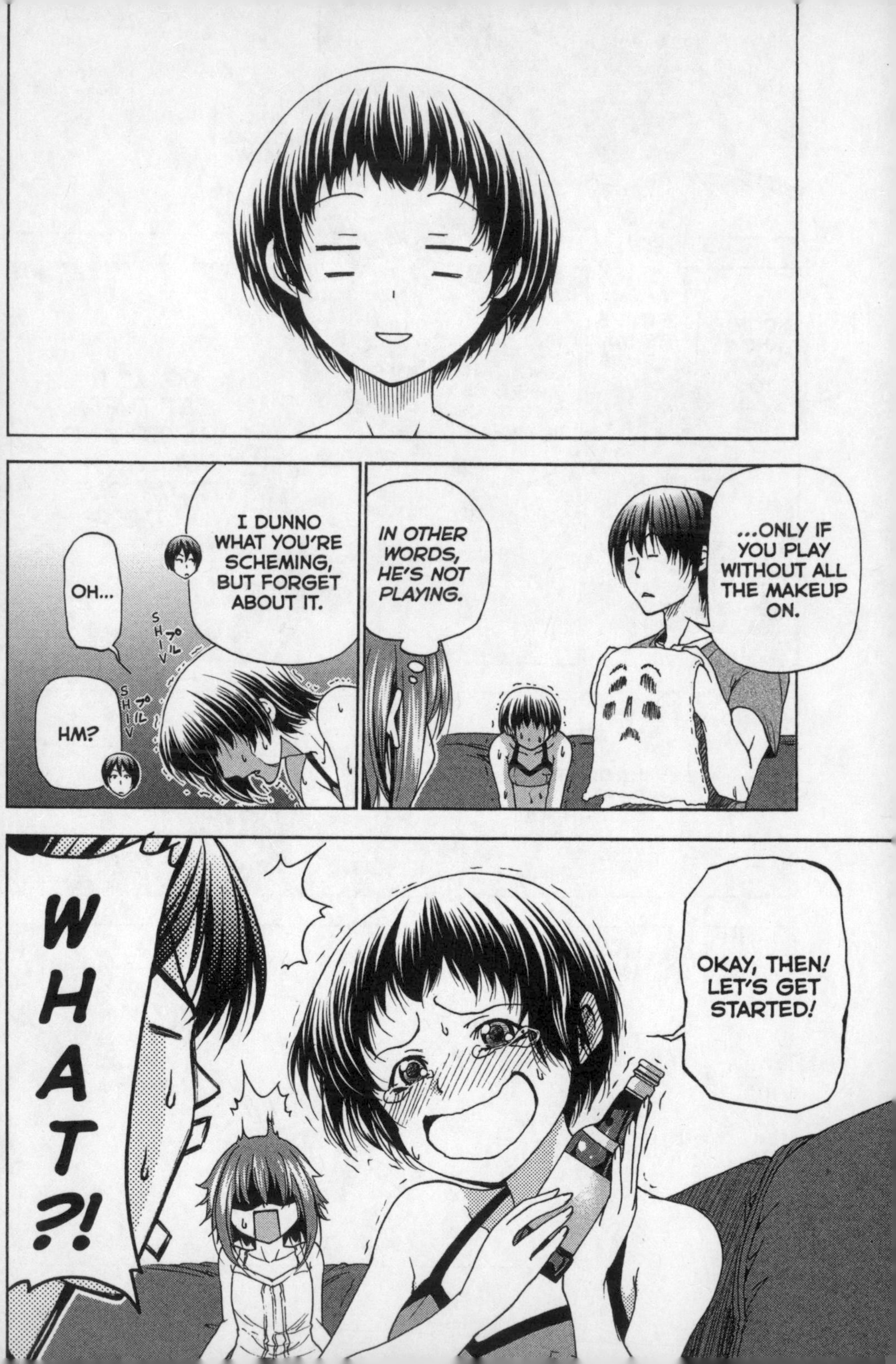
...ONLY IF YOU PLAY WITHOUT ALL THE MAKEUP ON.
IN OTHER WORDS, HE'S NOT PLAYING.
I DUNNO WHAT YOU'RE SCHEMING, BUT FORGET ABOUT IT.
SHIV
OH...
SHIV
HM?
OKAY, THEN! LET'S GET STARTED!
WHAT?!

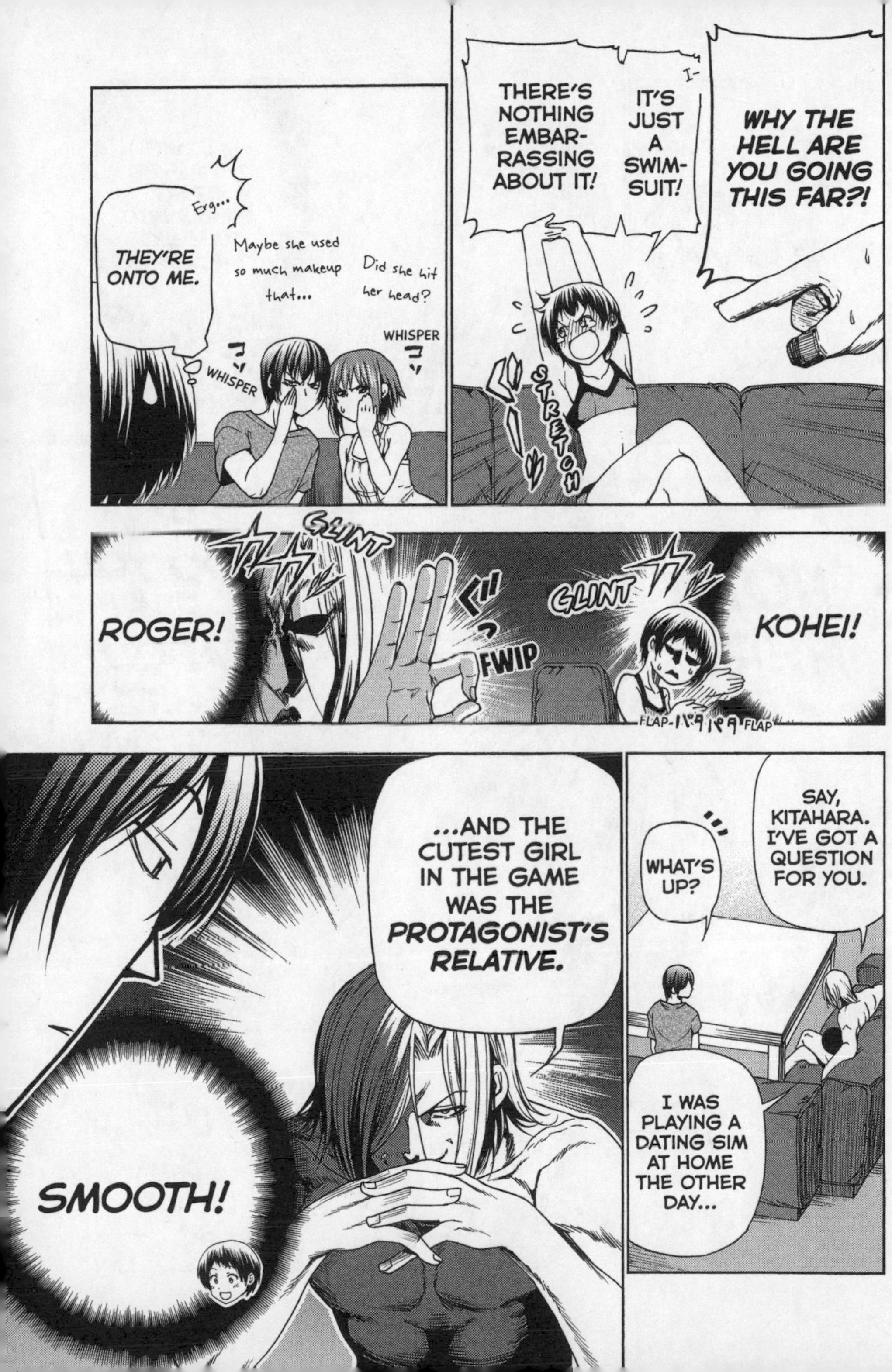
I-
WHY THE HELL ARE YOU GOING THIS FAR?!
IT'S JUST A SWIM-SUIT!
THERE'S NOTHING EMBAR-RASSING ABOUT IT!
STRETCH
Erg...
Did she hit her head?
WHISPER
Maybe she used so much makeup that...
WHISPER
THEY'RE ONTO ME.
KOHEI!
GLINT
FLAP FLAP
FWIP
GLINT
ROGER!
SAY, KITAHARA. I'VE GOT A QUESTION FOR YOU.
WHAT'S UP?
I WAS PLAYING A DATING SIM AT HOME THE OTHER DAY...
...AND THE CUTEST GIRL IN THE GAME WAS THE PROTAGONIST'S RELATIVE.
SMOOTH!

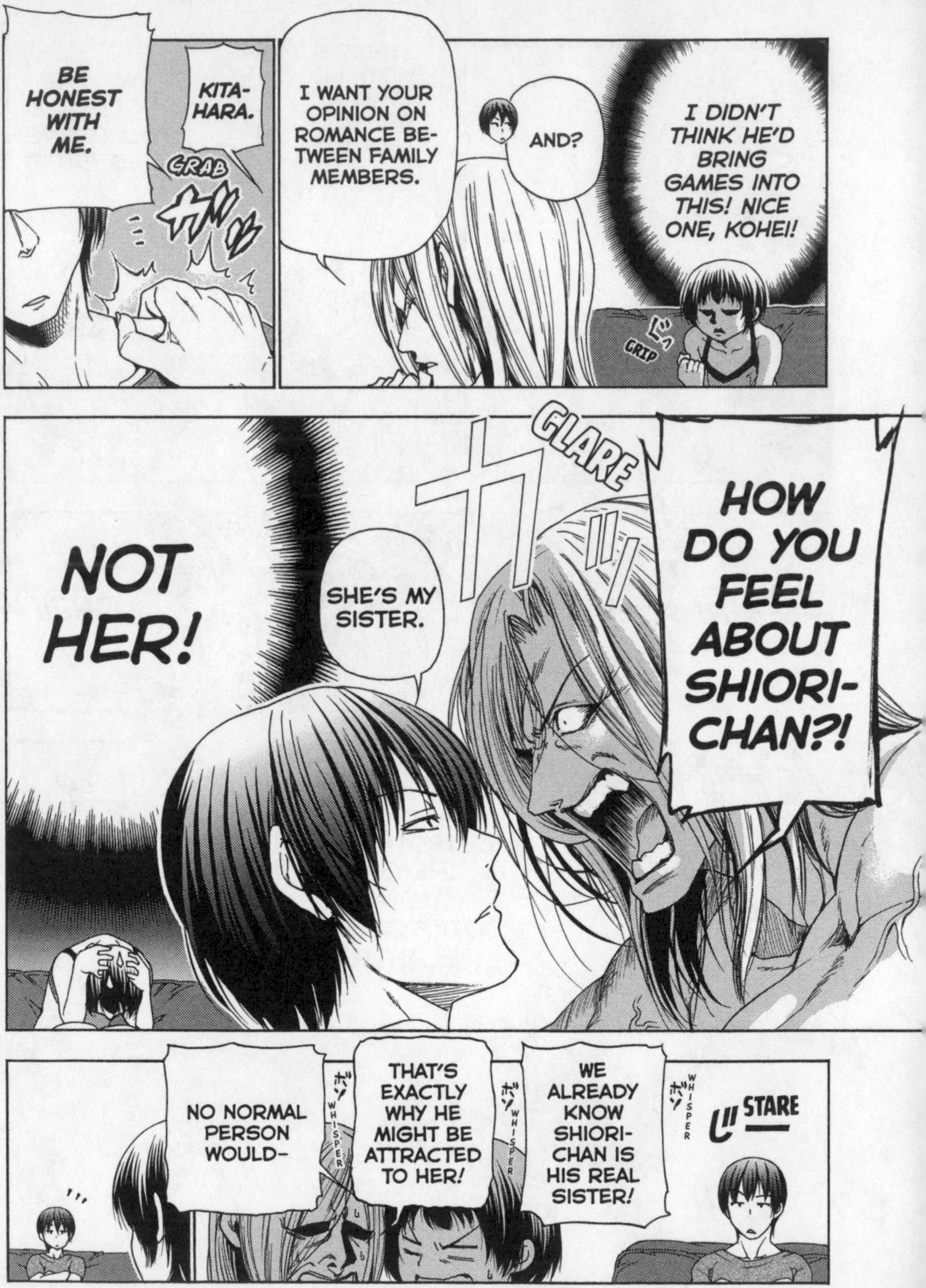
I DIDN'T THINK HE'D BRING GAMES INTO THIS! NICE ONE, KOHEI!
AND?
I WANT YOUR OPINION ON ROMANCE BETWEEN FAMILY MEMBERS.
GRIP
KITA-HARA.
BE HONEST WITH ME.
GRAB
GLARE
HOW DO YOU FEEL ABOUT SHIORI-CHAN?!
SHE'S MY SISTER.
NOT HER!
STARE
WHISPER
WE ALREADY KNOW SHIORI-CHAN IS HIS REAL SISTER!
WHISPER
THAT'S EXACTLY WHY HE MIGHT BE ATTRACTED TO HER!
WHISPER
NO NORMAL PERSON WOULD-

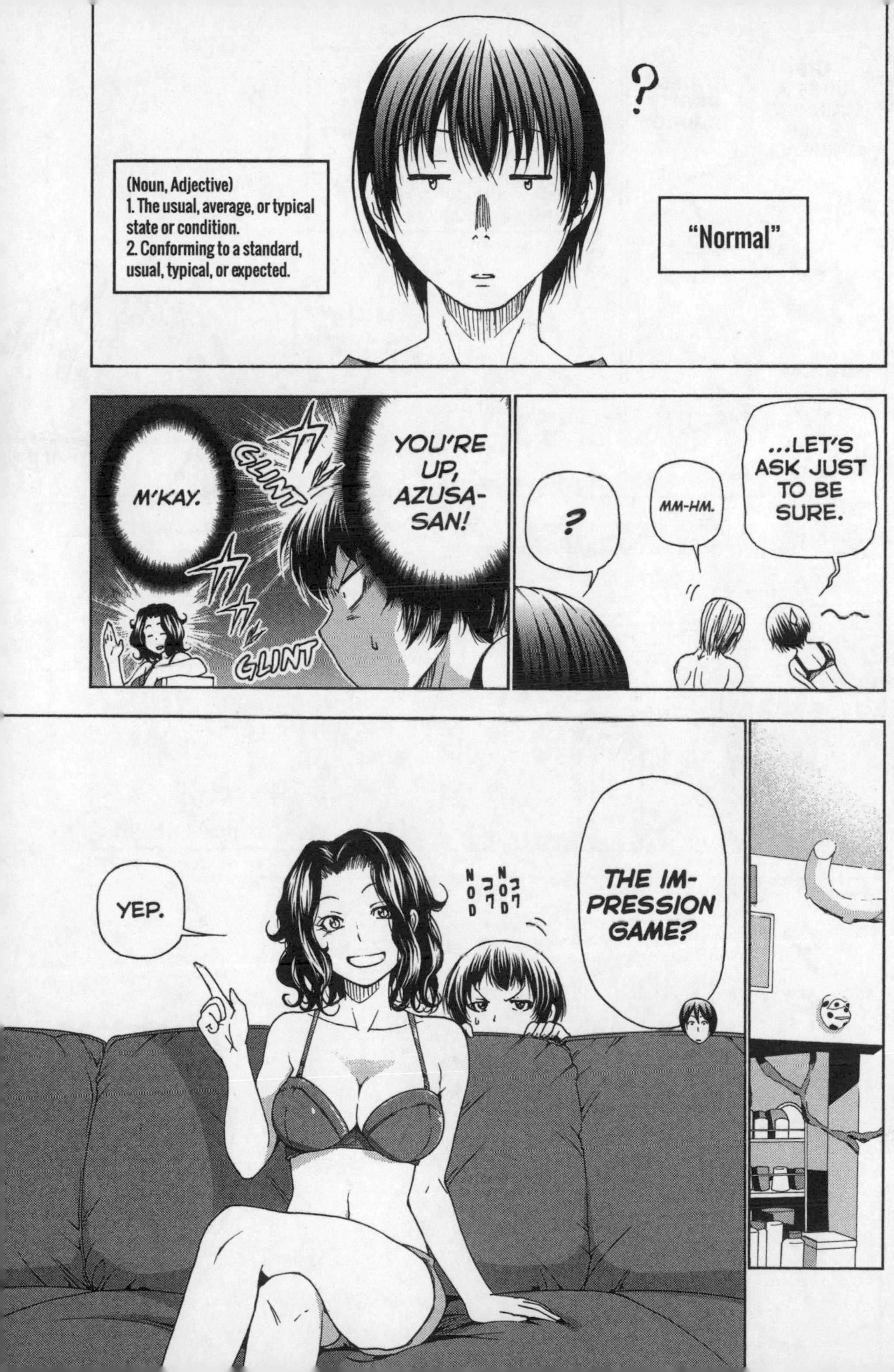
?
"Normal"
(Noun, Adjective)
1. The usual, average, or typical state or condition.
2. Conforming to a standard, usual, typical, or expected.
...LET'S ASK JUST TO BE SURE.
MM-HM.
?
YOU'RE UP, AZUSA-SAN!
GLINT
M'KAY.
GLINT
THE IM-PRESSION GAME?
NOD NOD
YEP.

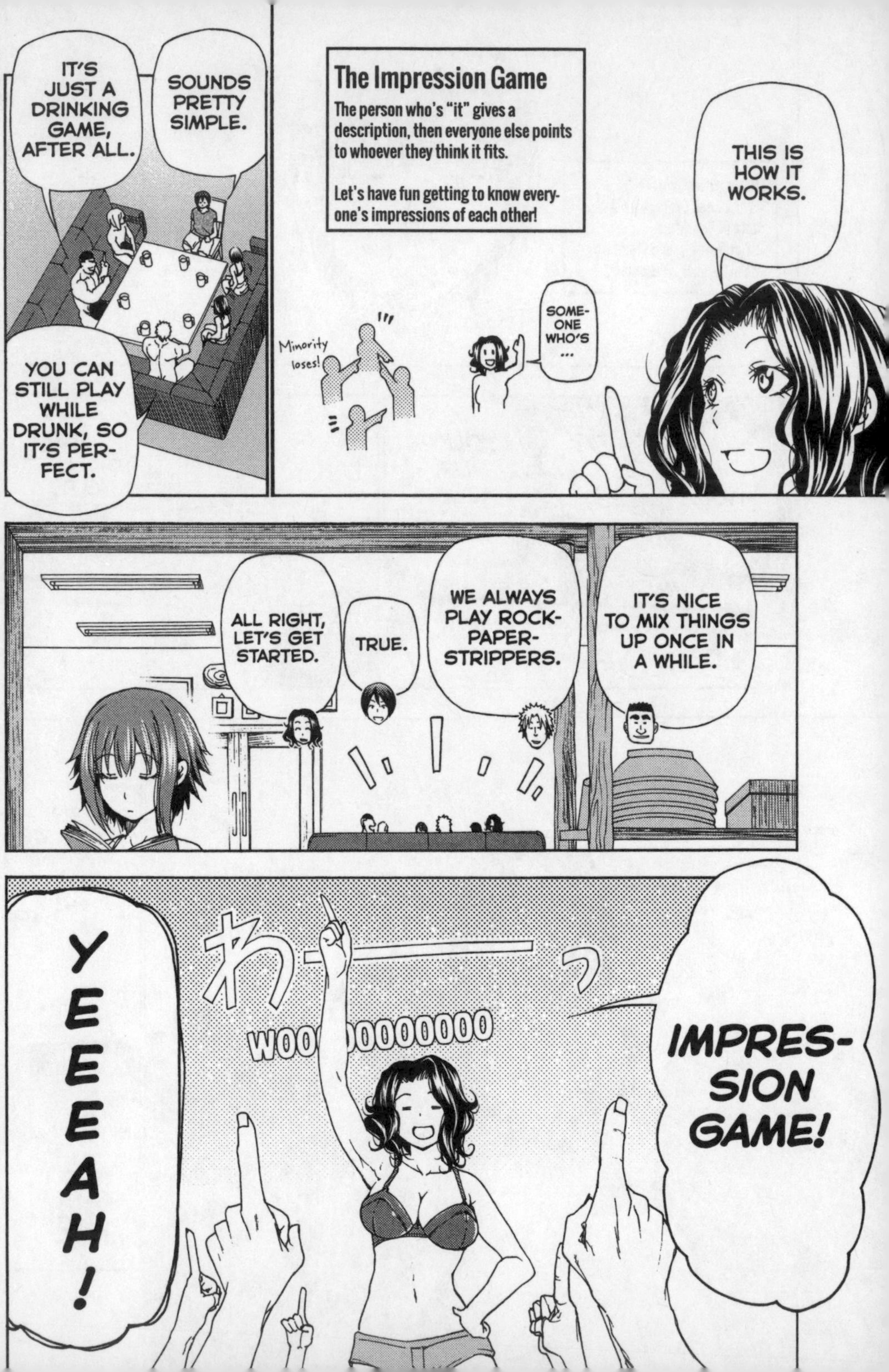
THIS IS HOW IT WORKS.
The Impression Game
The person who's "it" gives a description, then everyone else points to whoever they think it fits.
Let's have fun getting to know everyone's impressions of each other!
SOME-ONE WHO'S ...
Minority loses!
SOUNDS PRETTY SIMPLE.
IT'S JUST A DRINKING GAME, AFTER ALL.
YOU CAN STILL PLAY WHILE DRUNK, SO IT'S PERFECT.
IT'S NICE TO MIX THINGS UP ONCE IN A WHILE.
WE ALWAYS PLAY ROCK-PAPER-STRIPPERS.
TRUE.
ALL RIGHT, LET'S GET STARTED.
IMPRES-SION GAME!
わーーっ
WOOOOOOOOOOO
YEEEAH!

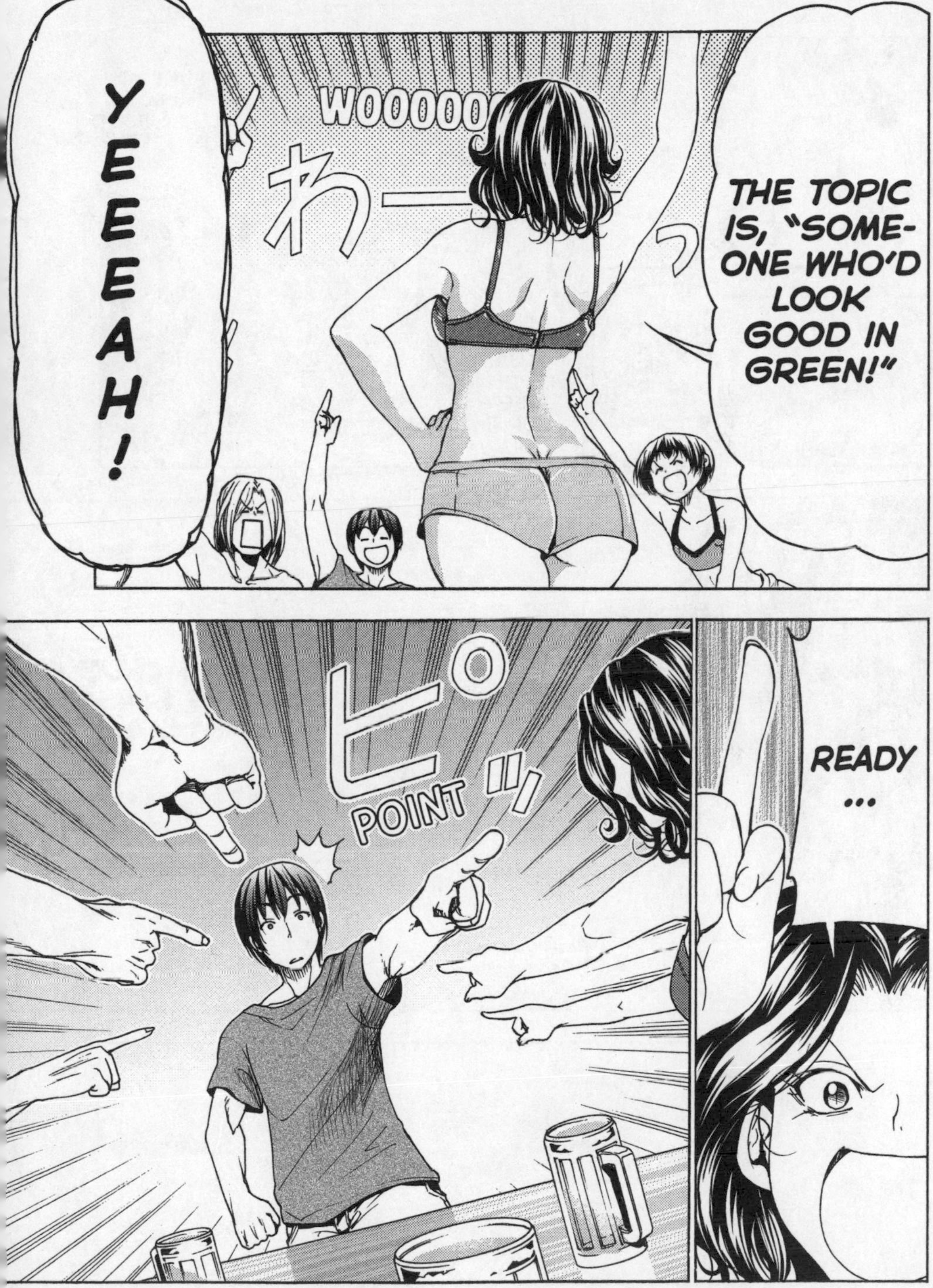
THE TOPIC IS, "SOME-ONE WHO'D LOOK GOOD IN GREEN!"
WOOOOOO
わーっ
YEEEAH!
READY ...
ピッ
POINT

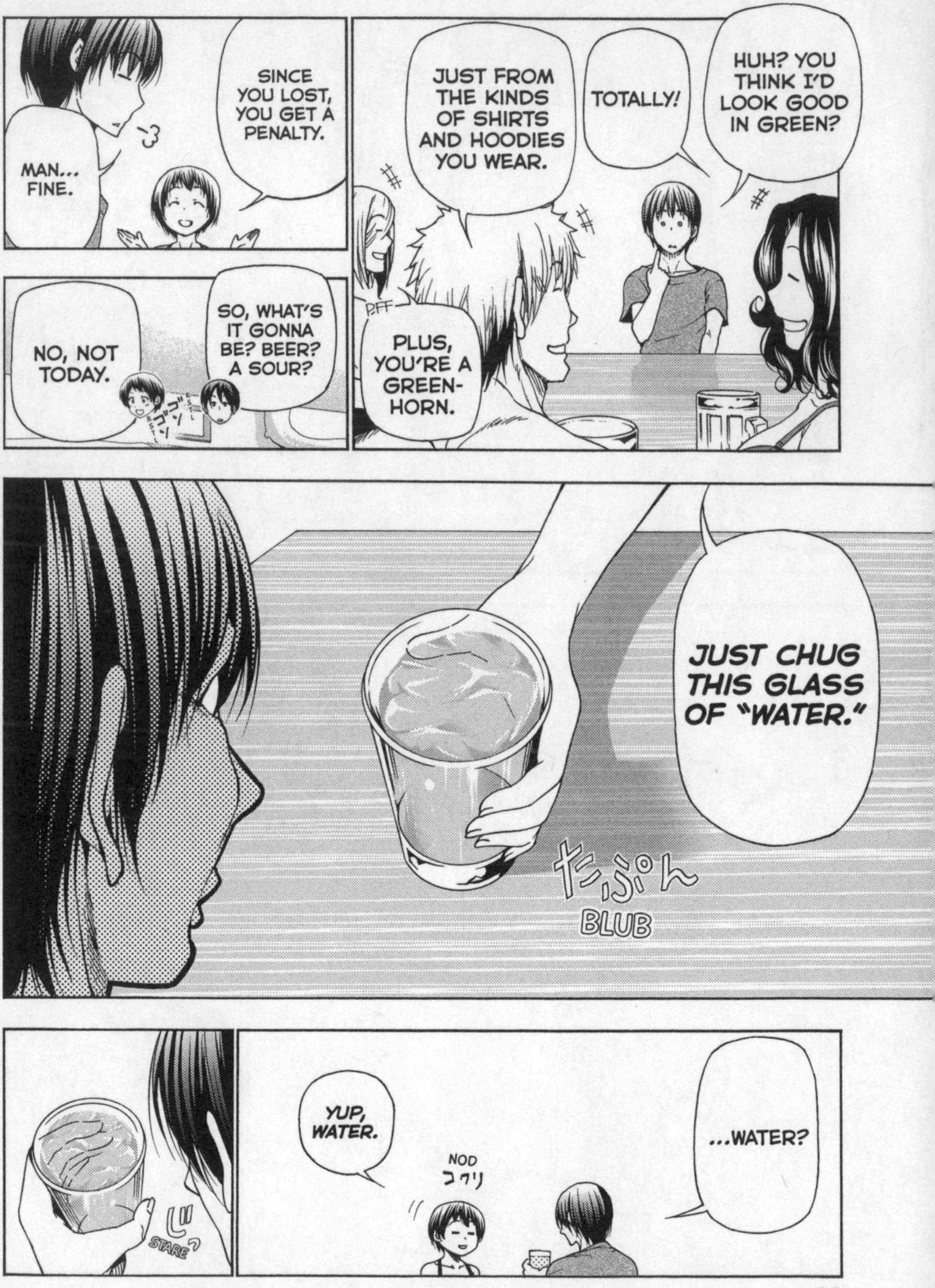
HUH? YOU THINK I'D LOOK GOOD IN GREEN?
TOTALLY!
JUST FROM THE KINDS OF SHIRTS AND HOODIES YOU WEAR.
PFF
PLUS, YOU'RE A GREEN-HORN.
SINCE YOU LOST, YOU GET A PENALTY.
MAN... FINE.
SO, WHAT'S IT GONNA BE? BEER? A SOUR?
RSTL
NO, NOT TODAY.
JUST CHUG THIS GLASS OF "WATER."
BLUB
...WATER?
NOD
YUP, WATER.
STARE

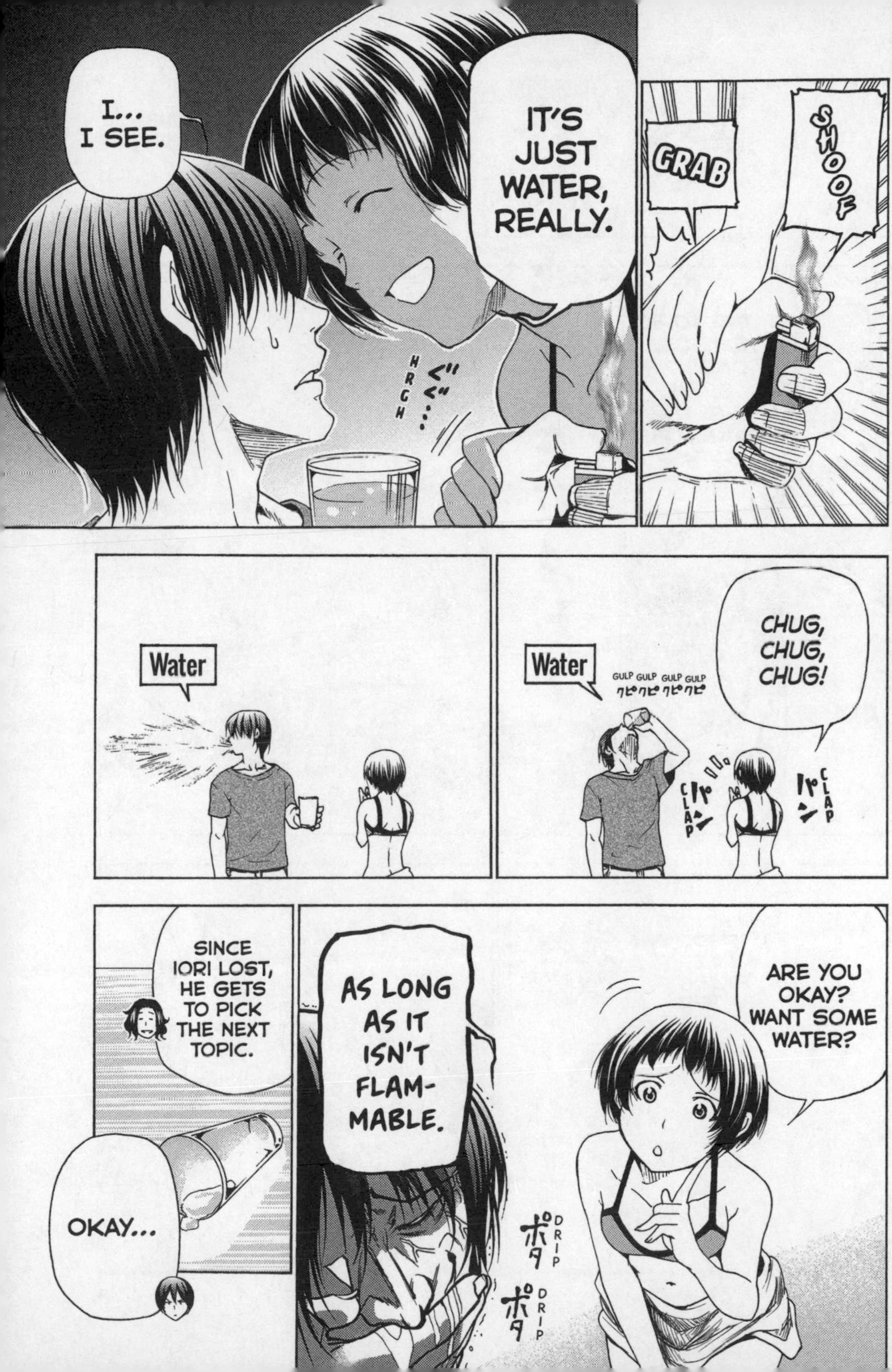

GRAB
SHOOF
IT'S JUST WATER, REALLY.
I... I SEE.
HRGH
ぐぐ…
Water
GULP GULP GULP GULP
クピクピクピクピ
CHUG, CHUG, CHUG!
パン CLAP
パン CLAP
Water
ARE YOU OKAY? WANT SOME WATER?
AS LONG AS IT ISN'T FLAM-MABLE.
ポタ DRIP
ポタ DRIP
SINCE IORI LOST, HE GETS TO PICK THE NEXT TOPIC.
OKAY...

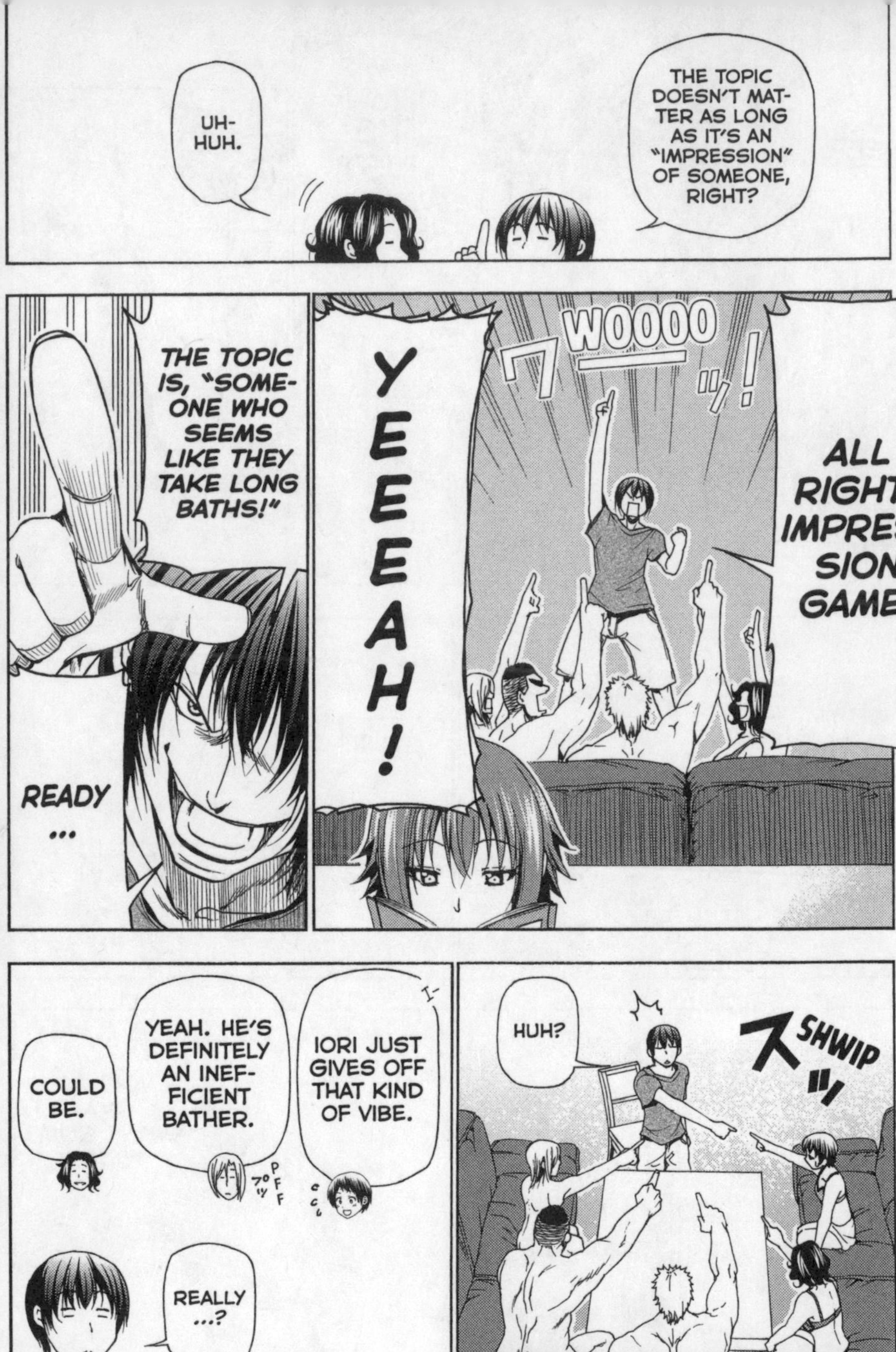
THE TOPIC DOESN'T MATTER AS LONG AS IT'S AN "IMPRESSION" OF SOMEONE, RIGHT?
UH-HUH.
ALL RIGHT! IMPRESSION GAME!
WOOOO
YEEEAH!
THE TOPIC IS, "SOMEONE WHO SEEMS LIKE THEY TAKE LONG BATHS!"
READY ...
HUH?
SHWIP
IORI JUST GIVES OFF THAT KIND OF VIBE.
YEAH. HE'S DEFINITELY AN INEFFICIENT BATHER.
PFF
COULD BE.
REALLY ...?

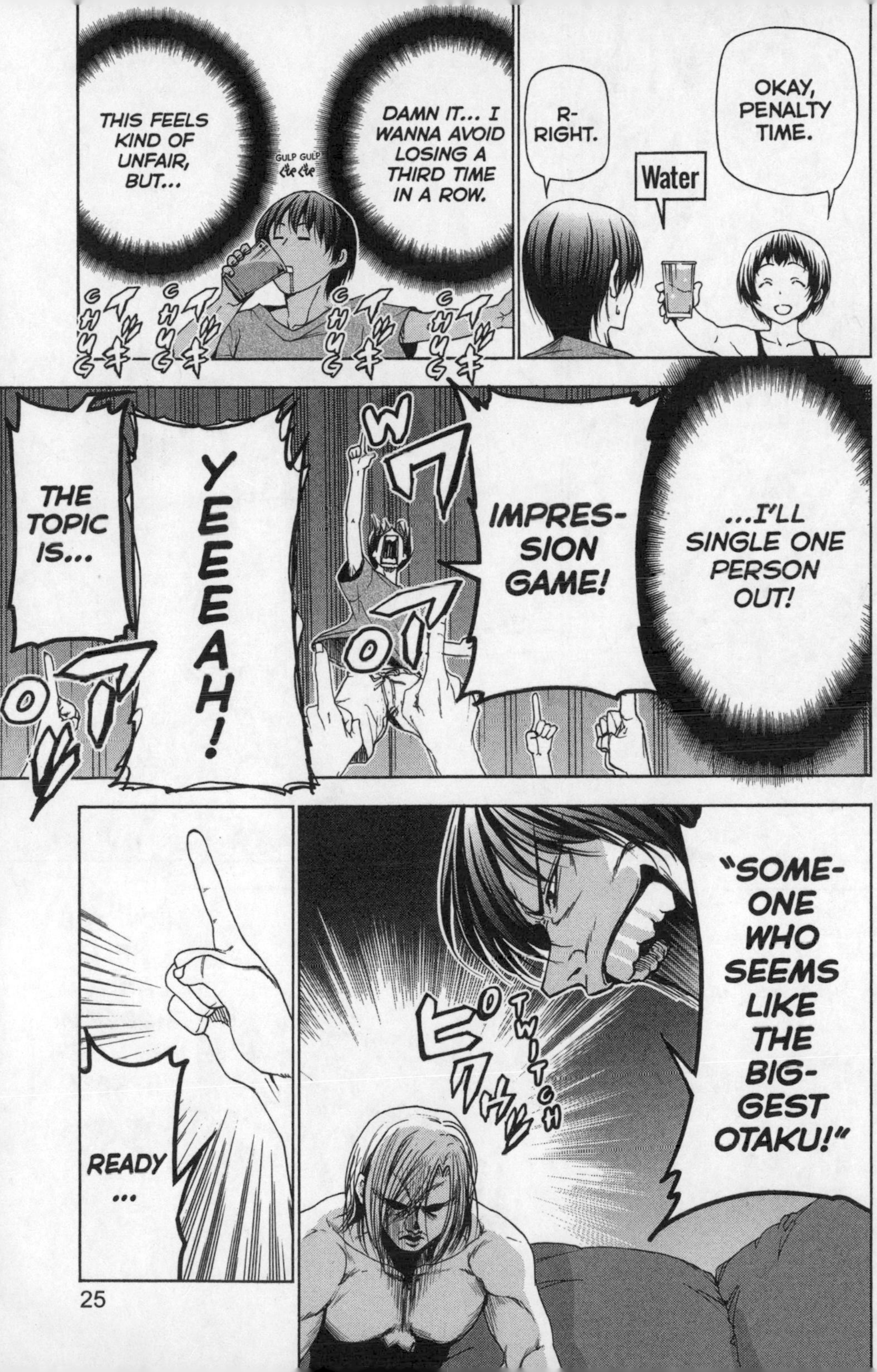
OKAY, PENALTY TIME.
Water
R- RIGHT.
DAMN IT... I WANNA AVOID LOSING A THIRD TIME IN A ROW.
THIS FEELS KIND OF UNFAIR, BUT...
GULP GULP
CHUG CHUG CHUG CHUG
...I'LL SINGLE ONE PERSON OUT!
IMPRESSION GAME!
WO
YEEEEAH!
THE TOPIC IS...
O
"SOMEONE WHO SEEMS LIKE THE BIGGEST OTAKU!"
TWITCH
READY...

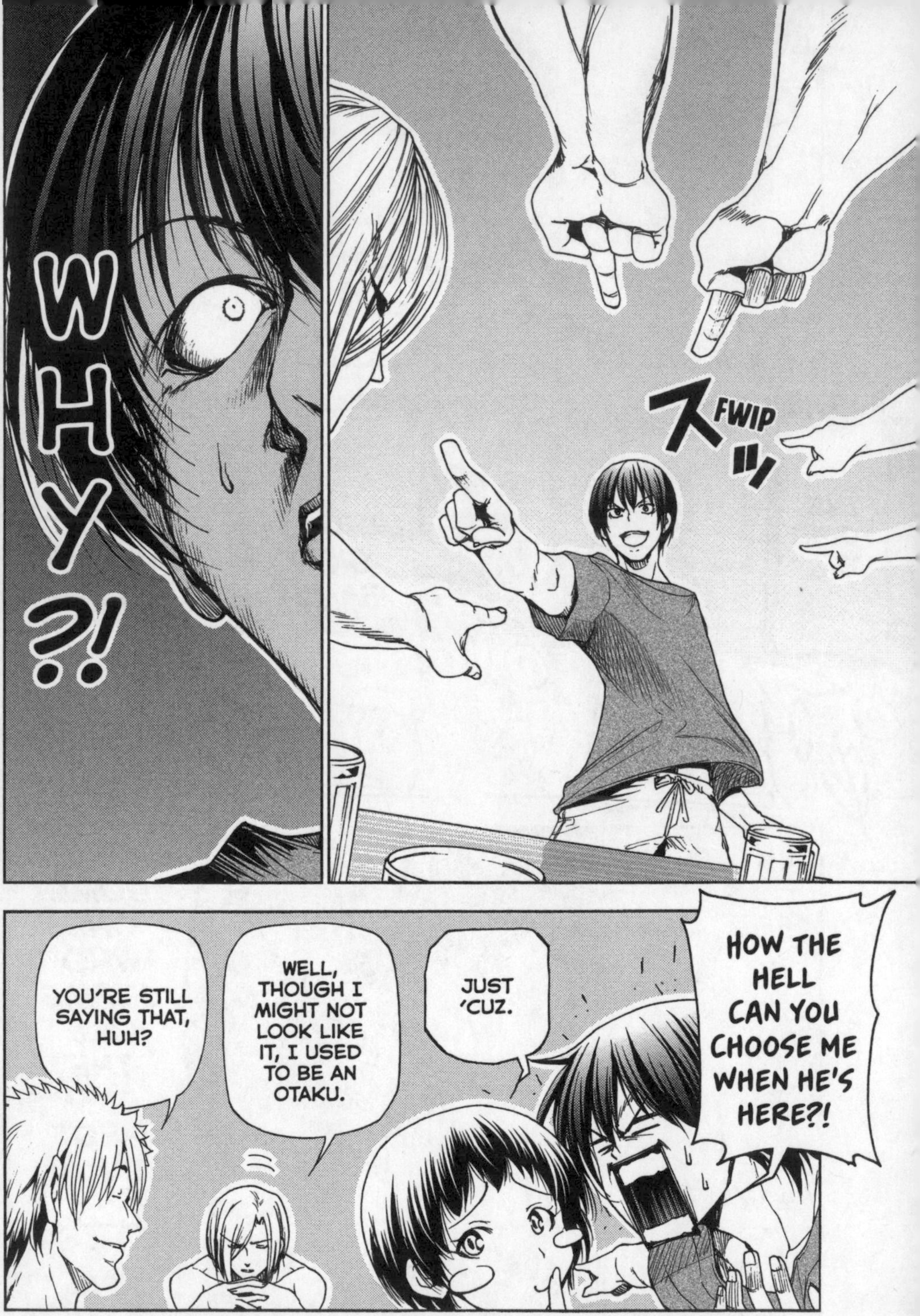
スッ
FWIP
WHY?!
HOW THE HELL CAN YOU CHOOSE ME WHEN HE'S HERE?!
JUST 'CUZ.
WELL, THOUGH I MIGHT NOT LOOK LIKE IT, I USED TO BE AN OTAKU.
YOU'RE STILL SAYING THAT, HUH?

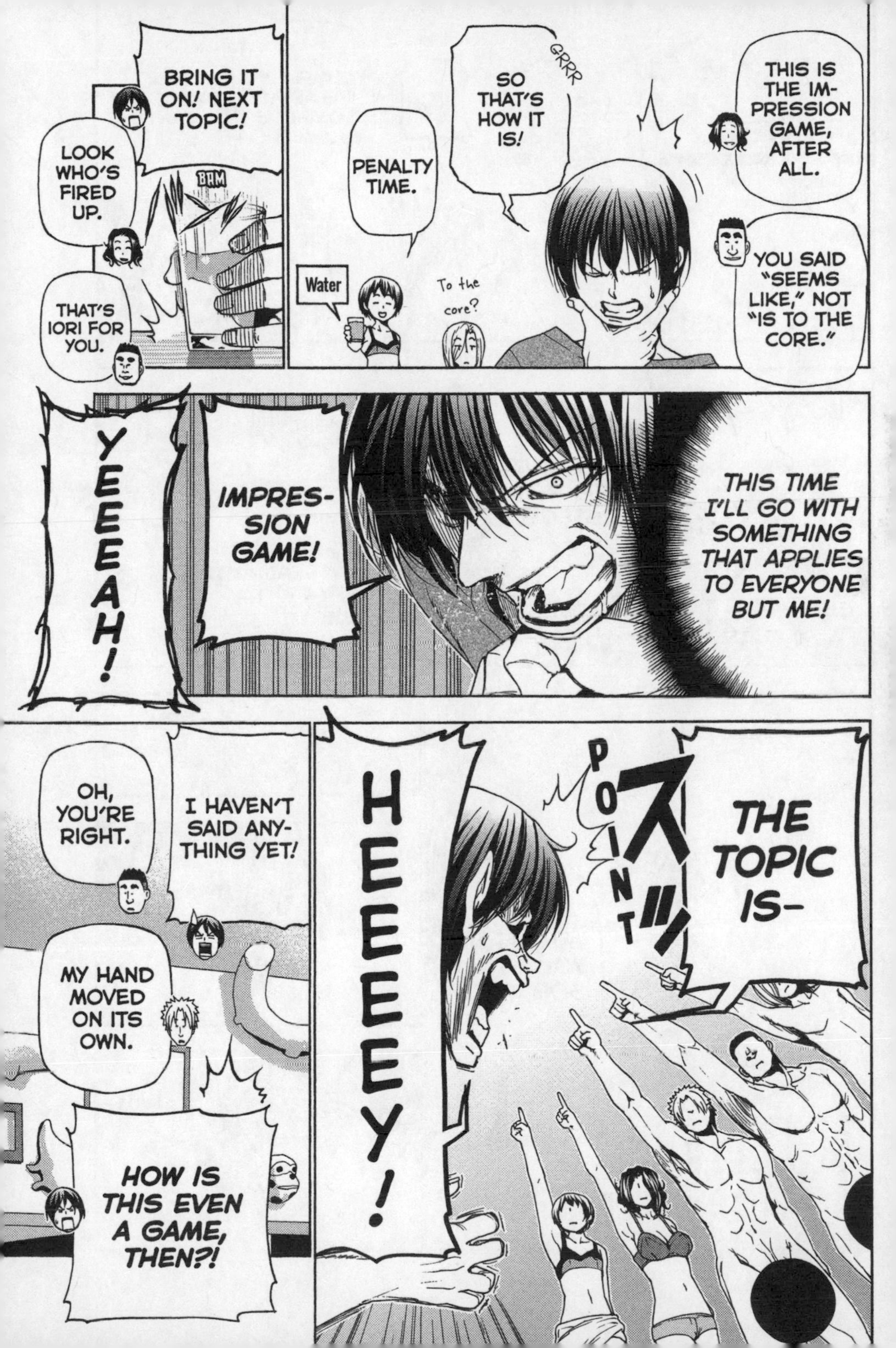
THIS IS THE IMPRESSION GAME, AFTER ALL.
YOU SAID "SEEMS LIKE," NOT "IS TO THE CORE."
GRRR
SO THAT'S HOW IT IS!
PENALTY TIME.
To the core?
Water
BRING IT ON! NEXT TOPIC!
BAM
LOOK WHO'S FIRED UP.
THAT'S IORI FOR YOU.
THIS TIME I'LL GO WITH SOMETHING THAT APPLIES TO EVERYONE BUT ME!
IMPRESSION GAME!
YEEEAH!
THE TOPIC IS-
POINT
HEEEEEY!
I HAVEN'T SAID ANYTHING YET!
OH, YOU'RE RIGHT.
MY HAND MOVED ON ITS OWN.
HOW IS THIS EVEN A GAME, THEN?!

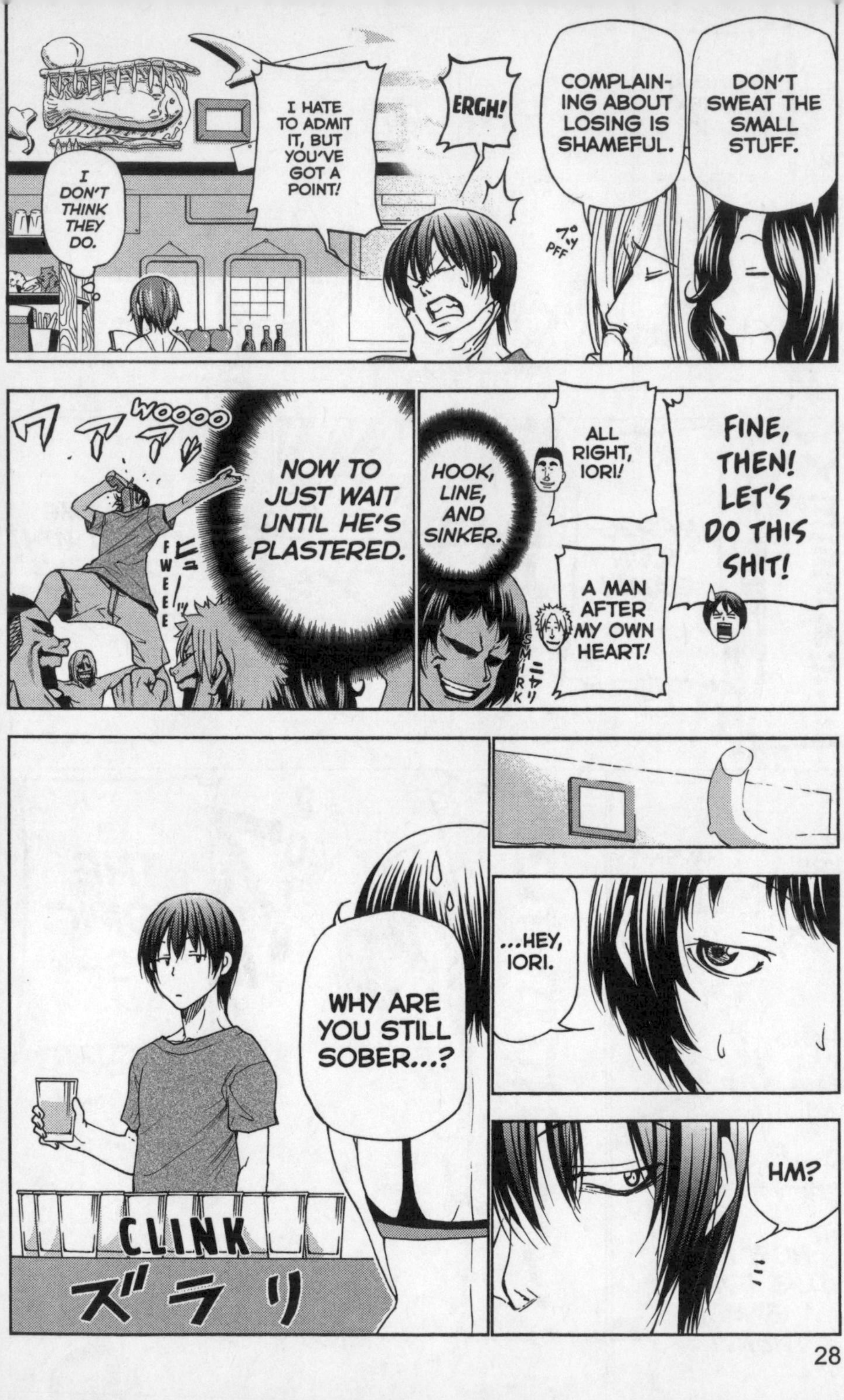
DON'T SWEAT THE SMALL STUFF.
COMPLAINING ABOUT LOSING IS SHAMEFUL.
PFF
ERGH!
I HATE TO ADMIT IT, BUT YOU'VE GOT A POINT!
I DON'T THINK THEY DO.
FINE, THEN! LET'S DO THIS SHIT!
ALL RIGHT, IORI!
A MAN AFTER MY OWN HEART!
HOOK, LINE, AND SINKER.
SMIRK
NOW TO JUST WAIT UNTIL HE'S PLASTERED.
WOOOO
FWEEE
...HEY, IORI.
HM?
WHY ARE YOU STILL SOBER...?
CLINK

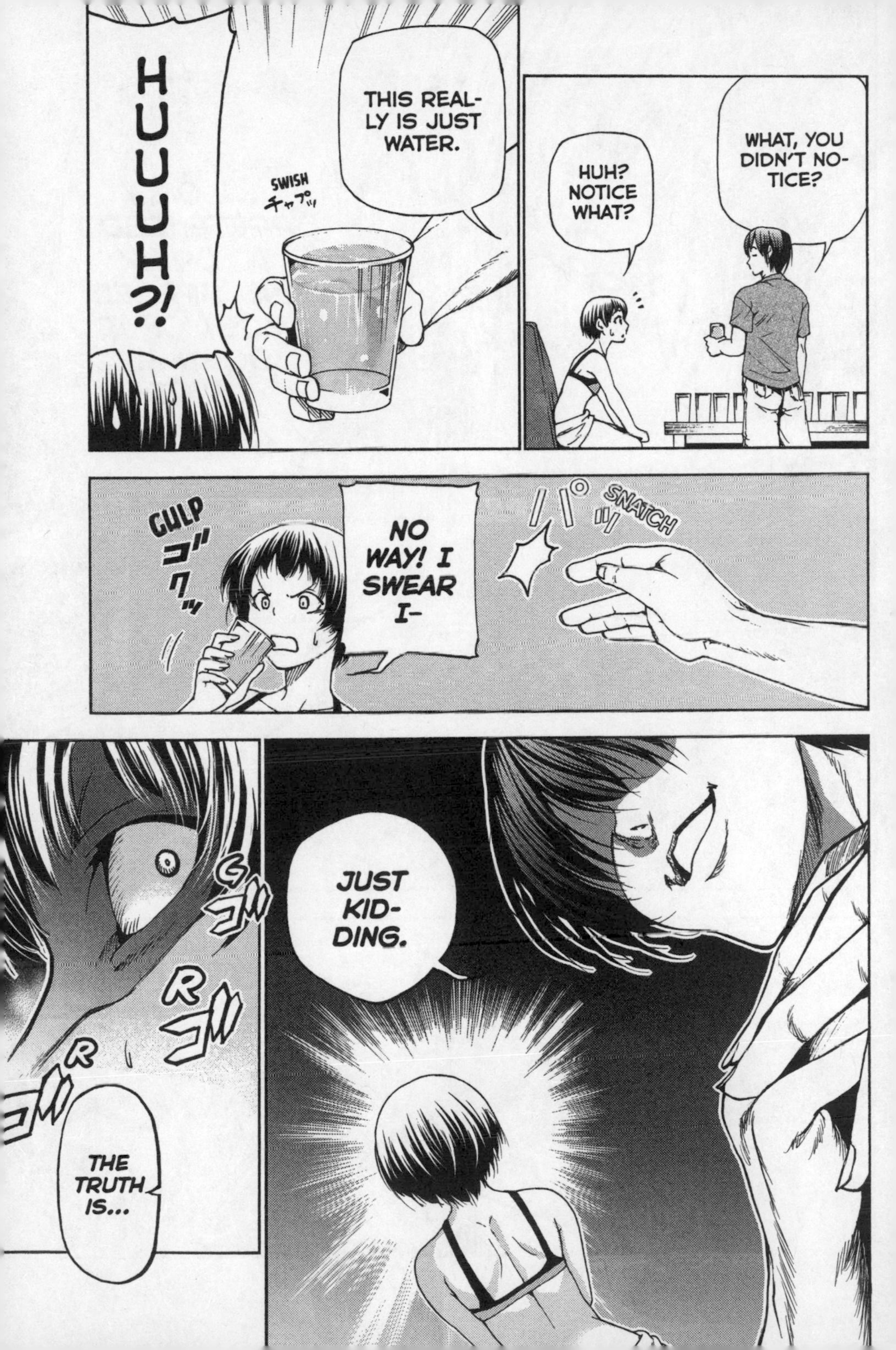
WHAT, YOU DIDN'T NOTICE?
HUH? NOTICE WHAT?
THIS REALLY IS JUST WATER.
SWISH
チャプッ
HUUUH?!
SNATCH
パッ
NO WAY! I SWEAR I-
GULP
ゴクッ
JUST KIDDING.
G
ゴ
R
ゴ
R
ゴ
THE TRUTH IS...

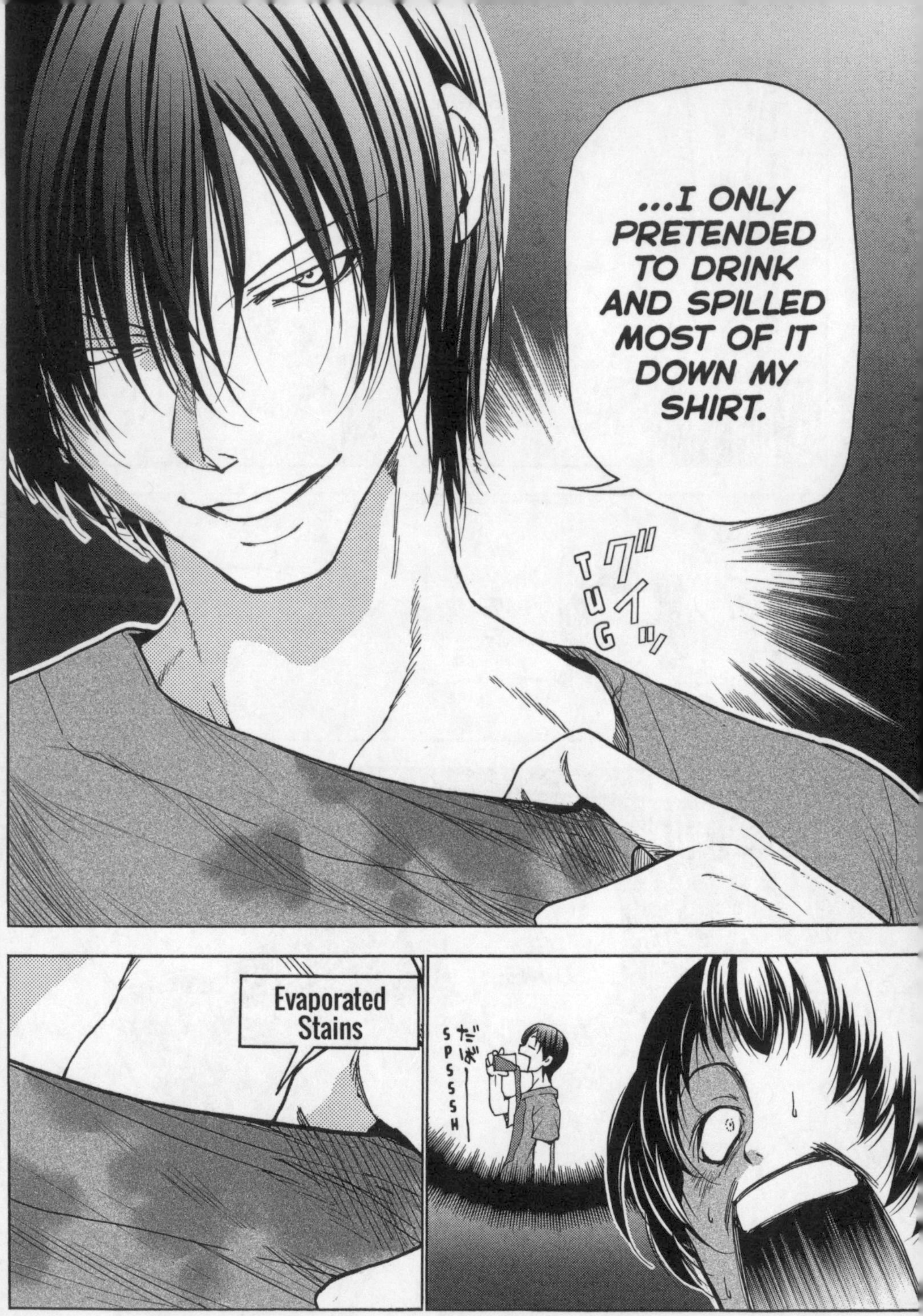
...I ONLY PRETENDED TO DRINK AND SPILLED MOST OF IT DOWN MY SHIRT.
グイッ
TUG
Evaporated Stains
だばー
SPSSSH

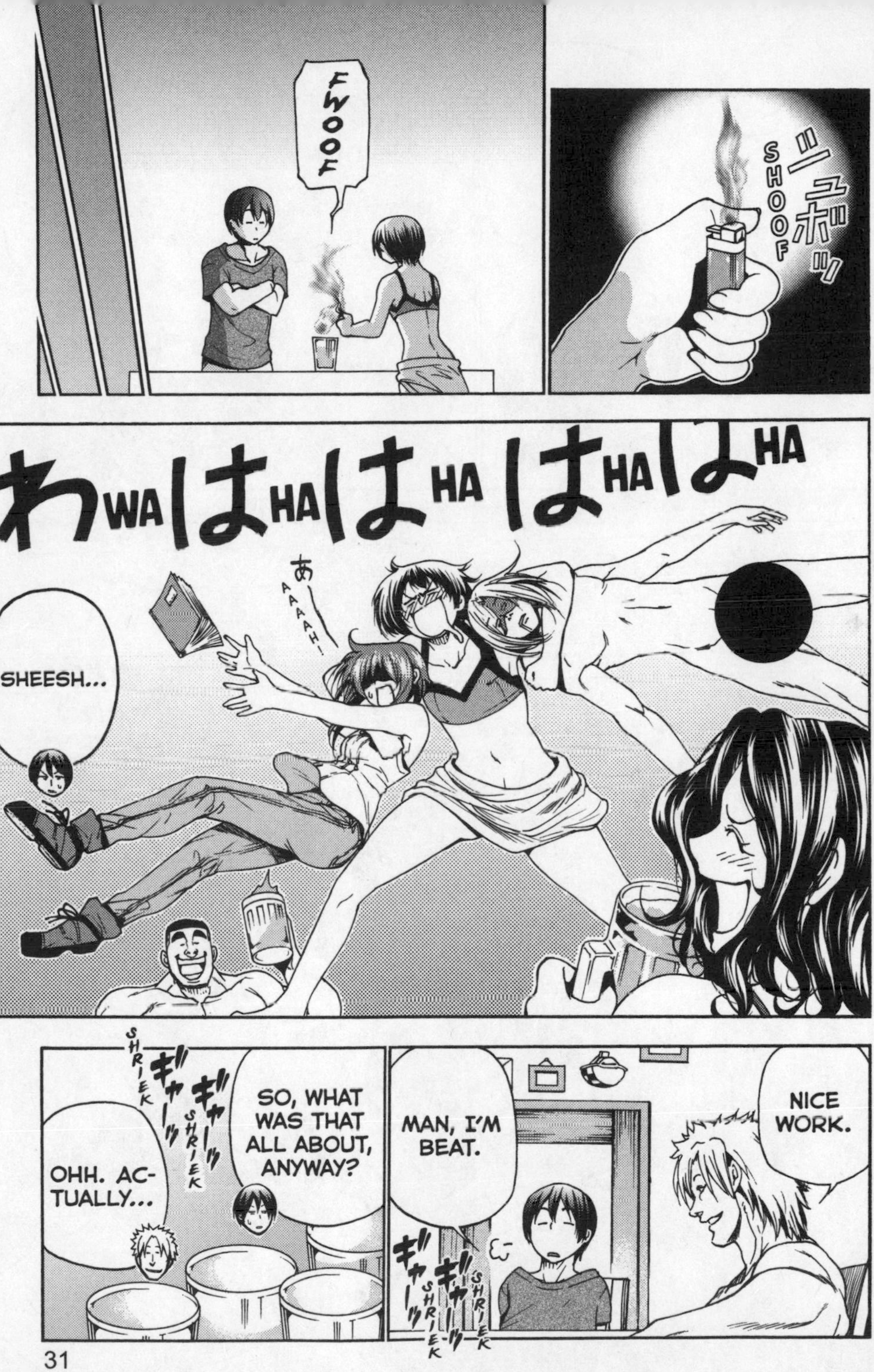
ジュボッ
SHOOF
FWOOF
わWAはHAはHAはHAはHA
あーAAAAH!
SHEESH...
NICE WORK.
MAN, I'M BEAT.
ギャーッ SHRIEK
ギャーッ SHRIEK
SO, WHAT WAS THAT ALL ABOUT, ANYWAY?
ギャーッ SHRIEK
ギャーッ SHRIEK
OHH. AC-TUALLY...

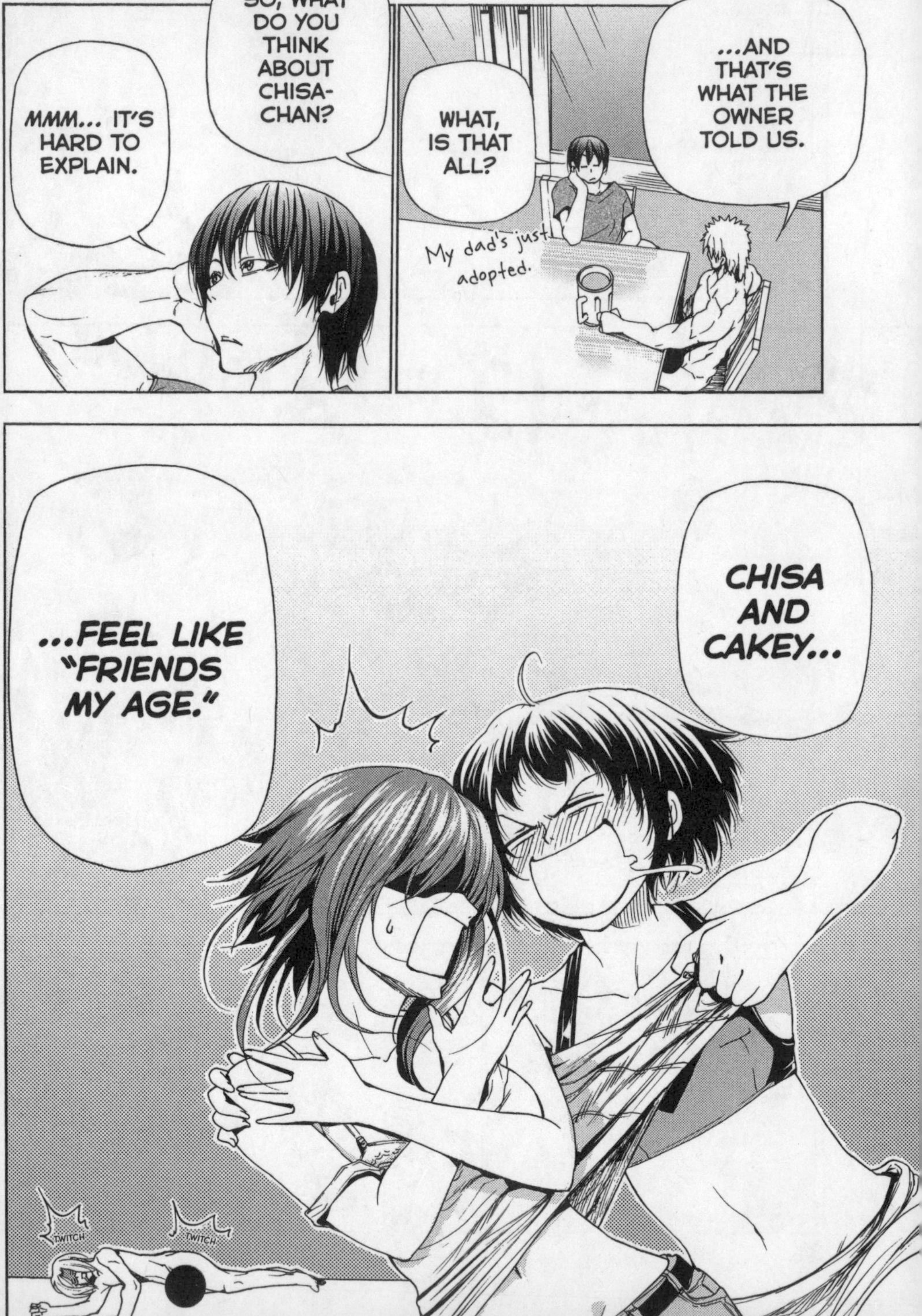
...AND THAT'S WHAT THE OWNER TOLD US.
WHAT, IS THAT ALL?
My dad's just adopted.
SO, WHAT DO YOU THINK ABOUT CHISA-CHAN?
MMM... IT'S HARD TO EXPLAIN.
CHISA AND CAKEY...
...FEEL LIKE "FRIENDS MY AGE."
TWITCH
TWITCH

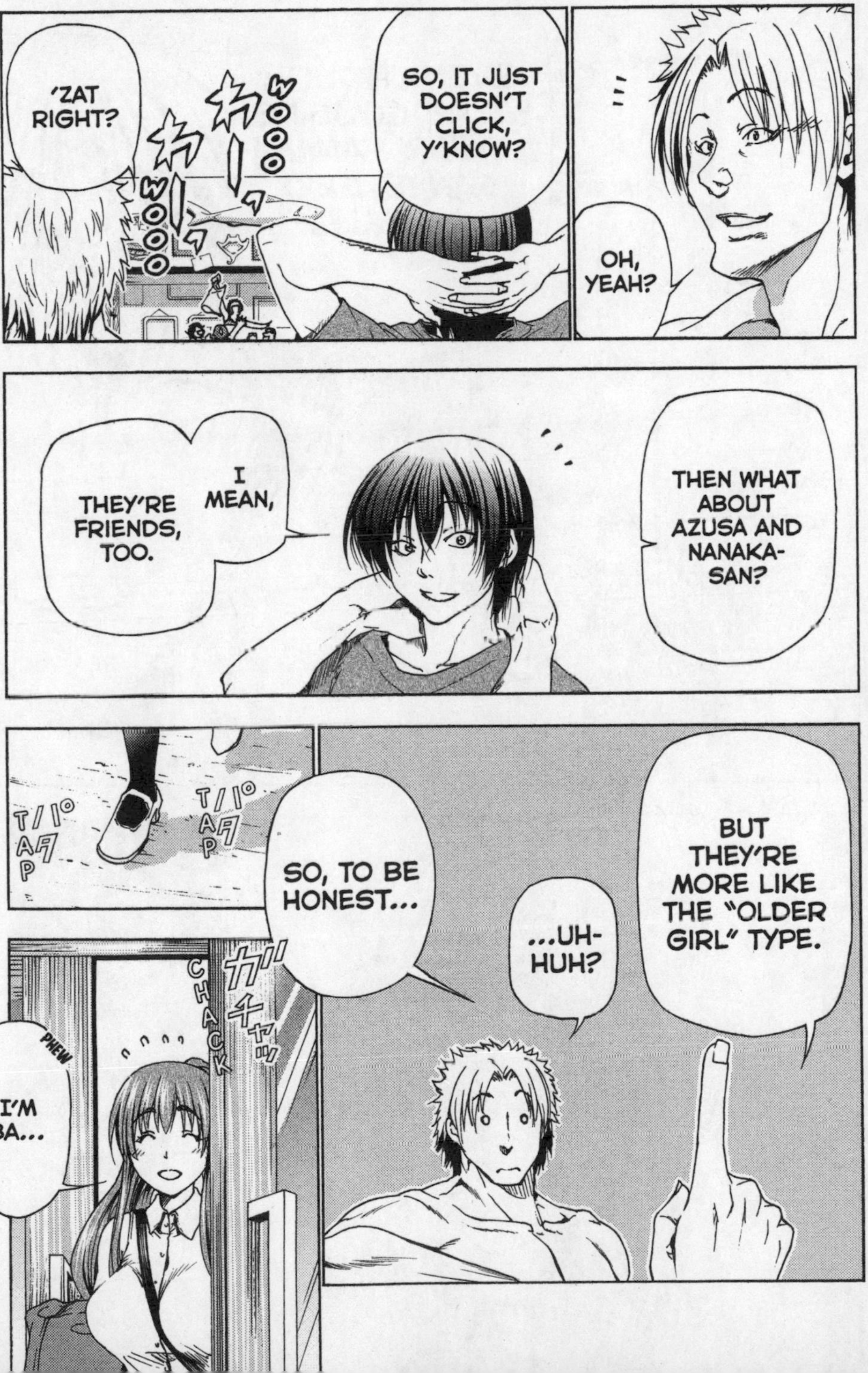
OH, YEAH?
SO, IT JUST DOESN'T CLICK, Y'KNOW?
WOOOO
WOOOO
'ZAT RIGHT?
THEN WHAT ABOUT AZUSA AND NANAKA-SAN?
I MEAN, THEY'RE FRIENDS, TOO.
BUT THEY'RE MORE LIKE THE "OLDER GIRL" TYPE.
...UH-HUH?
SO, TO BE HONEST...
TAP
TAP
CHACK
PHEW
I'M BA...

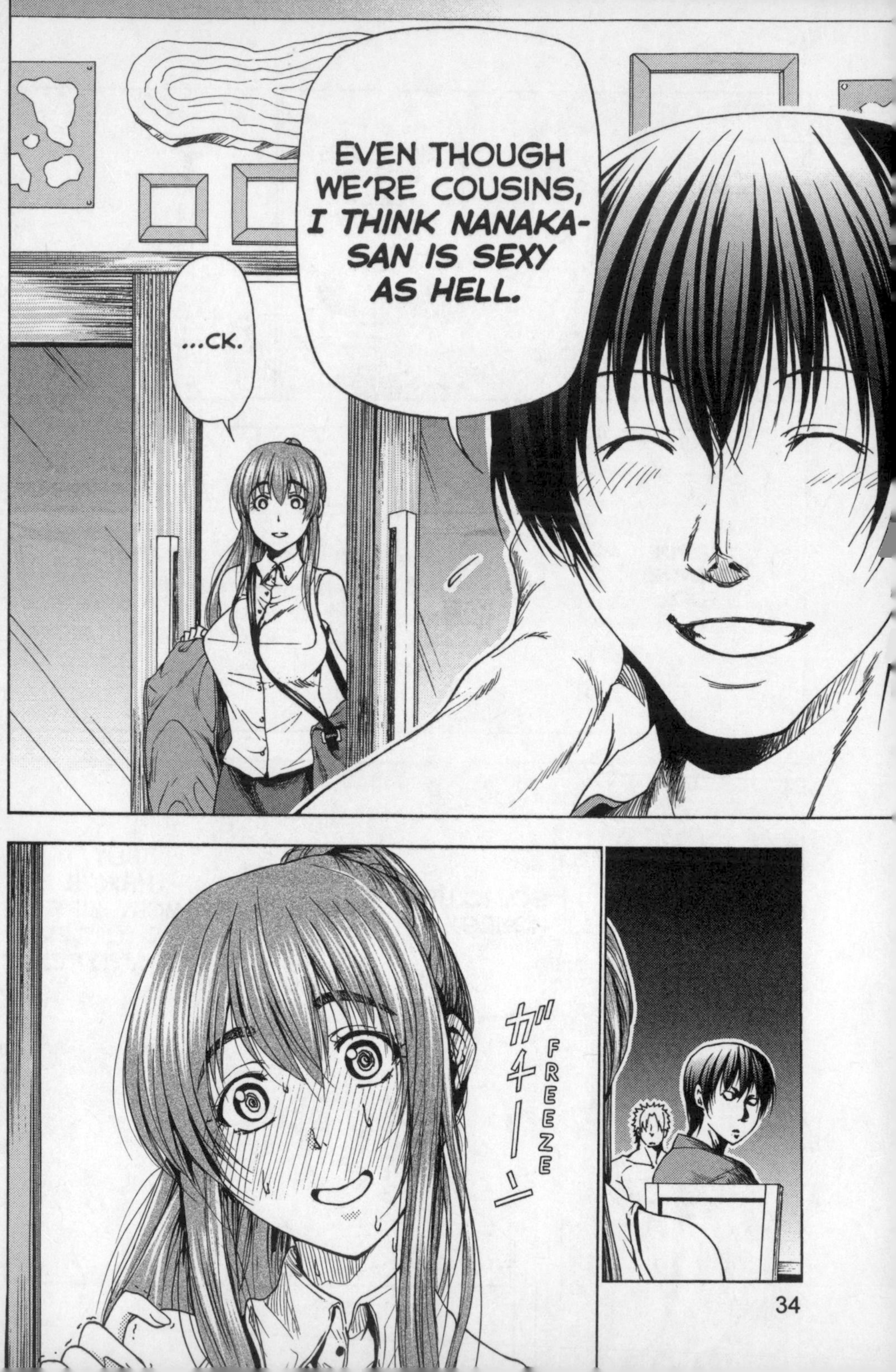
EVEN THOUGH WE'RE COUSINS, *I THINK NANAKA-SAN IS SEXY AS HELL.*
...CK.
FREEZE

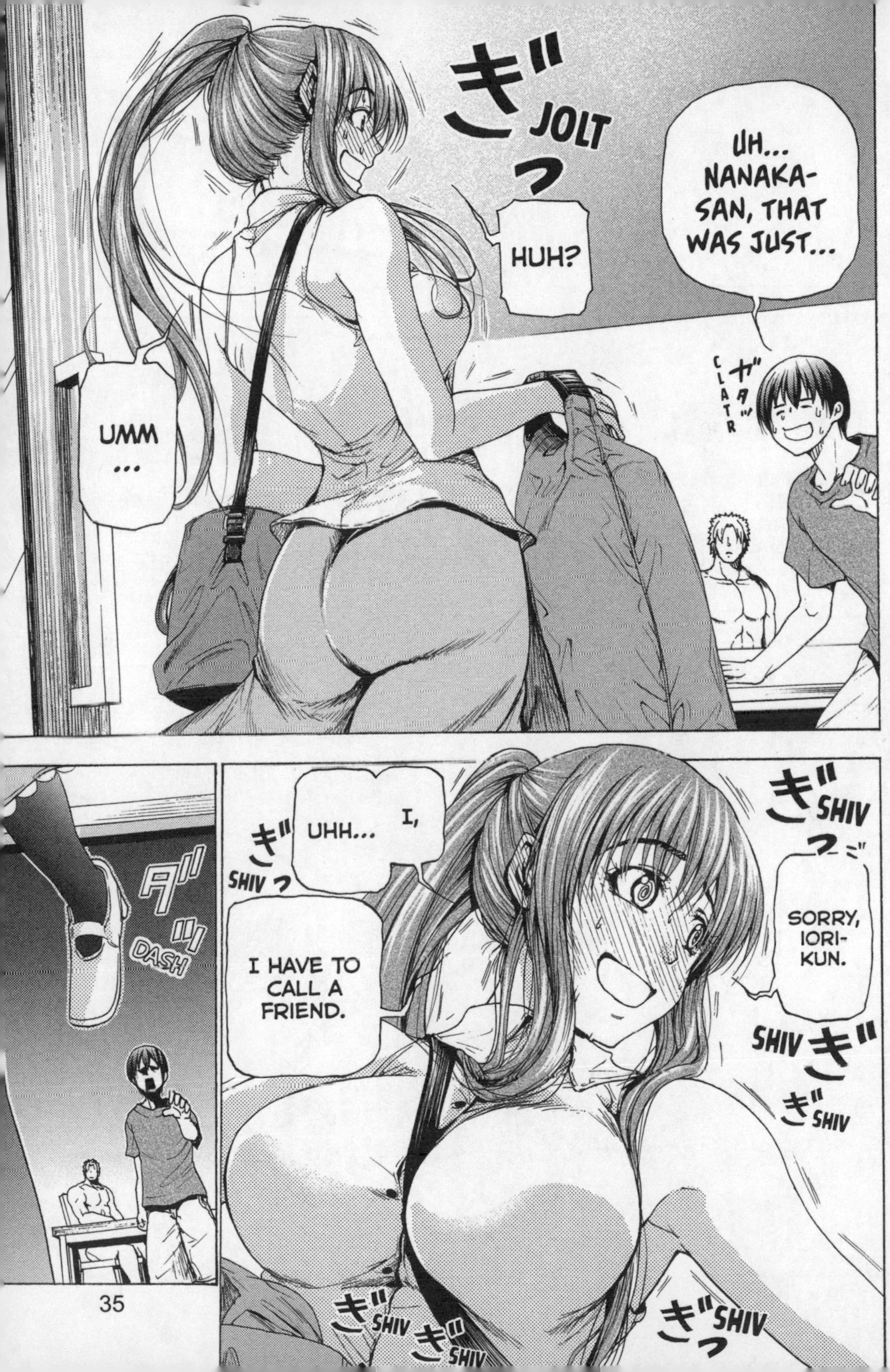

ぎっ JOLT
UH... NANAKA-SAN, THAT WAS JUST...
HUH?
ガタッ CLATR
UMM ...
ぎっ SHIV
SORRY, IORI-KUN.
I, UHH...
ぎっ SHIV
I HAVE TO CALL A FRIEND.
ぎ SHIV
ぎ SHIV
ぎっ SHIV
ぎ SHIV
ぎ SHIV
ダッ DASH

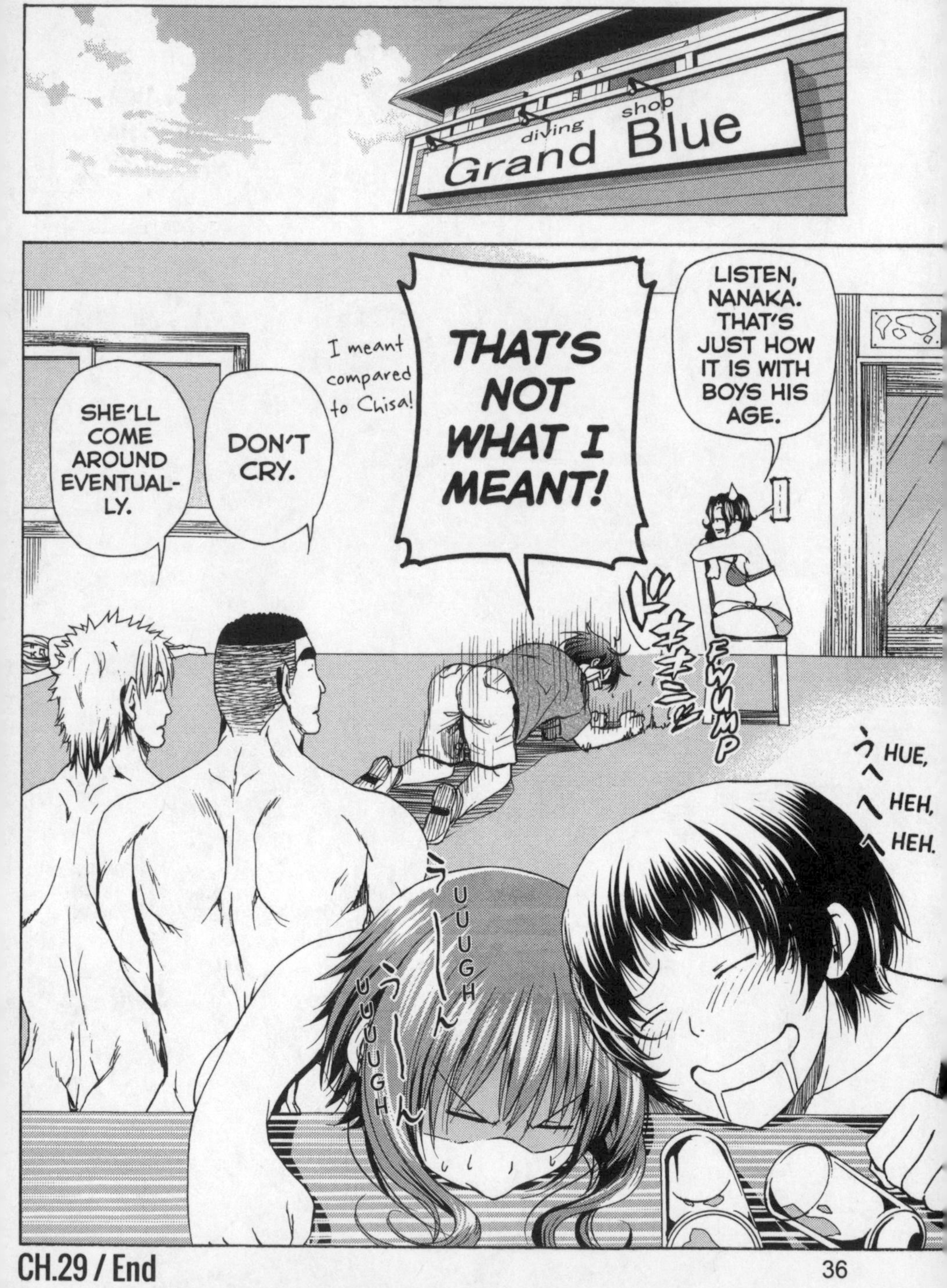
diving shop
Grand Blue
LISTEN, NANAKA. THAT'S JUST HOW IT IS WITH BOYS HIS AGE.
THAT'S NOT WHAT I MEANT!
I meant compared to Chisa!
FWUMP
DON'T CRY.
SHE'LL COME AROUND EVENTUAL-LY.
HUE, HEH, HEH.
UUUGH
UUUUGH

CH.29 / End

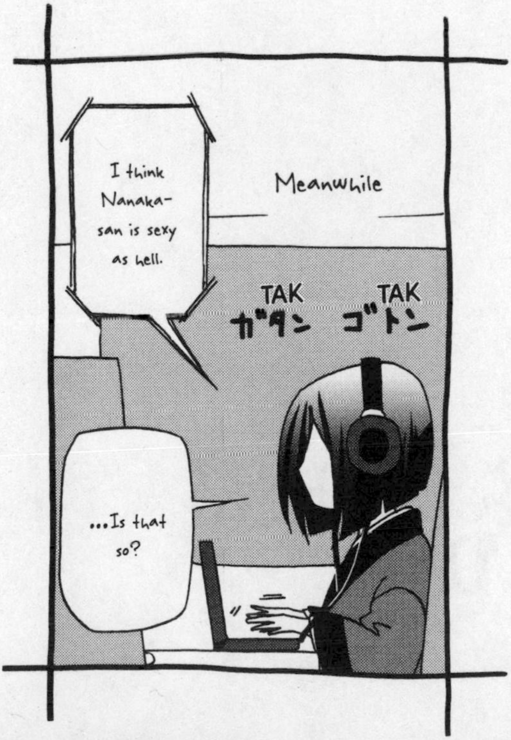
Meanwhile
TAK TAK
ガタン ゴトン
I think Nanaka-san is sexy as hell.
...Is that so?

Grand Blue
Dreaming

# Ch. 30 I'm Not Stripping, Okay?

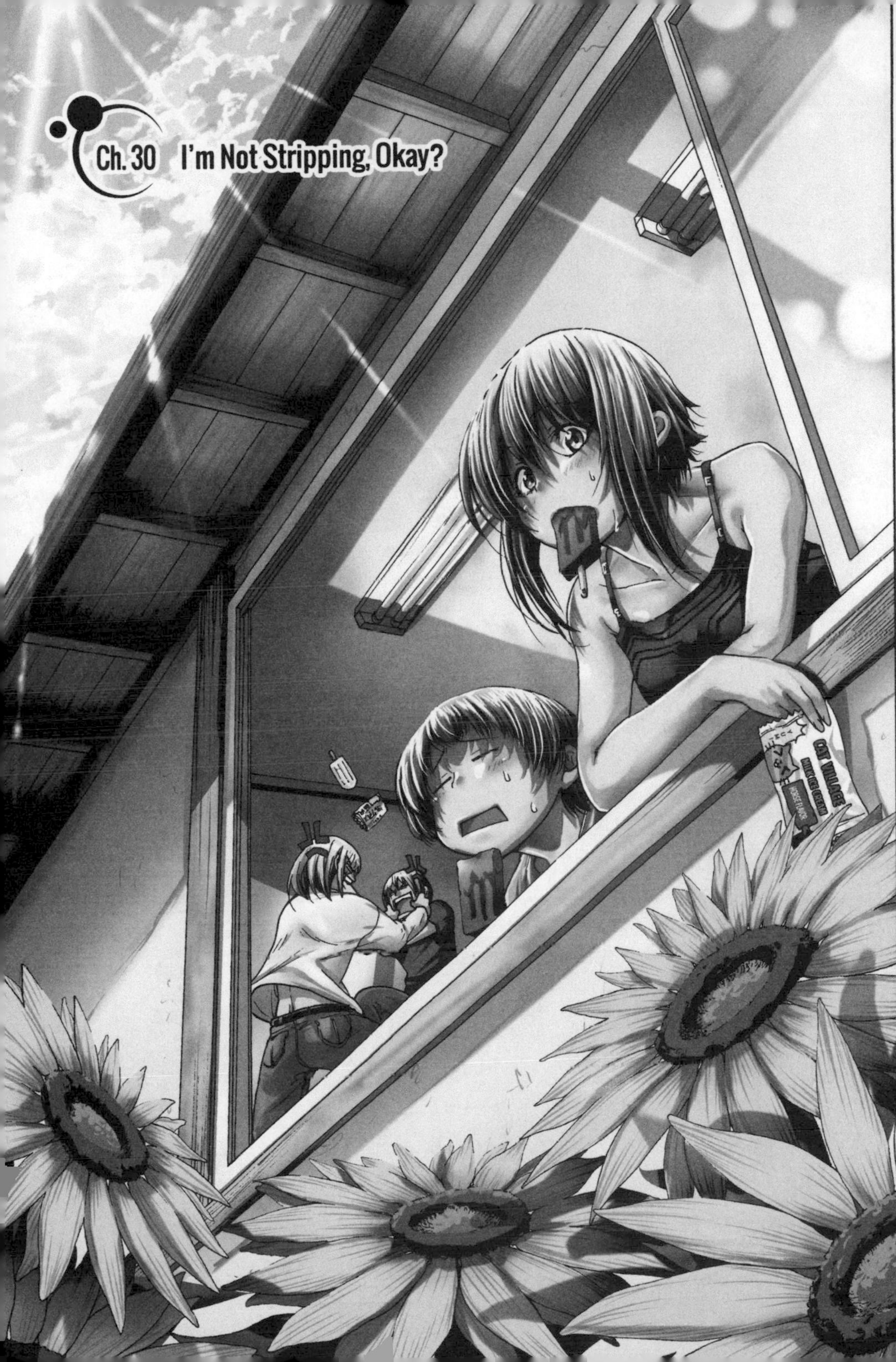
CAT VILLAGE
MILK ICE CREAM
HORSE FLAVOR

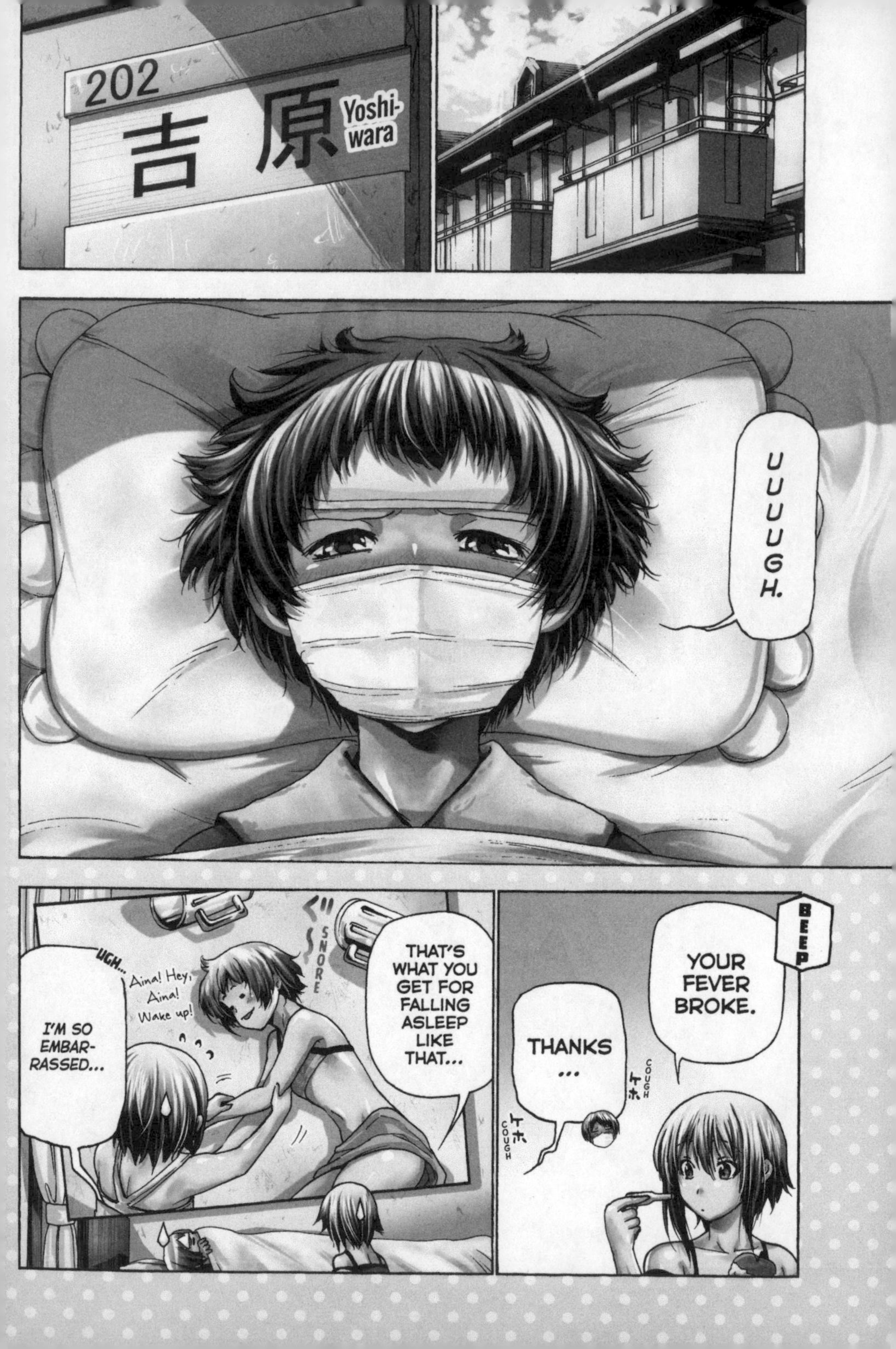
202
吉原
Yoshi-wara
UUUUGH.
BEEP
YOUR FEVER BROKE.
ケホ COUGH
THANKS ...
ケホ COUGH
SNORE
THAT'S WHAT YOU GET FOR FALLING ASLEEP LIKE THAT...
Aina! Hey, Aina! Wake up!
UGH...
I'M SO EMBARRASSED...

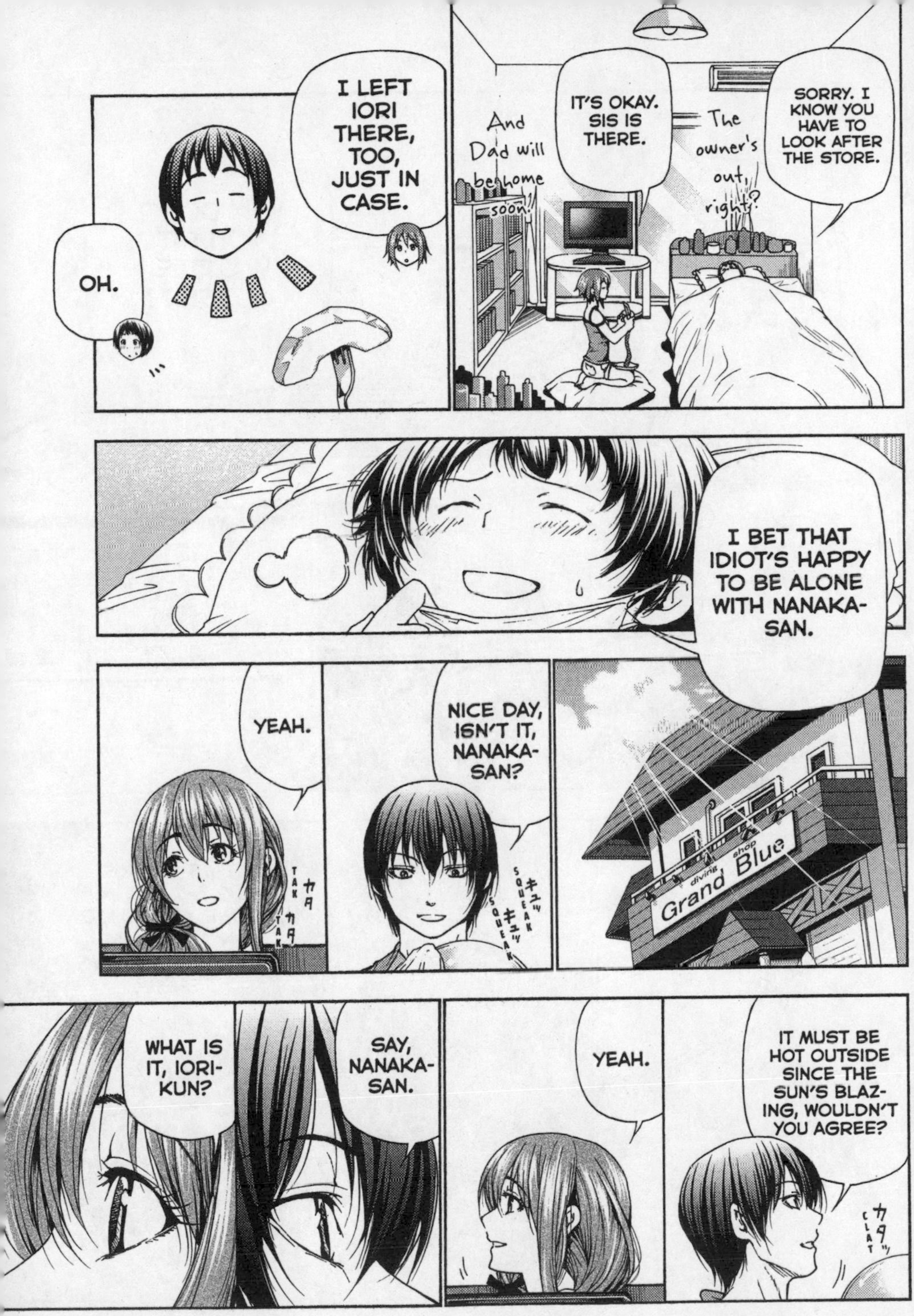
SORRY. I KNOW YOU HAVE TO LOOK AFTER THE STORE.
The owner's out, right?
IT'S OKAY. SIS IS THERE.
And Dad will be home soon!
I LEFT IORI THERE, TOO, JUST IN CASE.
OH.
I BET THAT IDIOT'S HAPPY TO BE ALONE WITH NANAKA-SAN.
diving shop Grand Blue
NICE DAY, ISN'T IT, NANAKA-SAN?
SQUEAK SQUEAK
YEAH.
TAK TAK
IT MUST BE HOT OUTSIDE SINCE THE SUN'S BLAZING, WOULDN'T YOU AGREE?
CLAT
YEAH.
SAY, NANAKA-SAN.
WHAT IS IT, IORI-KUN?

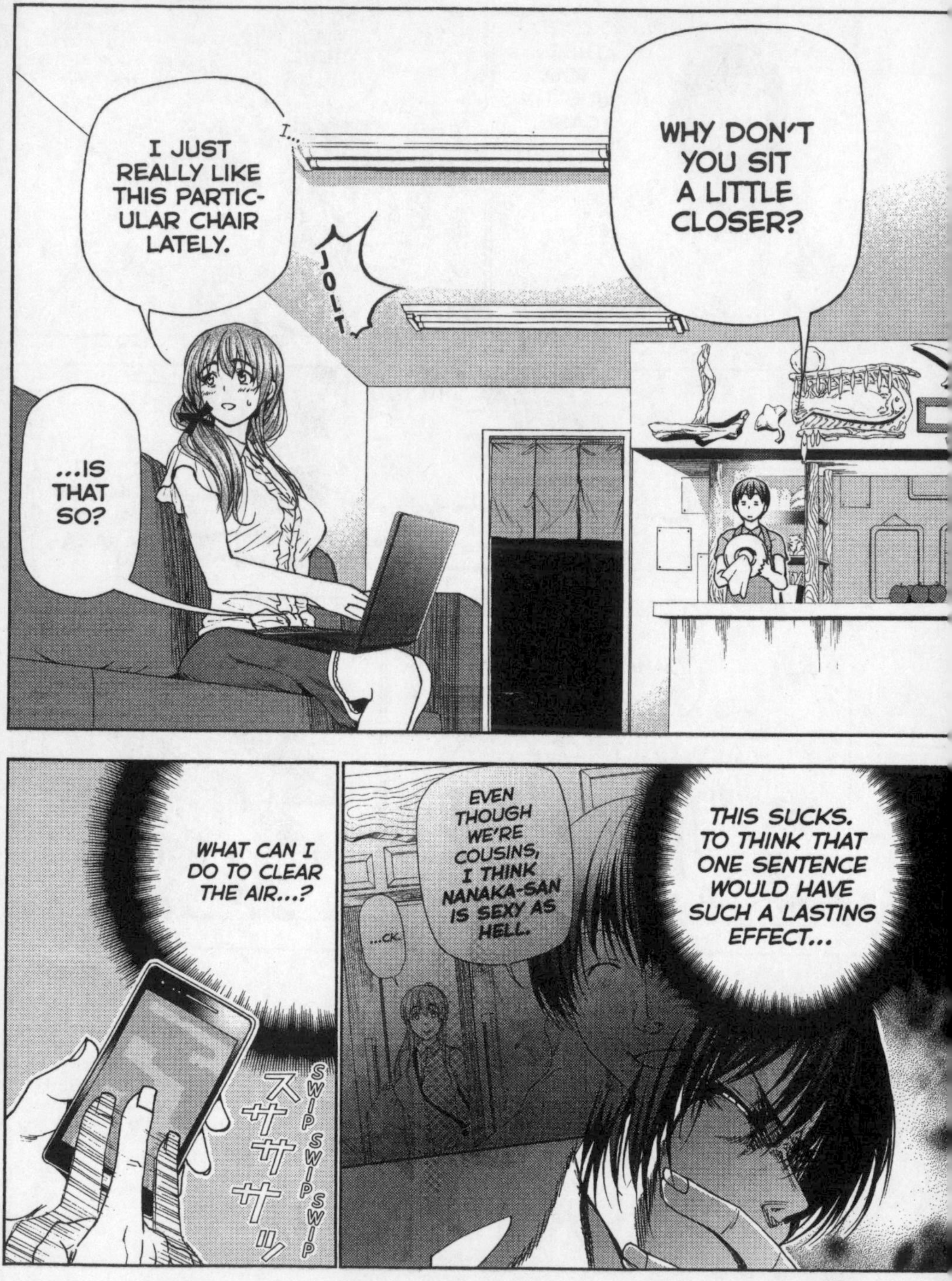
WHY DON'T YOU SIT A LITTLE CLOSER?
I...
JOLT
I JUST REALLY LIKE THIS PARTICULAR CHAIR LATELY.
...IS THAT SO?
THIS SUCKS. TO THINK THAT ONE SENTENCE WOULD HAVE SUCH A LASTING EFFECT...
EVEN THOUGH WE'RE COUSINS, I THINK NANAKA-SAN IS SEXY AS HELL.
...CK.
WHAT CAN I DO TO CLEAR THE AIR...?
スサササッ
SWIP SWIP SWIP

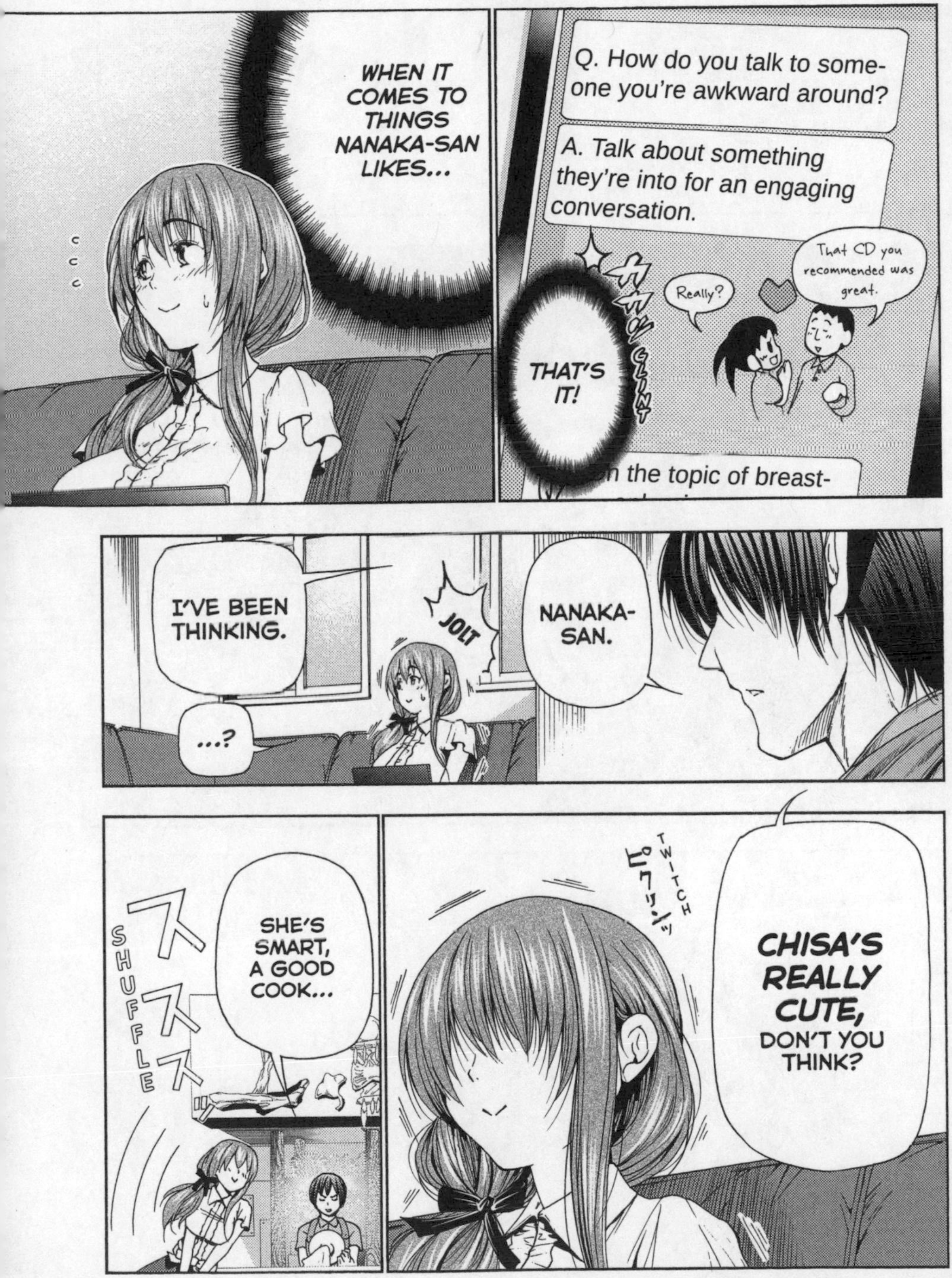
Q. How do you talk to some-one you're awkward around?
A. Talk about something they're into for an engaging conversation.
That CD you recommended was great.
Really?
GLINT
THAT'S IT!
the topic of breast-
WHEN IT COMES TO THINGS NANAKA-SAN LIKES...
NANAKA-SAN.
JOLT
I'VE BEEN THINKING.
...?
TWITCH
CHISA'S REALLY CUTE, DON'T YOU THINK?
SHE'S SMART, A GOOD COOK...
SHUFFLE

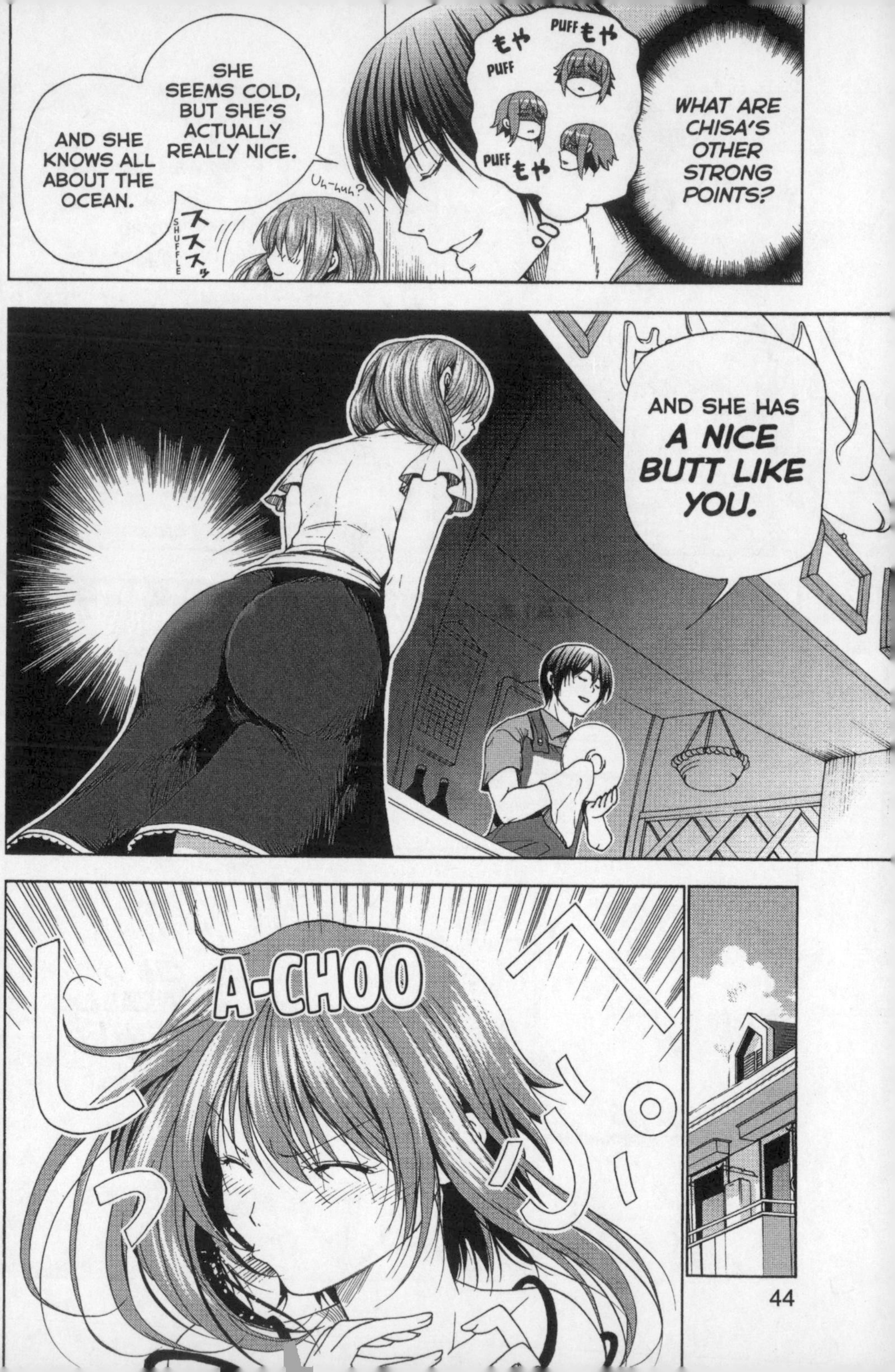
WHAT ARE CHISA'S OTHER STRONG POINTS?
もや PUFF もや
PUFF
PUFF もや
Uh-huh?
SHE SEEMS COLD, BUT SHE'S ACTUALLY REALLY NICE.
AND SHE KNOWS ALL ABOUT THE OCEAN.
スススッ SHUFFLE
AND SHE HAS A NICE BUTT LIKE YOU.
A-CHOO

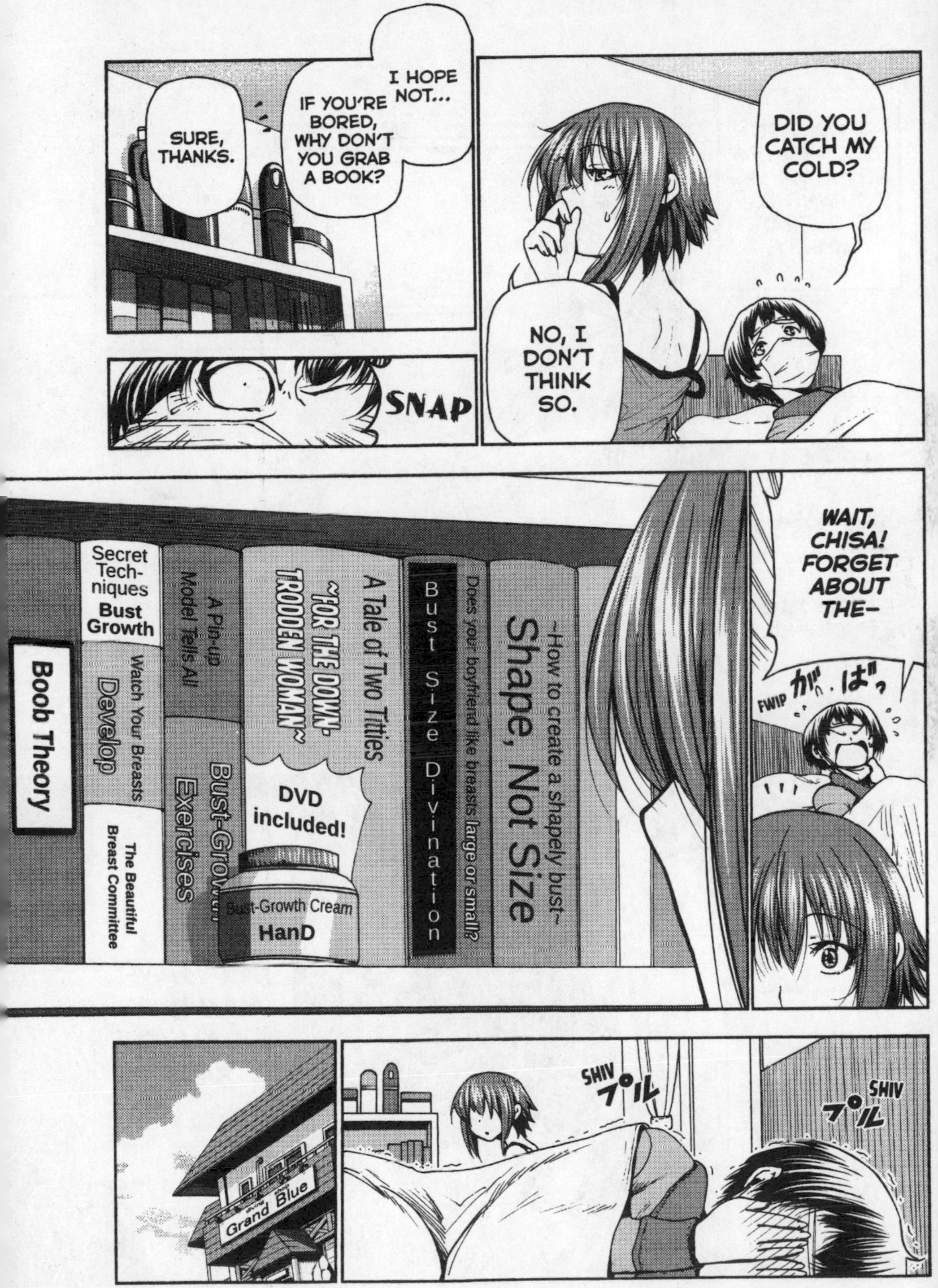
DID YOU CATCH MY COLD?
NO, I DON'T THINK SO.
I HOPE NOT...
IF YOU'RE BORED, WHY DON'T YOU GRAB A BOOK?
SURE, THANKS.
SNAP
WAIT, CHISA! FORGET ABOUT THE-
FWIP がばっ
~How to create a shapely bust~
Shape, Not Size
Does your boyfriend like breasts large or small?
Bust Size Divination
A Tale of Two Titties
~FOR THE DOWNTRODDEN WOMAN~
DVD included!
Bust-Growth Cream
HanD
A Pin-up Model Tells All
Exercises
Secret Techniques
Bust Growth
Watch Your Breasts
Develop
The Beautiful Breast Committee
Boob Theory
SHIV プル
SHIV プル
Grand Blue

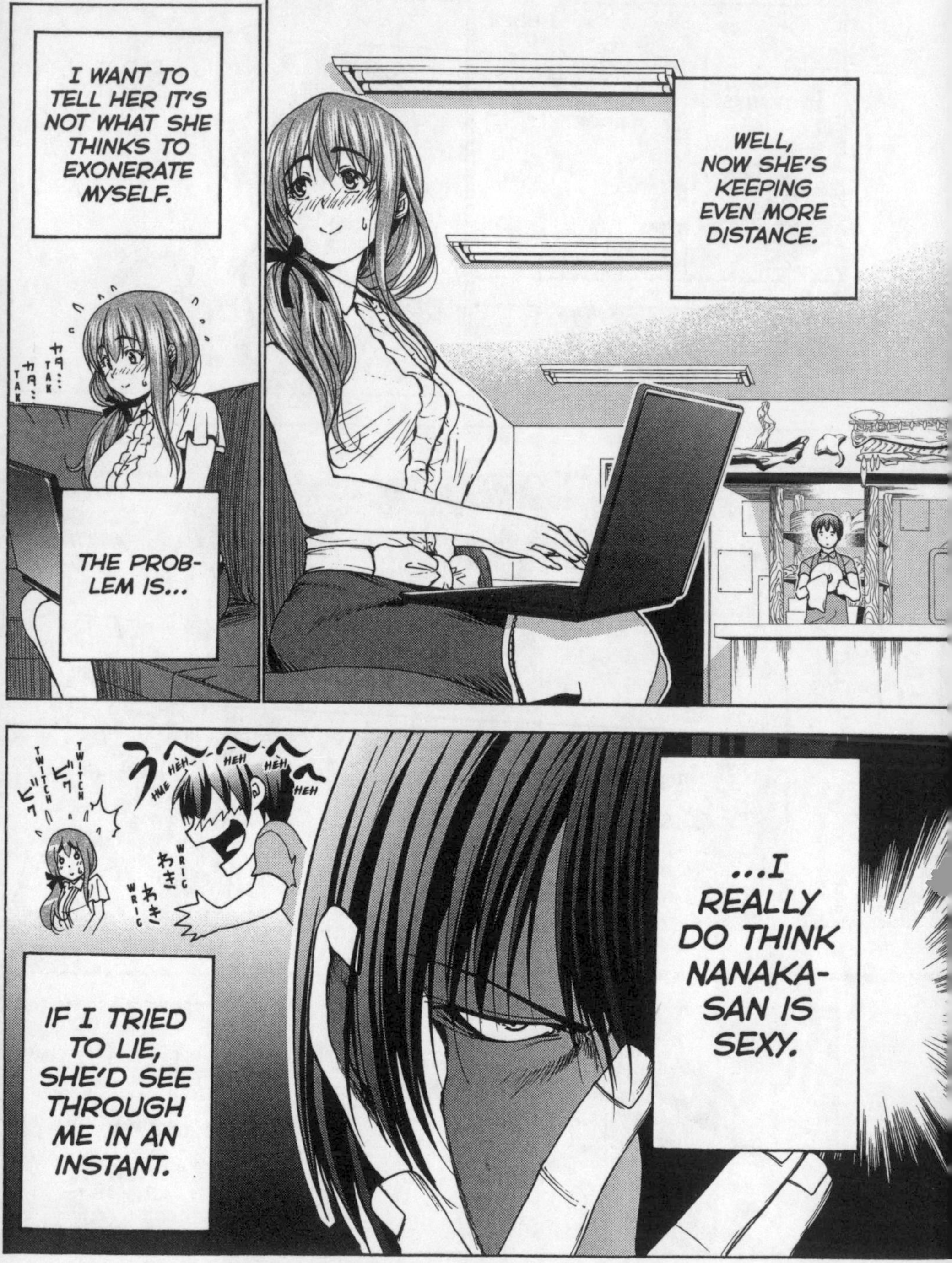
WELL, NOW SHE'S KEEPING EVEN MORE DISTANCE.
I WANT TO TELL HER IT'S NOT WHAT SHE THINKS TO EXONERATE MYSELF.
カタ… TAK
カタ… TAK
THE PROB-LEM IS...
...I REALLY DO THINK NANAKA-SAN IS SEXY.
うへへへへ HWAE HEH HEH HEH HEH
ビク TWITCH
ビク TWITCH
わき WRIG
わき WRIG
IF I TRIED TO LIE, SHE'D SEE THROUGH ME IN AN INSTANT.

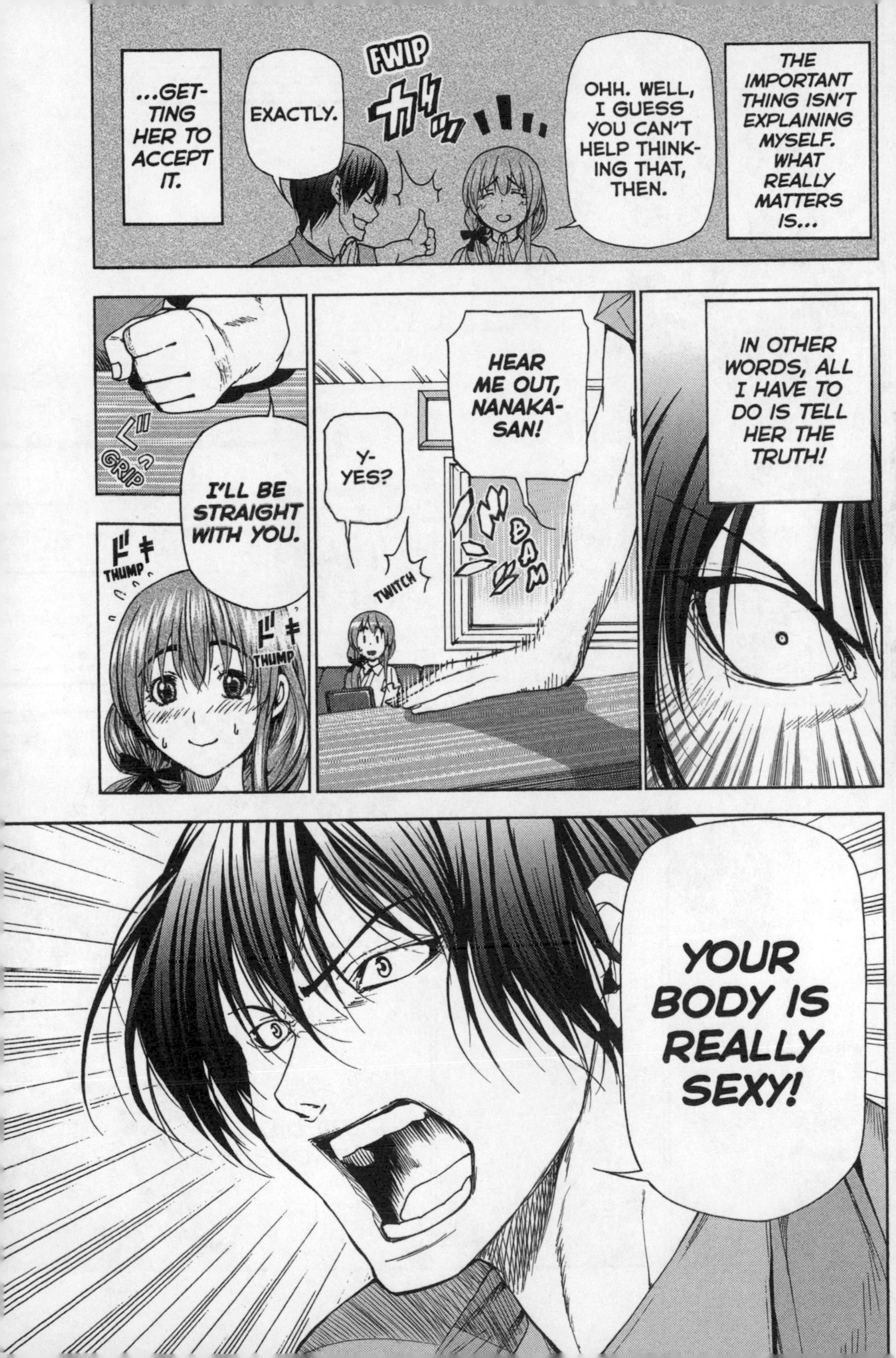
THE IMPORTANT THING ISN'T EXPLAINING MYSELF. WHAT REALLY MATTERS IS...
OHH. WELL, I GUESS YOU CAN'T HELP THINKING THAT, THEN.
FWIP
EXACTLY.
...GETTING HER TO ACCEPT IT.
IN OTHER WORDS, ALL I HAVE TO DO IS TELL HER THE TRUTH!
HEAR ME OUT, NANAKA-SAN!
BAM
Y-YES?
TWITCH
GRIP
I'LL BE STRAIGHT WITH YOU.
THUMP
THUMP
YOUR BODY IS REALLY SEXY!

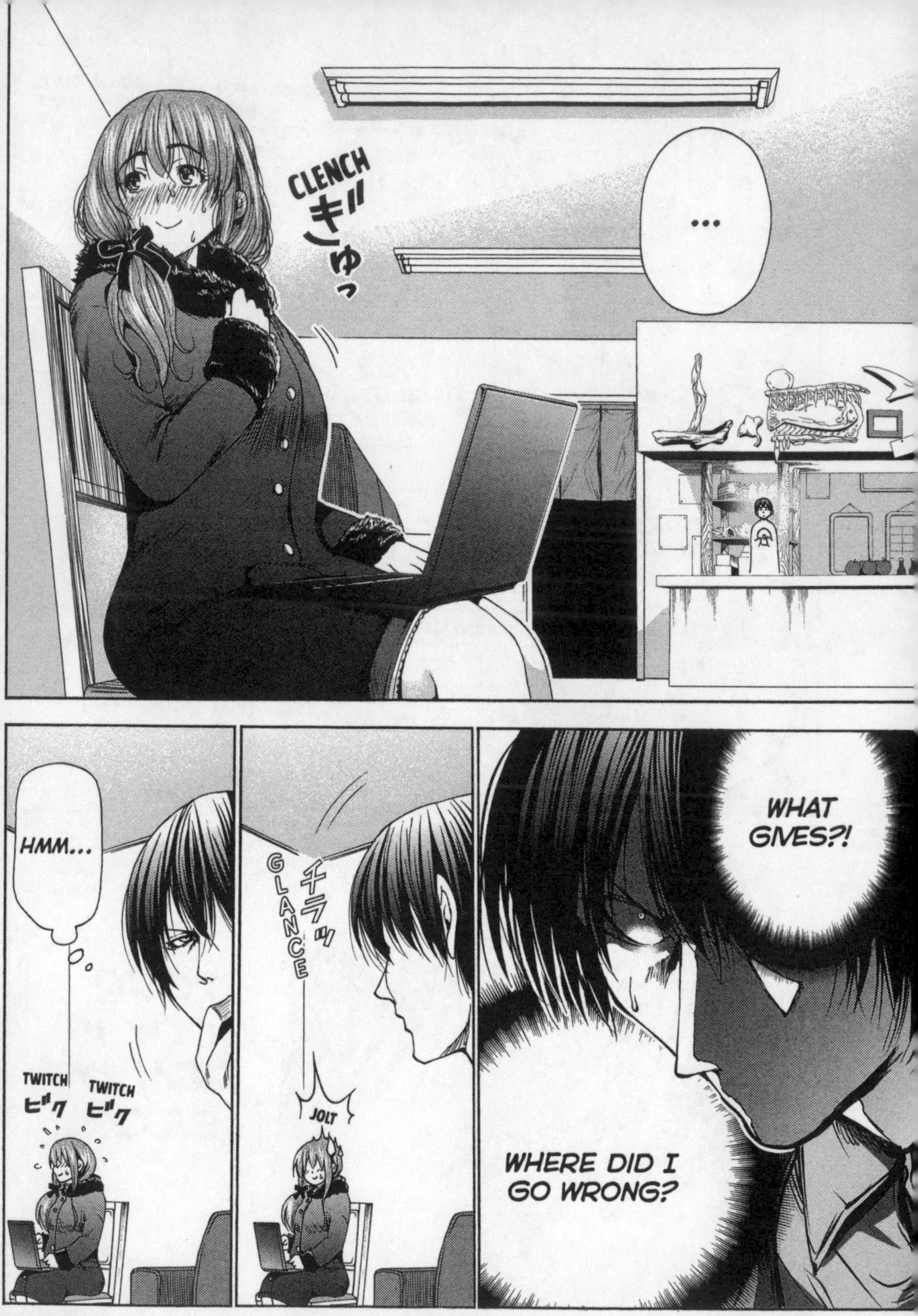
...
CLENCH
キゅっ
WHAT GIVES?!
WHERE DID I GO WRONG?
GLANCE
チラッ
JOLT
HMM...
TWITCH
ビク
TWITCH
ビク

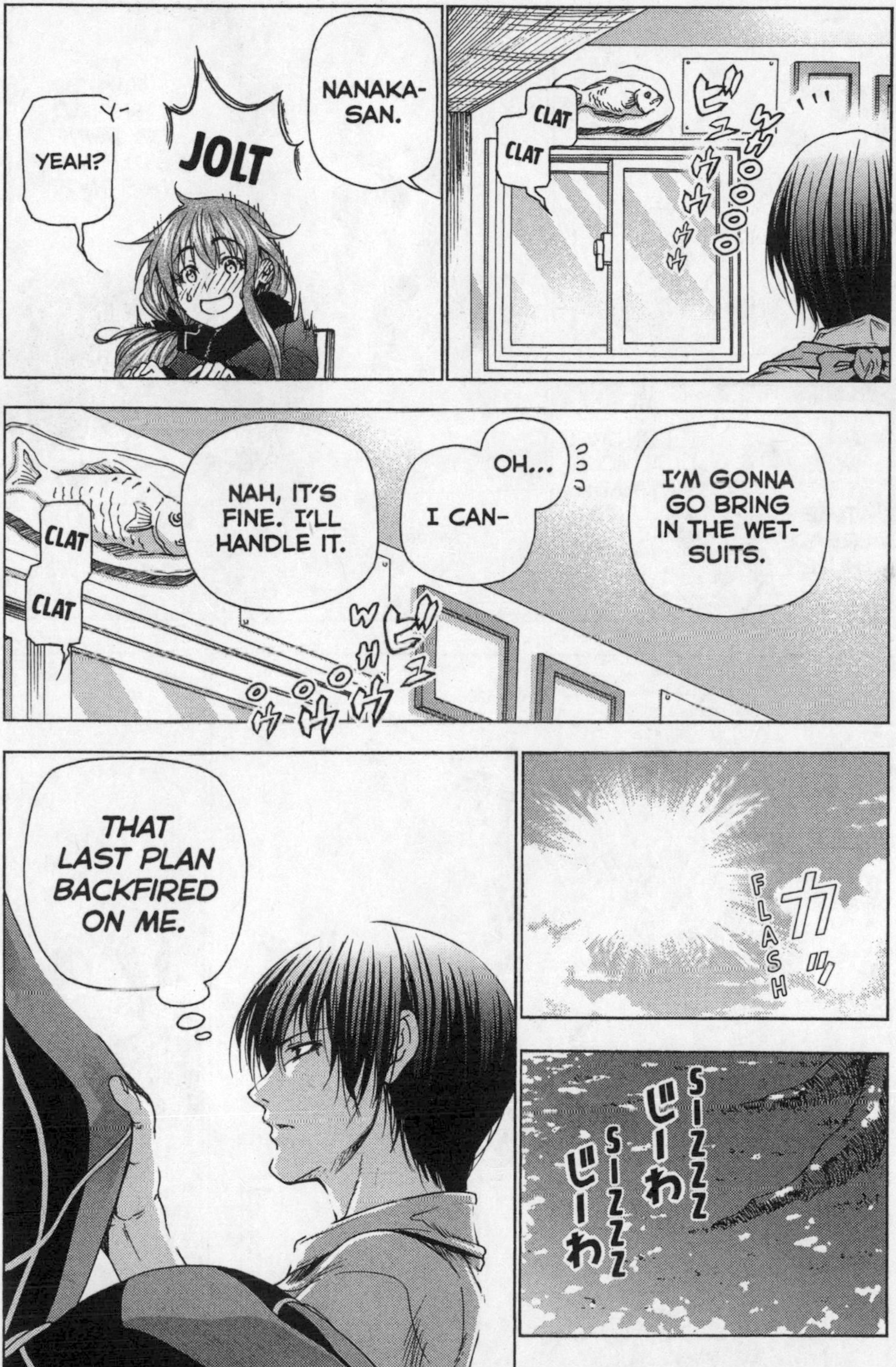
CLAT
CLAT
WHOOOOO
ビュウウウウ
NANAKA-SAN.
JOLT
Y-
YEAH?
I'M GONNA GO BRING IN THE WET-SUITS.
OH...
I CAN-
NAH, IT'S FINE. I'LL HANDLE IT.
CLAT
CLAT
WHOOO
ビュウウウ
FLASH
カッ
SIZZZ
じーわ
SIZZZ
じーわ
THAT LAST PLAN BACKFIRED ON ME.

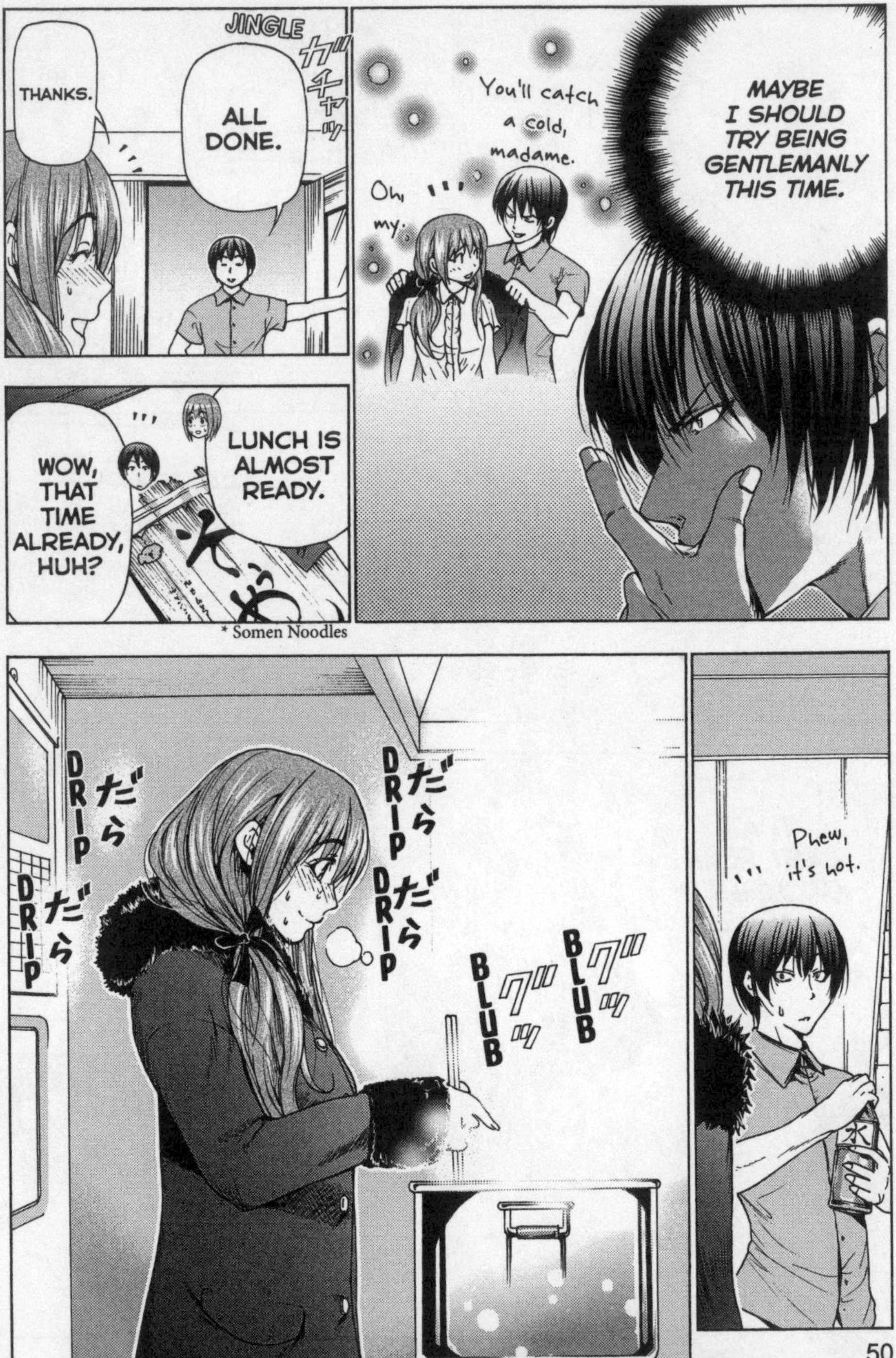
MAYBE I SHOULD TRY BEING GENTLEMANLY THIS TIME.
You'll catch a cold, madame.
Oh, my.
JINGLE
ALL DONE.
THANKS.
LUNCH IS ALMOST READY.
WOW, THAT TIME ALREADY, HUH?
Phew, it's hot.
DRIP
DRIP
DRIP
BLUB
BLUB

* Somen Noodles

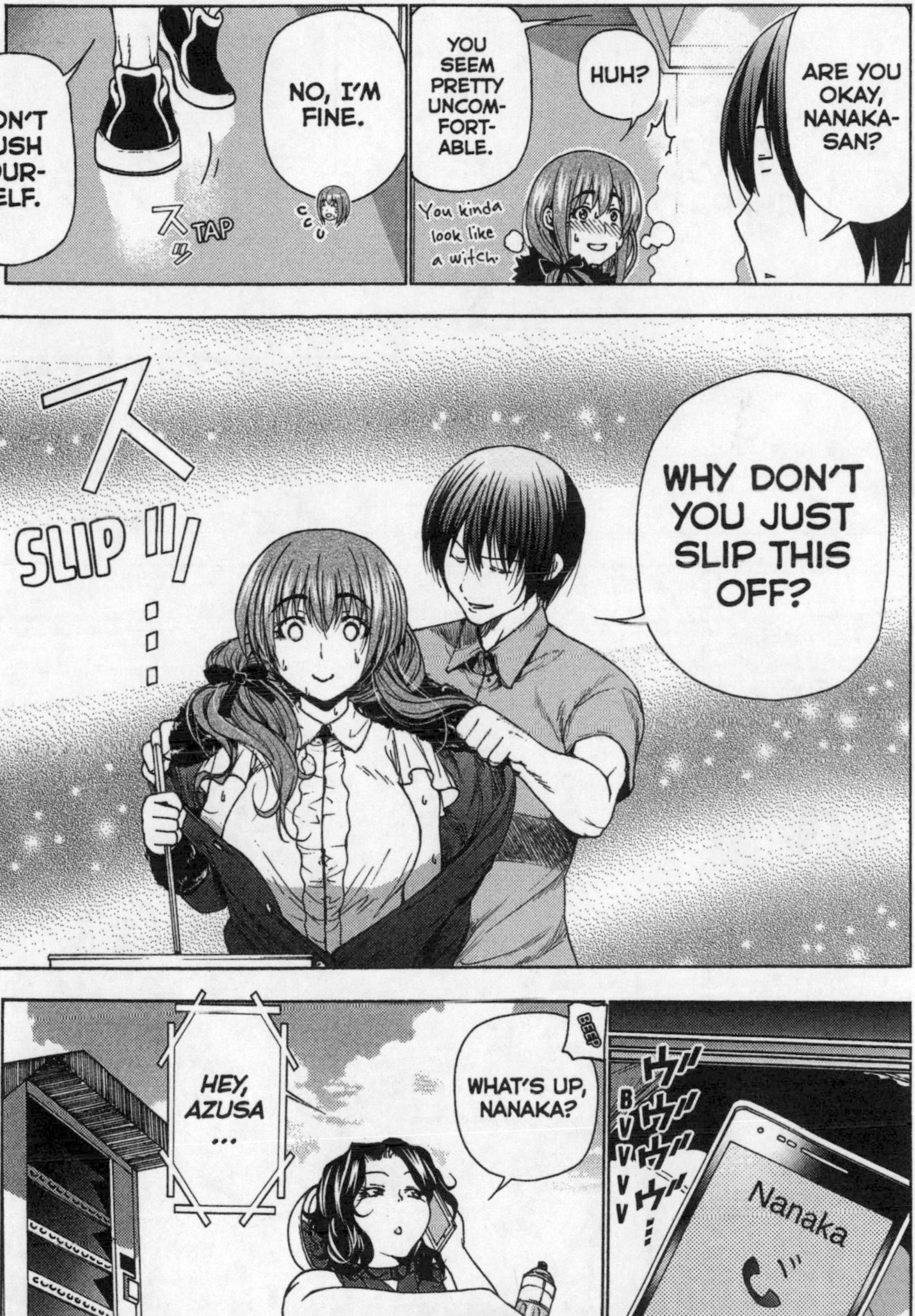
ARE YOU OKAY, NANAKA-SAN?
HUH?
YOU SEEM PRETTY UNCOMFORTABLE.
You kinda look like a witch.
NO, I'M FINE.
TAP
DON'T PUSH YOURSELF.
WHY DON'T YOU JUST SLIP THIS OFF?
SLIP
...
BVVVVV
Nanaka
BEEP
WHAT'S UP, NANAKA?
HEY, AZUSA...

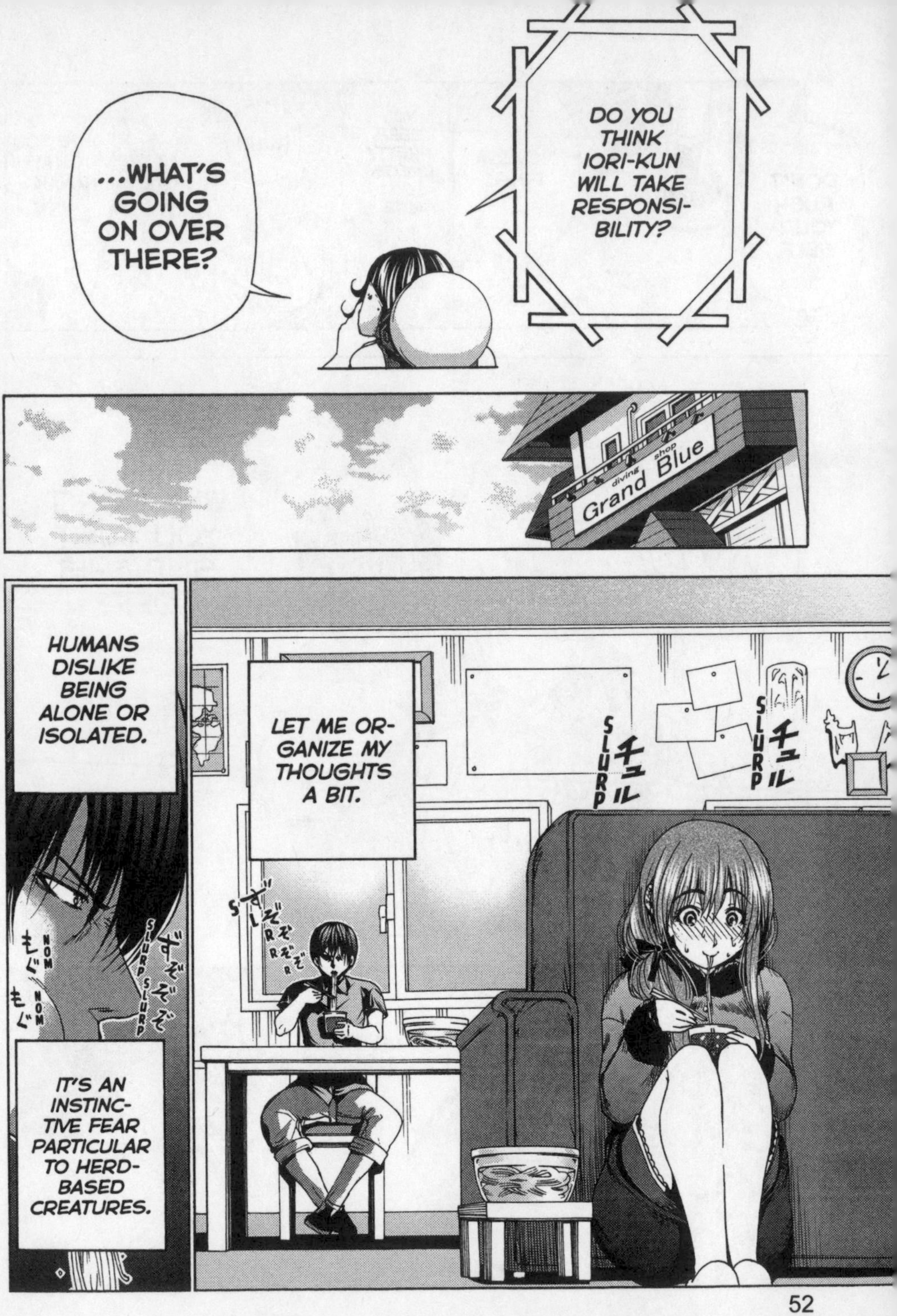
DO YOU THINK IORI-KUN WILL TAKE RESPONSI-BILITY?
...WHAT'S GOING ON OVER THERE?
diving shop Grand Blue
SLURP チュル
SLURP チュル
LET ME OR-GANIZE MY THOUGHTS A BIT.
ずぞぞぞ SLRRR
HUMANS DISLIKE BEING ALONE OR ISOLATED.
ずぞぞぞ SLURP SLURP
もぐもぐ NOM NOM
IT'S AN INSTINC-TIVE FEAR PARTICULAR TO HERD-BASED CREATURES.

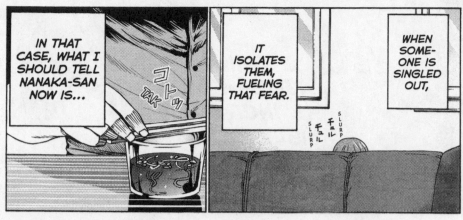

WHEN SOMEONE IS SINGLED OUT,
IT ISOLATES THEM, FUELING THAT FEAR.
チュル チュル
SLURP SLURP
IN THAT CASE, WHAT I SHOULD TELL NANAKA-SAN NOW IS...
コトッ
TAK
CLATR
カタッ
NANAKA-SAN.
JOLT
ビクッ
I- I'M NOT STRIPPING, OKAY?
NO, LET'S SET THAT ASIDE FOR NOW.
SO WE'RE ONLY SETTING IT ASIDE...
PLEASE JUST KEEP THIS IN MIND.
O- OKAY.
ドキ ドキ
THUMP THUMP

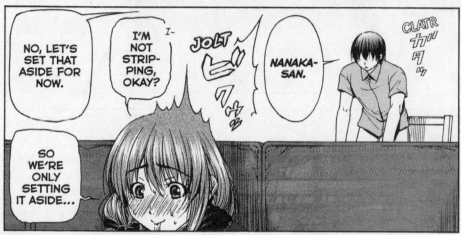

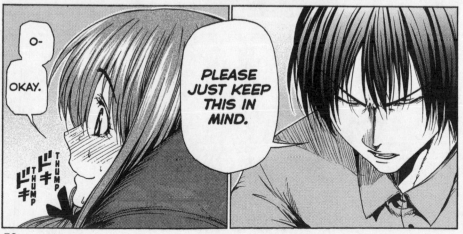

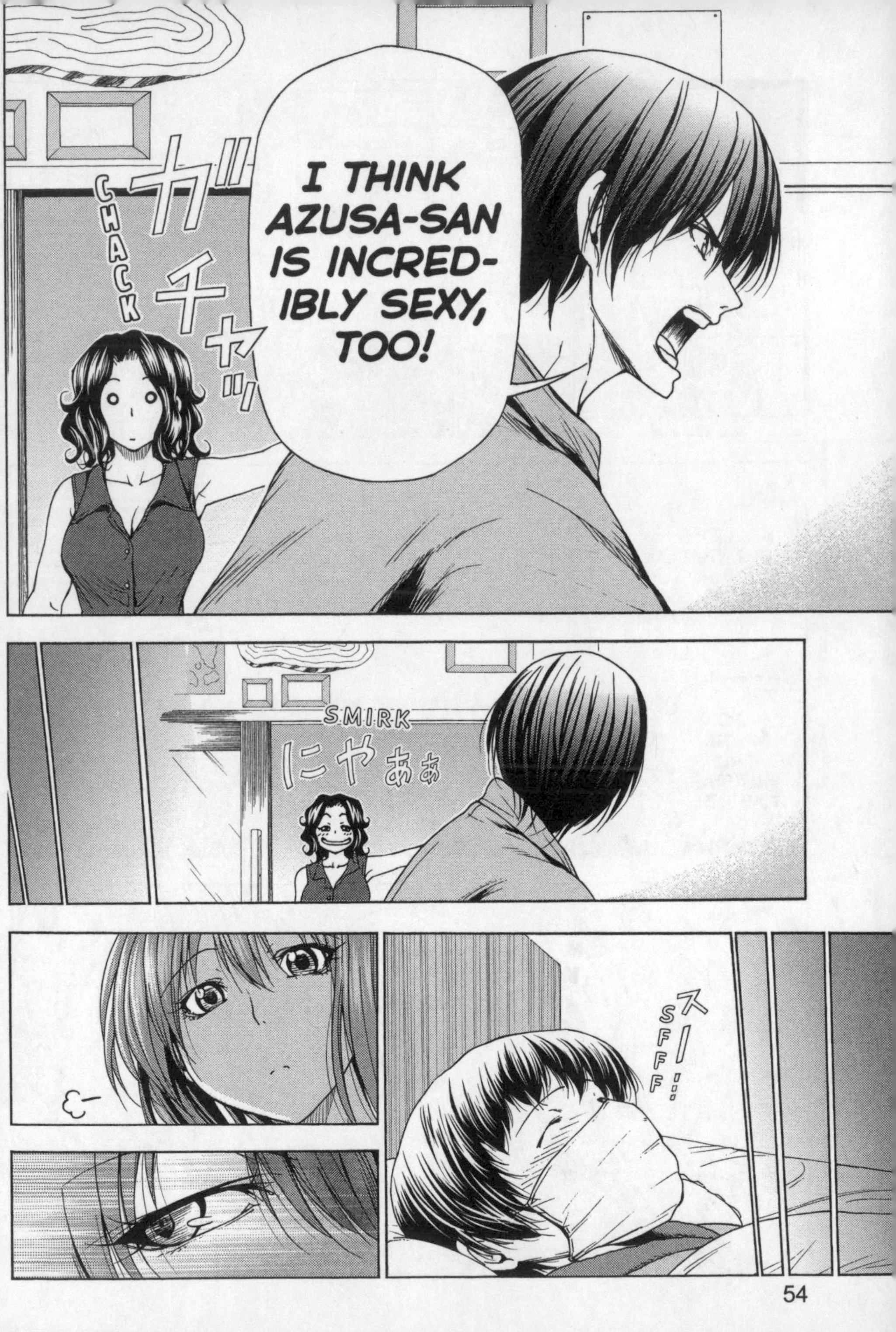
ガチャッ
CHACK
I THINK AZUSA-SAN IS INCREDIBLY SEXY, TOO!
にやぁぁ
SMIRK
スー!!
SFFF

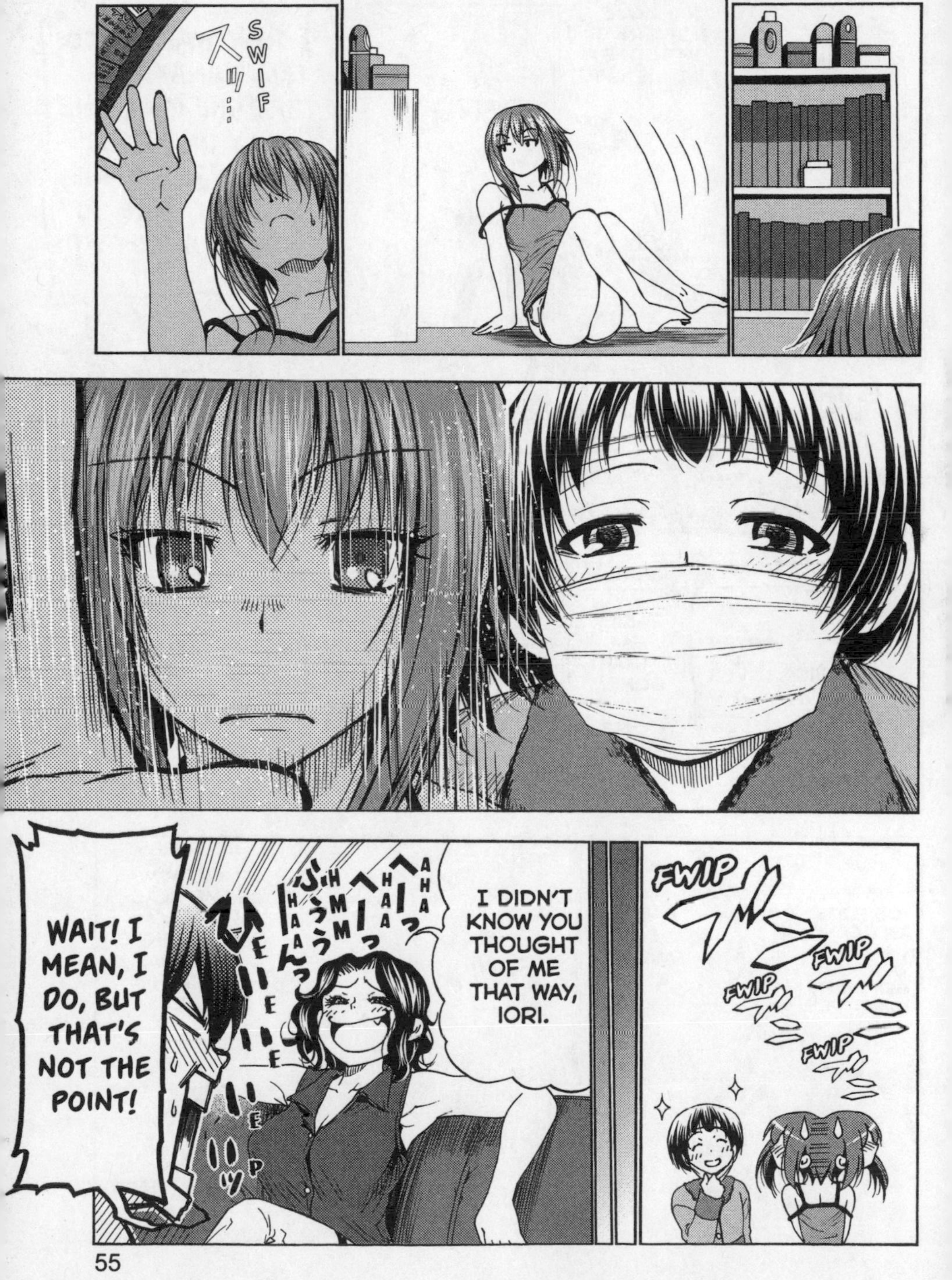
SWIF
FWIP
FWIP
FWIP
FWIP
AHA
HAA
HMM
HAA
I DIDN'T KNOW YOU THOUGHT OF ME THAT WAY, IORI.
EEEEE
EEP
WAIT! I MEAN, I DO, BUT THAT'S NOT THE POINT!

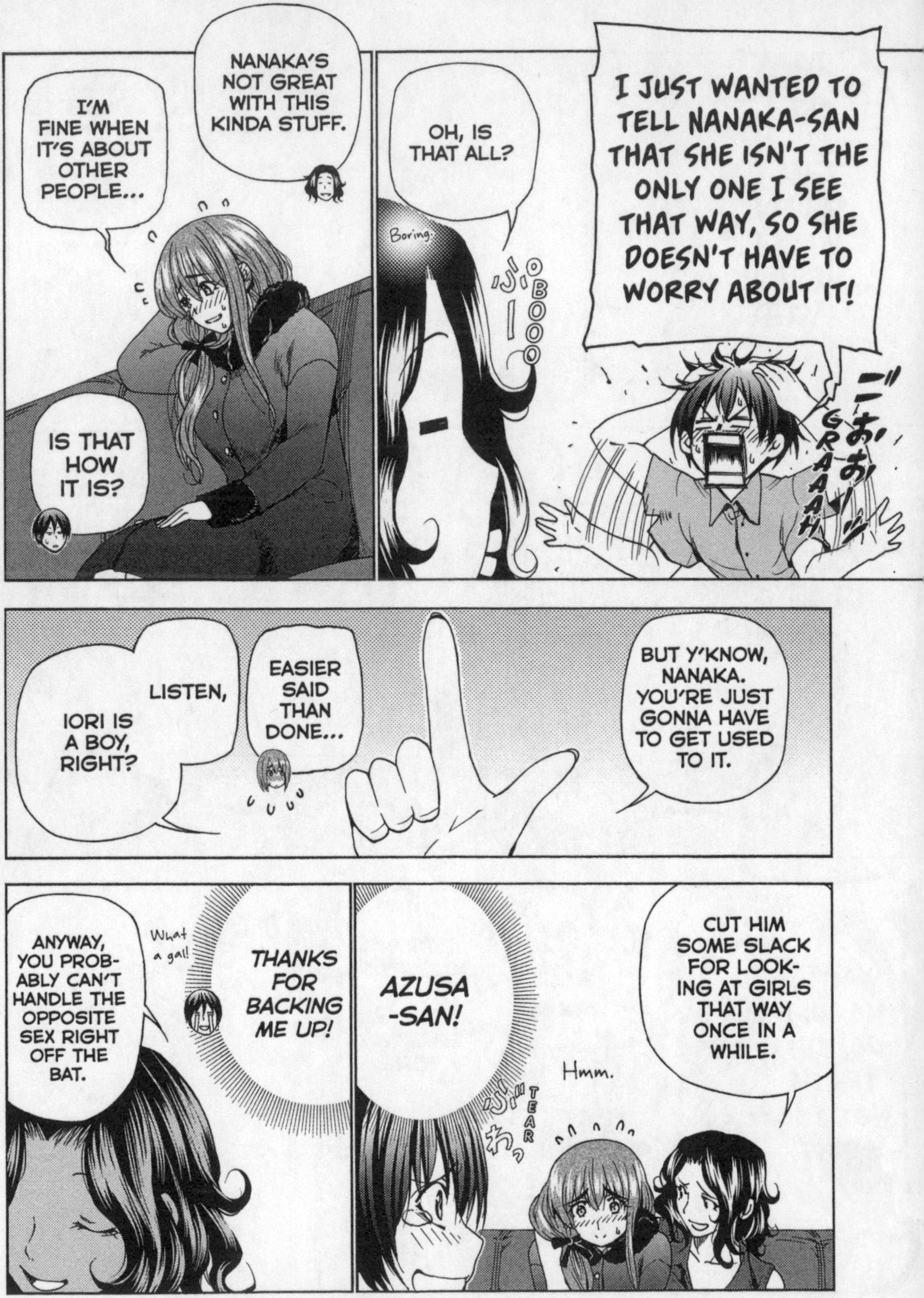
I JUST WANTED TO TELL NANAKA-SAN THAT SHE ISN'T THE ONLY ONE I SEE THAT WAY, SO SHE DOESN'T HAVE TO WORRY ABOUT IT!
GRAAAAH
OH, IS THAT ALL?
Boring.
BOOOO
NANAKA'S NOT GREAT WITH THIS KINDA STUFF.
I'M FINE WHEN IT'S ABOUT OTHER PEOPLE...
IS THAT HOW IT IS?
BUT Y'KNOW, NANAKA. YOU'RE JUST GONNA HAVE TO GET USED TO IT.
EASIER SAID THAN DONE...
LISTEN,
IORI IS A BOY, RIGHT?
CUT HIM SOME SLACK FOR LOOK-ING AT GIRLS THAT WAY ONCE IN A WHILE.
Hmm.
AZUSA -SAN!
TEAR
THANKS FOR BACKING ME UP!
What a gal!
ANYWAY, YOU PROB-ABLY CAN'T HANDLE THE OPPOSITE SEX RIGHT OFF THE BAT.

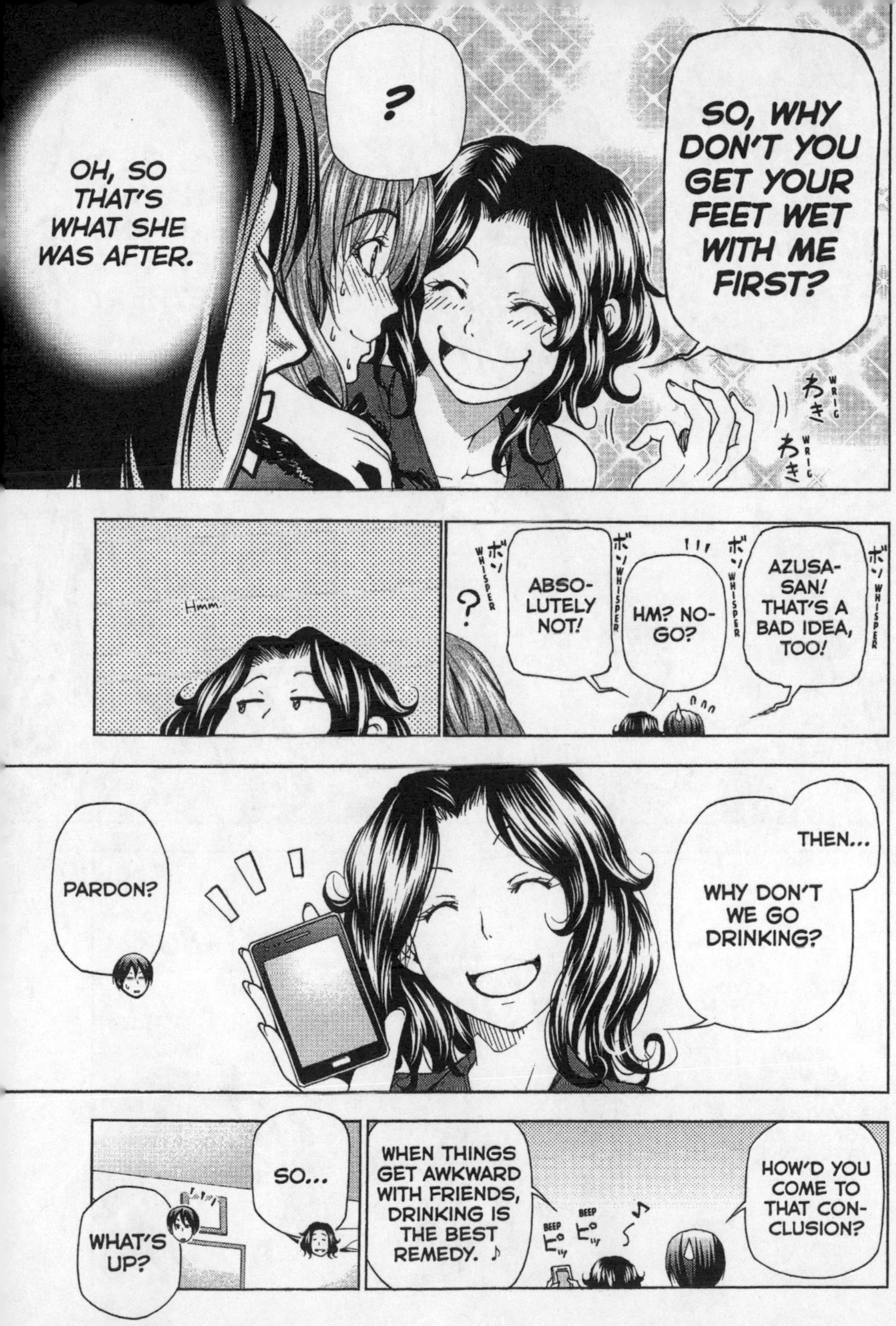
SO, WHY DON'T YOU GET YOUR FEET WET WITH ME FIRST?
わき WRIG
わき WRIG
?
OH, SO THAT'S WHAT SHE WAS AFTER.
ボソ WHISPER
AZUSA-SAN! THAT'S A BAD IDEA, TOO!
ボソ WHISPER
HM? NO-GO?
ボソ WHISPER
ABSOLUTELY NOT!
ボソ WHISPER
?
Hmm
THEN...
WHY DON'T WE GO DRINKING?
PARDON?
HOW'D YOU COME TO THAT CONCLUSION?
ピッ BEEP
ピッ BEEP
WHEN THINGS GET AWKWARD WITH FRIENDS, DRINKING IS THE BEST REMEDY. ♪
SO...
WHAT'S UP?

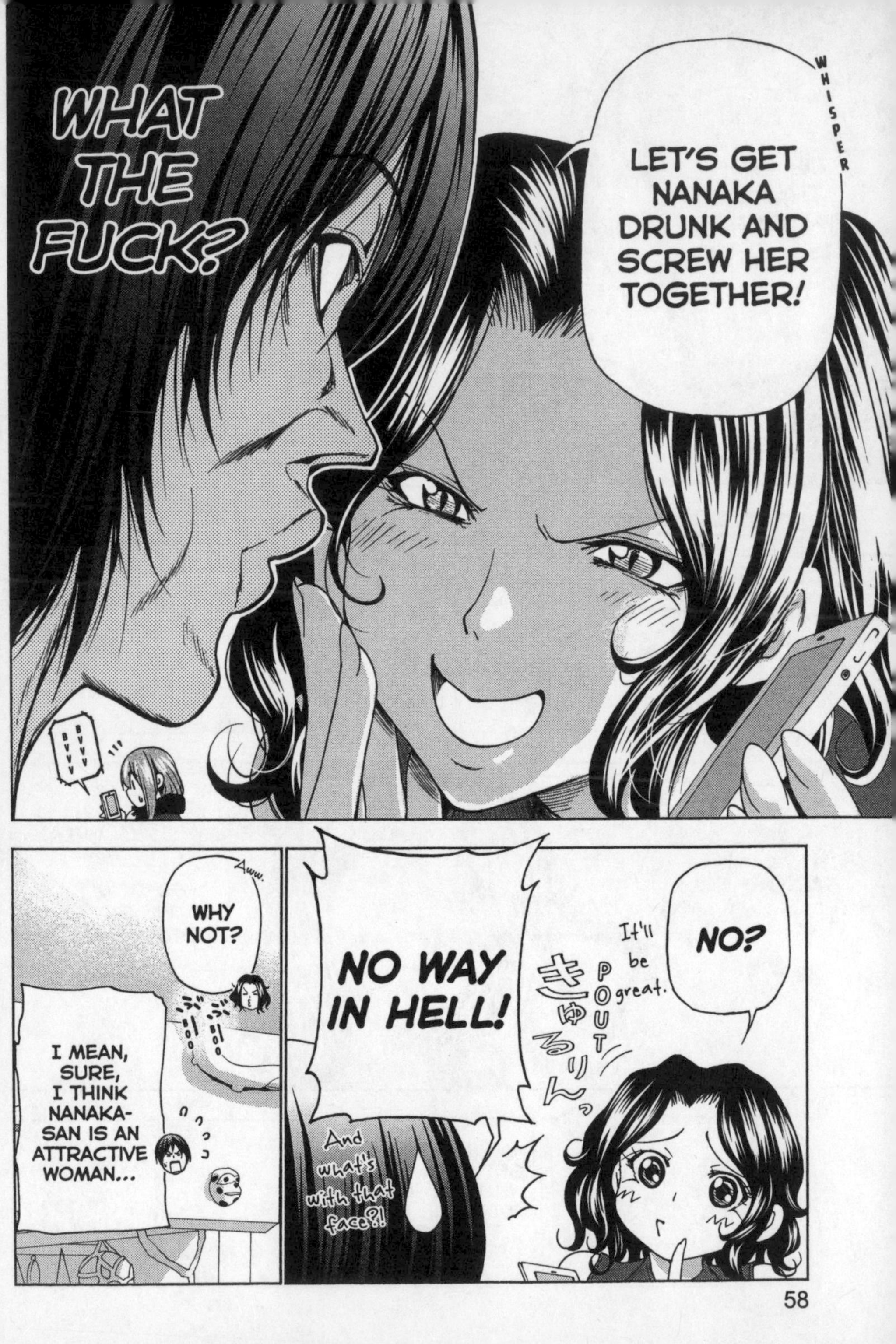
WHISPER
LET'S GET NANAKA DRUNK AND SCREW HER TOGETHER!
WHAT THE FUCK?
BVVV BVVV
NO?
It'll be great.
POUT
きゅるりんっ
NO WAY IN HELL!
And what's with that face?!
Aww.
WHY NOT?
ぶーぶー
I MEAN, SURE, I THINK NANAKA-SAN IS AN ATTRACTIVE WOMAN...

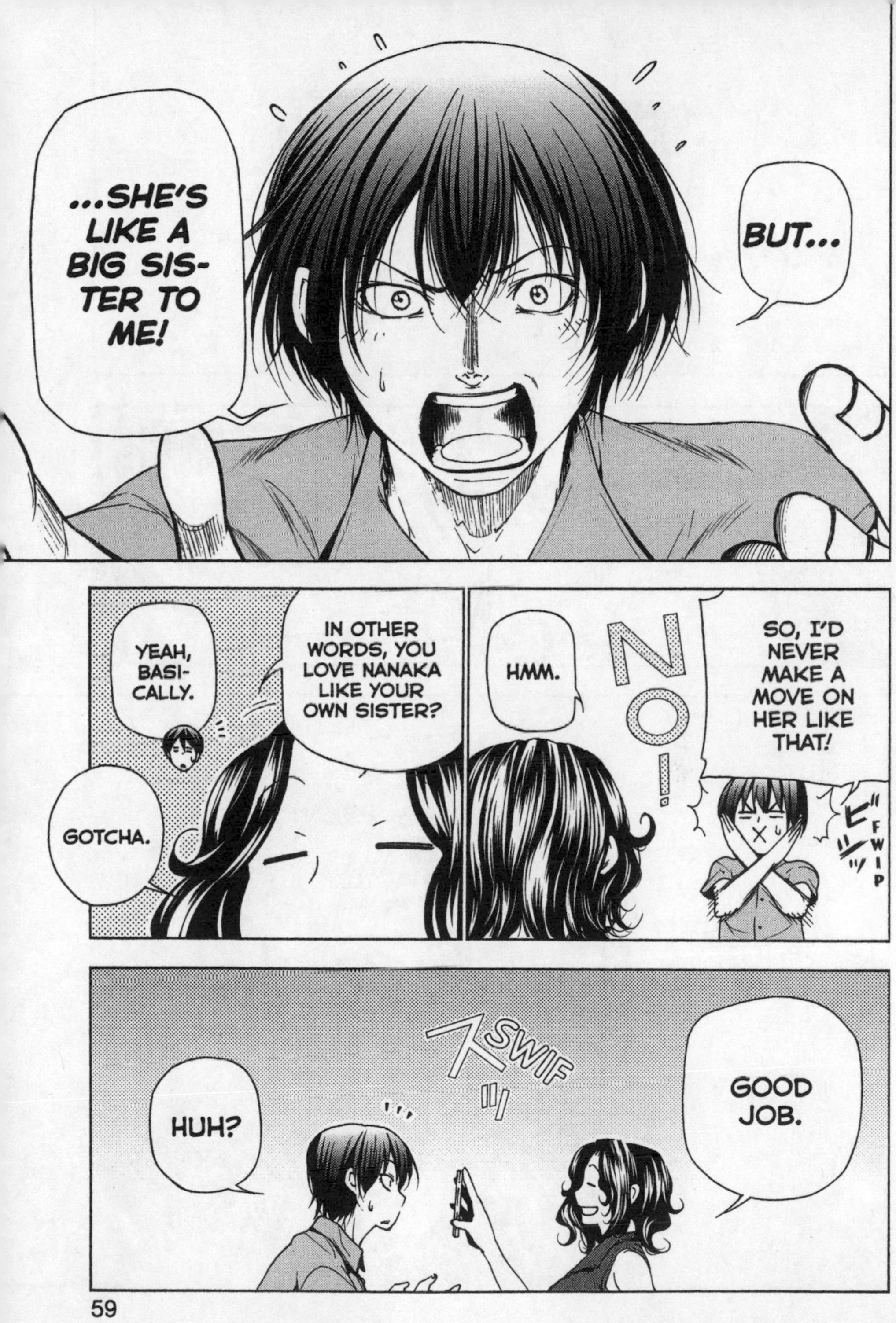
BUT...
...SHE'S LIKE A BIG SIS-TER TO ME!
SO, I'D NEVER MAKE A MOVE ON HER LIKE THAT!
NO!
FWIP
HMM.
IN OTHER WORDS, YOU LOVE NANAKA LIKE YOUR OWN SISTER?
YEAH, BASI-CALLY.
GOTCHA.
GOOD JOB.
SWIF
HUH?

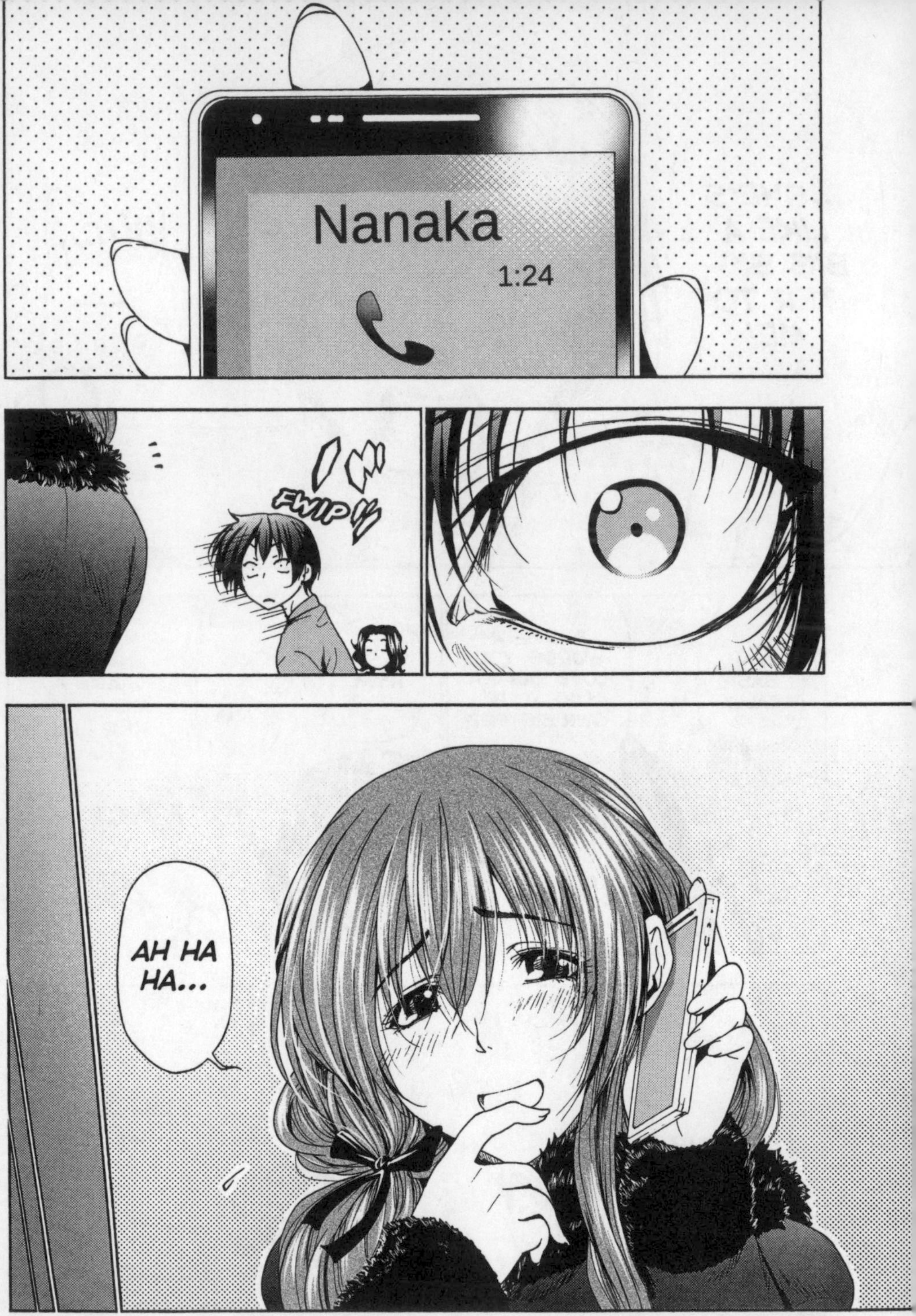
Nanaka
1:24
FWIP
AH HA HA...

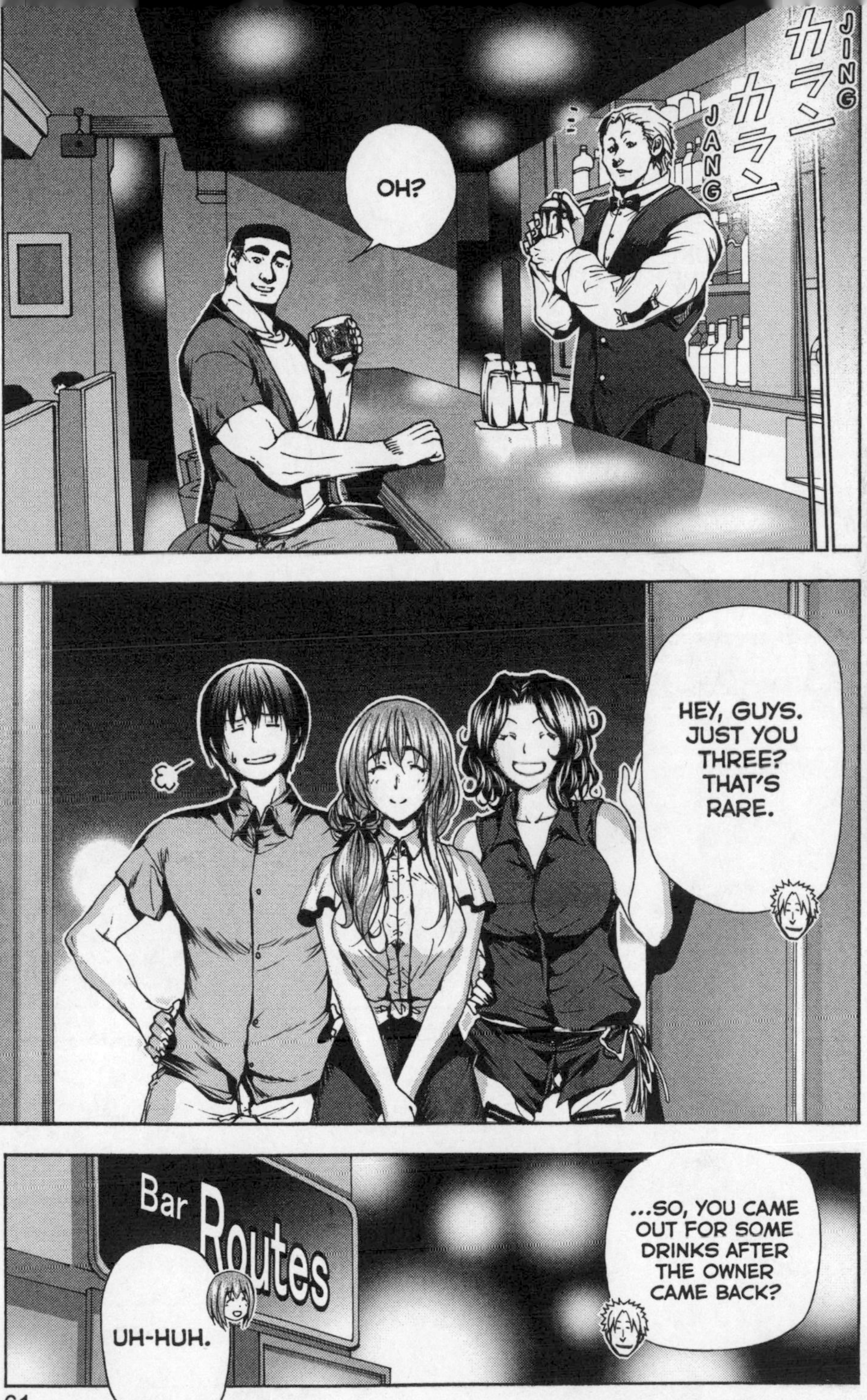
JING
JANG
カランカラン
OH?
HEY, GUYS. JUST YOU THREE? THAT'S RARE.
...SO, YOU CAME OUT FOR SOME DRINKS AFTER THE OWNER CAME BACK?
Bar Routes
UH-HUH.

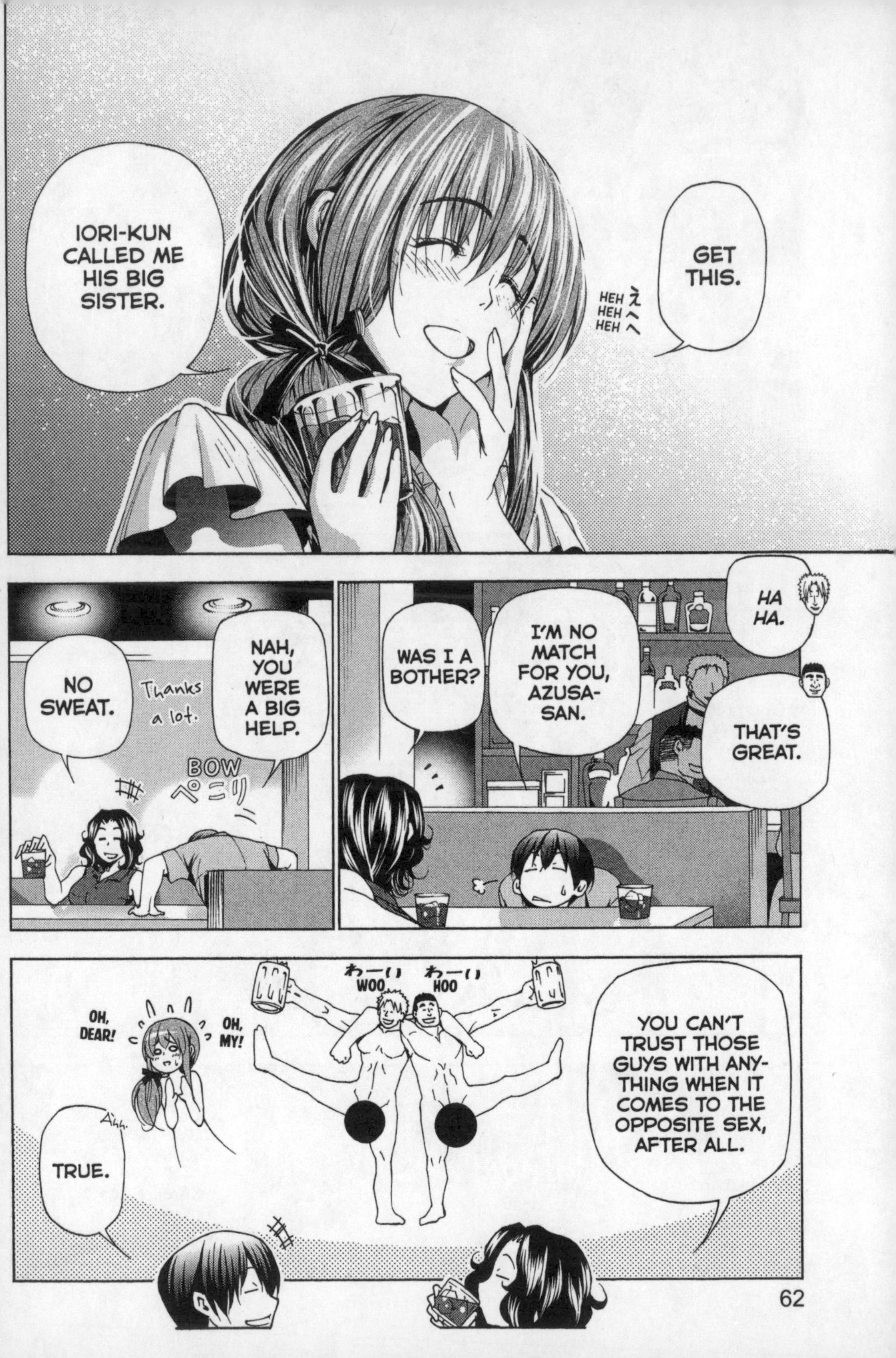

GET THIS.
HEH HEH HEH えへへ
IORI-KUN CALLED ME HIS BIG SISTER.
HA HA.
THAT'S GREAT.
I'M NO MATCH FOR YOU, AZUSA-SAN.
WAS I A BOTHER?
NAH, YOU WERE A BIG HELP.
BOW ぺこり
Thanks a lot.
NO SWEAT.
YOU CAN'T TRUST THOSE GUYS WITH ANY-THING WHEN IT COMES TO THE OPPOSITE SEX, AFTER ALL.
わーい HOO
わーい WOO
OH, MY!
OH, DEAR!
Ahh.
TRUE.

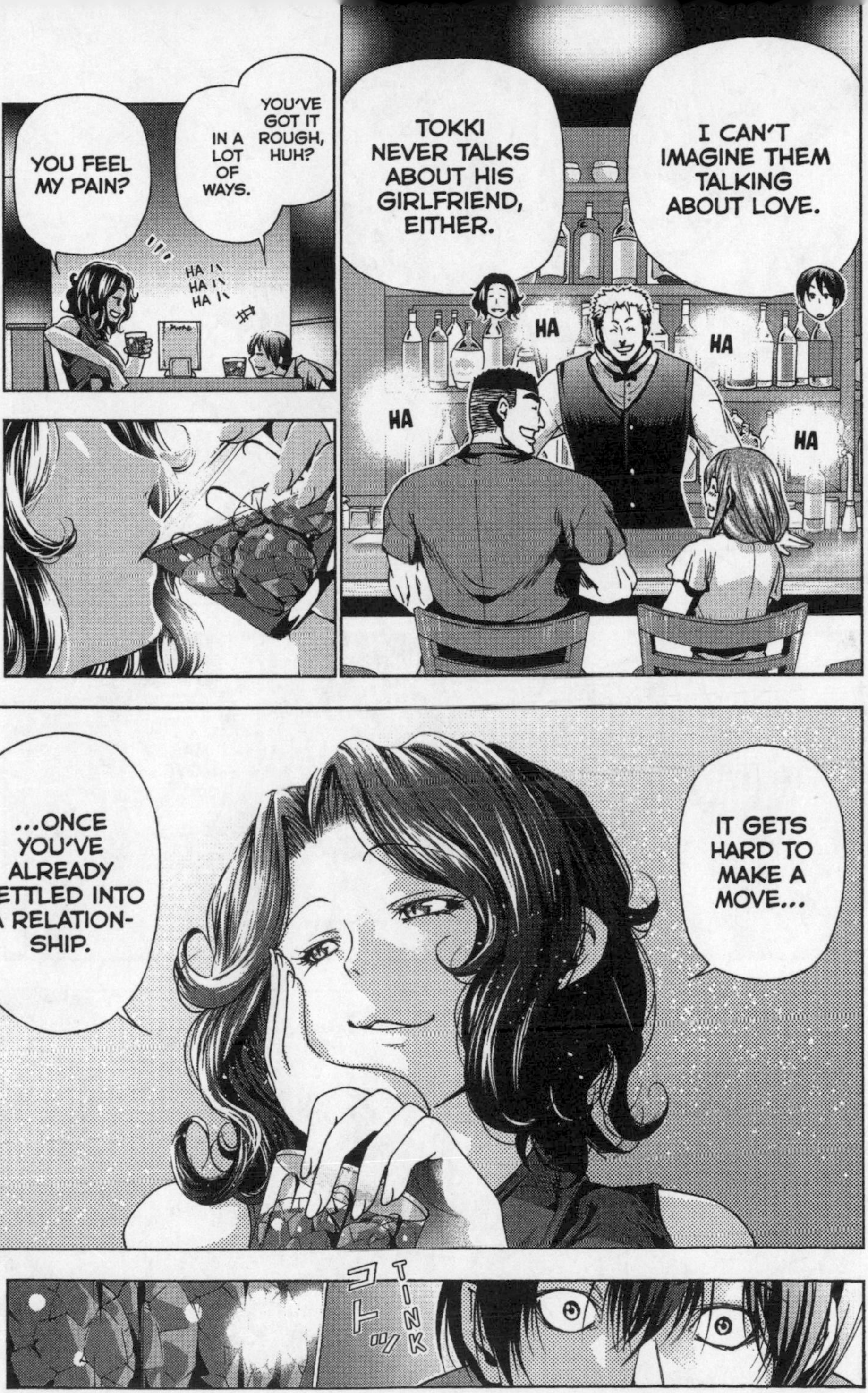
I CAN'T IMAGINE THEM TALKING ABOUT LOVE.
TOKKI NEVER TALKS ABOUT HIS GIRLFRIEND, EITHER.
HA
HA
HA
HA
YOU'VE GOT IT ROUGH, HUH?
IN A LOT OF WAYS.
YOU FEEL MY PAIN?
HA HA HA
IT GETS HARD TO MAKE A MOVE...
...ONCE YOU'VE ALREADY SETTLED INTO A RELATION-SHIP.
コトッ
TINK

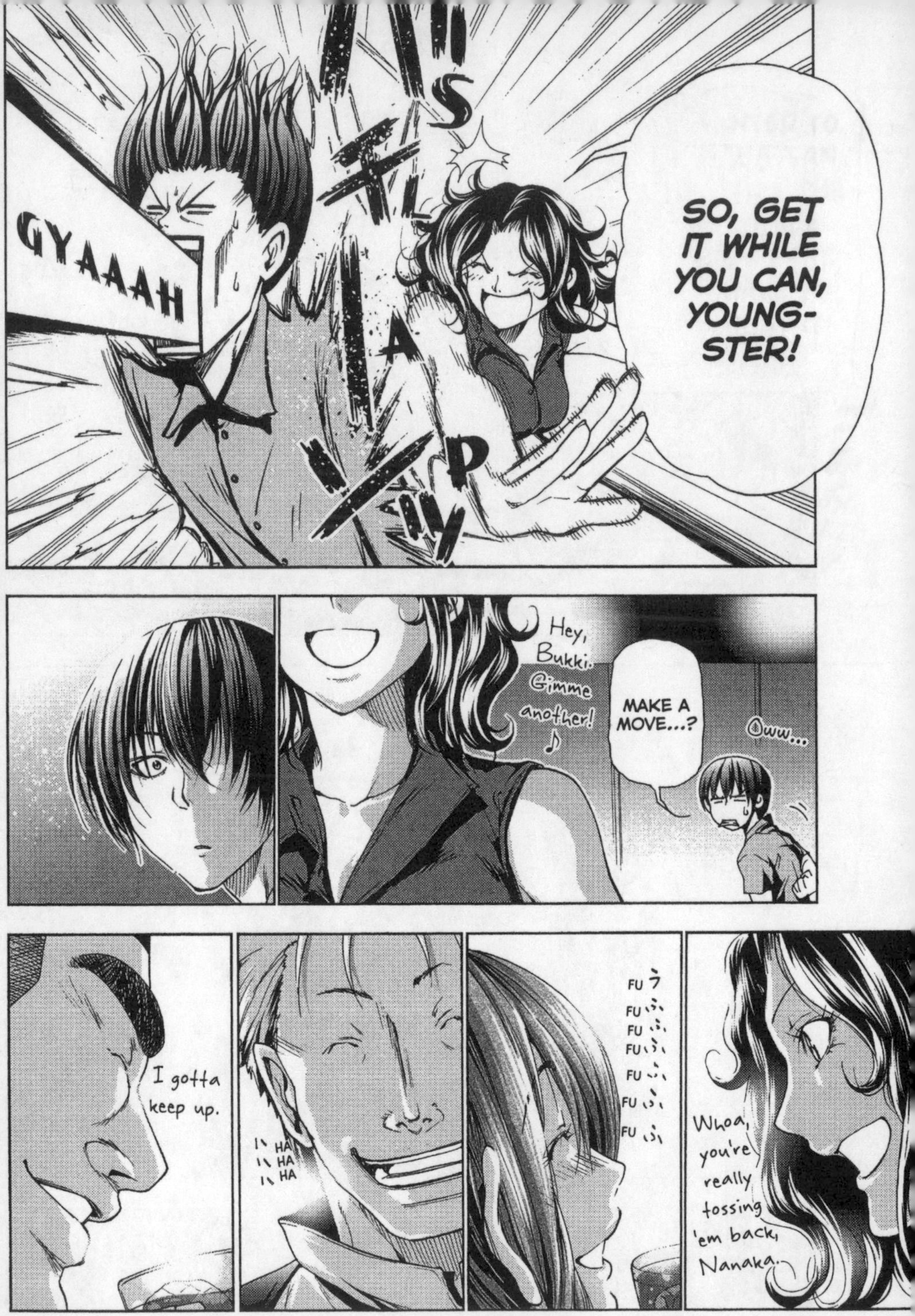
SO, GET IT WHILE YOU CAN, YOUNG-STER!
SLAP
GYAAAH
Oww...
MAKE A MOVE...?
Hey, Bukki. Gimme another! ♪
Whoa, you're really tossing 'em back, Nanaka.
FU FU FU FU FU FU FU
HA HA HA
I gotta keep up.

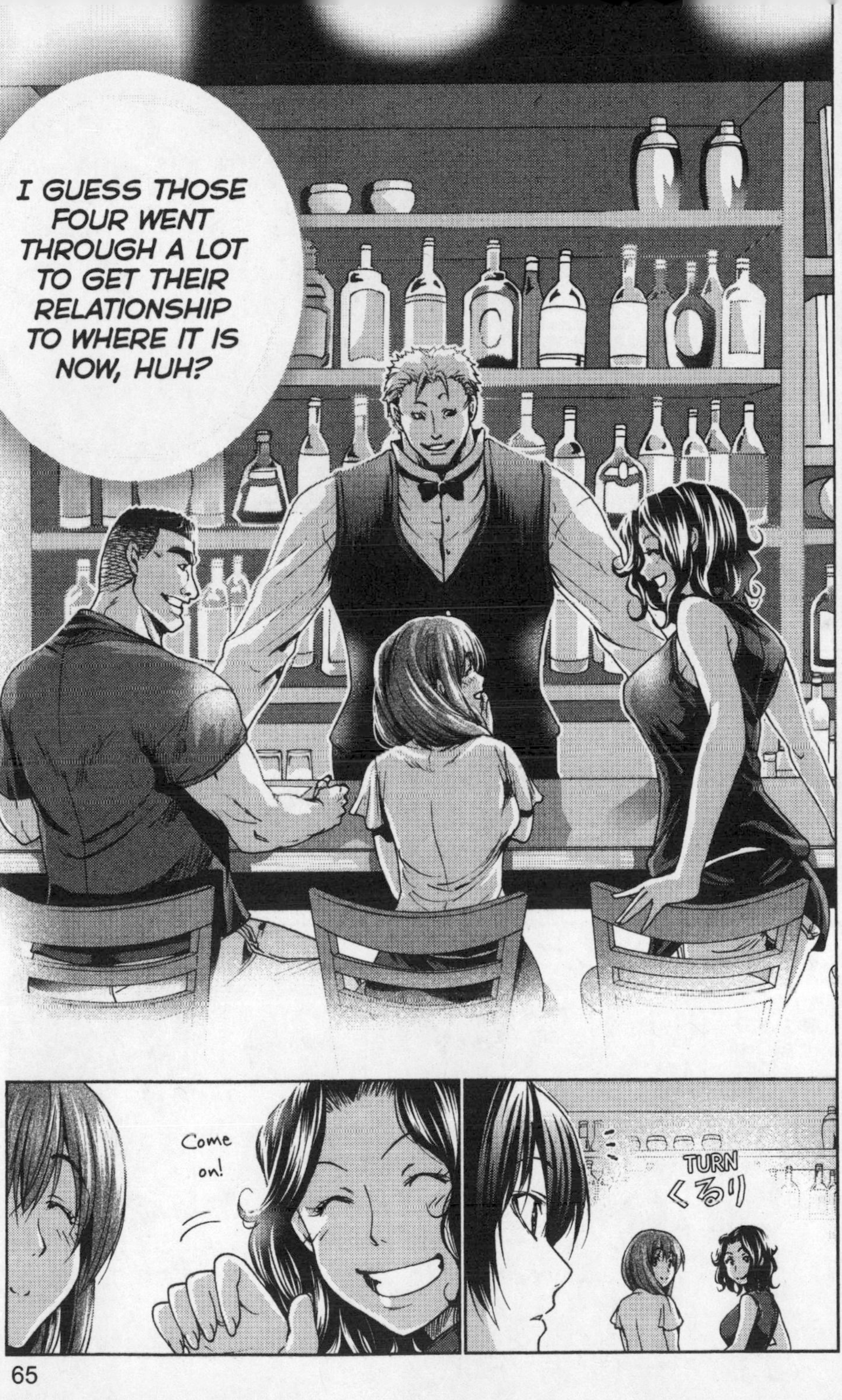
I GUESS THOSE FOUR WENT THROUGH A LOT TO GET THEIR RELATIONSHIP TO WHERE IT IS NOW, HUH?
TURN
くるり
Come on!

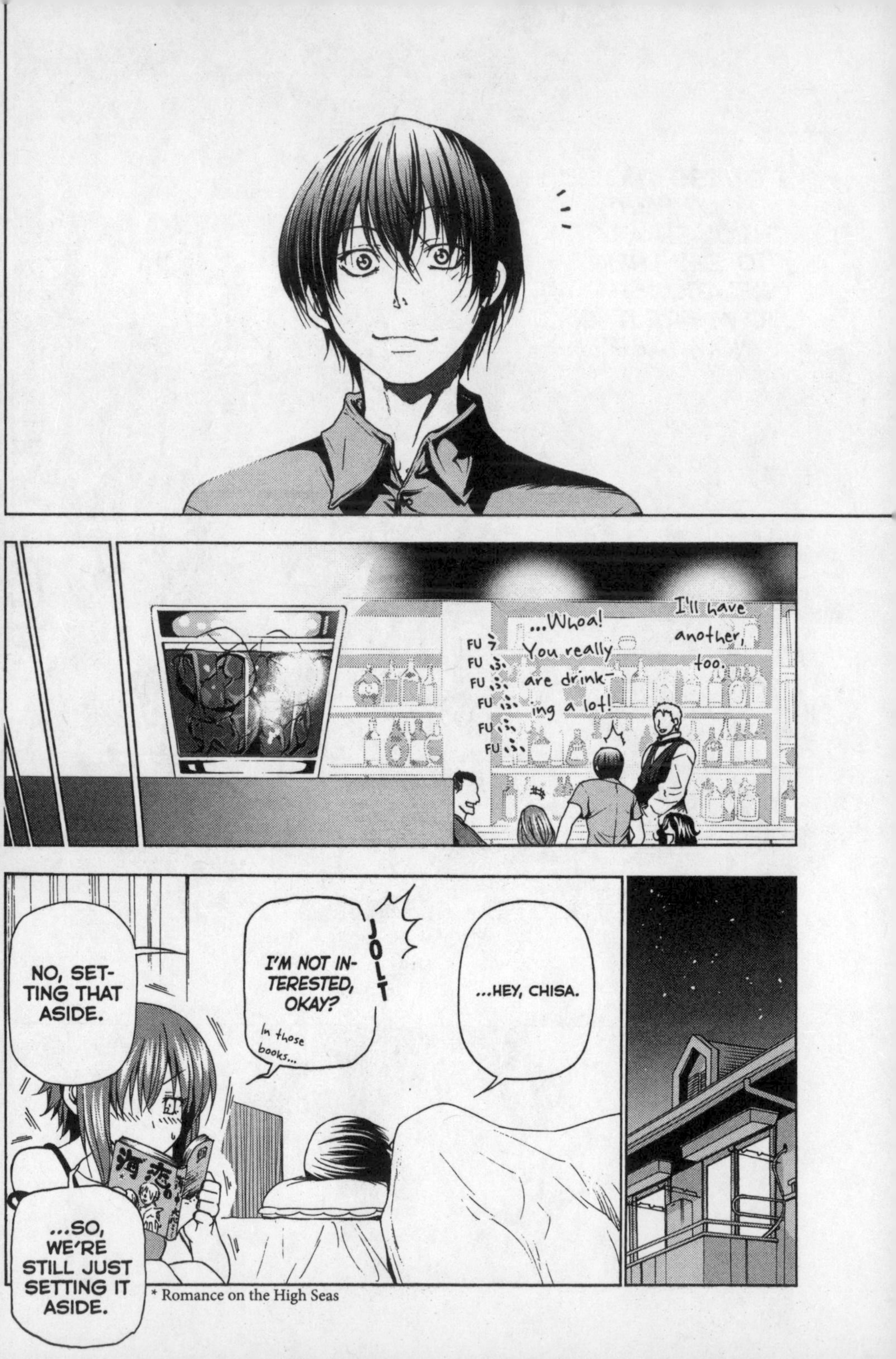
I'll have another, too.
...Whoa! You really are drink-ing a lot!
FU ふ
FU ふ
FU ふ
FU ふ
FU ふ
FU ふ
...HEY, CHISA.
JOLT
I'M NOT IN-TERESTED, OKAY?
In those books...
NO, SET-TING THAT ASIDE.
...SO, WE'RE STILL JUST SETTING IT ASIDE.

* Romance on the High Seas

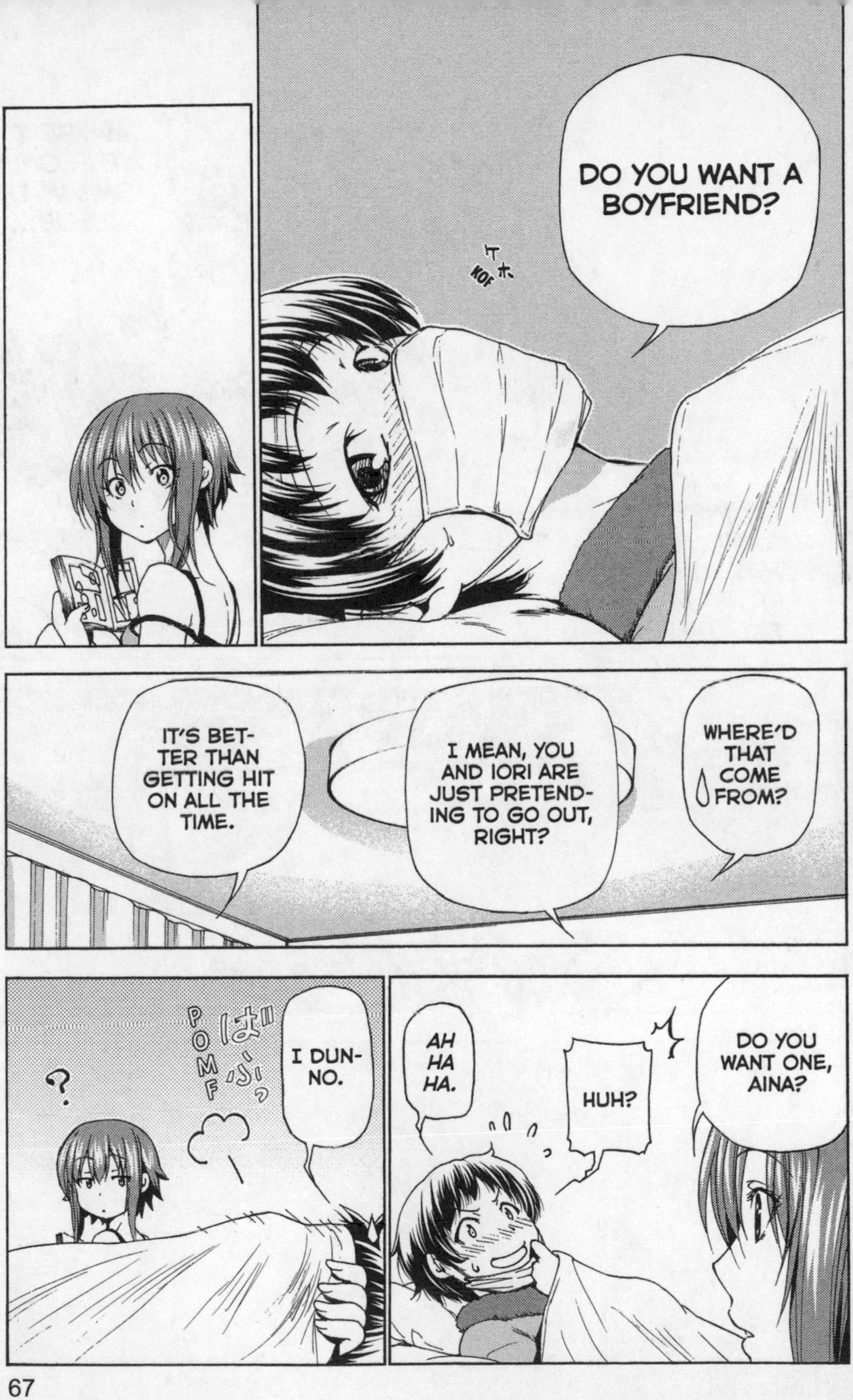
DO YOU WANT A BOYFRIEND?
KOF
WHERE'D THAT COME FROM?
I MEAN, YOU AND IORI ARE JUST PRETEND-ING TO GO OUT, RIGHT?
IT'S BET-TER THAN GETTING HIT ON ALL THE TIME.
DO YOU WANT ONE, AINA?
HUH?
AH HA HA.
I DUN-NO.
POMF

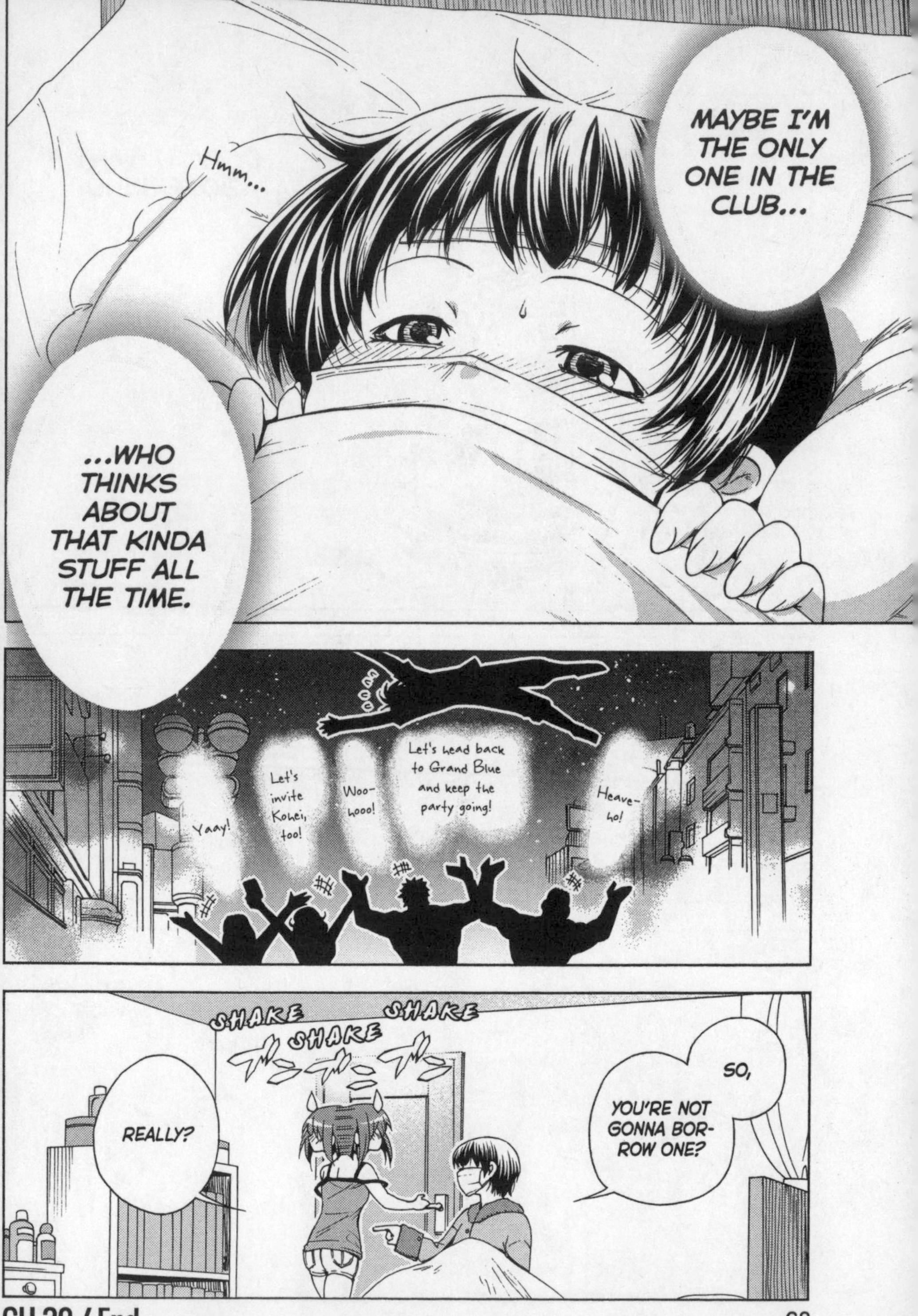
MAYBE I'M THE ONLY ONE IN THE CLUB...
Hmm...
...WHO THINKS ABOUT THAT KINDA STUFF ALL THE TIME.
Heave-ho!
Let's head back to Grand Blue and keep the party going!
Woo-hooo!
Let's invite Kohei, too!
Yaay!
SHAKE SHAKE
SHAKE
SO,
YOU'RE NOT GONNA BOR-ROW ONE?
REALLY?

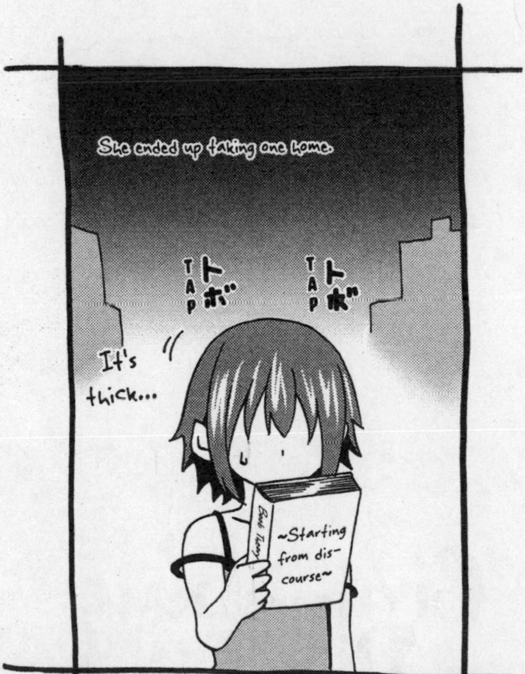

She ended up taking one home.
TAP トボ
TAP トボ
It's thick...
~Starting from dis-course~

Grand Blue Dreaming

THE HARD-EST PART OF SCIENCE COURSES ...

ISN'T THE LECTURES, LABS, OR EVEN THE EXAMS,

BUT THE REPORTS.

YOU MUST UNDER-STAND THE TOPIC,

GATHER SOURCES, READ THEM THOROUGHLY;

THEN WRITE A REPORT ABOUT IT.

REPORT

AFTER PAINSTAKINGLY OVERCOMING THAT STRUGGLE, NOW THAT IT'S FINALLY TIME TO PRESENT OUR WORK...

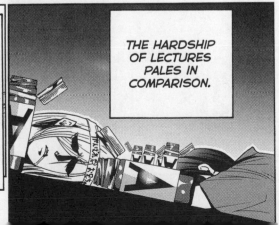

THE HARDSHIP OF LECTURES PALES IN COMPARISON.

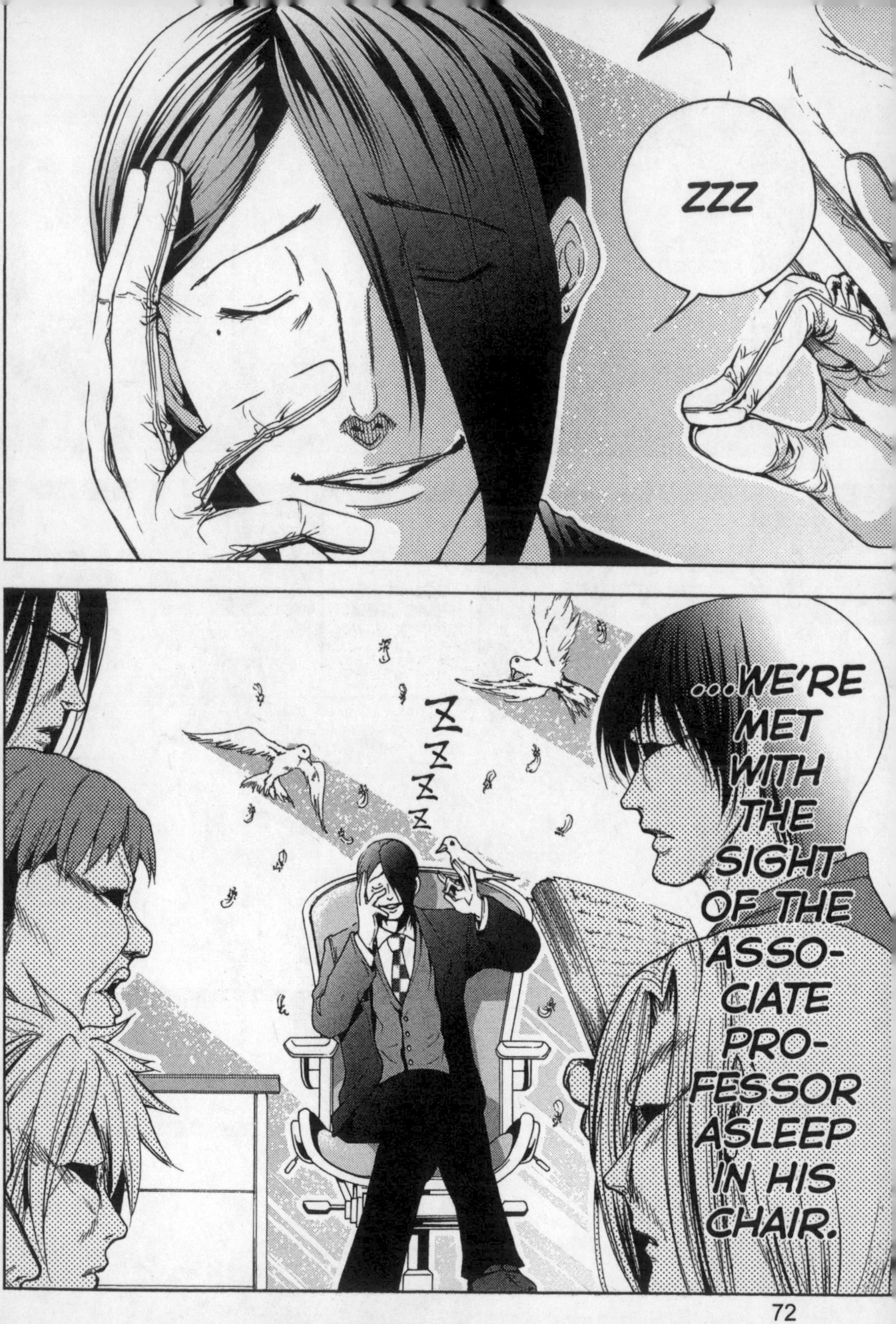
ZZZ
...WE'RE MET WITH THE SIGHT OF THE ASSO-CIATE PRO-FESSOR ASLEEP IN HIS CHAIR.
ZZZZZ

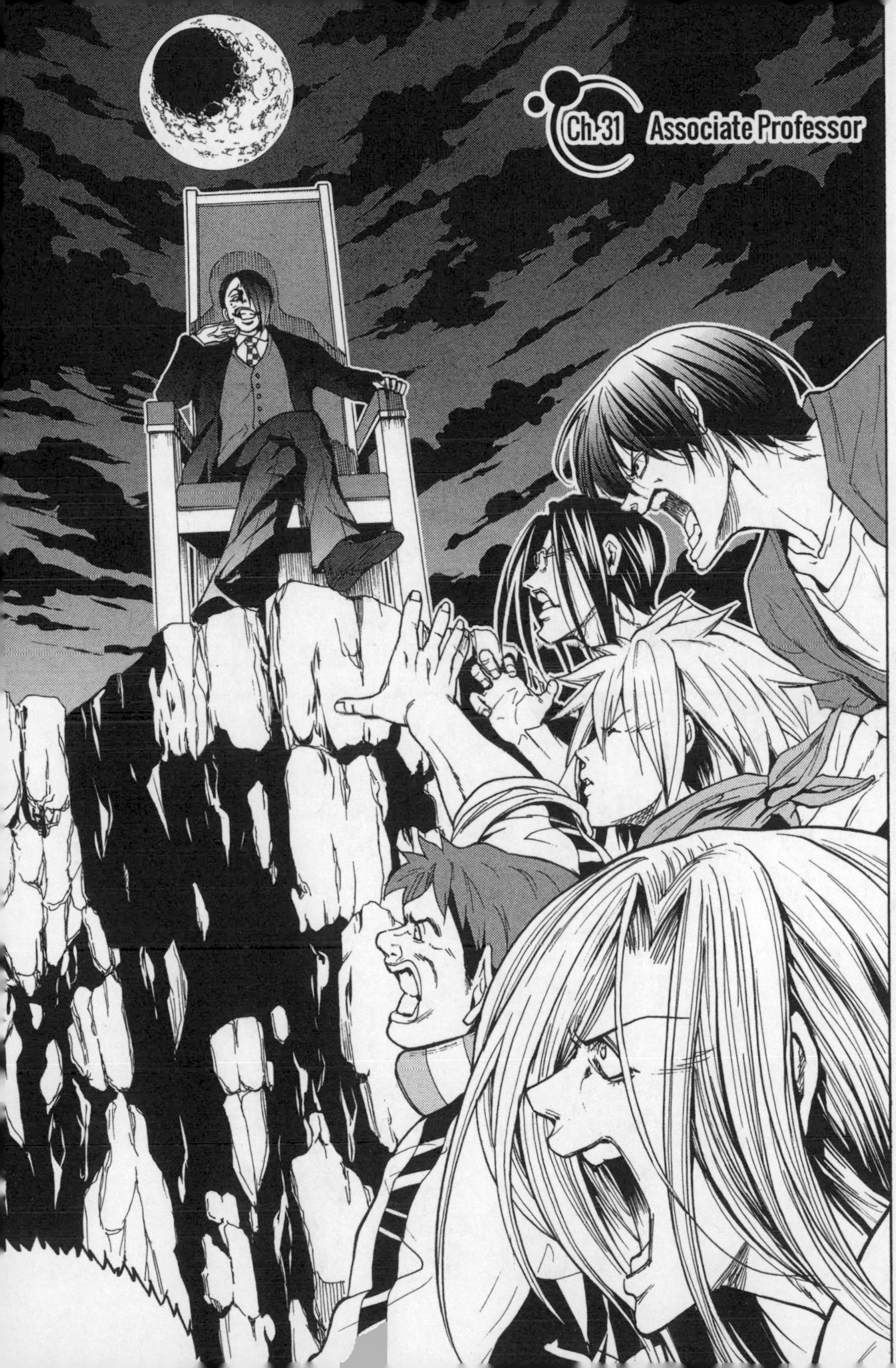
Ch. 31 Associate Professor

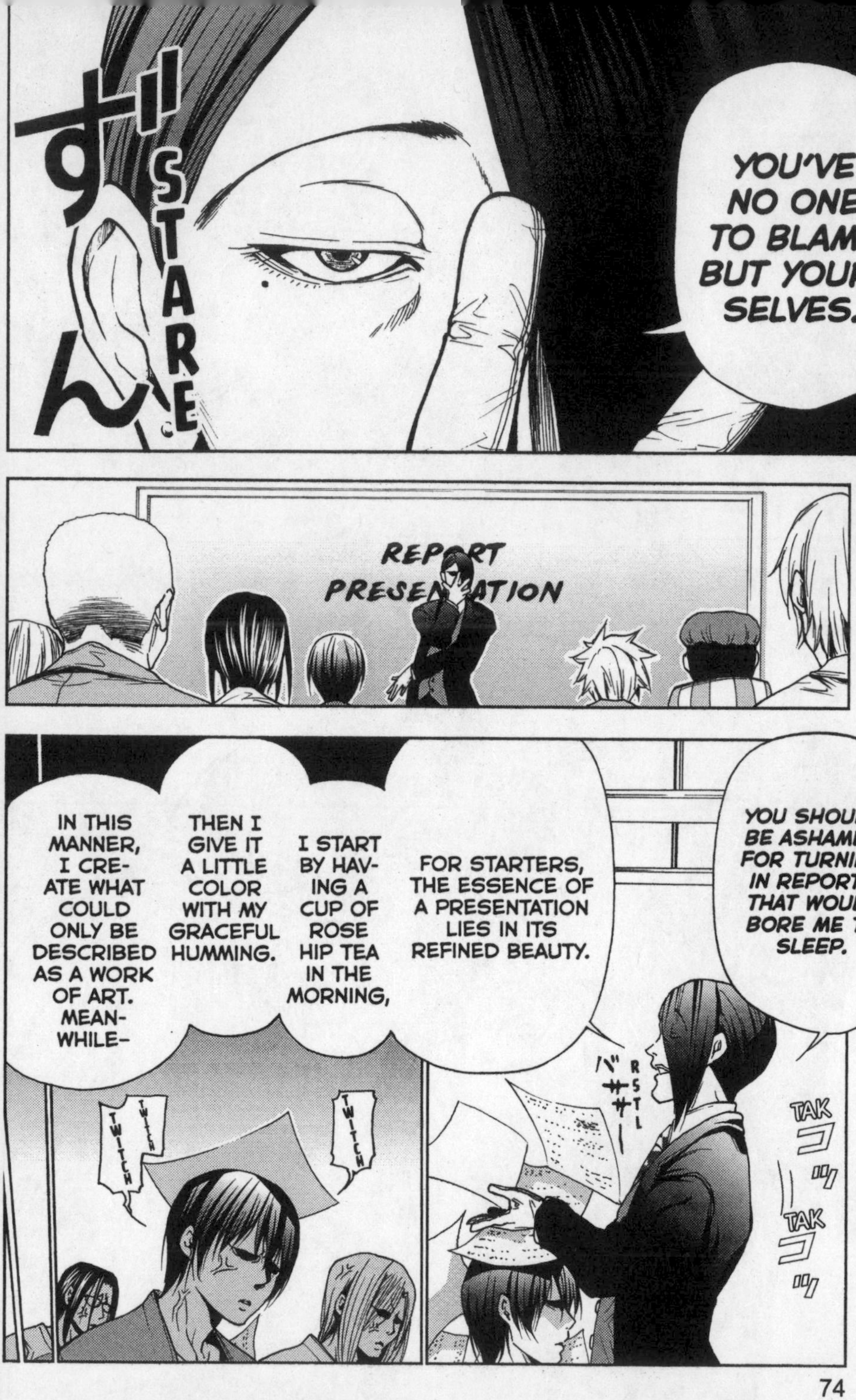

YOU'VE NO ONE TO BLAME BUT YOUR-SELVES.
ずーん
STARE
REPORT PRESENTATION
YOU SHOULD BE ASHAMED FOR TURNING IN REPORTS THAT WOULD BORE ME TO SLEEP.
TAK コッ
TAK コッ
FOR STARTERS, THE ESSENCE OF A PRESENTATION LIES IN ITS REFINED BEAUTY.
I START BY HAV-ING A CUP OF ROSE HIP TEA IN THE MORNING,
THEN I GIVE IT A LITTLE COLOR WITH MY GRACEFUL HUMMING.
IN THIS MANNER, I CRE-ATE WHAT COULD ONLY BE DESCRIBED AS A WORK OF ART. MEAN-WHILE-
バサッ
RSTL
TWITCH
TWITCH
TWITCH

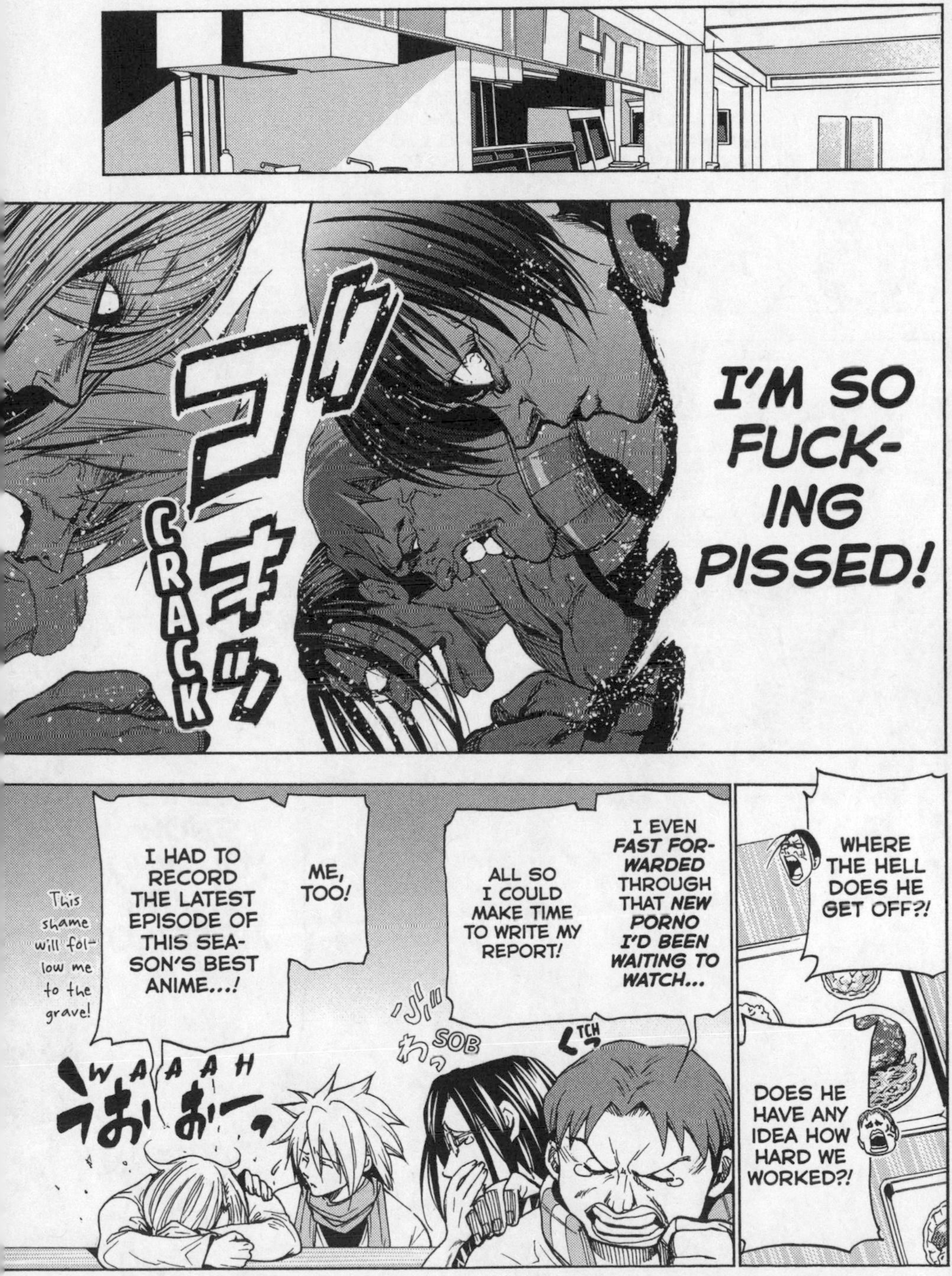
CRACK
I'M SO FUCKING PISSED!
WHERE THE HELL DOES HE GET OFF?!
DOES HE HAVE ANY IDEA HOW HARD WE WORKED?!
I EVEN FAST FORWARDED THROUGH THAT NEW PORNO I'D BEEN WAITING TO WATCH...
TCH
ALL SO I COULD MAKE TIME TO WRITE MY REPORT!
SOB
ME, TOO!
I HAD TO RECORD THE LATEST EPISODE OF THIS SEASON'S BEST ANIME...!
WAAAH
This shame will follow me to the grave!

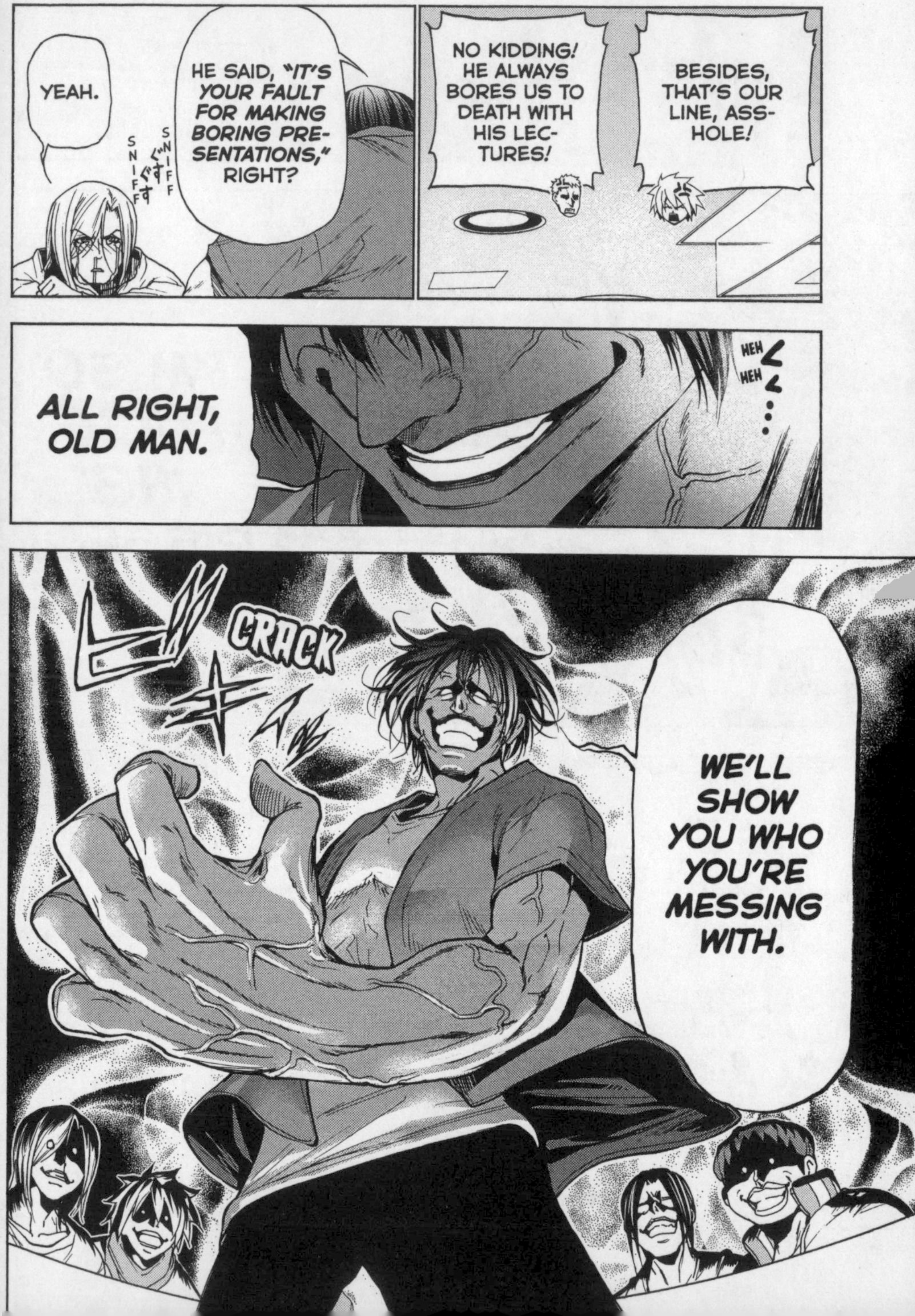

BESIDES, THAT'S OUR LINE, ASS-HOLE!
NO KIDDING! HE ALWAYS BORES US TO DEATH WITH HIS LEC-TURES!
HE SAID, "IT'S YOUR FAULT FOR MAKING BORING PRE-SENTATIONS," RIGHT?
SNIFF
ぐすぐす
SNIFF
YEAH.
HEH HEH...
ALL RIGHT, OLD MAN.
WE'LL SHOW YOU WHO YOU'RE MESSING WITH.
CRACK

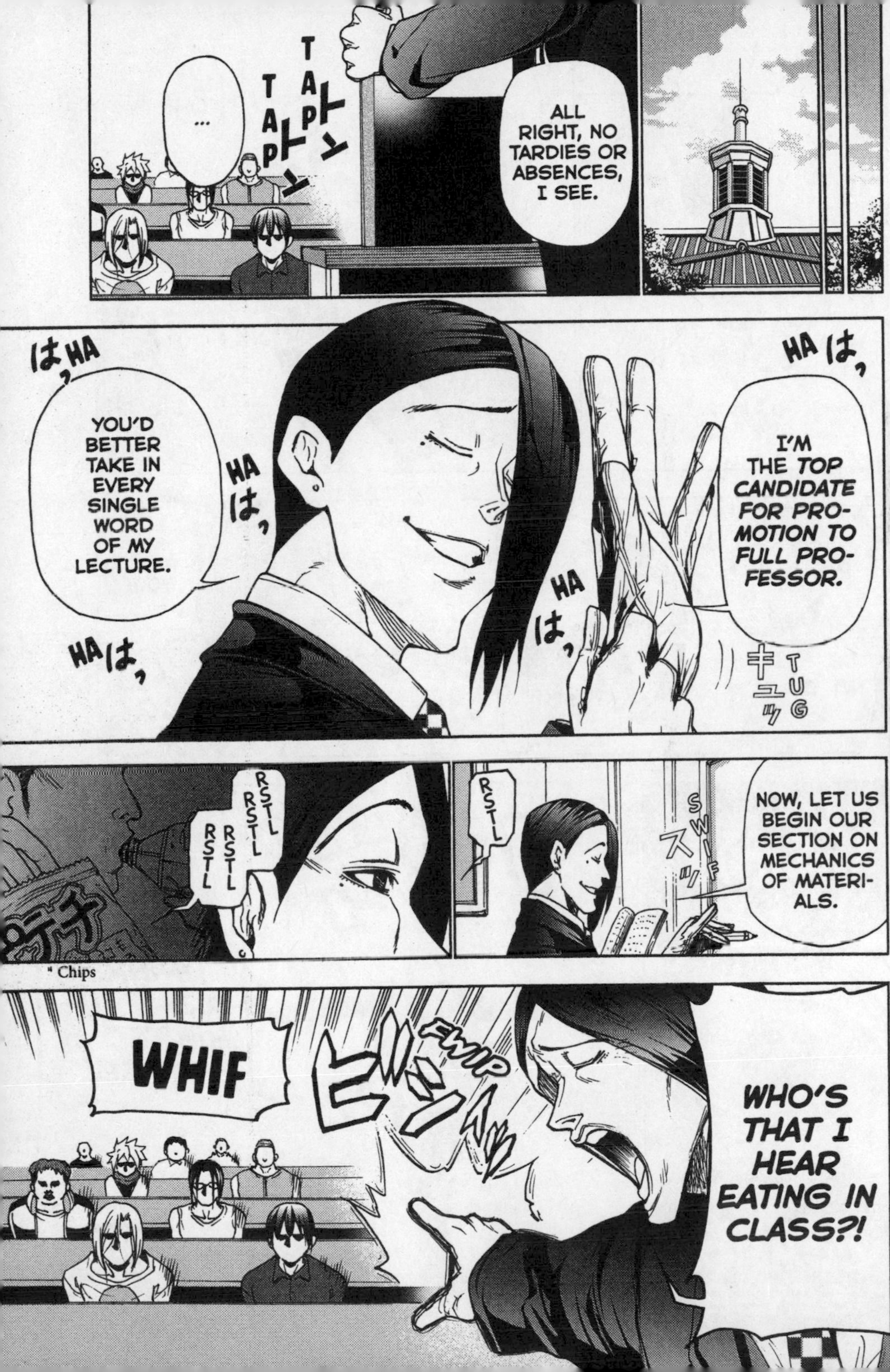
ALL RIGHT, NO TARDIES OR ABSENCES, I SEE.
TAP TAP
...
HA は
I'M THE TOP CANDIDATE FOR PROMOTION TO FULL PROFESSOR.
TUG キュッ
HA は
HA は
HA は
YOU'D BETTER TAKE IN EVERY SINGLE WORD OF MY LECTURE.
HA は
NOW, LET US BEGIN OUR SECTION ON MECHANICS OF MATERIALS.
SWIF スッ
RSTL
RSTL RSTL RSTL RSTL
WHO'S THAT I HEAR EATING IN CLASS?!
FWIP
WHIF

* Chips

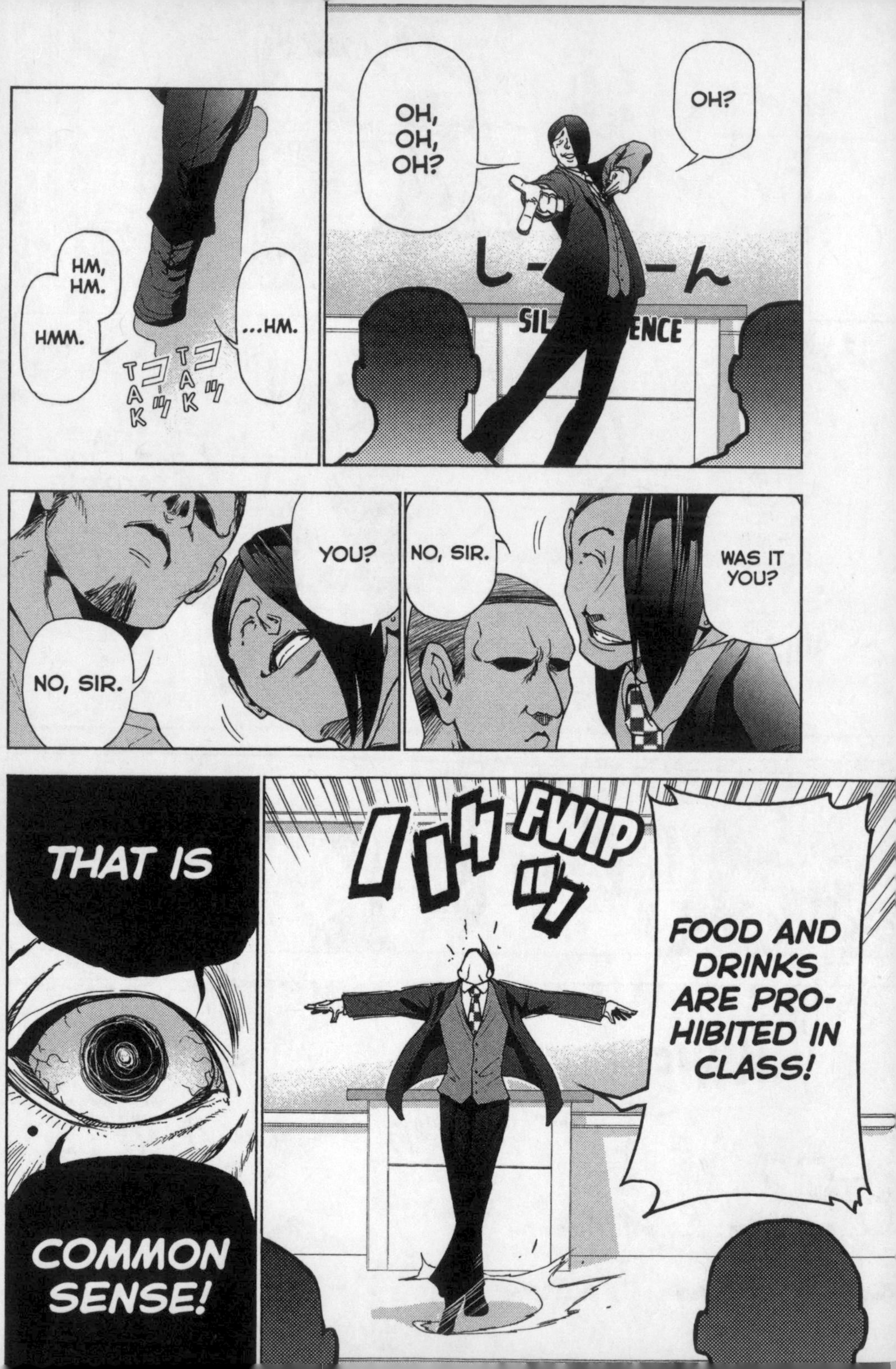
OH?
OH, OH, OH?
SILENCE
...HM.
HM, HM.
HMM.
TAK
TAK
WAS IT YOU?
NO, SIR.
YOU?
NO, SIR.
FWIP
FOOD AND DRINKS ARE PRO-HIBITED IN CLASS!
THAT IS
COMMON SENSE!

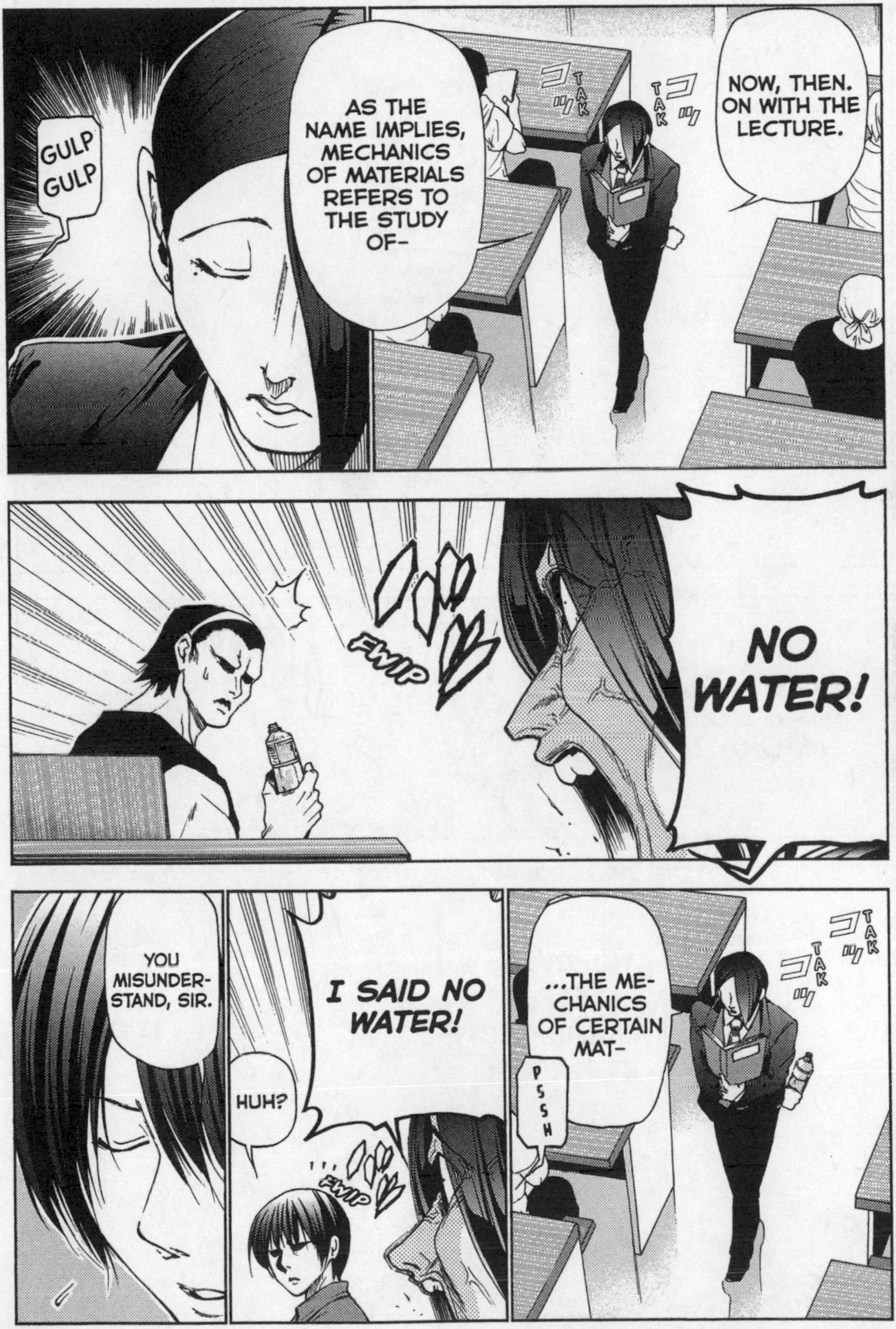
TAK
TAK
NOW, THEN. ON WITH THE LECTURE.
AS THE NAME IMPLIES, MECHANICS OF MATERIALS REFERS TO THE STUDY OF-
GULP GULP
NO WATER!
FWIP
TAK
TAK
...THE MECHANICS OF CERTAIN MAT-
PSSH
I SAID NO WATER!
HUH?
FWIP
YOU MISUNDERSTAND, SIR.

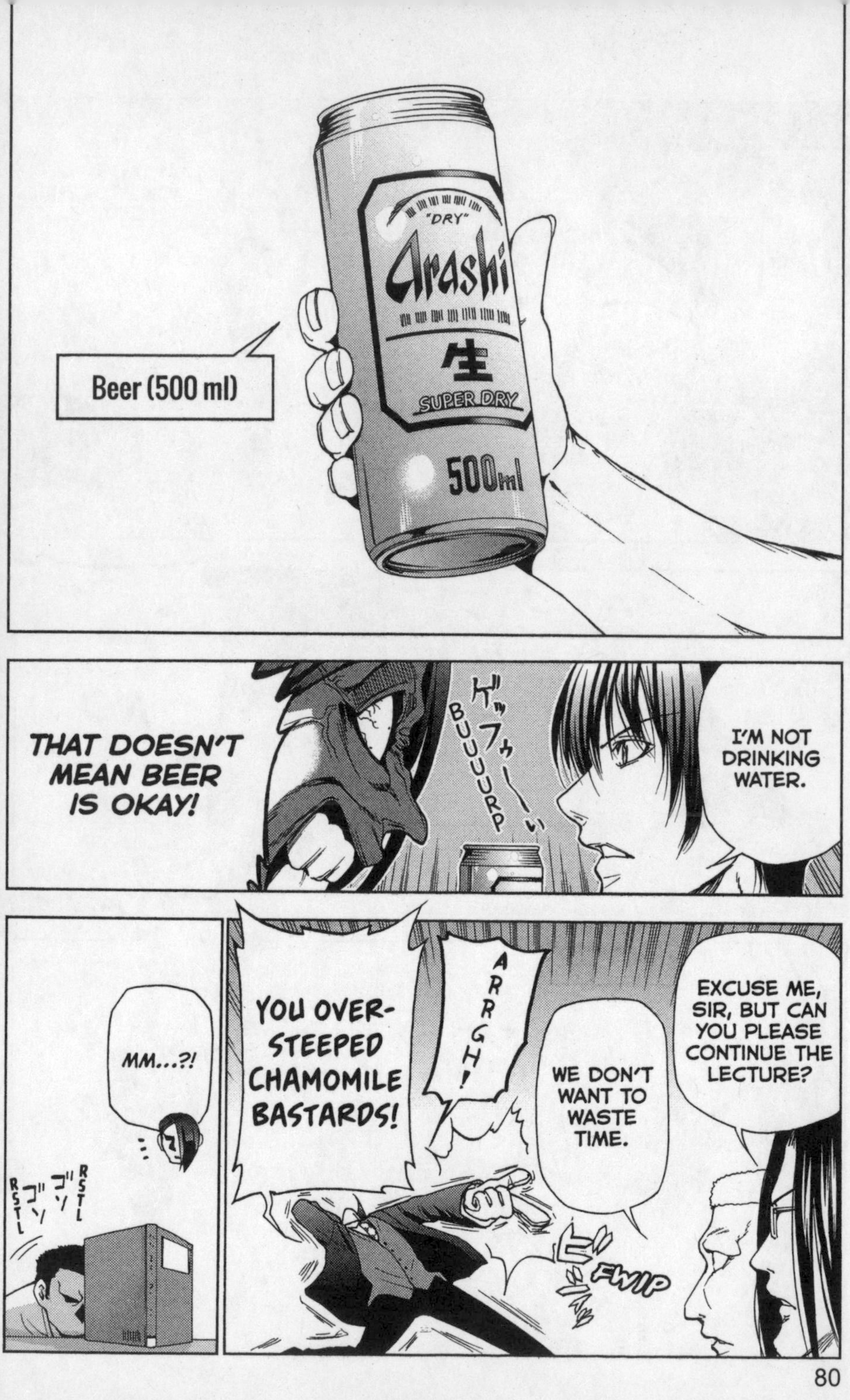
"DRY"
Arashi
生
SUPER DRY
500ml
Beer (500 ml)
I'M NOT DRINKING WATER.
ゲッフゥーぃ
BUUUURP
THAT DOESN'T MEAN BEER IS OKAY!
EXCUSE ME, SIR, BUT CAN YOU PLEASE CONTINUE THE LECTURE?
WE DON'T WANT TO WASTE TIME.
ARRGH!
YOU OVER-STEEPED CHAMOMILE BASTARDS!
ビシッ
FWIP
MM...?!
ゴソ
RSTL
ゴソ
RSTL

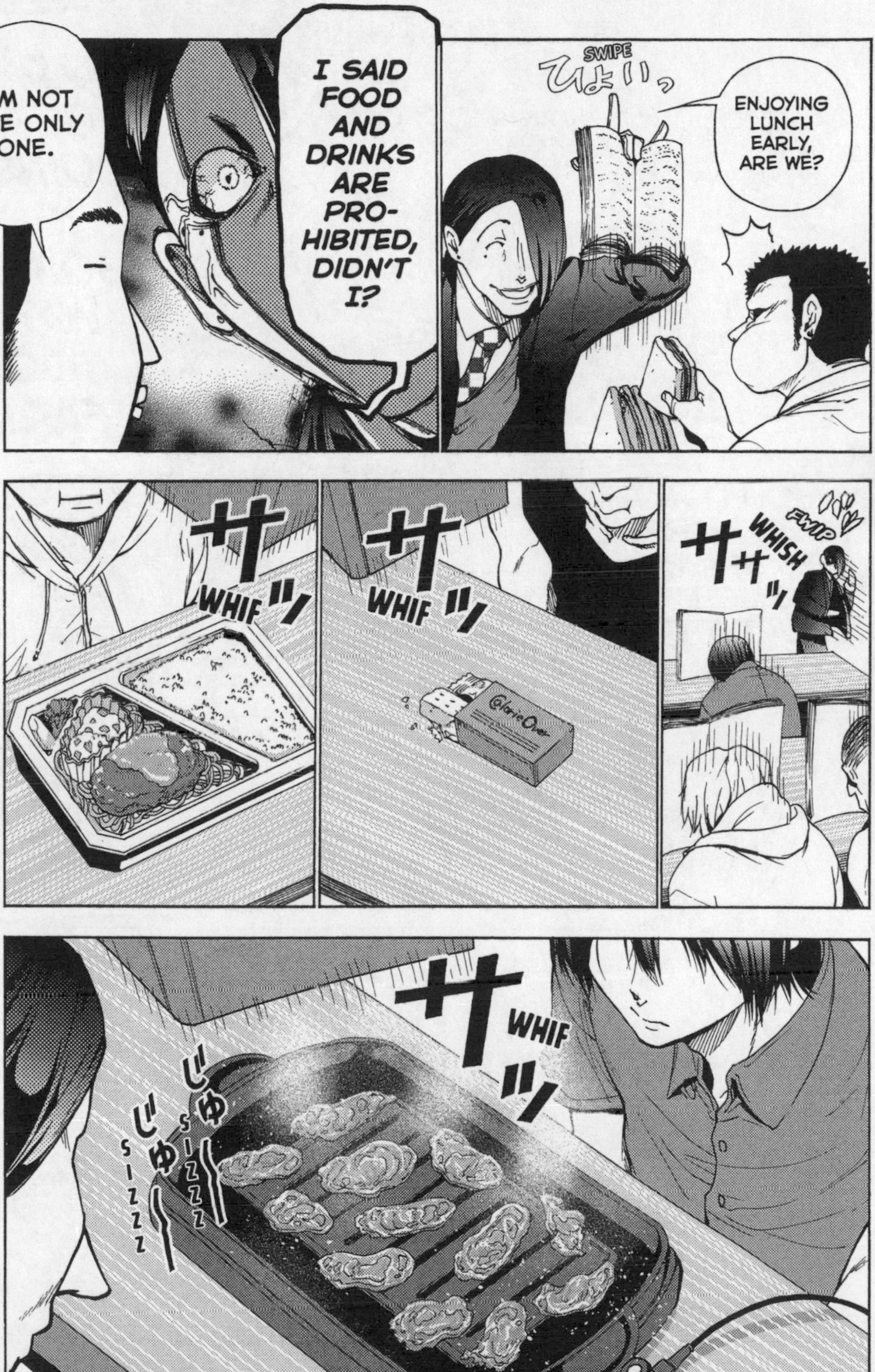
SWIPE
ひょいっ
ENJOYING LUNCH EARLY, ARE WE?
I SAID FOOD AND DRINKS ARE PRO-HIBITED, DIDN'T I?
I'M NOT THE ONLY ONE.
FWIP
WHISH
ササッ
サッ
WHIF
サッ
WHIF
サッ
WHIF
じゅ〜
SIZZZ
じゅ〜
SIZZZ

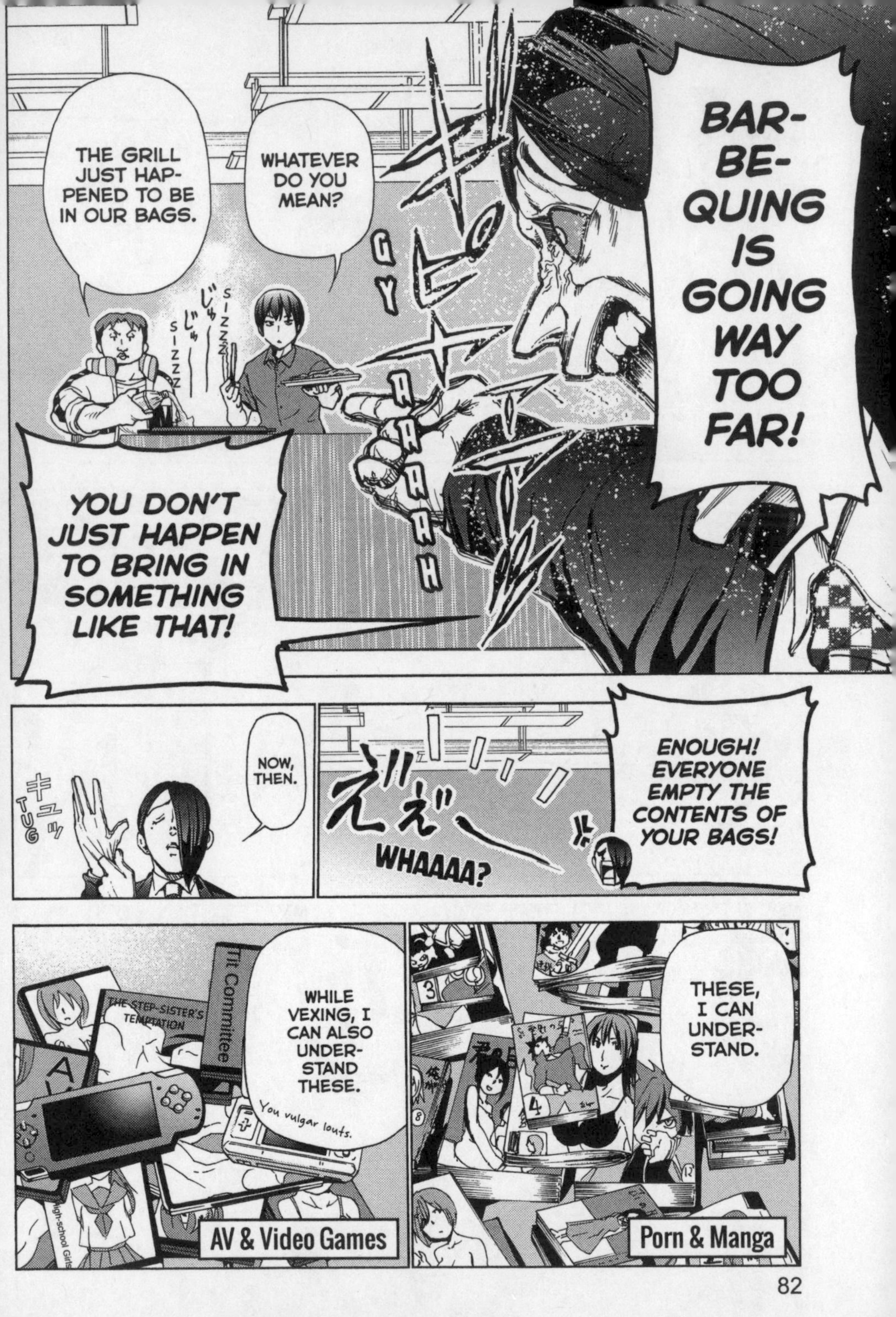
BAR-BE-QUING IS GOING WAY TOO FAR!
GYAAAAH
WHATEVER DO YOU MEAN?
THE GRILL JUST HAPPENED TO BE IN OUR BAGS.
SIZZZ
SIZZZ
YOU DON'T JUST HAPPEN TO BRING IN SOMETHING LIKE THAT!
ENOUGH! EVERYONE EMPTY THE CONTENTS OF YOUR BAGS!
WHAAAA?
NOW, THEN.
TUG
THESE, I CAN UNDERSTAND.
Porn & Manga
WHILE VEXING, I CAN ALSO UNDERSTAND THESE.
You vulgar louts.
Tit Committee
THE STEP-SISTER'S TEMPTATION
AV & Video Games

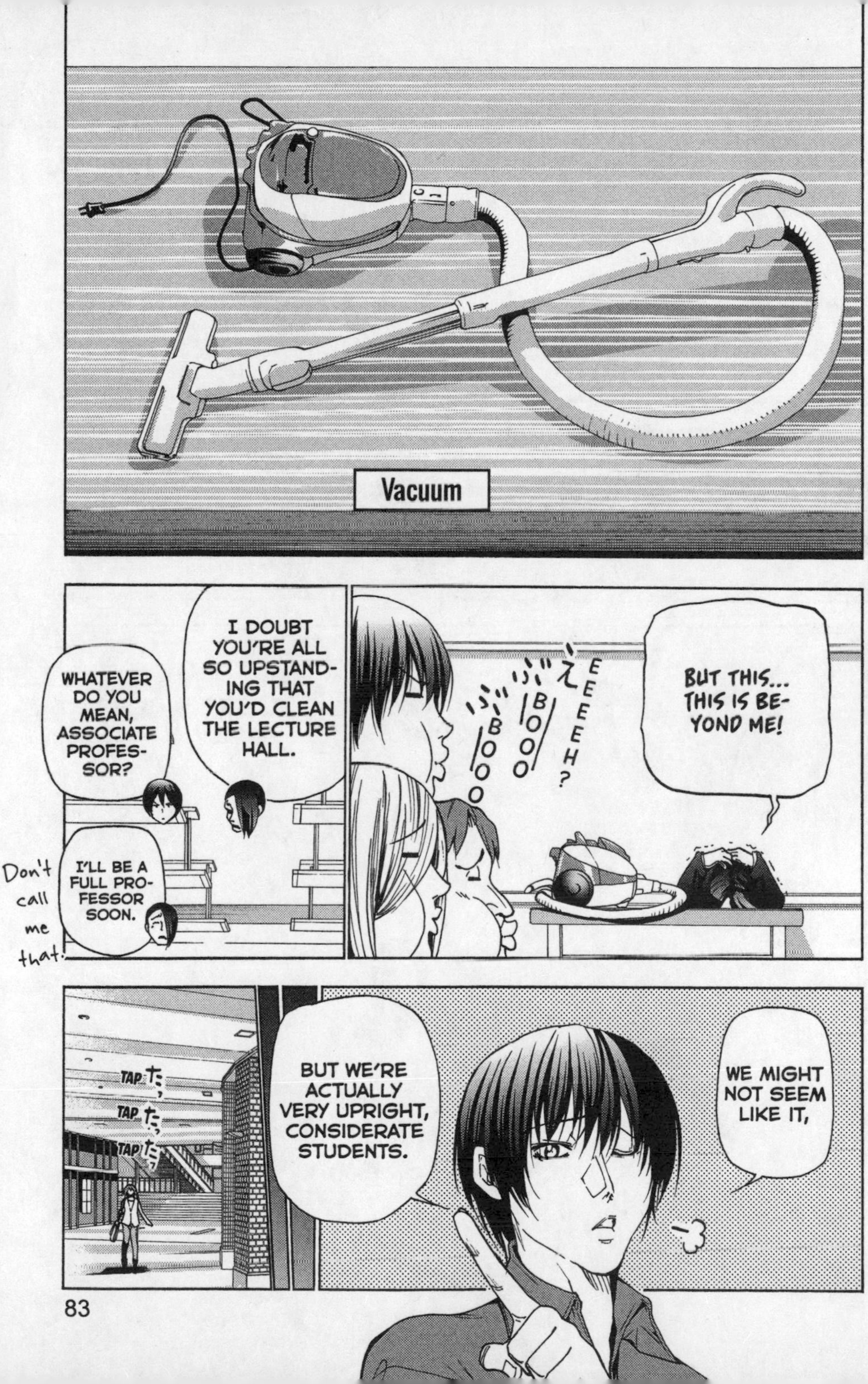
Vacuum
BUT THIS... THIS IS BE-YOND ME!
EEEEEH?
BOOO
BOOO
I DOUBT YOU'RE ALL SO UPSTANDING THAT YOU'D CLEAN THE LECTURE HALL.
WHATEVER DO YOU MEAN, ASSOCIATE PROFESSOR?
I'LL BE A FULL PROFESSOR SOON.
Don't call me that!
WE MIGHT NOT SEEM LIKE IT,
BUT WE'RE ACTUALLY VERY UPRIGHT, CONSIDERATE STUDENTS.
TAP
TAP
TAP

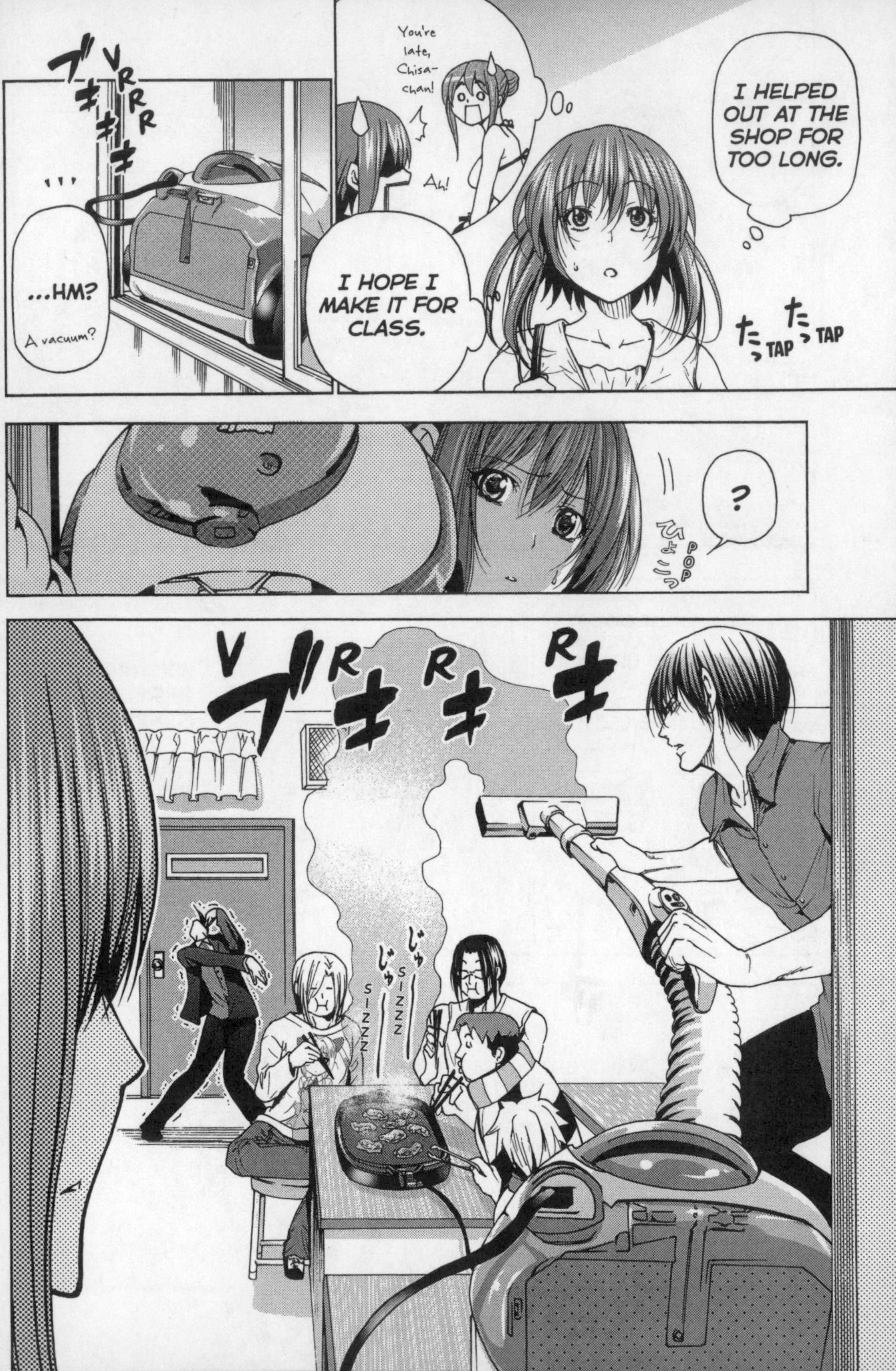
I HELPED OUT AT THE SHOP FOR TOO LONG.
たっ TAP たっ TAP
You're late, Chisa-chan!
Ah!
I HOPE I MAKE IT FOR CLASS.
ブギギギ VRRR
...HM?
A vacuum?
?
ひょこっ POP
ブギギギ VRRR
じゅー SIZZZ じゅー SIZZZ

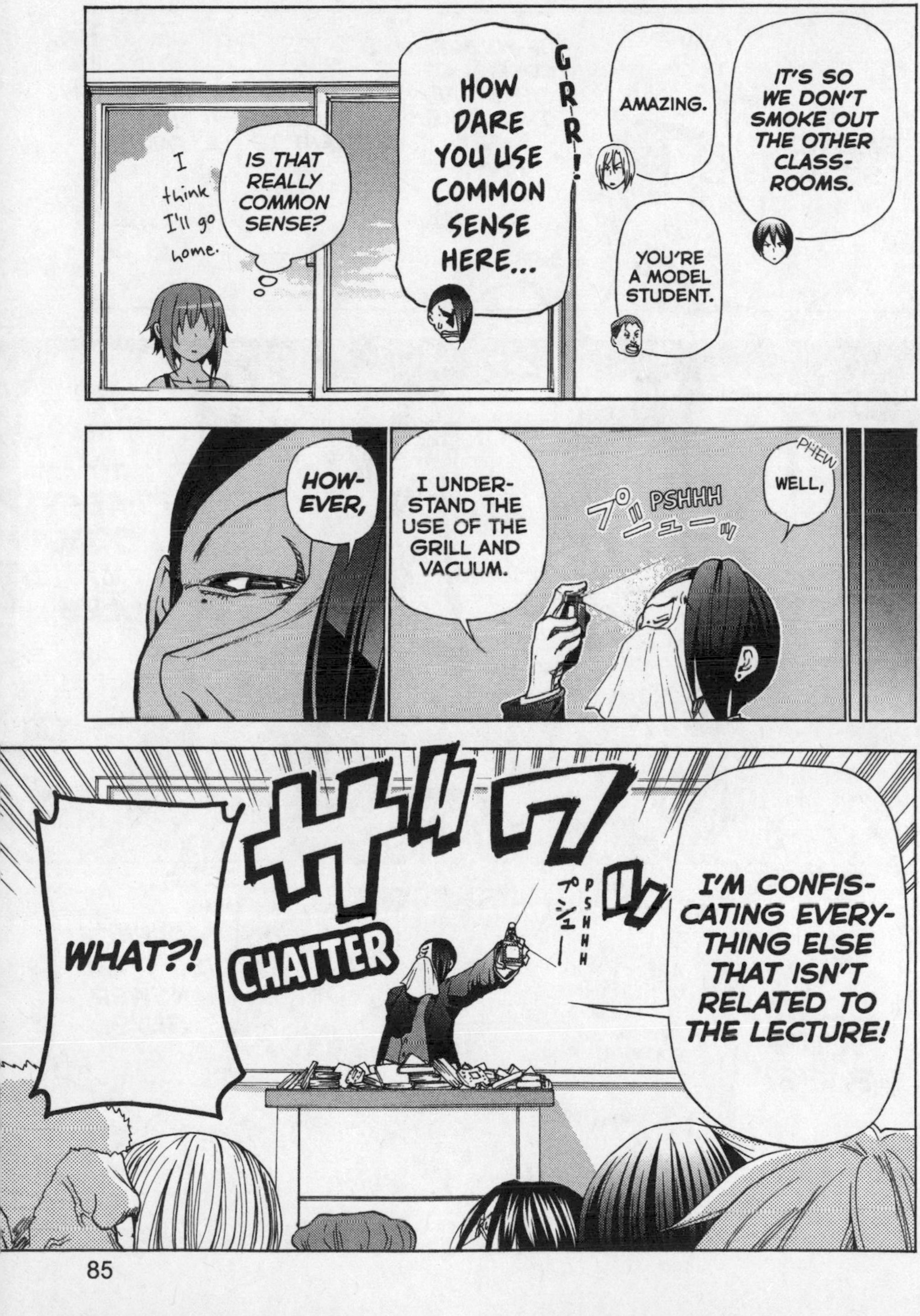
IT'S SO WE DON'T SMOKE OUT THE OTHER CLASSROOMS.
AMAZING.
YOU'RE A MODEL STUDENT.
GRR!
HOW DARE YOU USE COMMON SENSE HERE...
IS THAT REALLY COMMON SENSE?
I think I'll go home.
PHEW
WELL,
PSHHH
I UNDERSTAND THE USE OF THE GRILL AND VACUUM.
HOWEVER,
I'M CONFISCATING EVERYTHING ELSE THAT ISN'T RELATED TO THE LECTURE!
PSHHH
CHATTER
WHAT?!

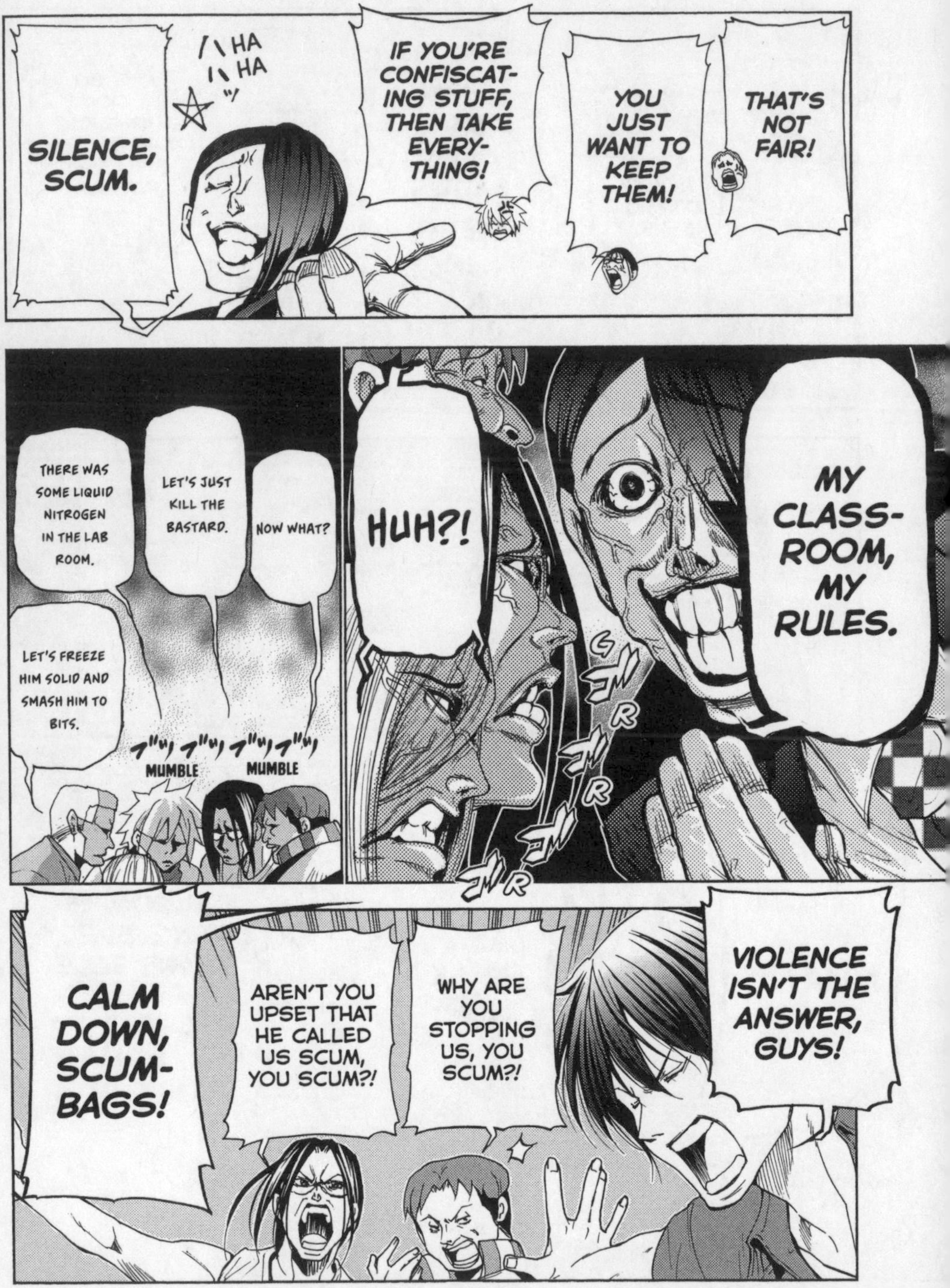
THAT'S NOT FAIR!
YOU JUST WANT TO KEEP THEM!
IF YOU'RE CONFISCATING STUFF, THEN TAKE EVERYTHING!
HA HA
SILENCE, SCUM.
MY CLASSROOM, MY RULES.
HUH?!
GRR GRR GRR GRR
NOW WHAT?
LET'S JUST KILL THE BASTARD.
THERE WAS SOME LIQUID NITROGEN IN THE LAB ROOM.
LET'S FREEZE HIM SOLID AND SMASH HIM TO BITS.
MUMBLE MUMBLE
VIOLENCE ISN'T THE ANSWER, GUYS!
WHY ARE YOU STOPPING US, YOU SCUM?!
AREN'T YOU UPSET THAT HE CALLED US SCUM, YOU SCUM?!
CALM DOWN, SCUMBAGS!

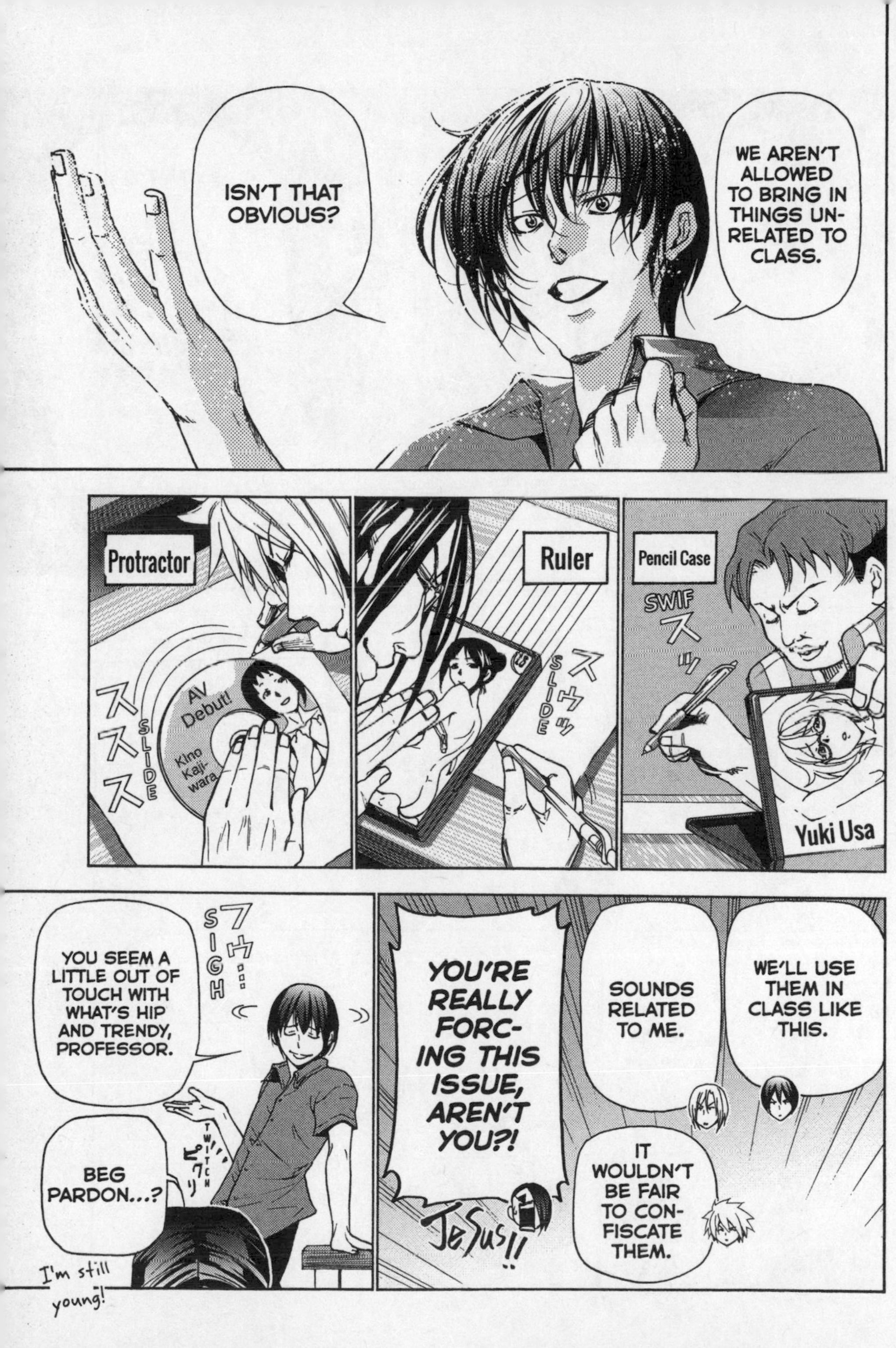
WE AREN'T ALLOWED TO BRING IN THINGS UN-RELATED TO CLASS.
ISN'T THAT OBVIOUS?
Pencil Case
SWIF
スッ
Yuki Usa
Ruler
スウッ
SLIDE
Protractor
AV Debut!
Kino Kajiwara
ススス
SLIDE
WE'LL USE THEM IN CLASS LIKE THIS.
SOUNDS RELATED TO ME.
IT WOULDN'T BE FAIR TO CONFISCATE THEM.
YOU'RE REALLY FORCING THIS ISSUE, AREN'T YOU?!
JeSus!!
フゥ…
SIGH
YOU SEEM A LITTLE OUT OF TOUCH WITH WHAT'S HIP AND TRENDY, PROFESSOR.
TWITCH
ピクリ
BEG PARDON...?
I'm still young!

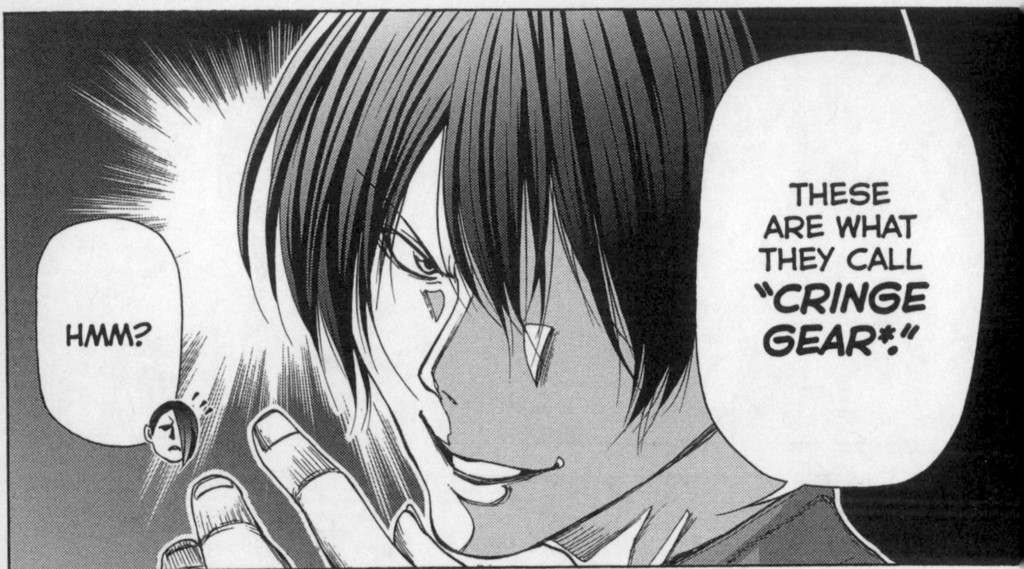
THESE ARE WHAT THEY CALL "CRINGE GEAR*."
HMM?

* Items, typically with anime characters printed on them, that make people cringe when they see them.

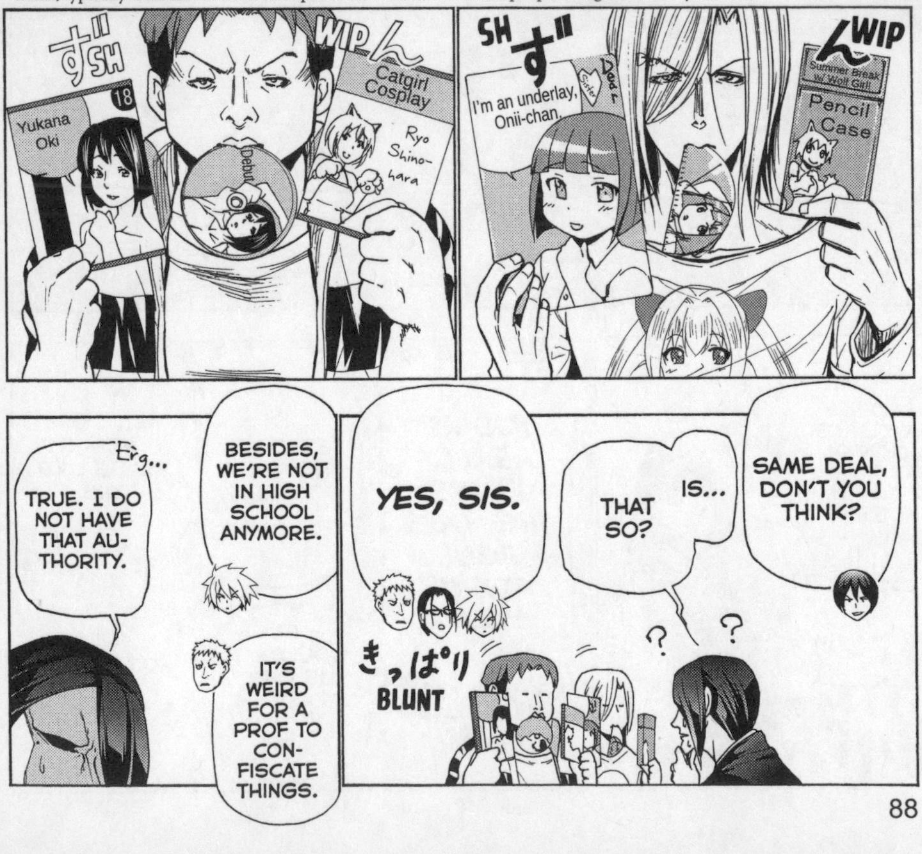
SH ず
WIP ん
Summer Break w/ Wolf Girl!
Pencil Case
I'm an underlay, Onii-chan.
ずSH
WIP ん
Catgirl Cosplay
18
Yukana Oki
Ryo Shino-hara
Debut
SAME DEAL, DON'T YOU THINK?
IS...
THAT SO?
YES, SIS.
きっぱり
BLUNT
BESIDES, WE'RE NOT IN HIGH SCHOOL ANYMORE.
Erg...
TRUE. I DO NOT HAVE THAT AU-THORITY.
IT'S WEIRD FOR A PROF TO CON-FISCATE THINGS.

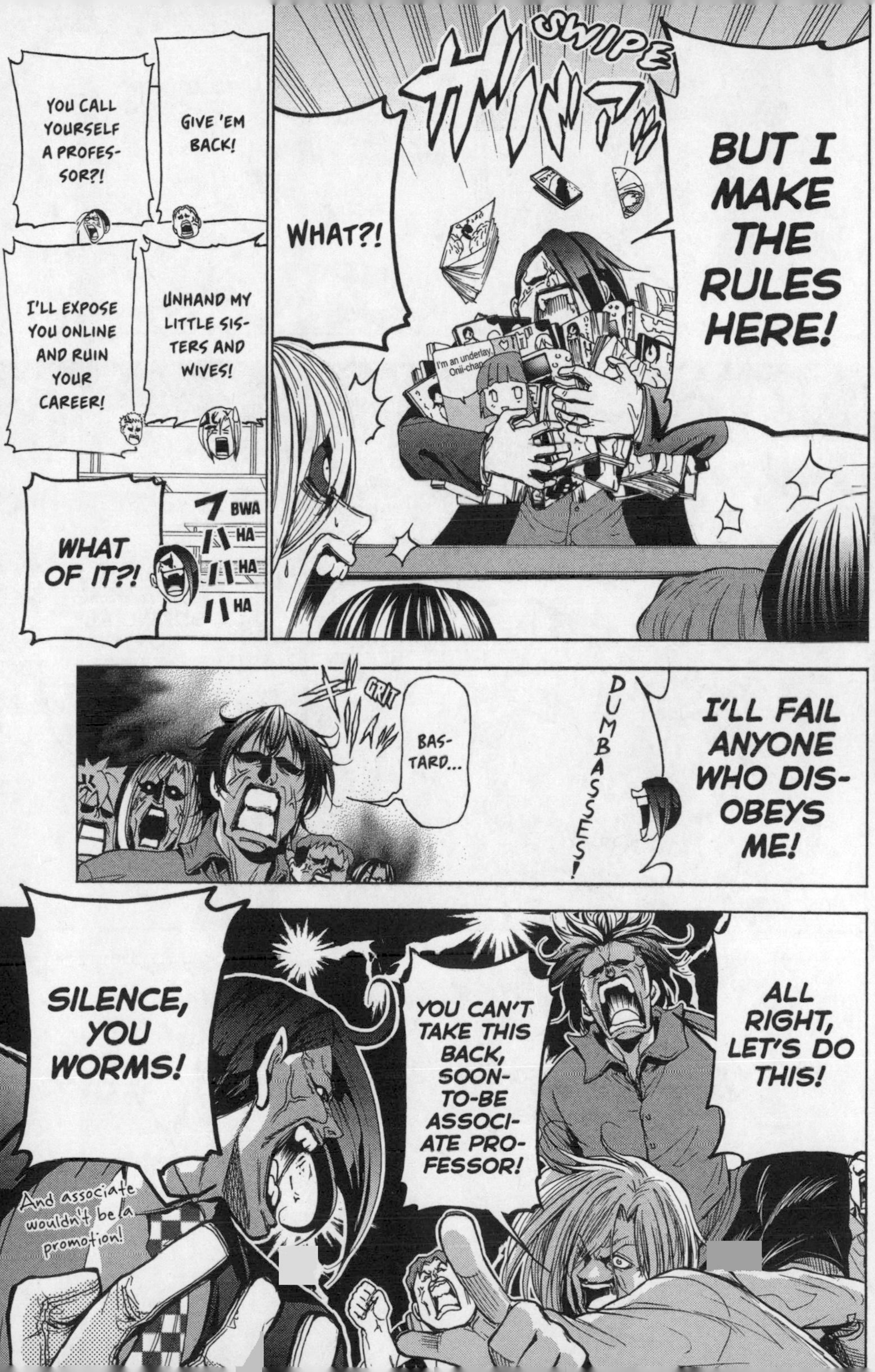
SWIPE
BUT I MAKE THE RULES HERE!
WHAT?!
I'm an underlay, Onii-cha
GIVE 'EM BACK!
YOU CALL YOURSELF A PROFES-SOR?!
UNHAND MY LITTLE SIS-TERS AND WIVES!
I'LL EXPOSE YOU ONLINE AND RUIN YOUR CAREER!
BWA HA HA HA
WHAT OF IT?!
I'LL FAIL ANYONE WHO DIS-OBEYS ME!
DUMBASSES!
BAS-TARD...
GRIT
ALL RIGHT, LET'S DO THIS!
YOU CAN'T TAKE THIS BACK, SOON-TO-BE ASSOCI-ATE PRO-FESSOR!
SILENCE, YOU WORMS!
And associate wouldn't be a promotion!

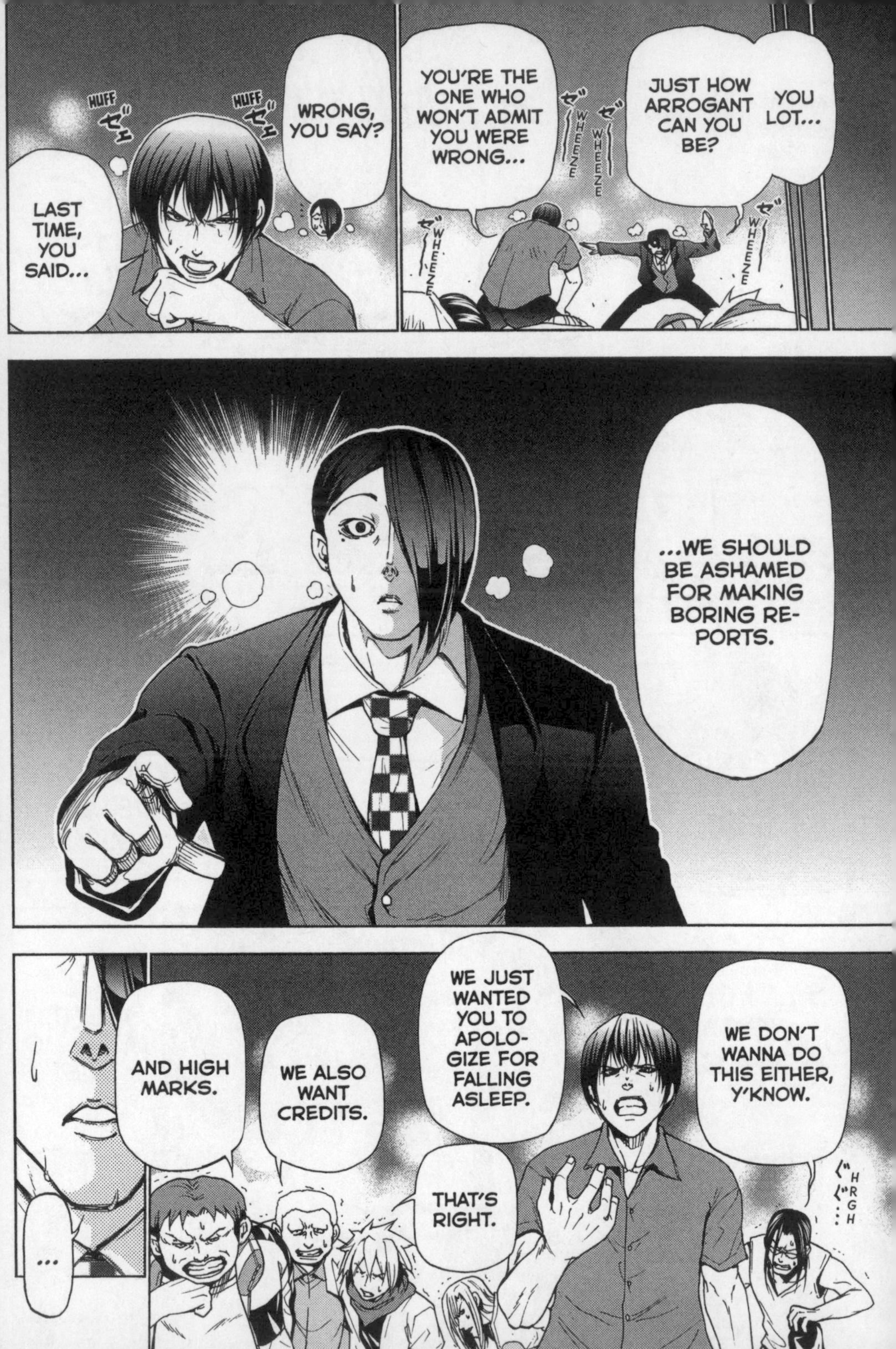
YOU LOT...
JUST HOW ARROGANT CAN YOU BE?
WHEEZE
WHEEZE
WHEEZE
YOU'RE THE ONE WHO WON'T ADMIT YOU WERE WRONG...
WHEEZE
HUFF
WRONG, YOU SAY?
HUFF
LAST TIME, YOU SAID...
...WE SHOULD BE ASHAMED FOR MAKING BORING RE-PORTS.
WE DON'T WANNA DO THIS EITHER, Y'KNOW.
HRGH
WE JUST WANTED YOU TO APOLO-GIZE FOR FALLING ASLEEP.
THAT'S RIGHT.
WE ALSO WANT CREDITS.
AND HIGH MARKS.
...

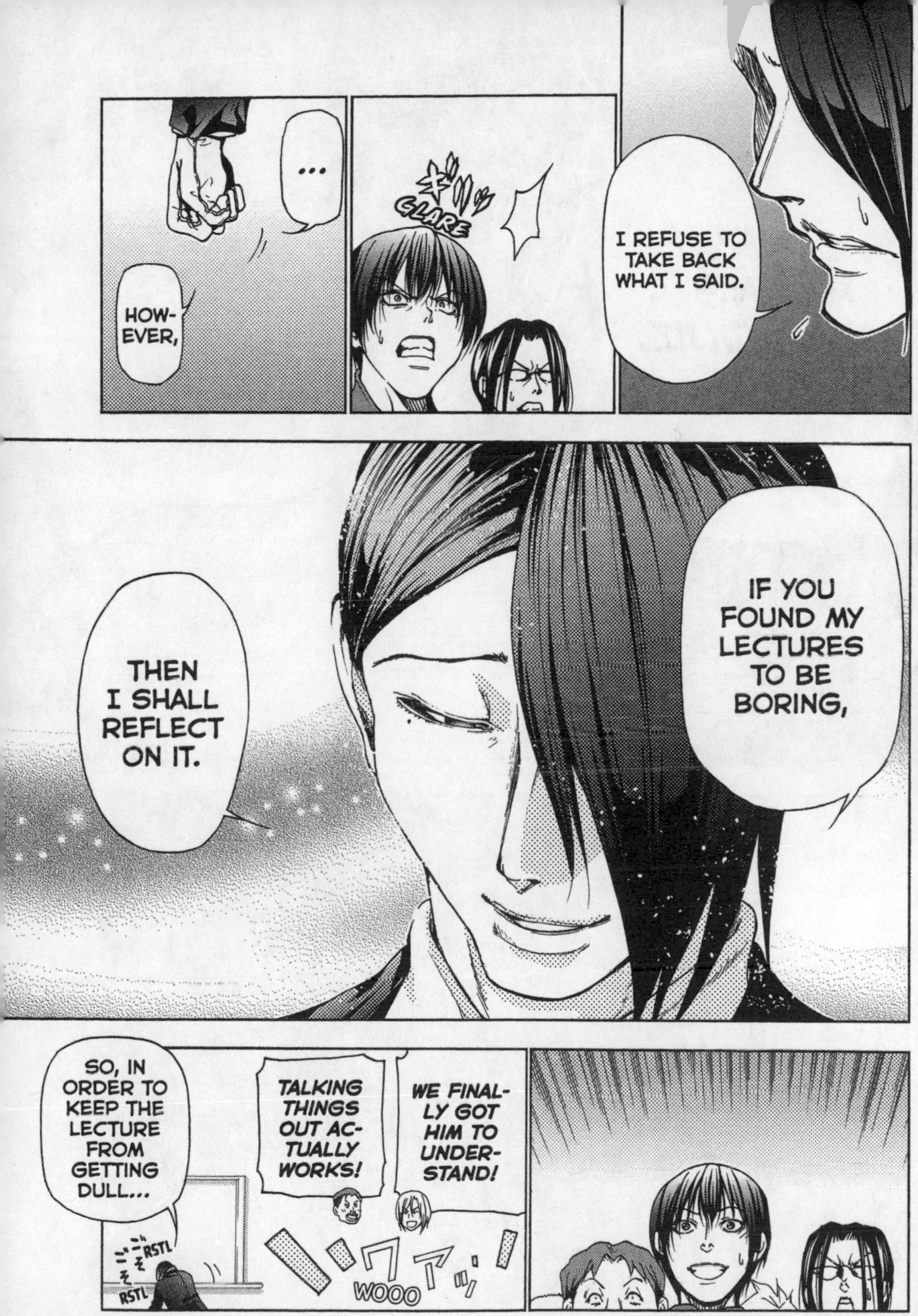
I REFUSE TO TAKE BACK WHAT I SAID.
GLARE
!
...
HOW-EVER,
IF YOU FOUND MY LECTURES TO BE BORING,
THEN I SHALL REFLECT ON IT.
WE FINAL-LY GOT HIM TO UNDER-STAND!
TALKING THINGS OUT AC-TUALLY WORKS!
SO, IN ORDER TO KEEP THE LECTURE FROM GETTING DULL...
RSTL
RSTL
WOOO

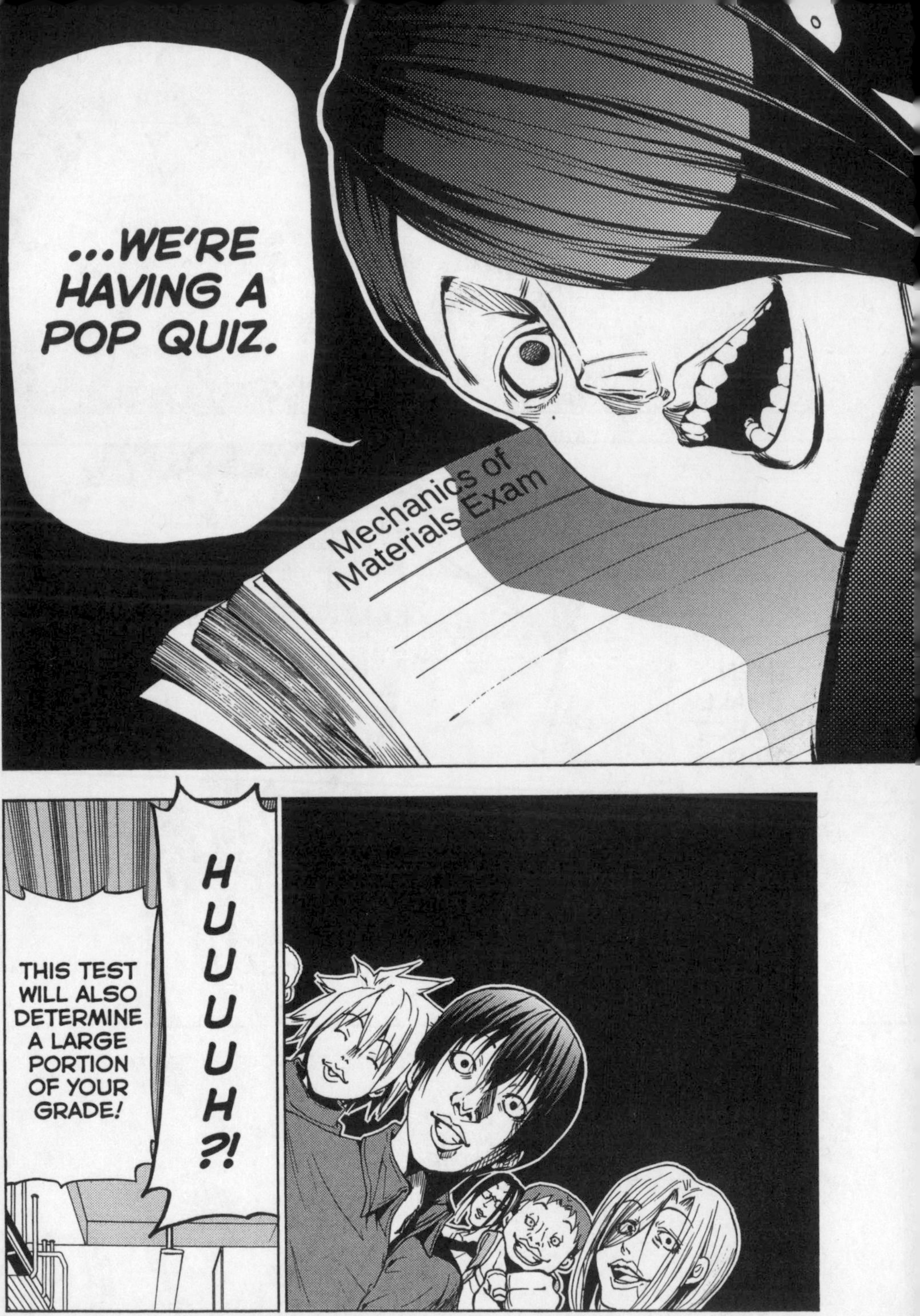
...WE'RE HAVING A POP QUIZ.
Mechanics of Materials Exam
HUUUUUH?!
THIS TEST WILL ALSO DETERMINE A LARGE PORTION OF YOUR GRADE!

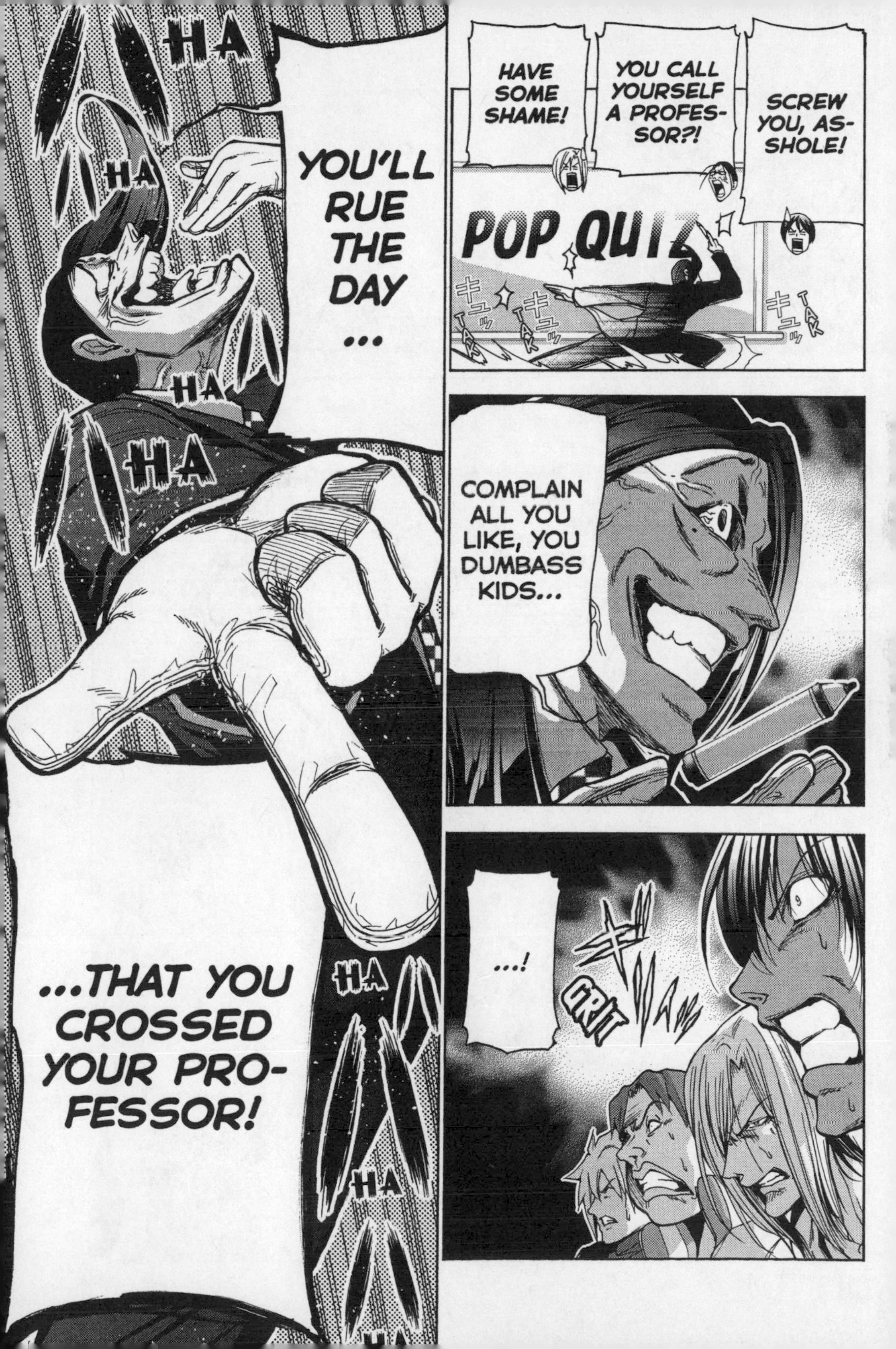
SCREW YOU, AS-SHOLE!
YOU CALL YOURSELF A PROFES-SOR?!
HAVE SOME SHAME!
TAK
キュッ
POP QUIZ
TAK
キュッ
TAK
キュッ
COMPLAIN ALL YOU LIKE, YOU DUMBASS KIDS...
GRIT
...!
HA
HA
YOU'LL RUE THE DAY ...
HA
HA
...THAT YOU CROSSED YOUR PRO-FESSOR!
HA
HA

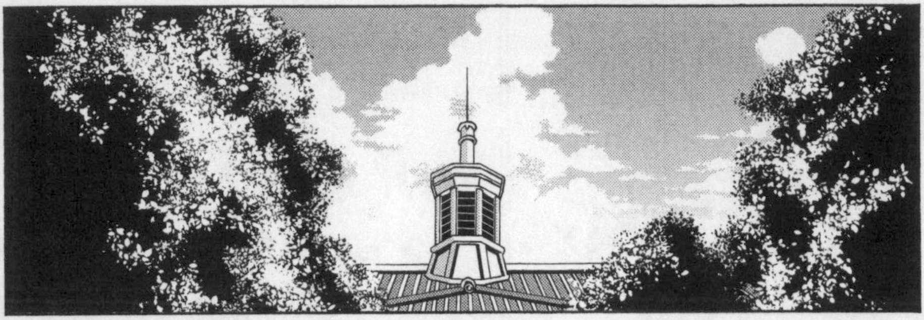

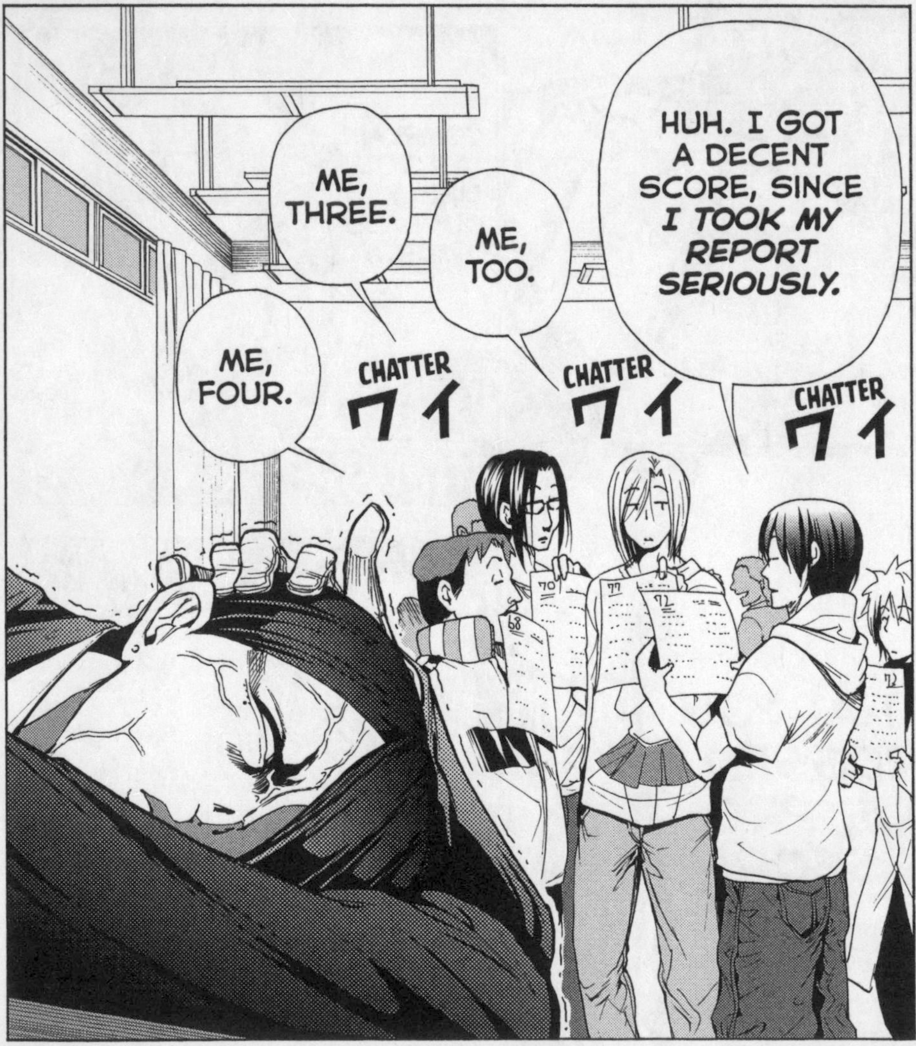
HUH. I GOT A DECENT SCORE, SINCE *I TOOK MY REPORT SERIOUSLY.*
CHATTER ワイ
ME, TOO.
CHATTER ワイ
ME, THREE.
CHATTER ワイ
ME, FOUR.

CH.31 / End

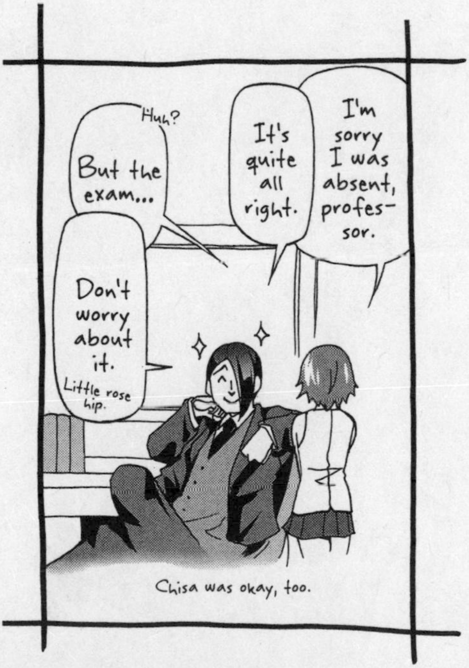
I'm sorry I was absent, profes- sor.
It's quite all right.
Huh?
But the exam...
Don't worry about it.
Little rose hip.
Chisa was okay, too.

Grand Blue Dreaming

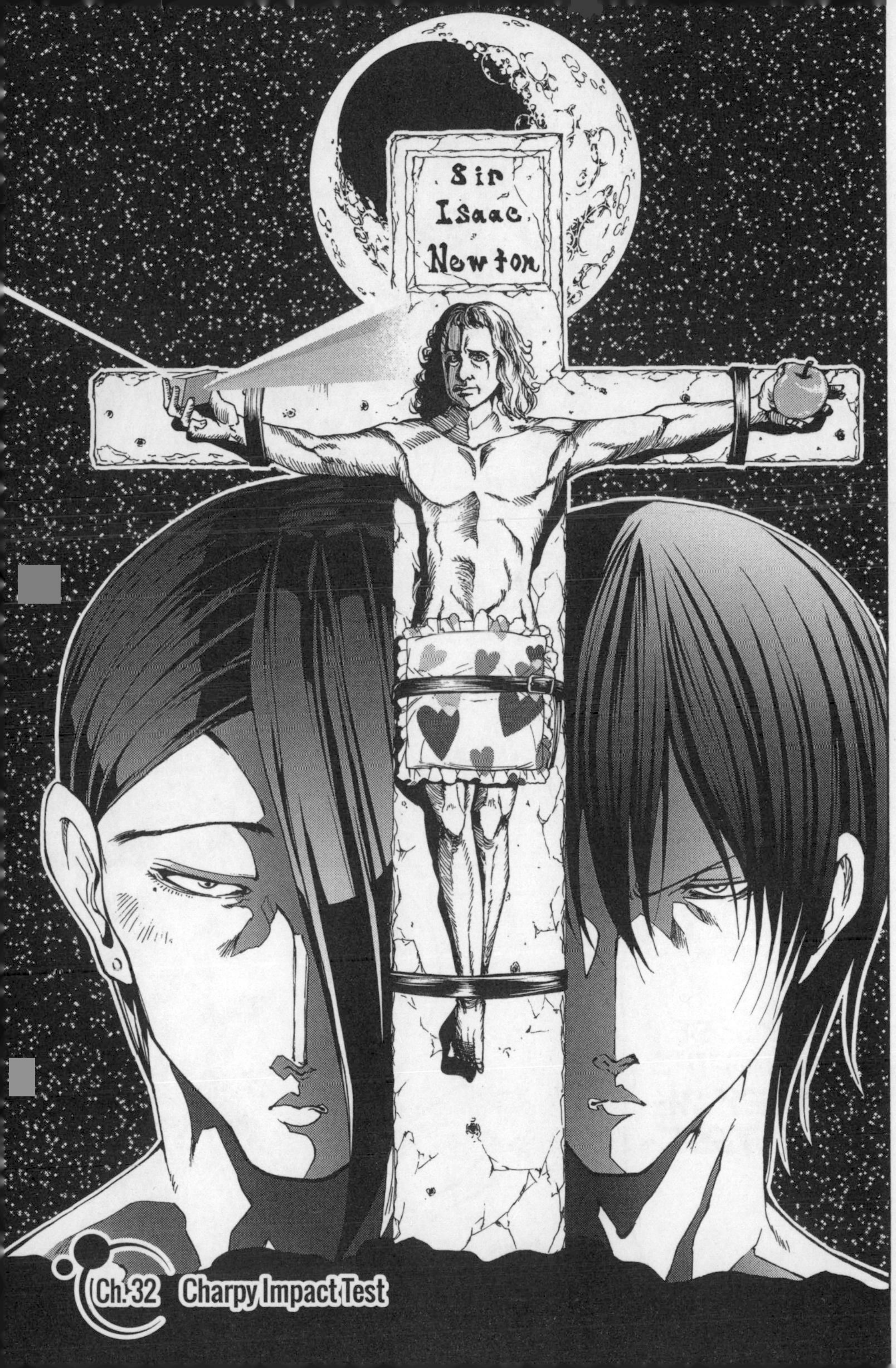
Sir Isaac Newton
Ch. 32 Charpy Impact Test

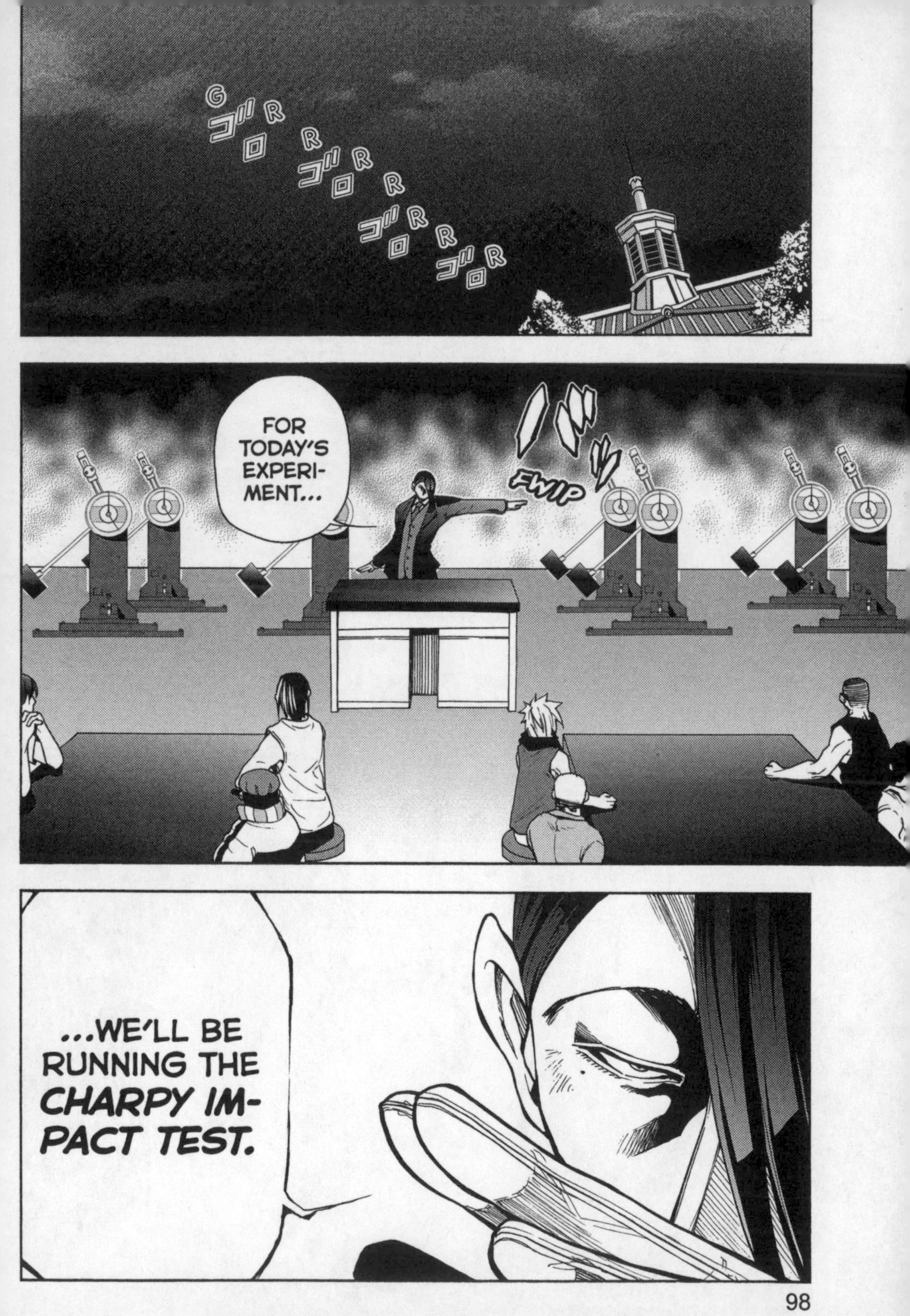
GRRRRRRR
ゴロゴロゴロゴロ
FWIP
FOR TODAY'S EXPERIMENT...
...WE'LL BE RUNNING THE *CHARPY IMPACT TEST.*

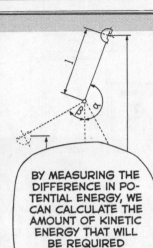

'KAAAY.
IN ES-SENCE,
M Mass of the hammer
l Distance from the center of the pivot to the hammer
h Initial height
h1 Final height
a Initial raised angle
β Angle after impact
If E equals the amount of energy required to destroy the sample and L represents the amount of energy lost in the rotation, the following is true
E = Mgh - Mgh1 - L
h = lcosa
h1 = lcosβ
l
α
β
BY MEASURING THE DIFFERENCE IN PO-TENTIAL ENERGY, WE CAN CALCULATE THE AMOUNT OF KINETIC ENERGY THAT WILL BE REQUIRED TO DESTROY THE SAMPLE.
FIRST, THE HAMMER IS RELEASED,
THEN, WE MEASURE THE FINAL ANGLE...
AFTER IT IMPACTS THE TEST SAMPLE.
BASI-CALLY, IT COMES DOWN TO THIS.
Height lost due as a result of impact
Initial Height
Calculate en-ergy expended from loss of height.
Impact & Destruction
Height after impact
キュッ
SQUEAK
FURTHER-MORE, SINCE L IS SIGNIFI-CANTLY SMALLER THAN E, WE CAN...
BLAH あーだ
SIGH...
Sheesh.
BLAH

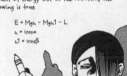

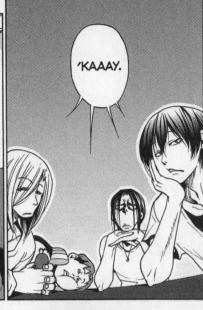

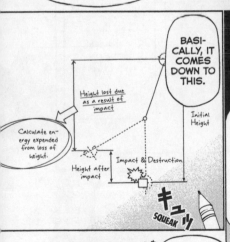

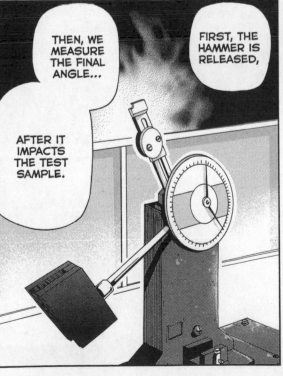

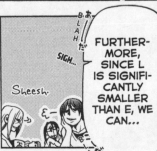

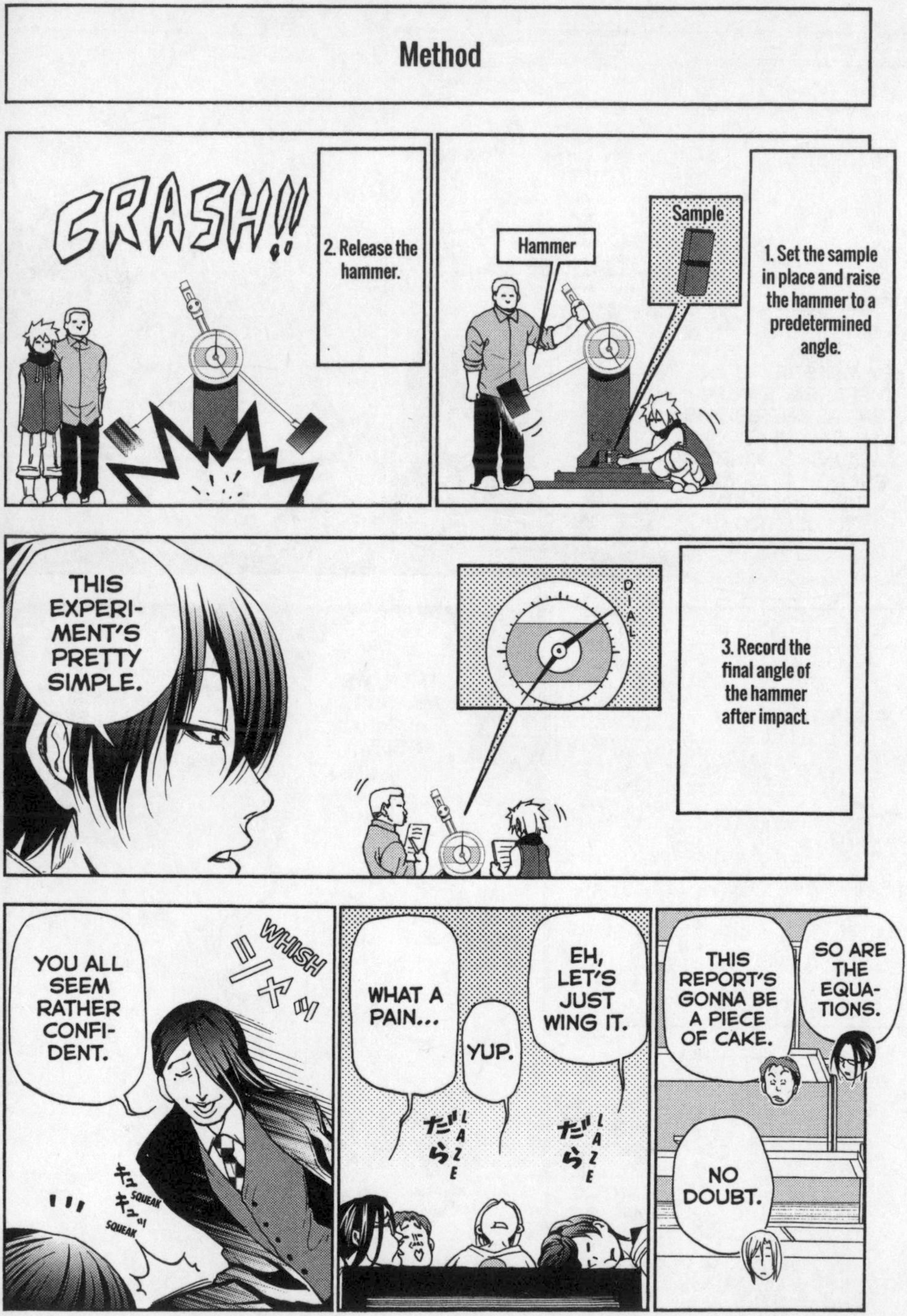
Method
1. Set the sample in place and raise the hammer to a predetermined angle.
Sample
Hammer
2. Release the hammer.
CRASH!!
3. Record the final angle of the hammer after impact.
DIAL
THIS EXPERIMENT'S PRETTY SIMPLE.
THIS REPORT'S GONNA BE A PIECE OF CAKE.
SO ARE THE EQUATIONS.
NO DOUBT.
EH, LET'S JUST WING IT.
WHAT A PAIN...
YUP.
LAZE
LAZE
WHISH
YOU ALL SEEM RATHER CONFIDENT.
SQUEAK
SQUEAK
!!!

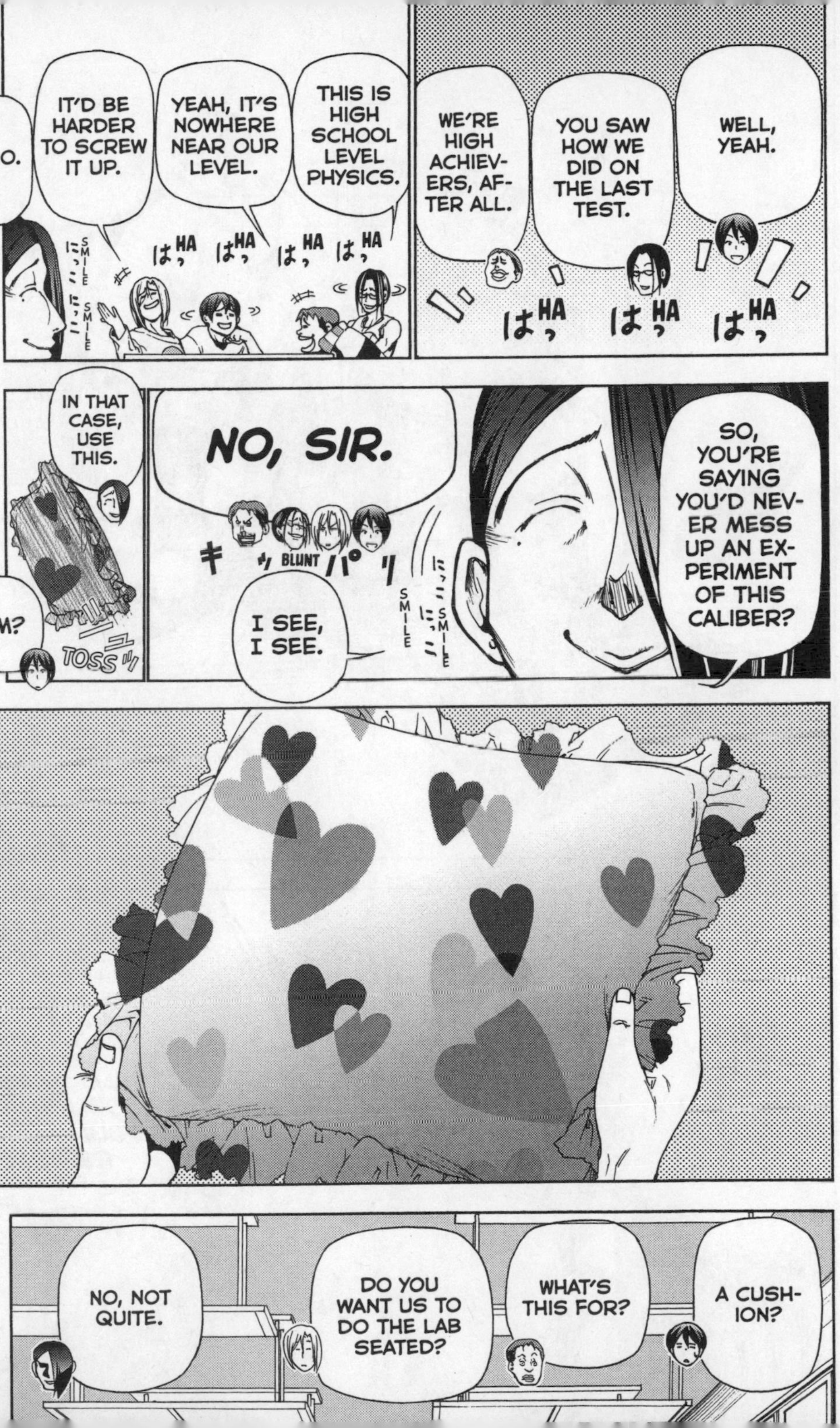
WELL, YEAH.
YOU SAW HOW WE DID ON THE LAST TEST.
WE'RE HIGH ACHIEVERS, AFTER ALL.
はっ HA
はっ HA
はっ HA
THIS IS HIGH SCHOOL LEVEL PHYSICS.
YEAH, IT'S NOWHERE NEAR OUR LEVEL.
IT'D BE HARDER TO SCREW IT UP.
はっ HA
はっ HA
はっ HA
はっ HA
O-HO.
にっこ SMILE
にっこ SMILE
SO, YOU'RE SAYING YOU'D NEVER MESS UP AN EXPERIMENT OF THIS CALIBER?
にっこ SMILE
にっこ SMILE
I SEE, I SEE.
NO, SIR.
キッパリ BLUNT
IN THAT CASE, USE THIS.
HM?
ニュッ TOSS
A CUSHION?
WHAT'S THIS FOR?
DO YOU WANT US TO DO THE LAB SEATED?
NO, NOT QUITE.

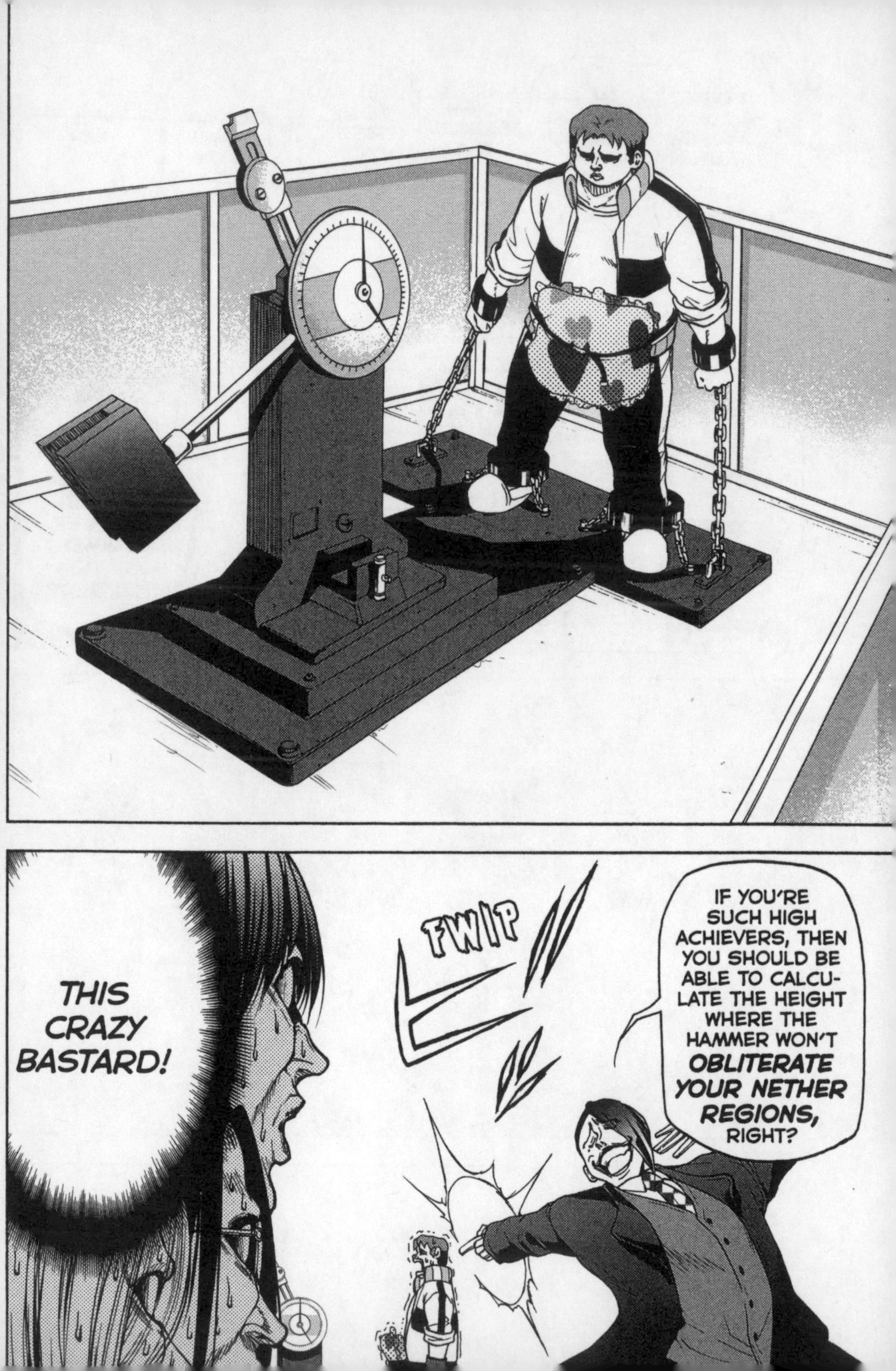
IF YOU'RE SUCH HIGH ACHIEVERS, THEN YOU SHOULD BE ABLE TO CALCULATE THE HEIGHT WHERE THE HAMMER WON'T *OBLITERATE YOUR NETHER REGIONS*, RIGHT?
FWIP
THIS CRAZY BASTARD!

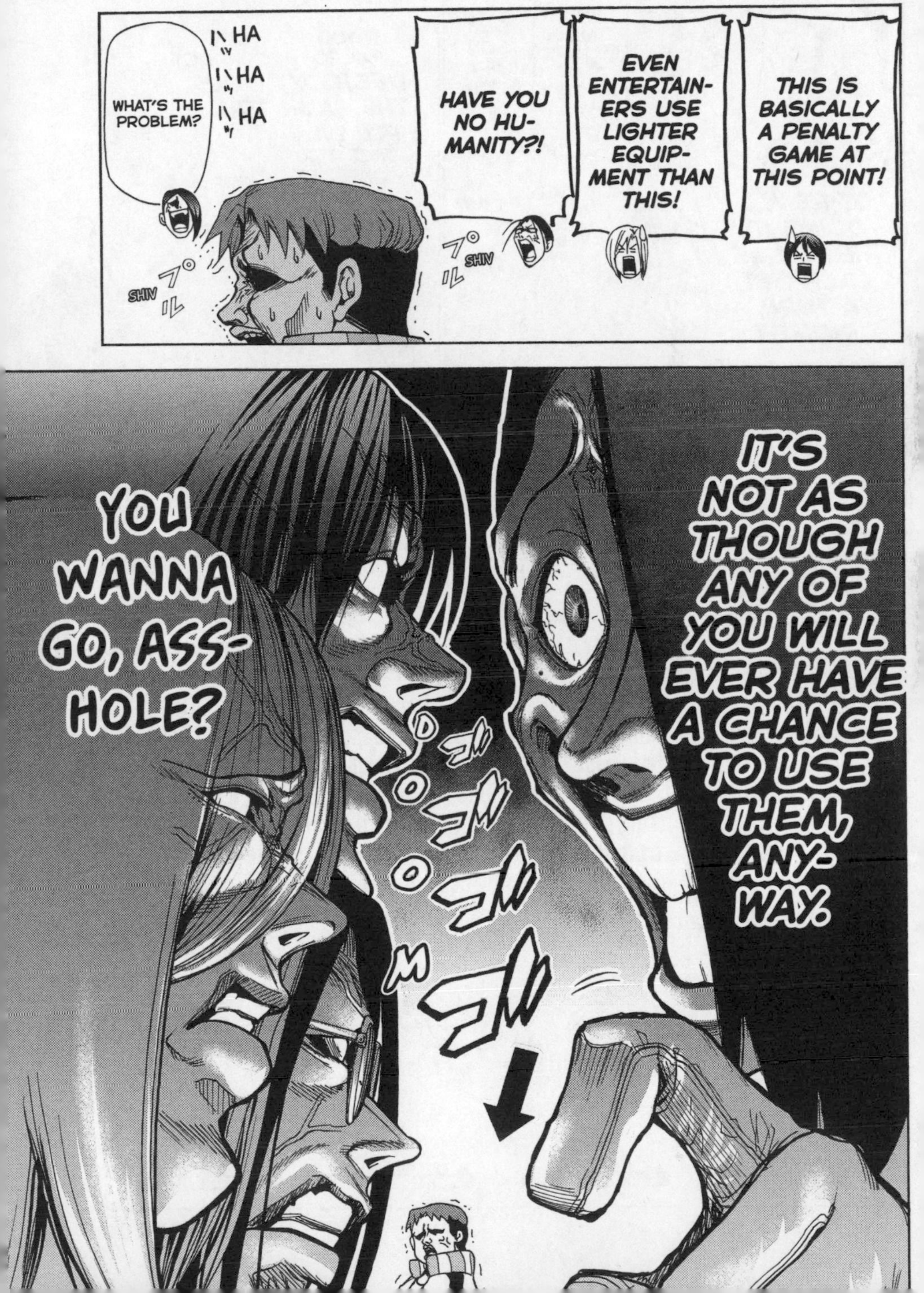
THIS IS BASICALLY A PENALTY GAME AT THIS POINT!
EVEN ENTERTAIN-ERS USE LIGHTER EQUIP-MENT THAN THIS!
HAVE YOU NO HU-MANITY?!
SHIV
HA
HA
HA
WHAT'S THE PROBLEM?
SHIV
IT'S NOT AS THOUGH ANY OF YOU WILL EVER HAVE A CHANCE TO USE THEM, ANY-WAY.
YOU WANNA GO, ASS-HOLE?
DOOOM

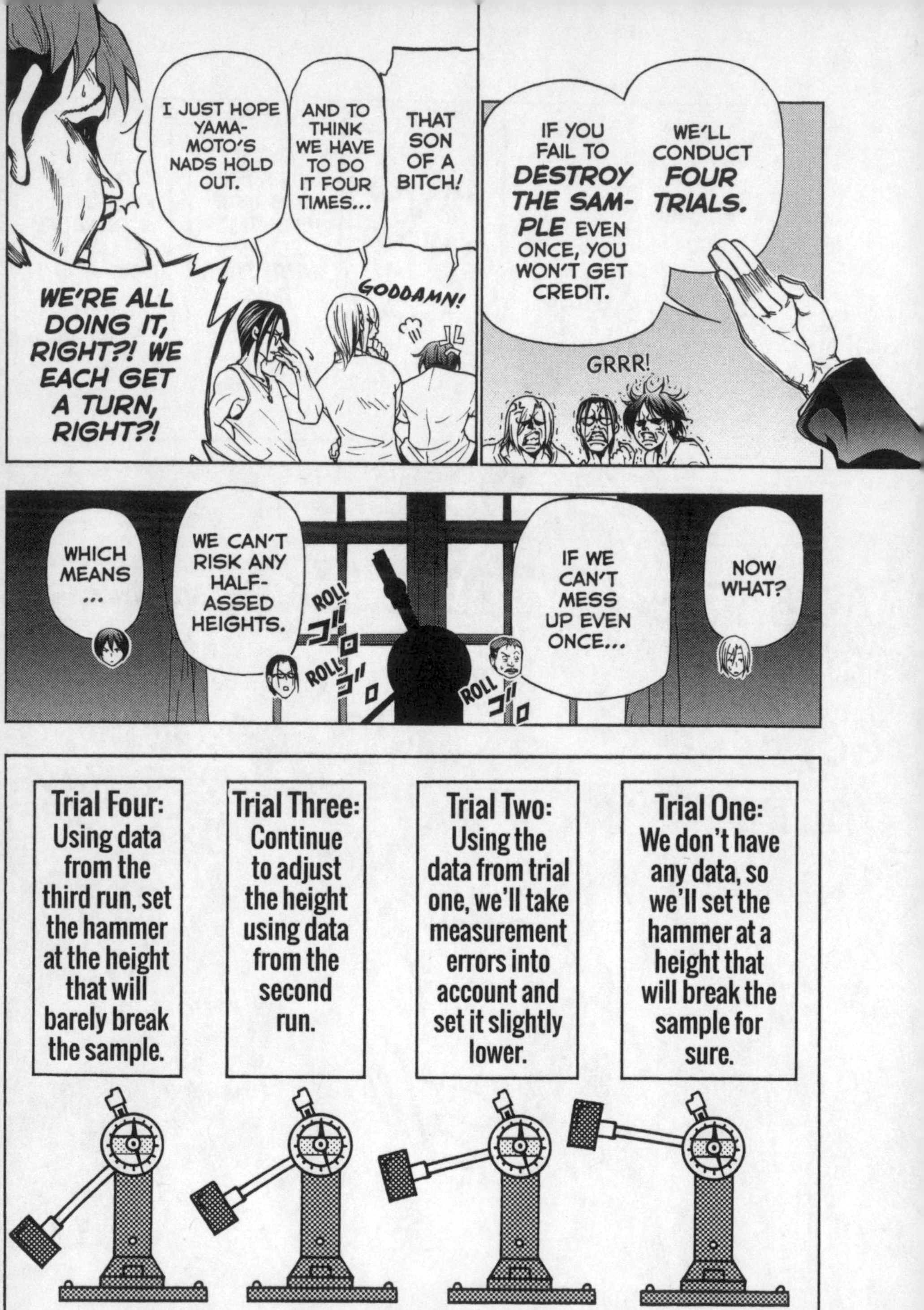
WE'LL CONDUCT FOUR TRIALS.
IF YOU FAIL TO DESTROY THE SAMPLE EVEN ONCE, YOU WON'T GET CREDIT.
GRRR!
THAT SON OF A BITCH!
AND TO THINK WE HAVE TO DO IT FOUR TIMES...
I JUST HOPE YAMAMOTO'S NADS HOLD OUT.
GODDAMN!
WE'RE ALL DOING IT, RIGHT?! WE EACH GET A TURN, RIGHT?!
NOW WHAT?
IF WE CAN'T MESS UP EVEN ONCE...
ROLL ゴロ
ROLL ゴロ
ROLL ゴロ
WE CAN'T RISK ANY HALF-ASSED HEIGHTS.
WHICH MEANS...
Trial One: We don't have any data, so we'll set the hammer at a height that will break the sample for sure.
Trial Two: Using the data from trial one, we'll take measurement errors into account and set it slightly lower.
Trial Three: Continue to adjust the height using data from the second run.
Trial Four: Using data from the third run, set the hammer at the height that will barely break the sample.

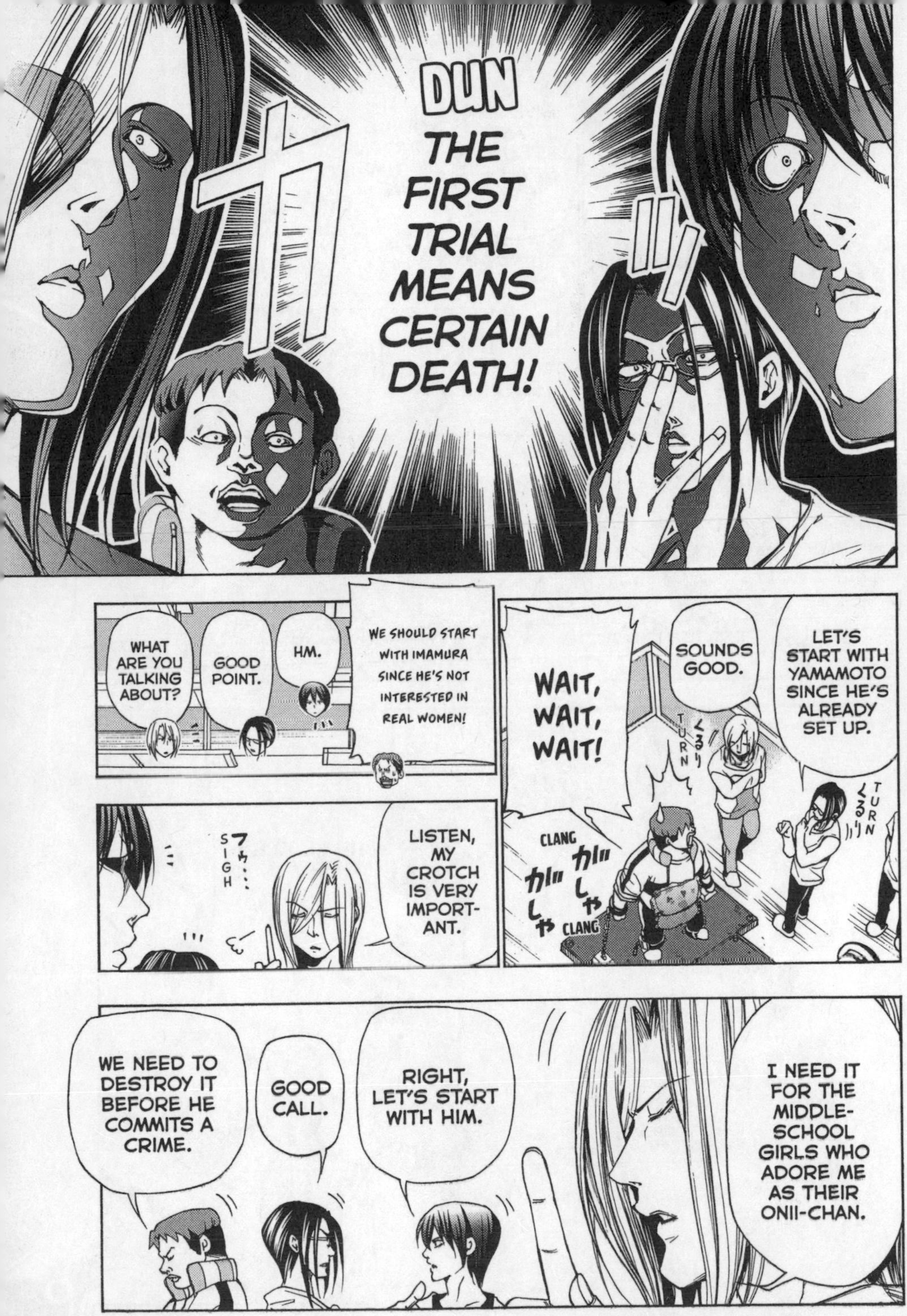
DUN
THE FIRST TRIAL MEANS CERTAIN DEATH!
LET'S START WITH YAMAMOTO SINCE HE'S ALREADY SET UP.
TURN
SOUNDS GOOD.
TURN
WAIT, WAIT, WAIT!
CLANG
CLANG
WE SHOULD START WITH IMAMURA SINCE HE'S NOT INTERESTED IN REAL WOMEN!
HM.
GOOD POINT.
WHAT ARE YOU TALKING ABOUT?
LISTEN, MY CROTCH IS VERY IMPORTANT.
SIGH
I NEED IT FOR THE MIDDLE-SCHOOL GIRLS WHO ADORE ME AS THEIR ONII-CHAN.
RIGHT, LET'S START WITH HIM.
GOOD CALL.
WE NEED TO DESTROY IT BEFORE HE COMMITS A CRIME.

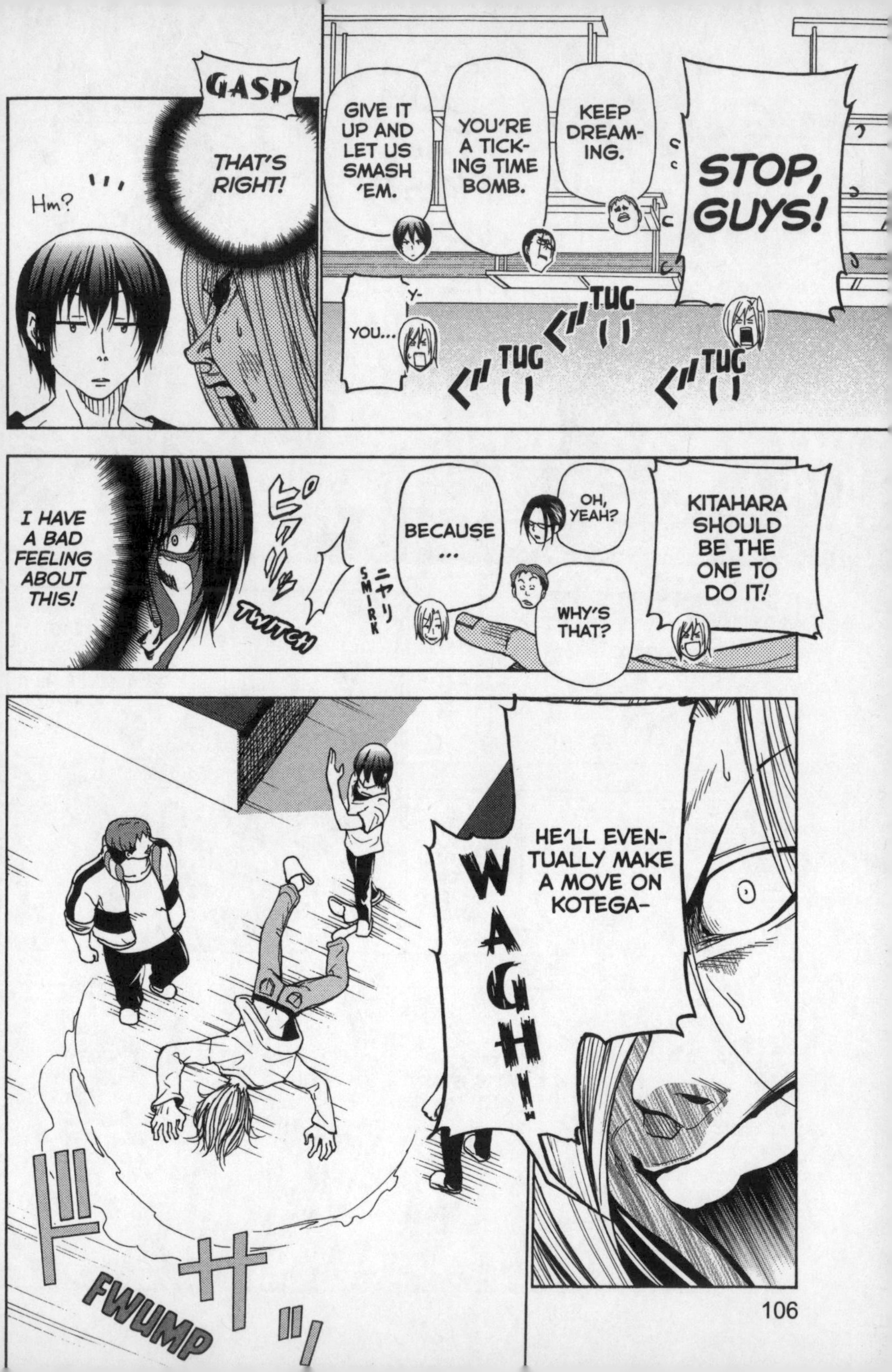
STOP, GUYS!
KEEP DREAM-ING.
YOU'RE A TICK-ING TIME BOMB.
GIVE IT UP AND LET US SMASH 'EM.
Y- YOU...
TUG
TUG
TUG
GASP
THAT'S RIGHT!
Hm?
KITAHARA SHOULD BE THE ONE TO DO IT!
OH, YEAH?
WHY'S THAT?
BECAUSE ...
ニヤリ SMIRK
TWITCH
I HAVE A BAD FEELING ABOUT THIS!
HE'LL EVEN-TUALLY MAKE A MOVE ON KOTEGA-
WAGH!!
FWUMP

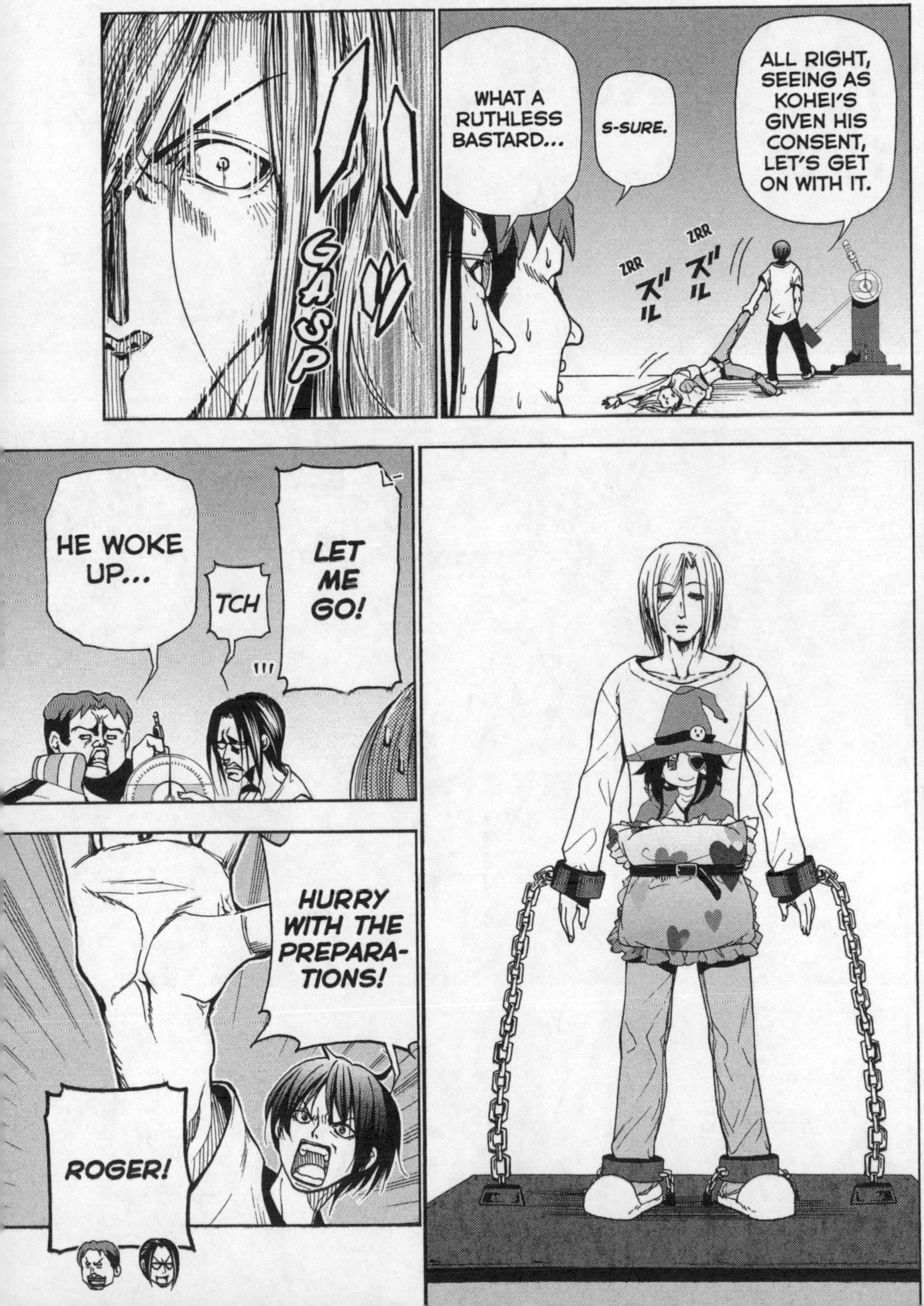
ALL RIGHT, SEEING AS KOHEI'S GIVEN HIS CONSENT, LET'S GET ON WITH IT.
ZRR
ZRR
S-SURE.
WHAT A RUTHLESS BASTARD...
GASP
LET ME GO!
TCH
HE WOKE UP...
HURRY WITH THE PREPARA-TIONS!
ROGER!

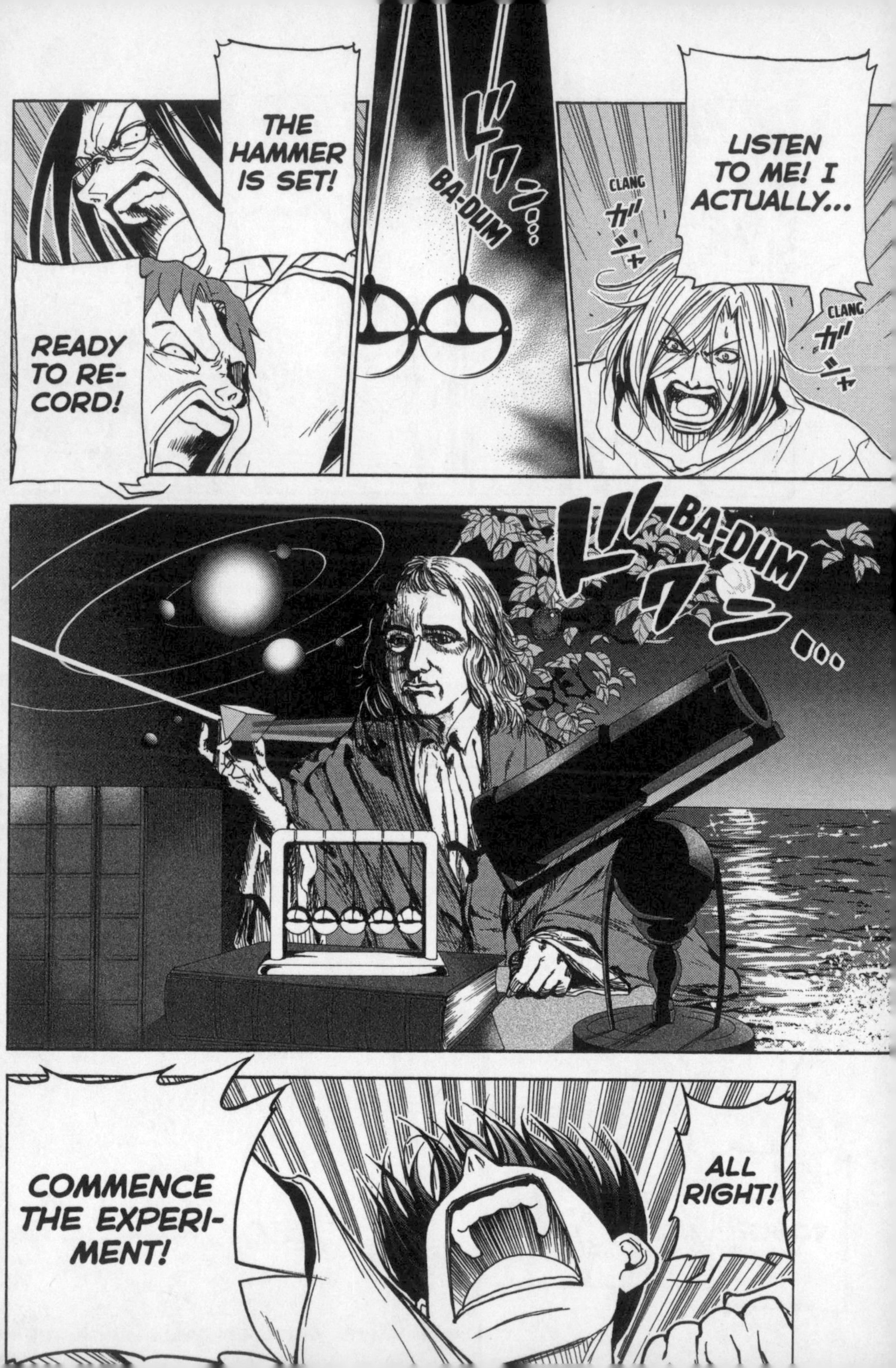
LISTEN TO ME! I ACTUALLY...
CLANG
ガシャ
CLANG
ガシャ
ドクン...
BA-DUM
THE HAMMER IS SET!
READY TO RE-CORD!
ドクン...
BA-DUM
ALL RIGHT!
COMMENCE THE EXPERI-MENT!

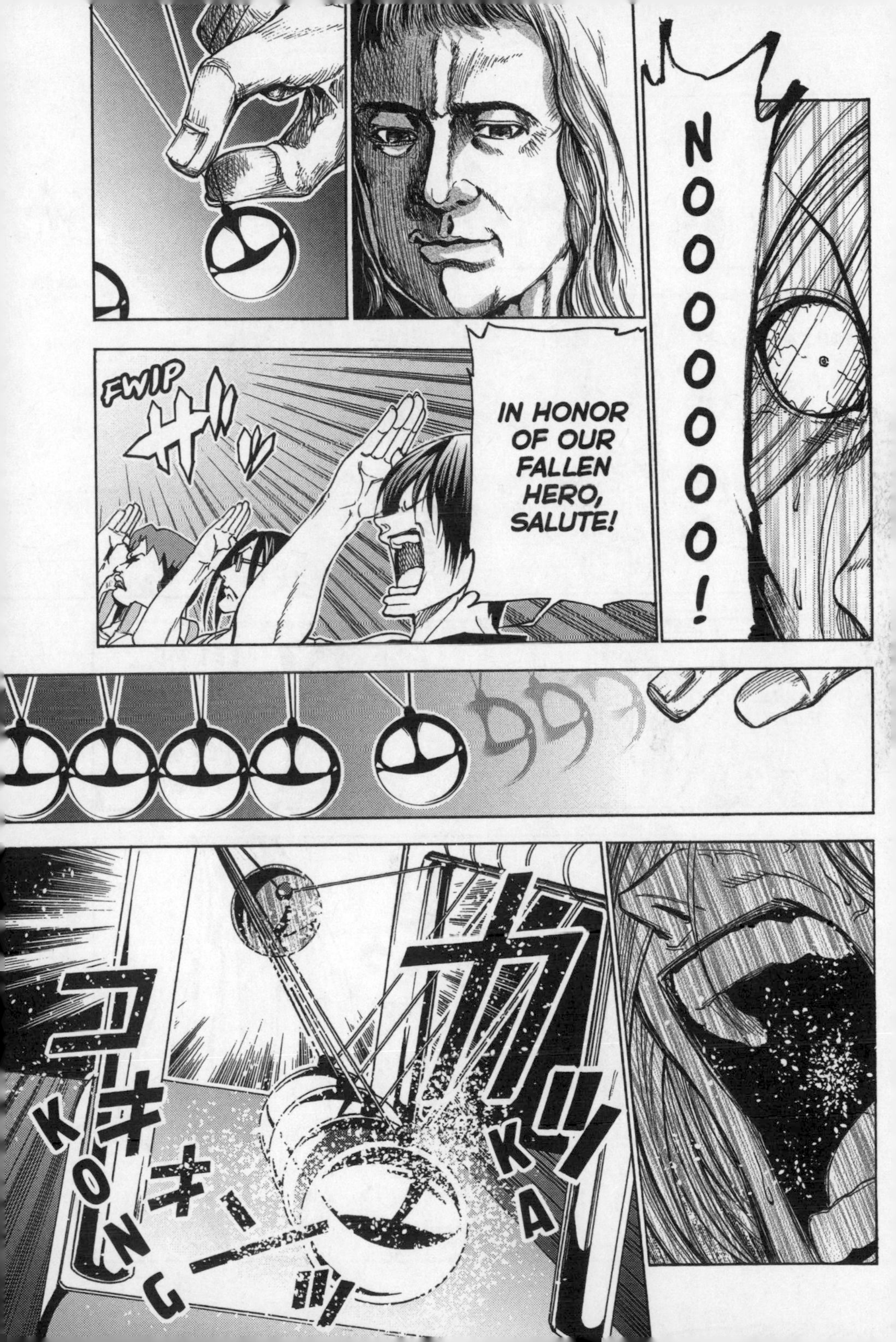
NOOOOOOO!
IN HONOR OF OUR FALLEN HERO, SALUTE!
FWIP
KA
KONG

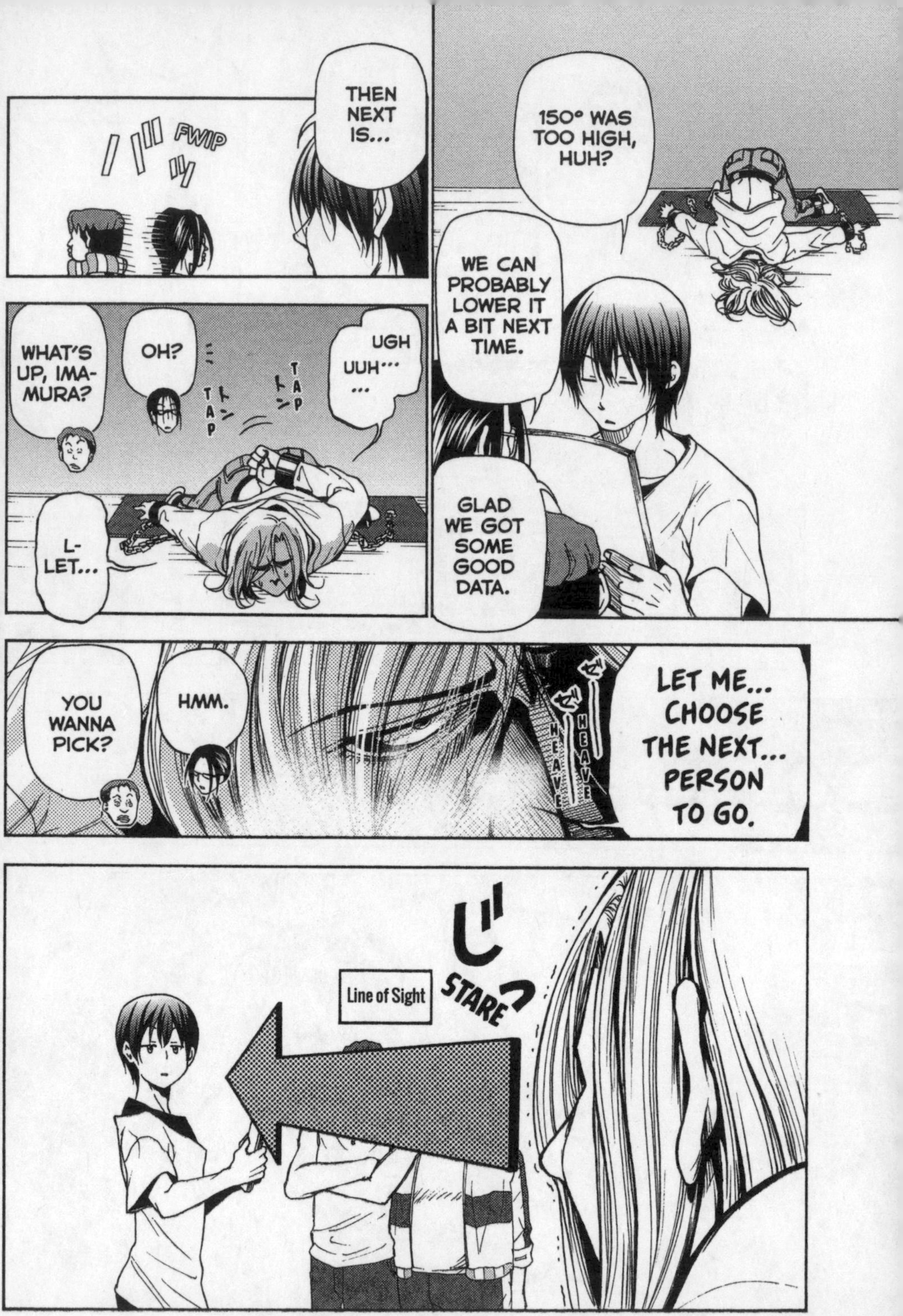
150° WAS TOO HIGH, HUH?
WE CAN PROBABLY LOWER IT A BIT NEXT TIME.
GLAD WE GOT SOME GOOD DATA.
FWIP
THEN NEXT IS...
UGH UUH... ...
TAP TAP
OH?
WHAT'S UP, IMAMURA?
L- LET...
LET ME... CHOOSE THE NEXT... PERSON TO GO.
HEAVE HEAVE
HMM.
YOU WANNA PICK?
STARE
Line of Sight

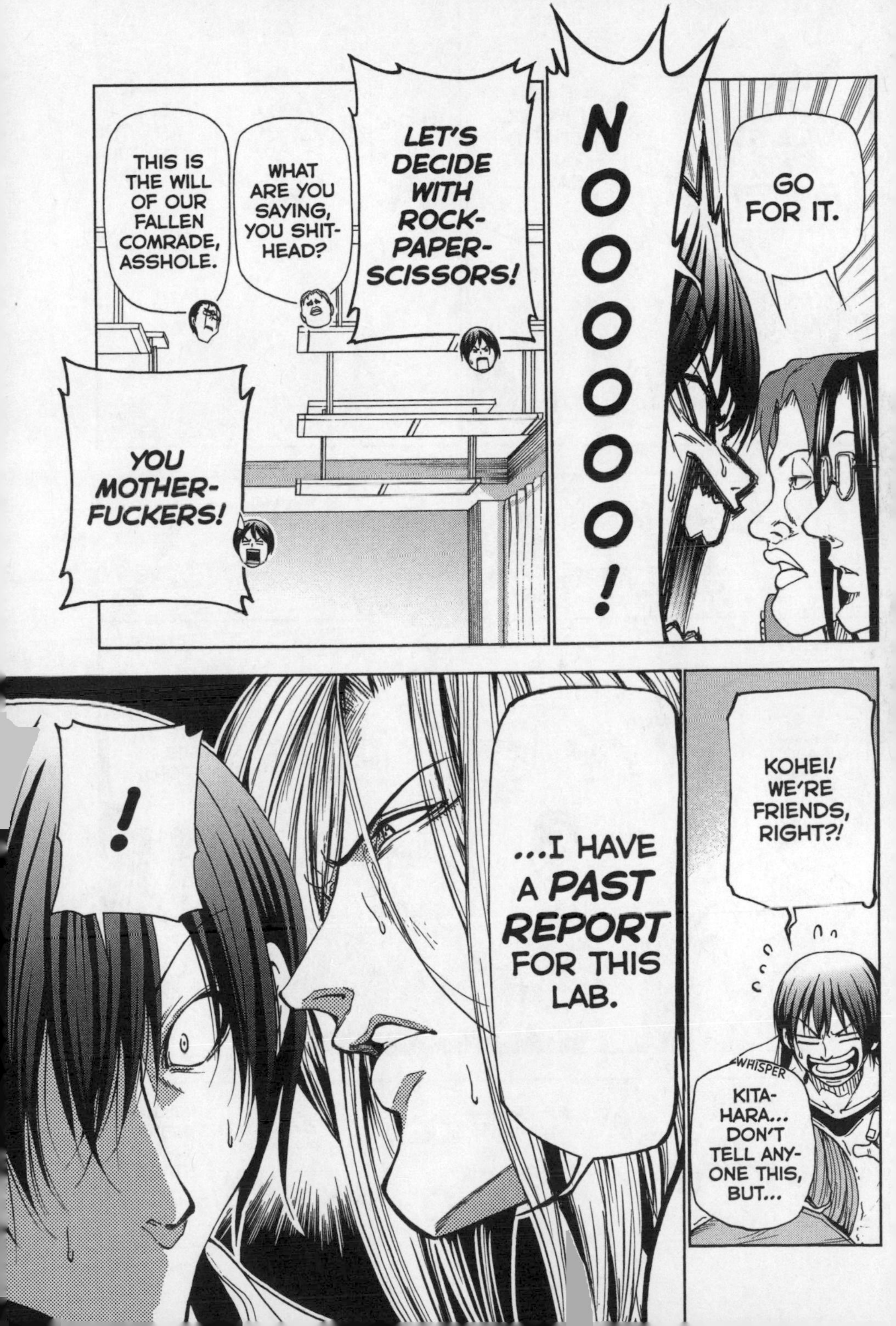
GO FOR IT.
NOOOOOOOO!
LET'S DECIDE WITH ROCK-PAPER-SCISSORS!
WHAT ARE YOU SAYING, YOU SHIT-HEAD?
THIS IS THE WILL OF OUR FALLEN COMRADE, ASSHOLE.
YOU MOTHER-FUCKERS!
KOHEI! WE'RE FRIENDS, RIGHT?!
WHISPER
KITA-HARA... DON'T TELL ANY-ONE THIS, BUT...
...I HAVE A PAST REPORT FOR THIS LAB.
!

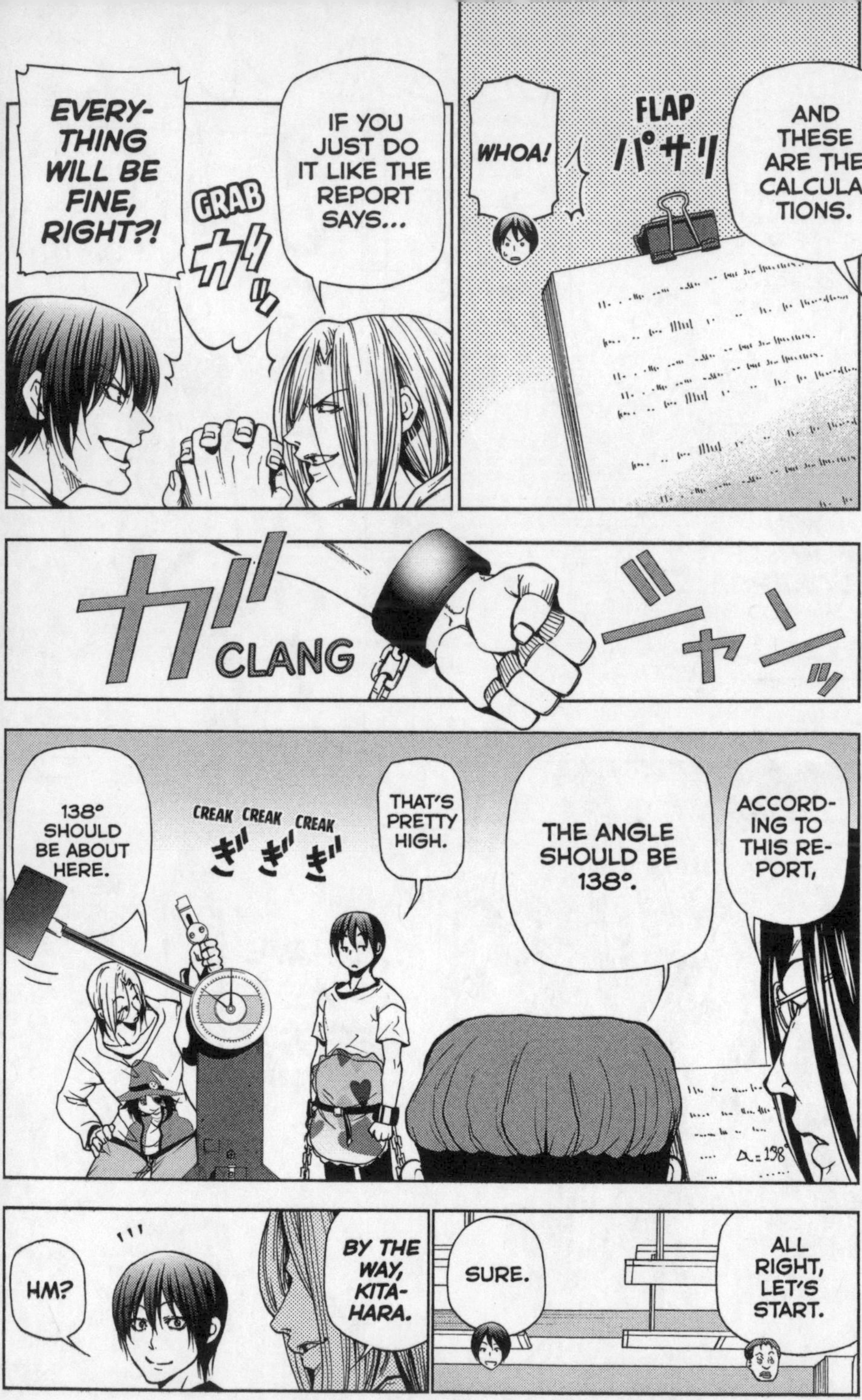
AND THESE ARE THE CALCULATIONS.
FLAP
パサリ
WHOA!
IF YOU JUST DO IT LIKE THE REPORT SAYS...
GRAB
ガシッ
EVERYTHING WILL BE FINE, RIGHT?!
ガシャーンッ
CLANG
ACCORDING TO THIS REPORT,
THE ANGLE SHOULD BE 138°.
THAT'S PRETTY HIGH.
CREAK CREAK CREAK
ぎぎぎ
138° SHOULD BE ABOUT HERE.
ALL RIGHT, LET'S START.
SURE.
BY THE WAY, KITAHARA.
HM?

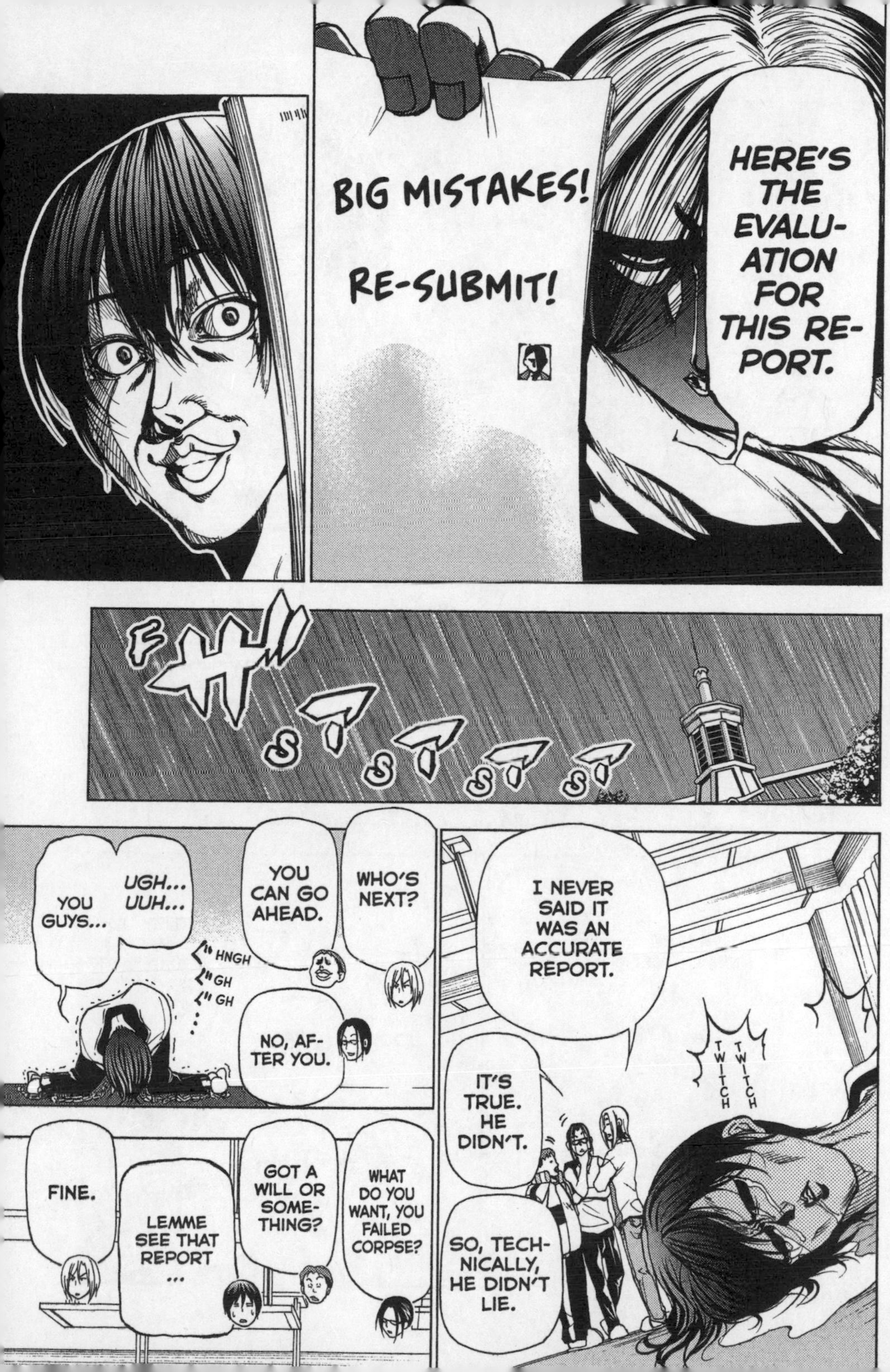
HERE'S THE EVALUATION FOR THIS REPORT.
BIG MISTAKES!
RE-SUBMIT!
I NEVER SAID IT WAS AN ACCURATE REPORT.
TWITCH TWITCH
IT'S TRUE. HE DIDN'T.
SO, TECHNICALLY, HE DIDN'T LIE.
WHO'S NEXT?
YOU CAN GO AHEAD.
UGH... UUH...
YOU GUYS...
HNGH
GH
GH
NO, AFTER YOU.
WHAT DO YOU WANT, YOU FAILED CORPSE?
GOT A WILL OR SOMETHING?
LEMME SEE THAT REPORT ...
FINE.

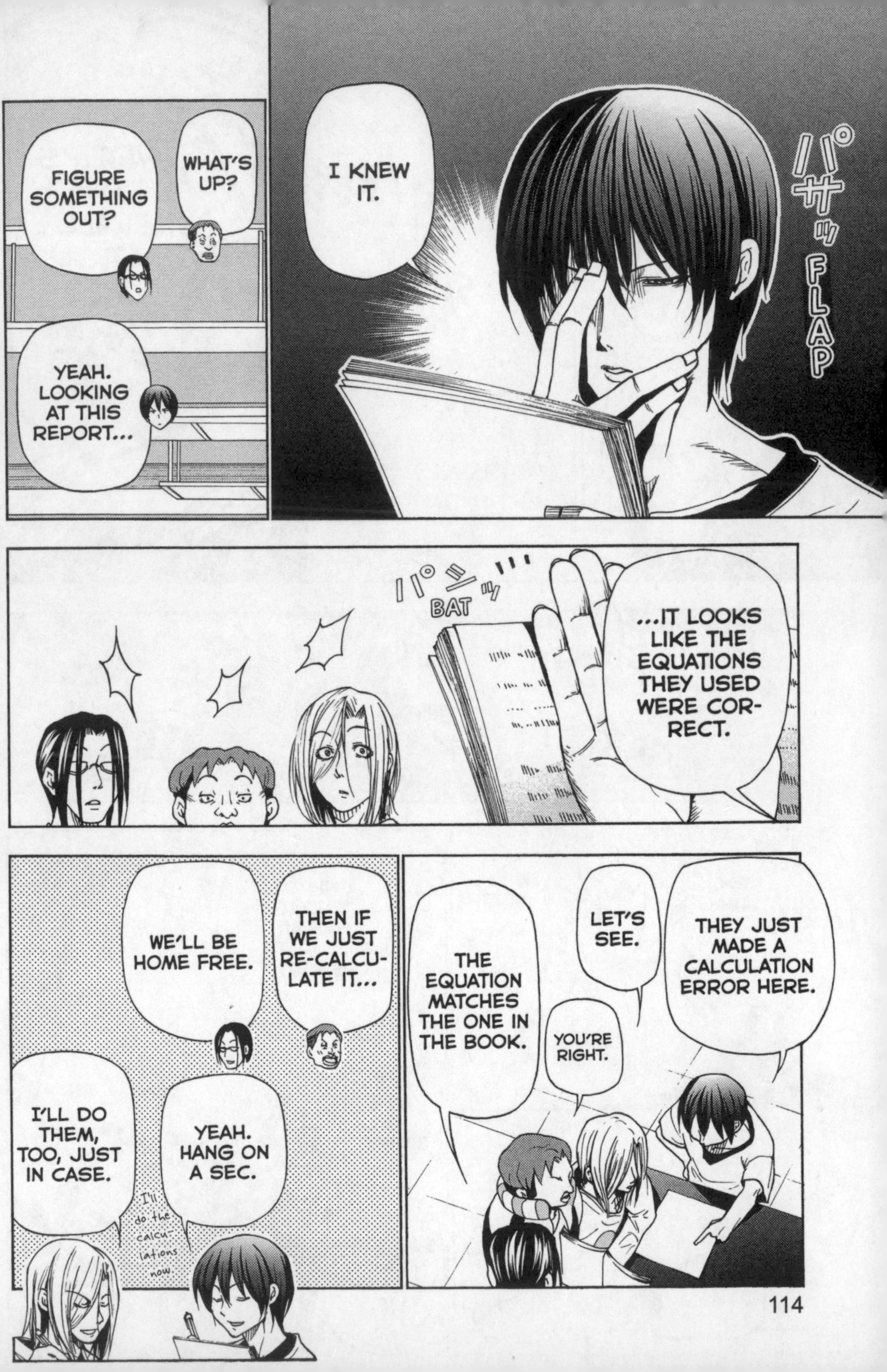
パサッ
FLAP
I KNEW IT.
WHAT'S UP?
FIGURE SOMETHING OUT?
YEAH. LOOKING AT THIS REPORT...
パシッ
BAT
...IT LOOKS LIKE THE EQUATIONS THEY USED WERE COR-RECT.
THEY JUST MADE A CALCULATION ERROR HERE.
LET'S SEE.
YOU'RE RIGHT.
THE EQUATION MATCHES THE ONE IN THE BOOK.
THEN IF WE JUST RE-CALCU-LATE IT...
WE'LL BE HOME FREE.
YEAH. HANG ON A SEC.
I'll do the calcu-lations now
I'LL DO THEM, TOO, JUST IN CASE.

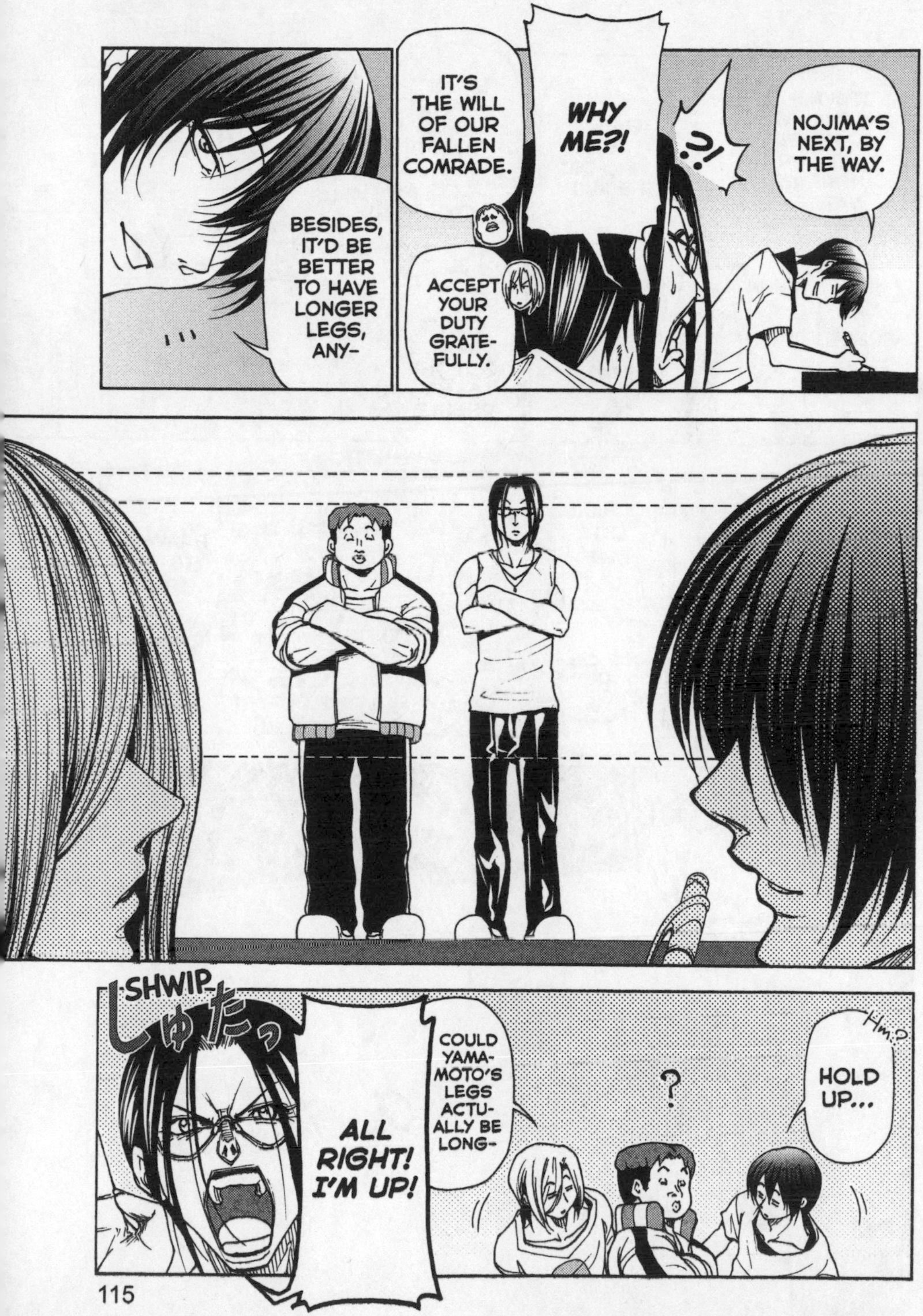
NOJIMA'S NEXT, BY THE WAY.
?!
WHY ME?!
IT'S THE WILL OF OUR FALLEN COMRADE.
ACCEPT YOUR DUTY GRATEFULLY.
BESIDES, IT'D BE BETTER TO HAVE LONGER LEGS, ANY-
Hm?
HOLD UP...
?
COULD YAMAMOTO'S LEGS ACTUALLY BE LONG-
ALL RIGHT! I'M UP!
SHWIP
しゅたっ

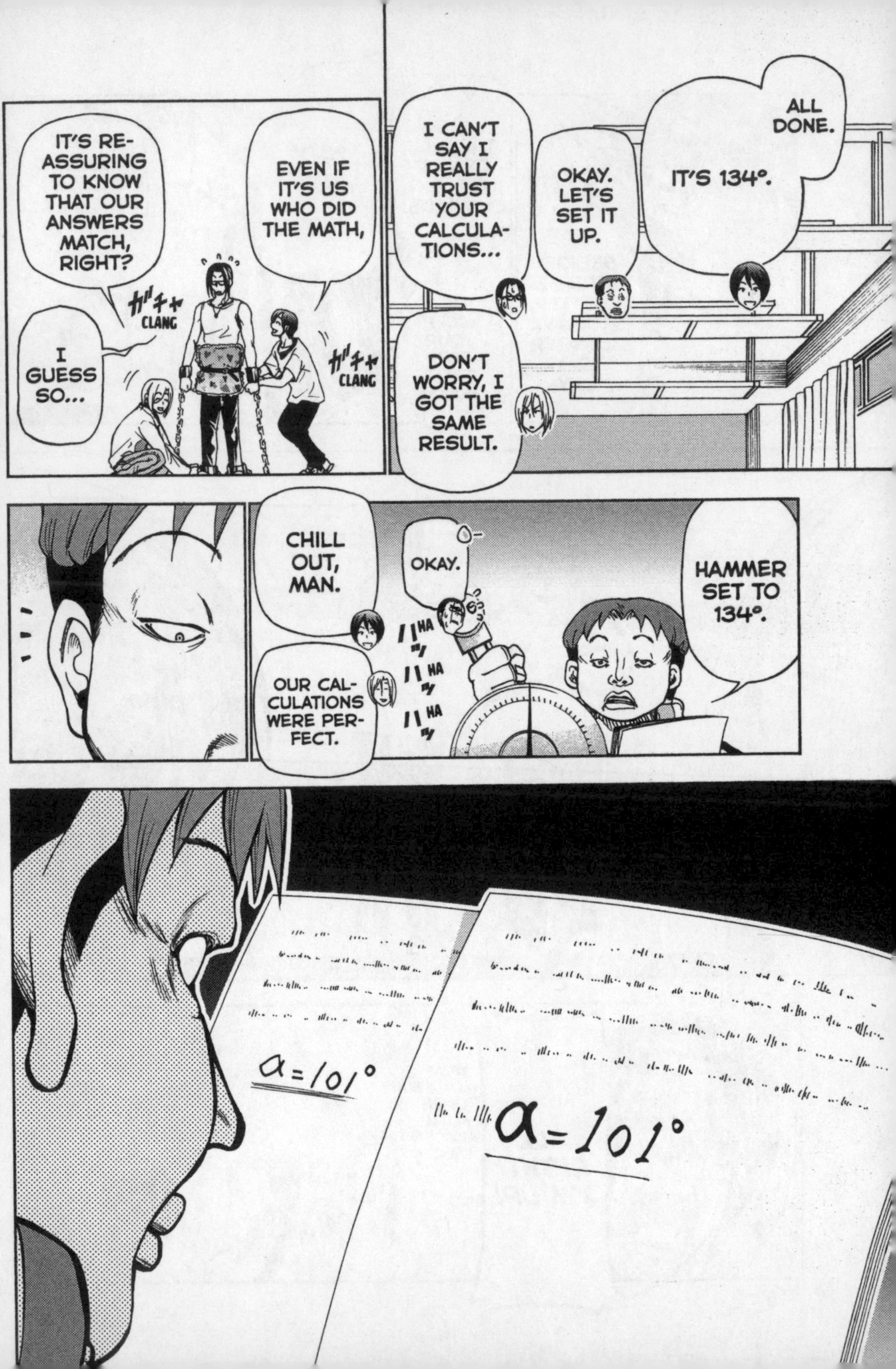
ALL DONE.
IT'S 134°.
OKAY. LET'S SET IT UP.
I CAN'T SAY I REALLY TRUST YOUR CALCULATIONS...
DON'T WORRY, I GOT THE SAME RESULT.
EVEN IF IT'S US WHO DID THE MATH,
IT'S RE-ASSURING TO KNOW THAT OUR ANSWERS MATCH, RIGHT?
ガチャ CLANG
ガチャ CLANG
I GUESS SO...
HAMMER SET TO 134°.
OKAY.
CHILL OUT, MAN.
ハ HA ハ HA ハ HA
OUR CAL-CULATIONS WERE PER-FECT.
α=101°
α=101°

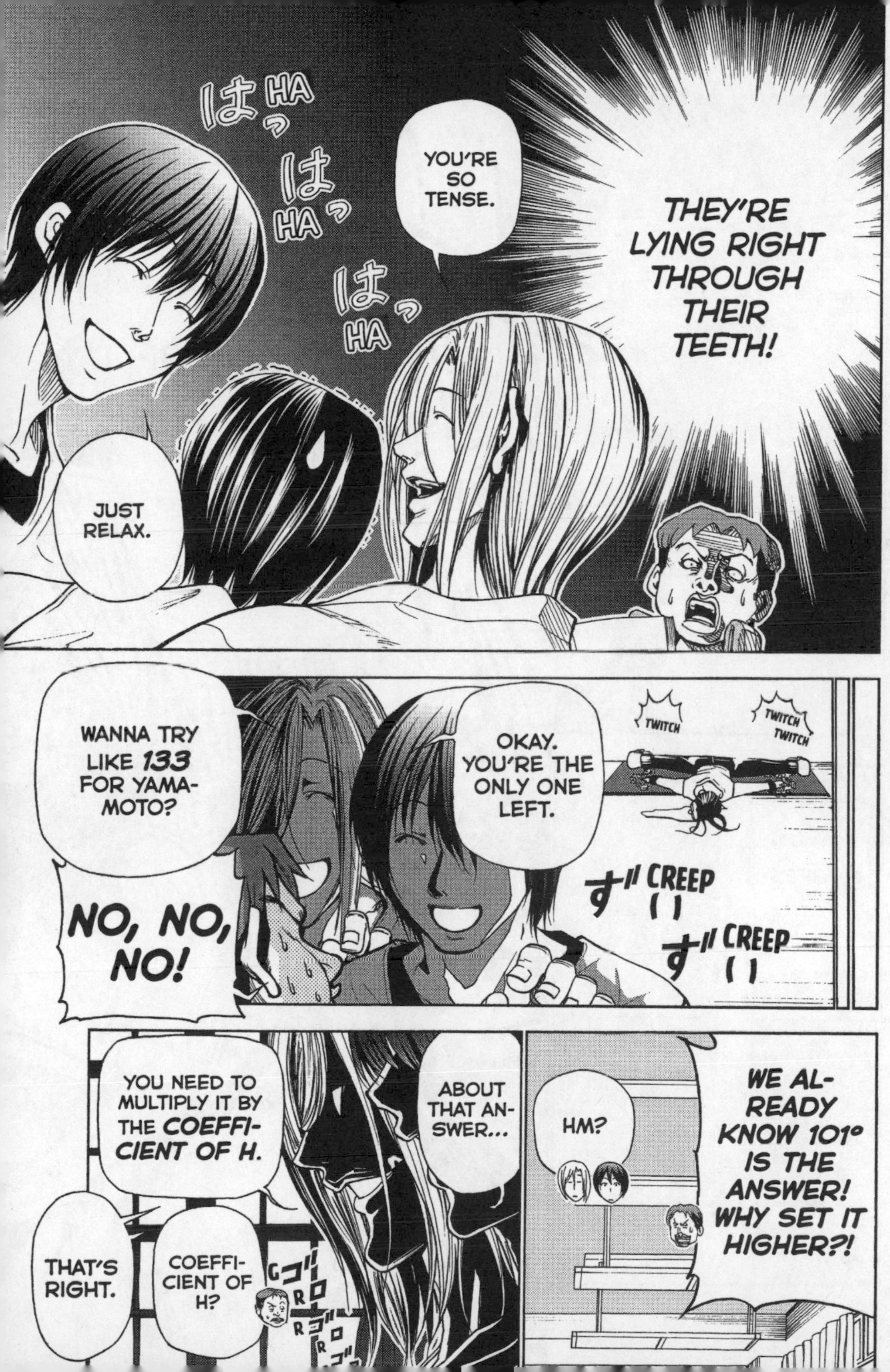
THEY'RE LYING RIGHT THROUGH THEIR TEETH!
YOU'RE SO TENSE.
はっ HA
はっ HA
はっ HA
JUST RELAX.
TWITCH
TWITCH TWITCH
すり CREEP
すり CREEP
OKAY. YOU'RE THE ONLY ONE LEFT.
WANNA TRY LIKE 133 FOR YAMA-MOTO?
NO, NO, NO!
WE AL-READY KNOW 101° IS THE ANSWER! WHY SET IT HIGHER?!
HM?
ABOUT THAT AN-SWER...
YOU NEED TO MULTIPLY IT BY THE COEFFI-CIENT OF H.
COEFFI-CIENT OF H?
THAT'S RIGHT.
ゴロ GRO
ゴロ GRO

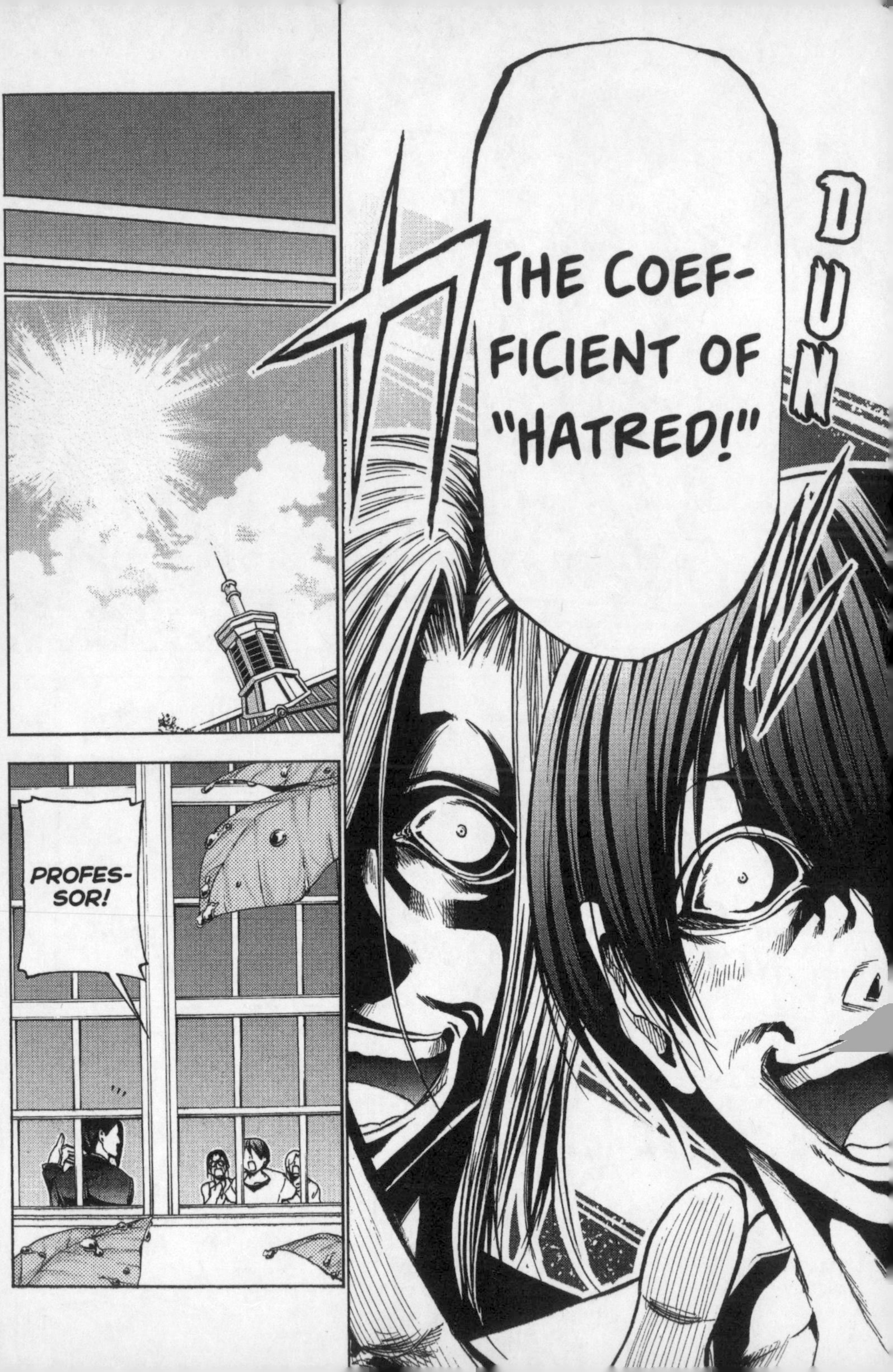
THE COEFFICIENT OF "HATRED!"
DUN
PROFESSOR!

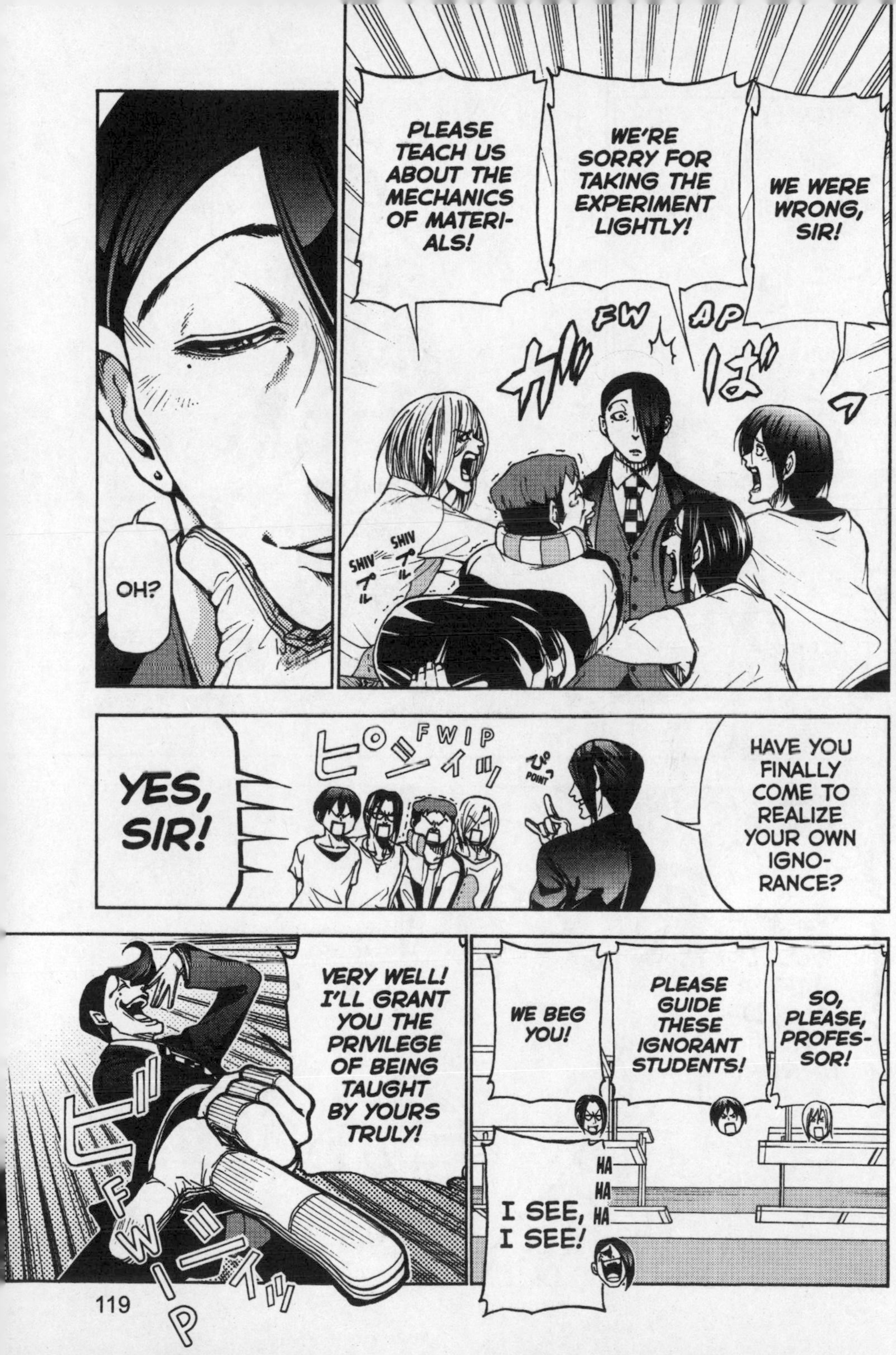
WE WERE WRONG, SIR!
WE'RE SORRY FOR TAKING THE EXPERIMENT LIGHTLY!
PLEASE TEACH US ABOUT THE MECHANICS OF MATERI-ALS!
FWAP
SHIV SHIV
OH?
HAVE YOU FINALLY COME TO REALIZE YOUR OWN IGNO-RANCE?
POINT
FWIP
YES, SIR!
SO, PLEASE, PROFES-SOR!
PLEASE GUIDE THESE IGNORANT STUDENTS!
WE BEG YOU!
HA HA HA
I SEE, I SEE!
VERY WELL! I'LL GRANT YOU THE PRIVILEGE OF BEING TAUGHT BY YOURS TRULY!
FWIP

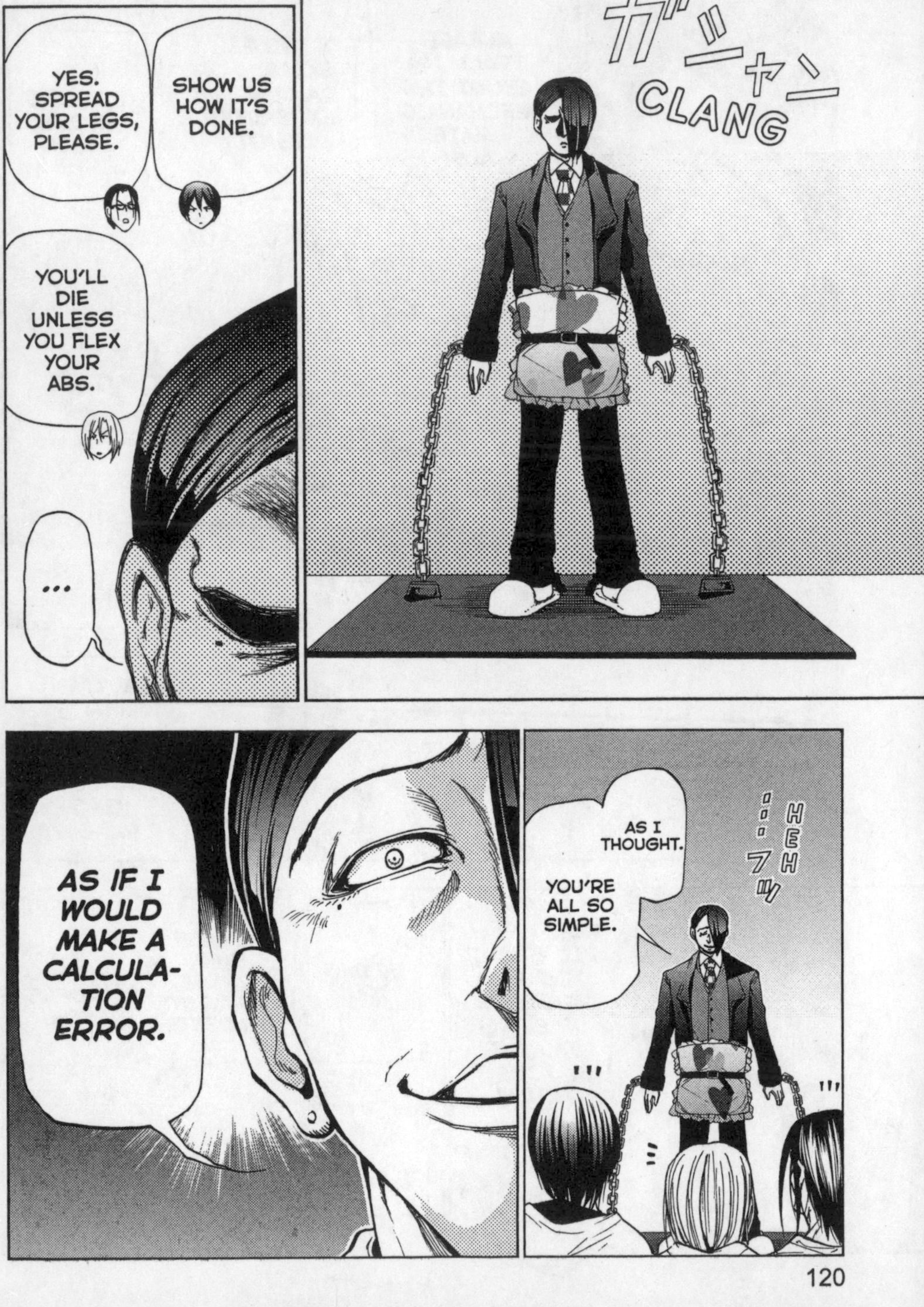
ガシャーン
CLANG
SHOW US HOW IT'S DONE.
YES. SPREAD YOUR LEGS, PLEASE.
YOU'LL DIE UNLESS YOU FLEX YOUR ABS.
...
HEH...
フッ
AS I THOUGHT.
YOU'RE ALL SO SIMPLE.
AS IF I WOULD MAKE A CALCULATION ERROR.

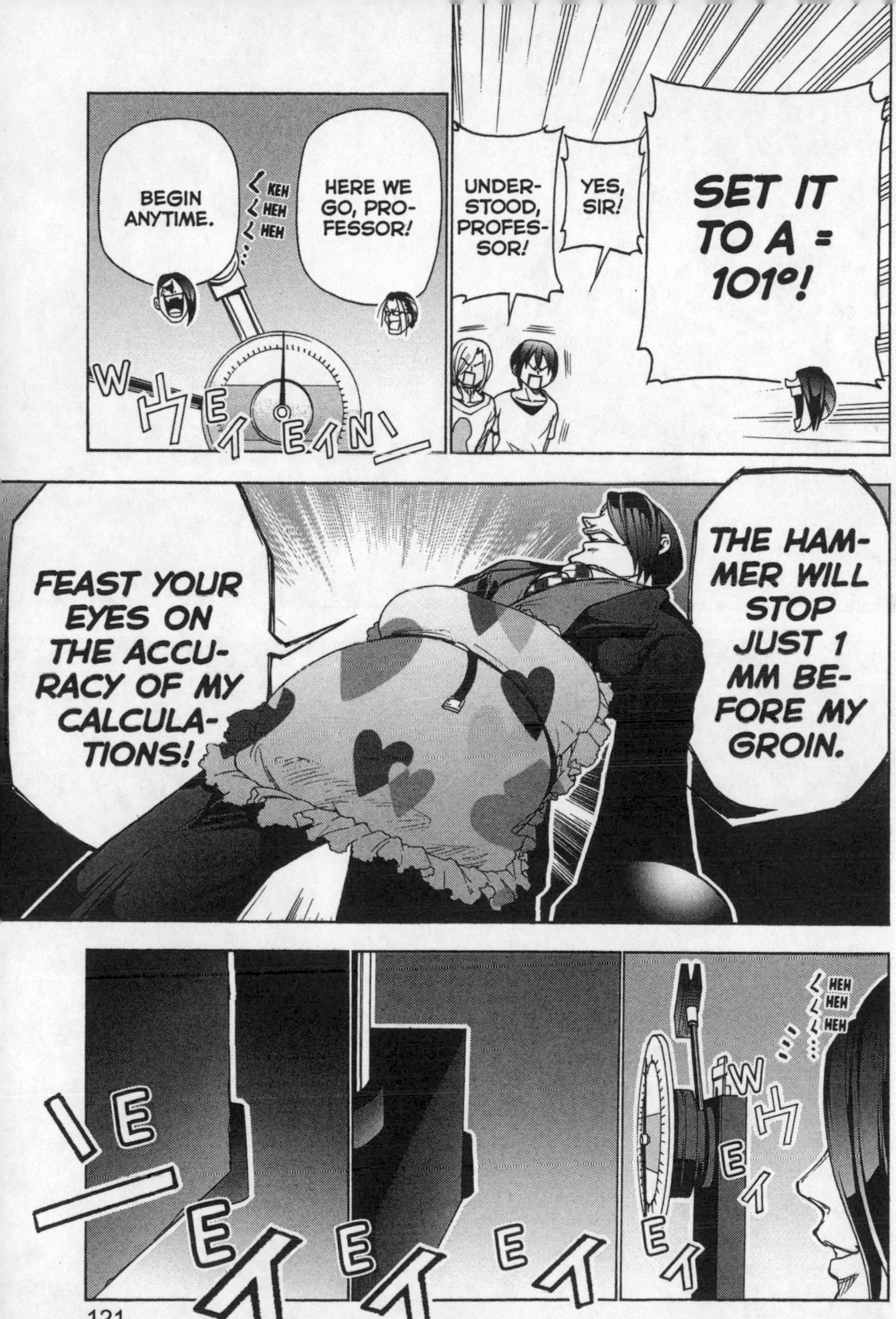
SET IT TO A = 101°!
YES, SIR!
UNDER-STOOD, PROFES-SOR!
HERE WE GO, PRO-FESSOR!
KEH HEH HEH...
BEGIN ANYTIME.
WHEEEN—
THE HAM-MER WILL STOP JUST 1 MM BE-FORE MY GROIN.
FEAST YOUR EYES ON THE ACCU-RACY OF MY CALCULA-TIONS!
HEH HEH HEH...
WHEE
EEEEE—

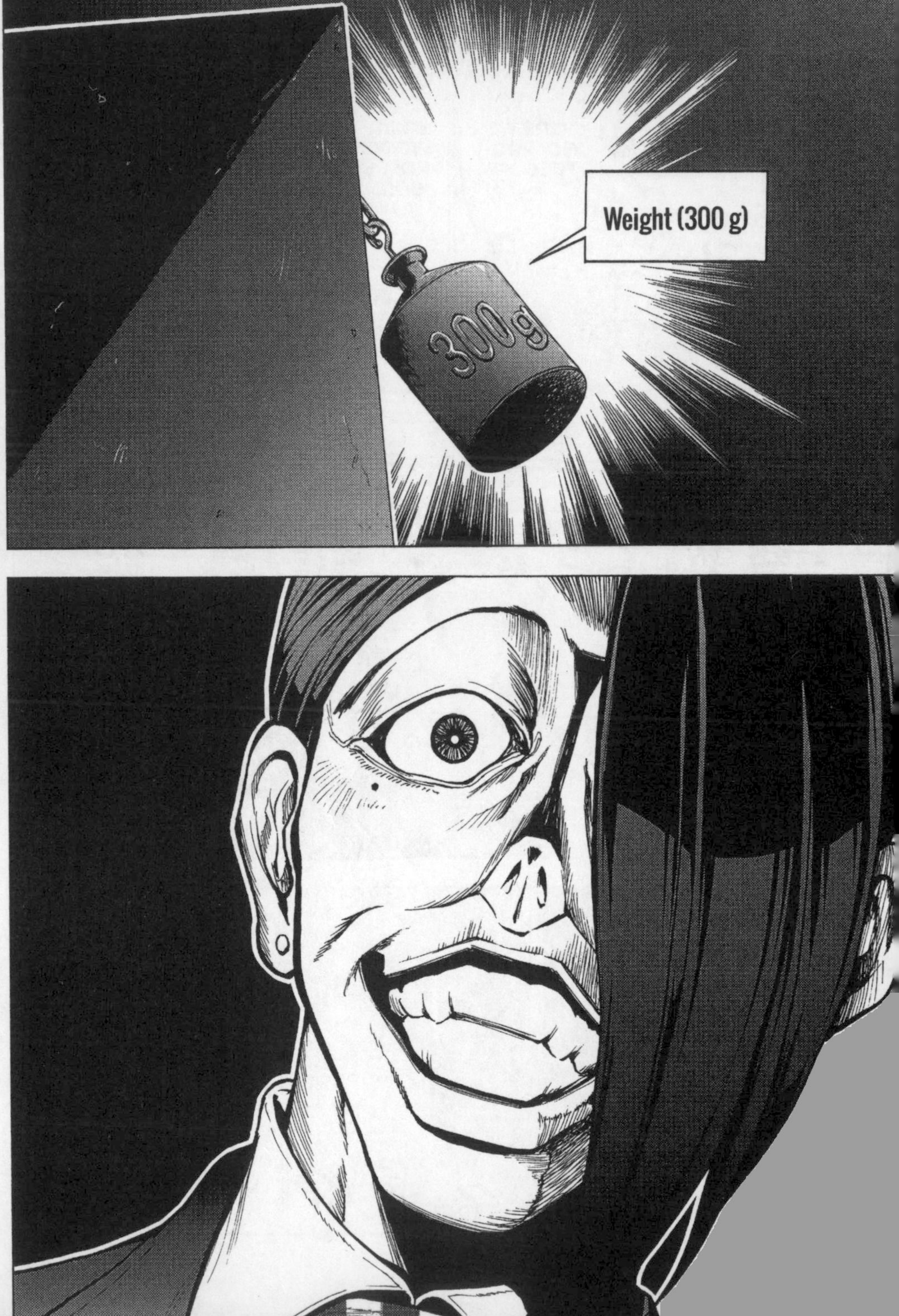
Weight (300 g)
300g

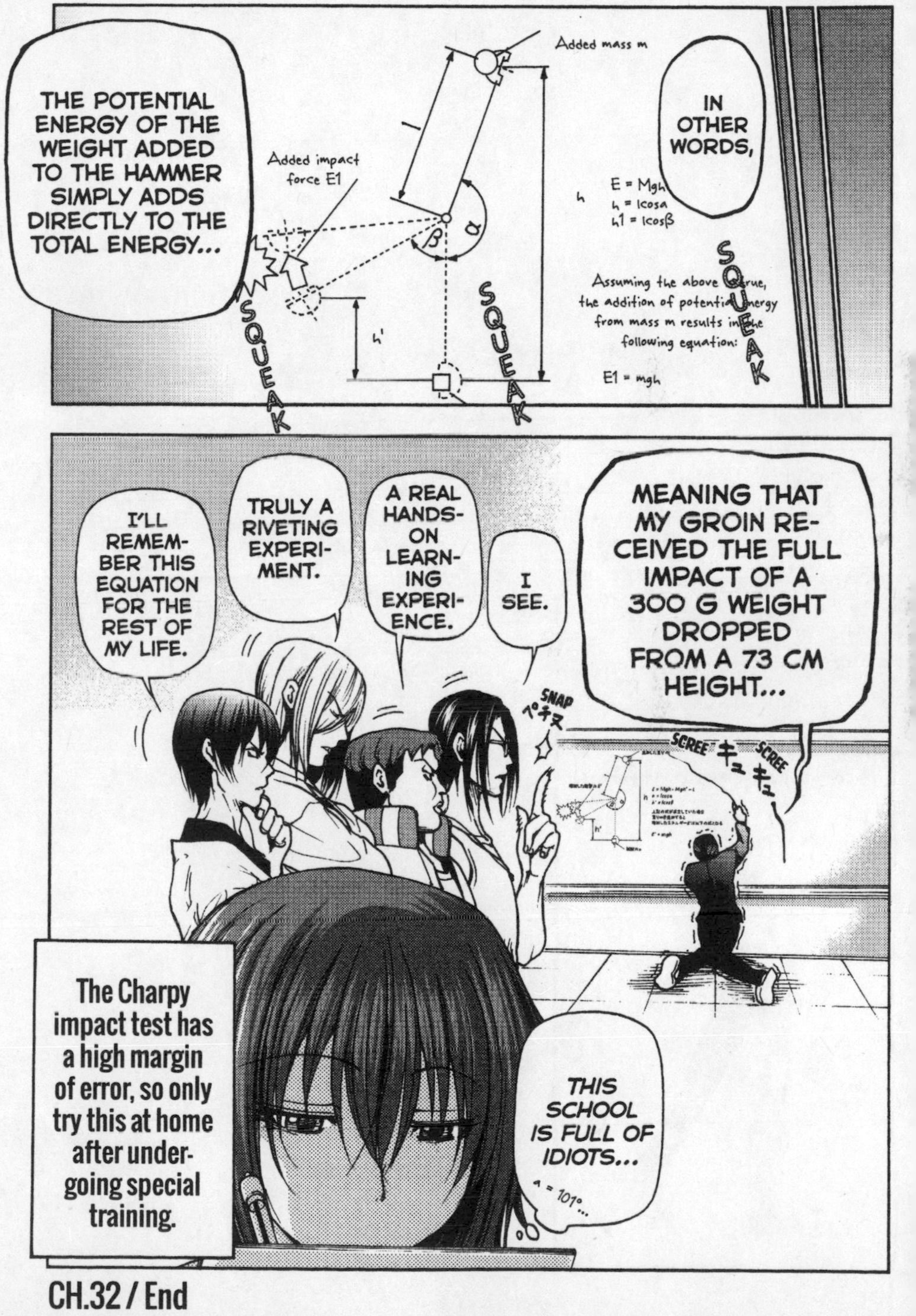

IN OTHER WORDS,
THE POTENTIAL ENERGY OF THE WEIGHT ADDED TO THE HAMMER SIMPLY ADDS DIRECTLY TO THE TOTAL ENERGY...
Added mass m
l
Added impact force E1
h'
h
E = Mgh
h = lcosα
h1 = lcosβ
Assuming the above is true, the addition of potential energy from mass m results in the following equation:
E1 = mgh
SQUEAK
SQUEAK
SQUEAK
MEANING THAT MY GROIN RECEIVED THE FULL IMPACT OF A 300 G WEIGHT DROPPED FROM A 73 CM HEIGHT...
I SEE.
A REAL HANDS-ON LEARNING EXPERIENCE.
TRULY A RIVETING EXPERIMENT.
I'LL REMEMBER THIS EQUATION FOR THE REST OF MY LIFE.
SCREE キュ
SCREE キュ
SNAP ペチヌ
THIS SCHOOL IS FULL OF IDIOTS...
α = 101°...
The Charpy impact test has a high margin of error, so only try this at home after undergoing special training.


CH.32 / End

Normally wears platforms.

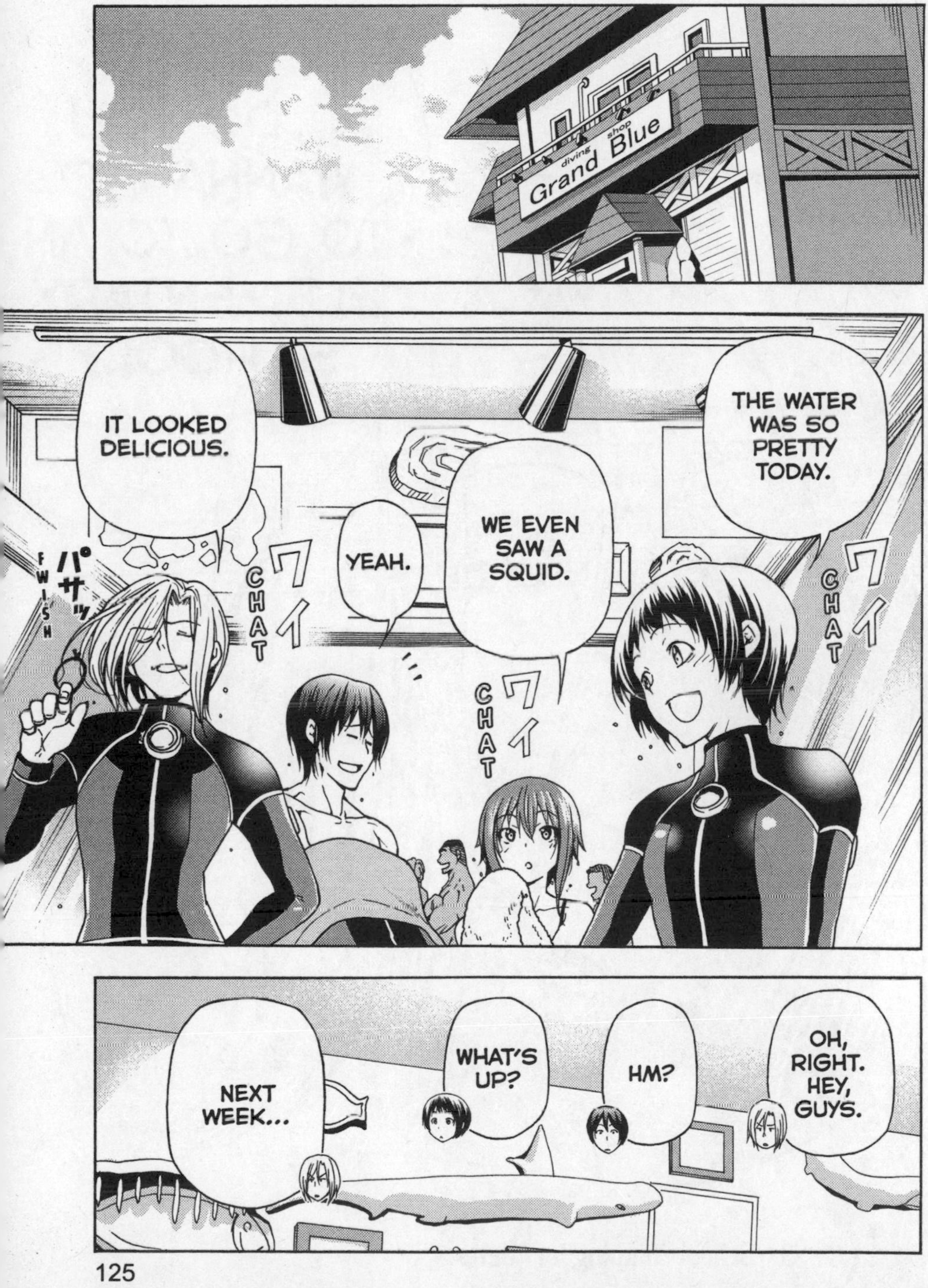
diving shop
Grand Blue
THE WATER WAS SO PRETTY TODAY.
ワイ
CHAT
WE EVEN SAW A SQUID.
ワイ
CHAT
YEAH.
ワイ
CHAT
IT LOOKED DELICIOUS.
パサッ
FWISH
OH, RIGHT. HEY, GUYS.
HM?
WHAT'S UP?
NEXT WEEK...

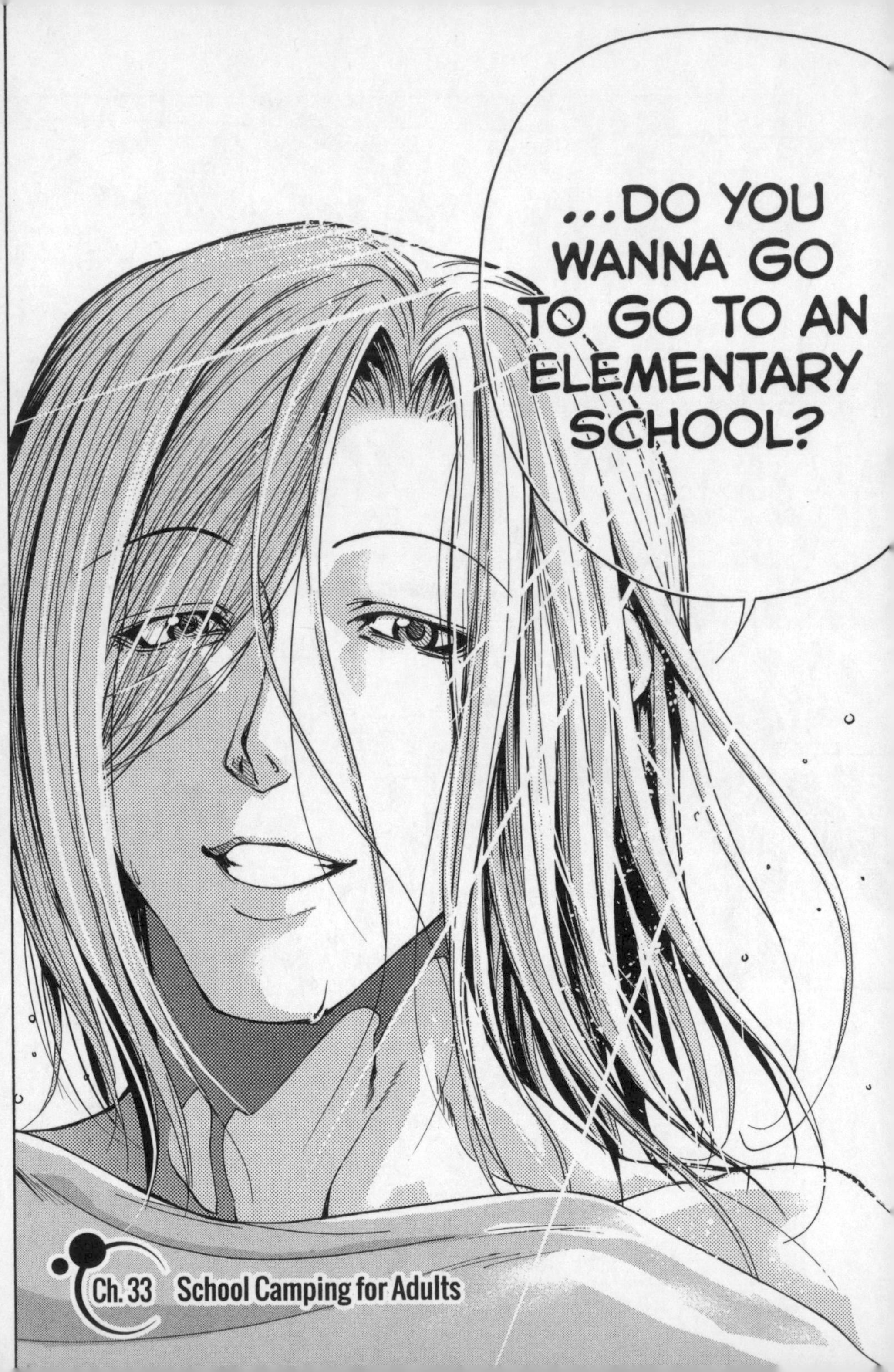
...DO YOU WANNA GO TO GO TO AN ELEMENTARY SCHOOL?
Ch. 33 School Camping for Adults

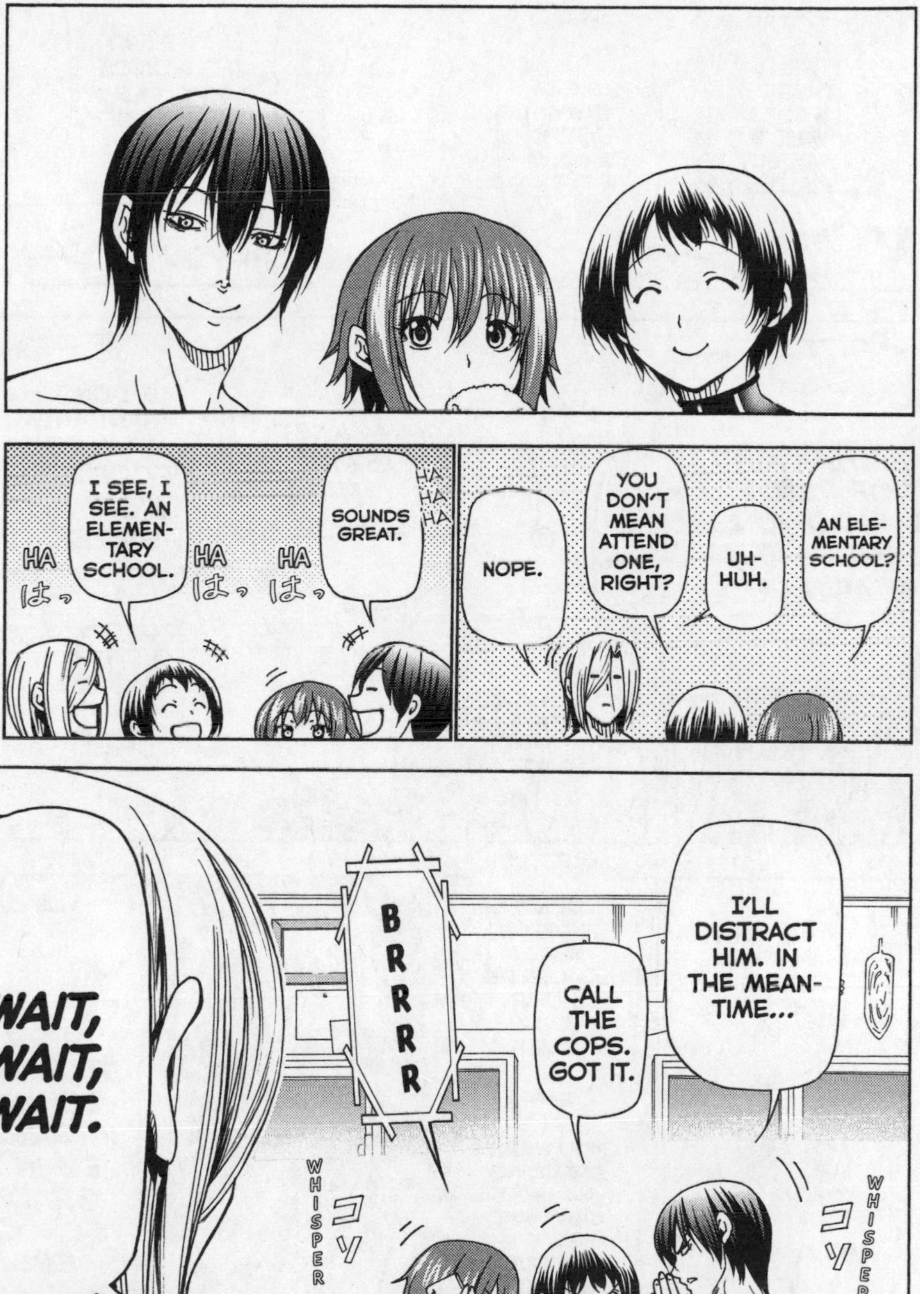
AN ELEMENTARY SCHOOL?
UH-HUH.
YOU DON'T MEAN ATTEND ONE, RIGHT?
NOPE.
HA HA HA
SOUNDS GREAT.
HA はっ
HA はっ
I SEE, I SEE. AN ELEMENTARY SCHOOL.
HA はっ
WHISPER コソ
I'LL DISTRACT HIM. IN THE MEANTIME...
CALL THE COPS. GOT IT.
BRRRR
WHISPER コソ
WAIT, WAIT, WAIT.

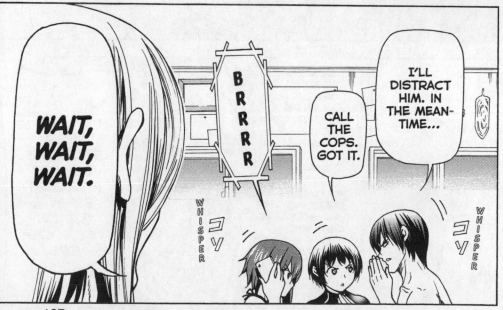

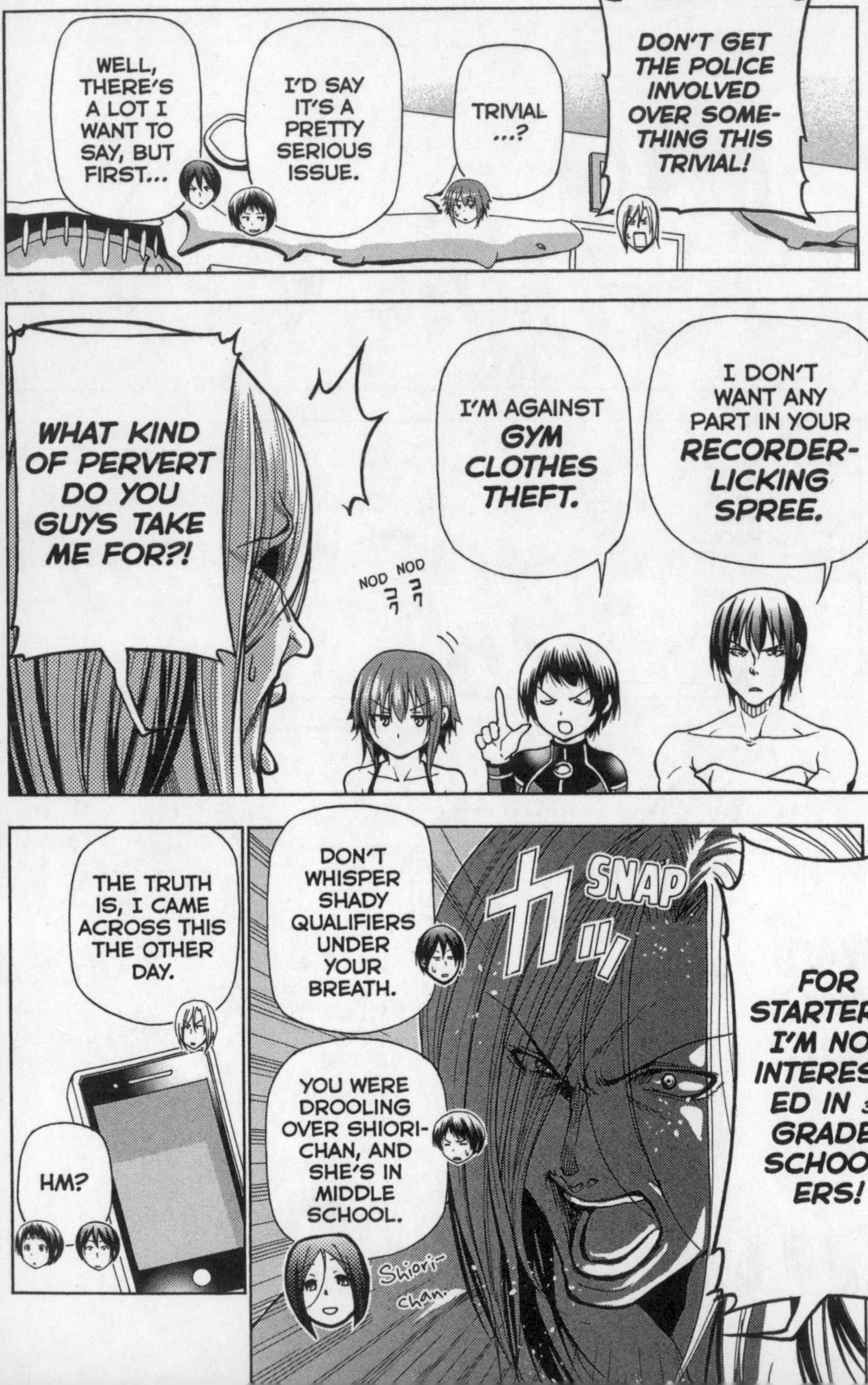
DON'T GET THE POLICE INVOLVED OVER SOME-THING THIS TRIVIAL!
TRIVIAL ...?
I'D SAY IT'S A PRETTY SERIOUS ISSUE.
WELL, THERE'S A LOT I WANT TO SAY, BUT FIRST...
I DON'T WANT ANY PART IN YOUR RECORDER-LICKING SPREE.
I'M AGAINST GYM CLOTHES THEFT.
NOD NOD
WHAT KIND OF PERVERT DO YOU GUYS TAKE ME FOR?!
SNAP
FOR STARTERS, I'M NOT INTEREST-ED IN 3D GRADE-SCHOOL-ERS!
DON'T WHISPER SHADY QUALIFIERS UNDER YOUR BREATH.
YOU WERE DROOLING OVER SHIORI-CHAN, AND SHE'S IN MIDDLE SCHOOL.
Shiori-chan.
THE TRUTH IS, I CAME ACROSS THIS THE OTHER DAY.
HM?

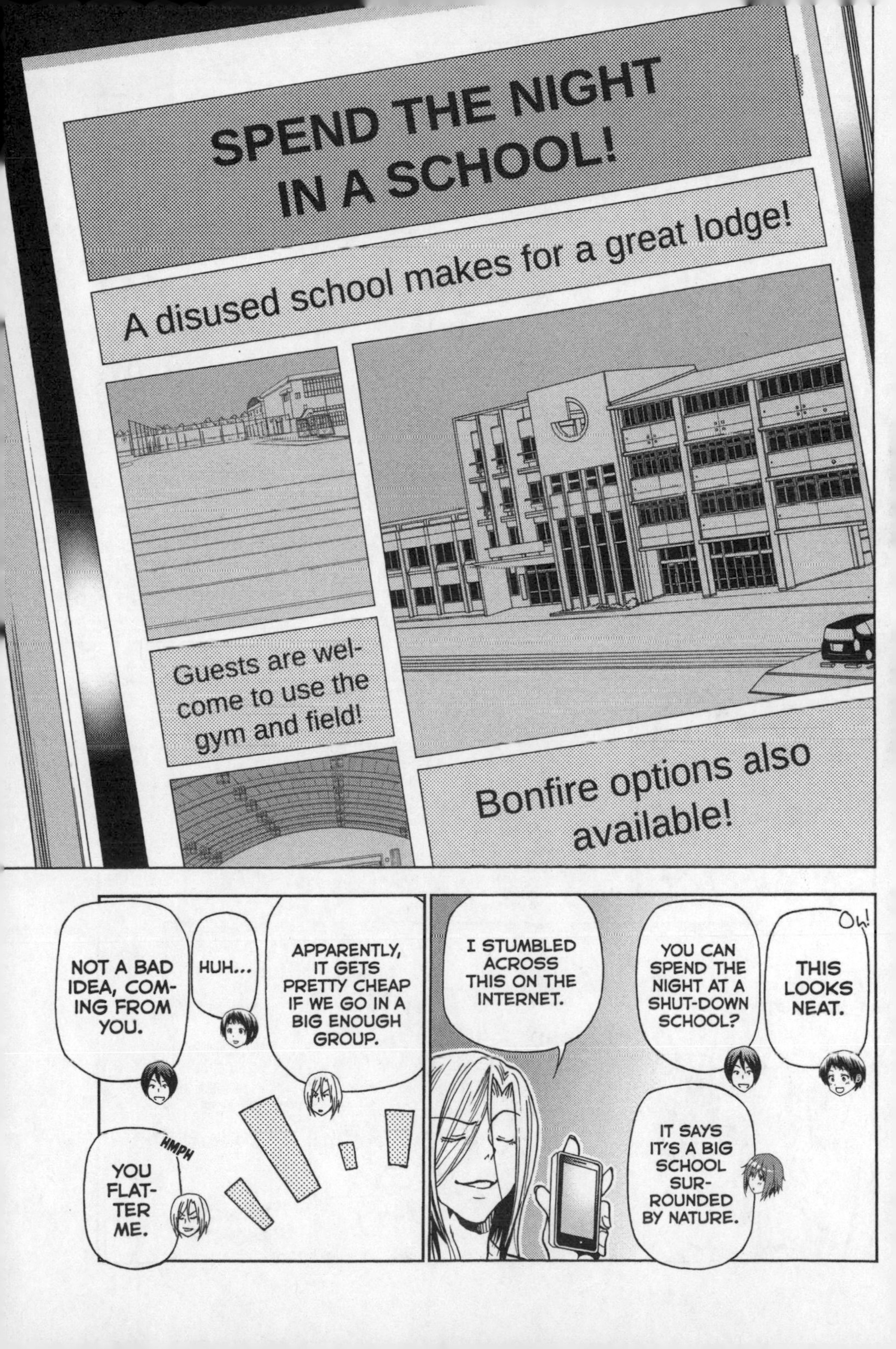
SPEND THE NIGHT IN A SCHOOL!
A disused school makes for a great lodge!
Guests are wel-come to use the gym and field!
Bonfire options also available!
Oh!
THIS LOOKS NEAT.
YOU CAN SPEND THE NIGHT AT A SHUT-DOWN SCHOOL?
I STUMBLED ACROSS THIS ON THE INTERNET.
IT SAYS IT'S A BIG SCHOOL SUR-ROUNDED BY NATURE.
APPARENTLY, IT GETS PRETTY CHEAP IF WE GO IN A BIG ENOUGH GROUP.
HUH...
NOT A BAD IDEA, COM-ING FROM YOU.
HMPH
YOU FLAT-TER ME.

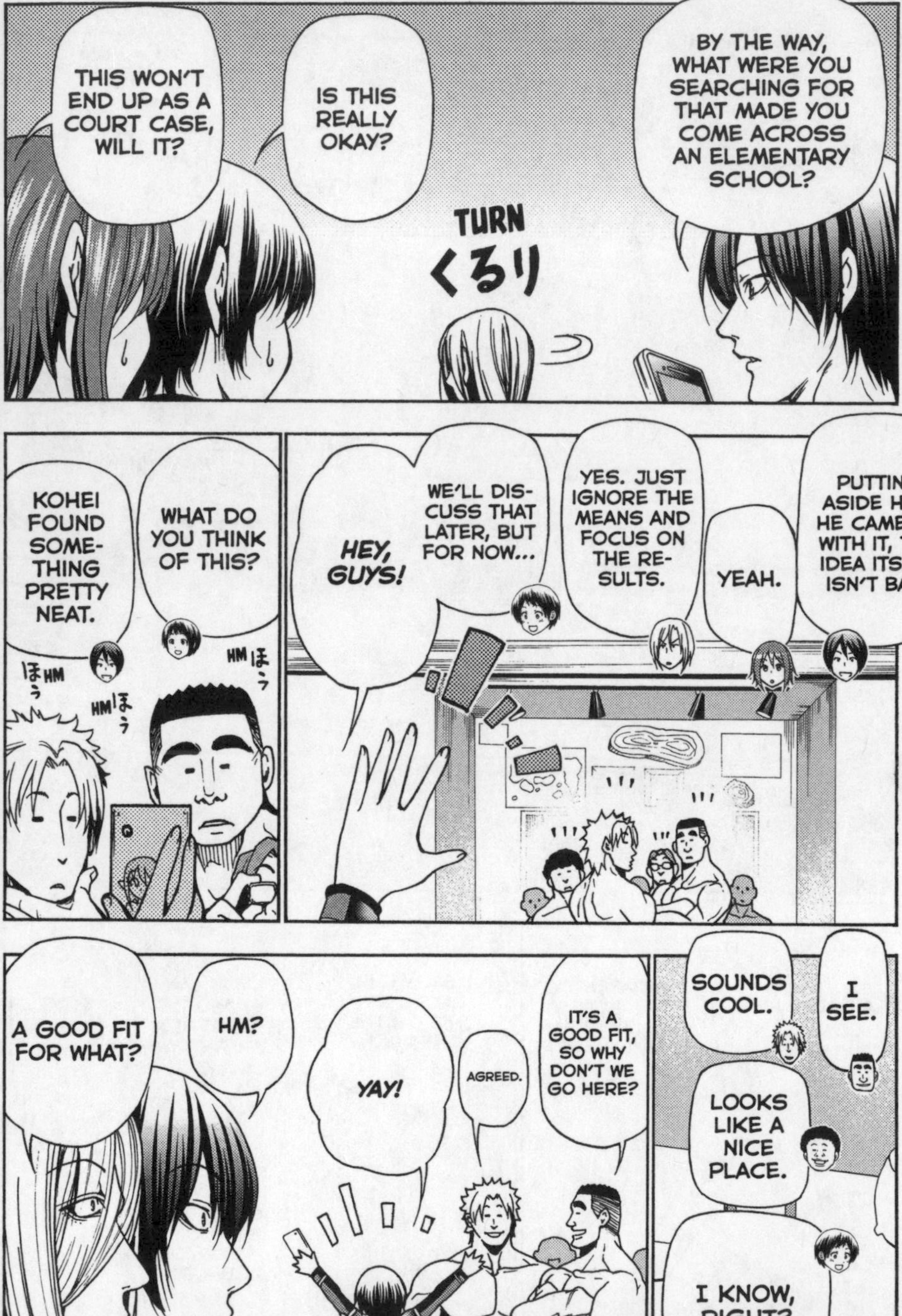
BY THE WAY, WHAT WERE YOU SEARCHING FOR THAT MADE YOU COME ACROSS AN ELEMENTARY SCHOOL?
TURN
くるり
IS THIS REALLY OKAY?
THIS WON'T END UP AS A COURT CASE, WILL IT?
PUTTING ASIDE HOW HE CAME UP WITH IT, THE IDEA ITSELF ISN'T BAD.
YEAH.
YES. JUST IGNORE THE MEANS AND FOCUS ON THE RE-SULTS.
WE'LL DIS-CUSS THAT LATER, BUT FOR NOW...
HEY, GUYS!
WHAT DO YOU THINK OF THIS?
KOHEI FOUND SOME-THING PRETTY NEAT.
HM ほう
HM ほう
HM ほう
I SEE.
SOUNDS COOL.
LOOKS LIKE A NICE PLACE.
I KNOW, RIGHT?
IT'S A GOOD FIT, SO WHY DON'T WE GO HERE?
AGREED.
YAY!
HM?
A GOOD FIT FOR WHAT?

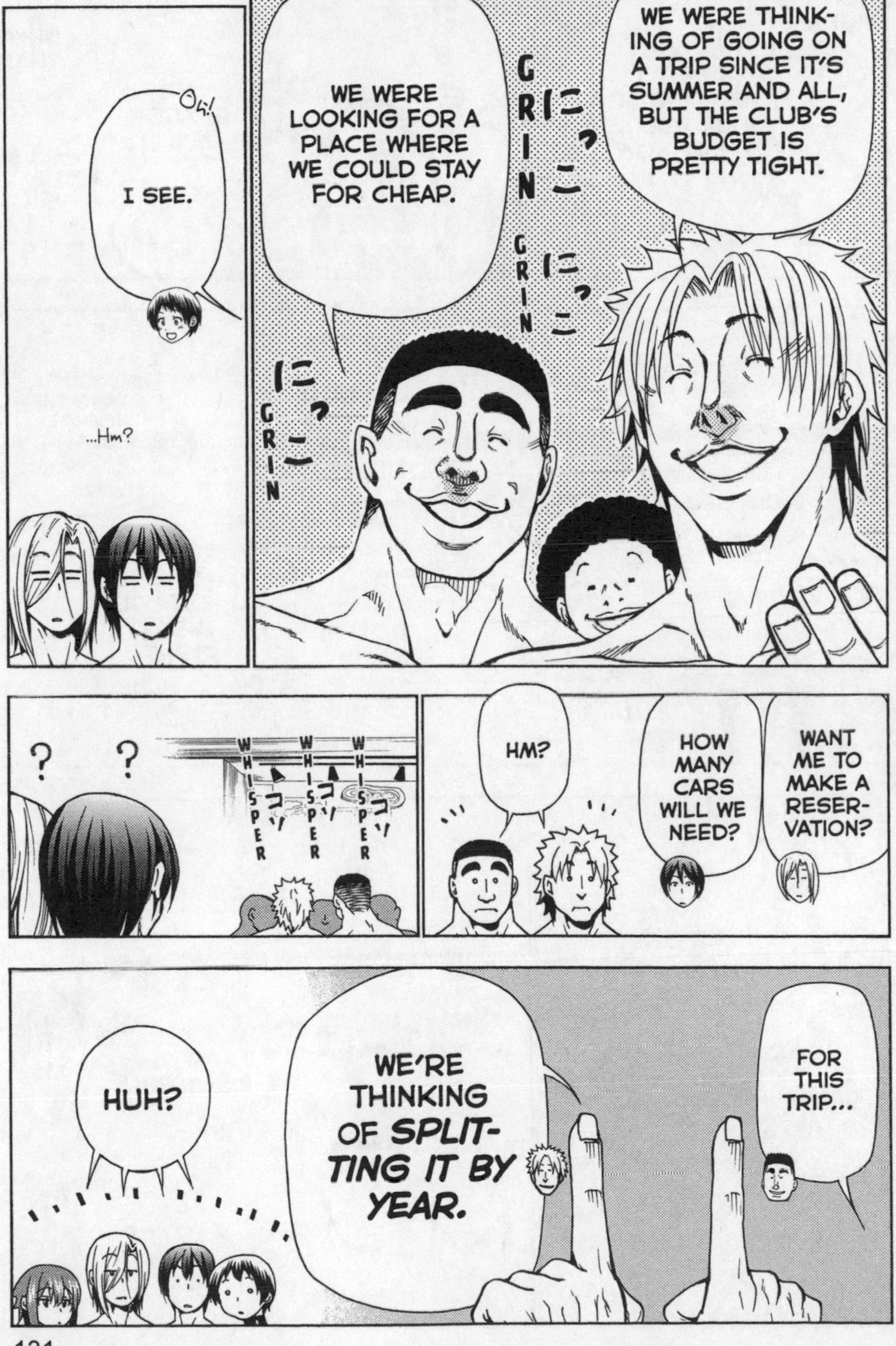
WE WERE THINKING OF GOING ON A TRIP SINCE IT'S SUMMER AND ALL, BUT THE CLUB'S BUDGET IS PRETTY TIGHT.
GRIN
GRIN
WE WERE LOOKING FOR A PLACE WHERE WE COULD STAY FOR CHEAP.
GRIN
Oh!
I SEE.
...Hm?
WANT ME TO MAKE A RESERVATION?
HOW MANY CARS WILL WE NEED?
HM?
? ?
WHISPER
WHISPER
WHISPER
FOR THIS TRIP...
WE'RE THINKING OF SPLITTING IT BY YEAR.
HUH?

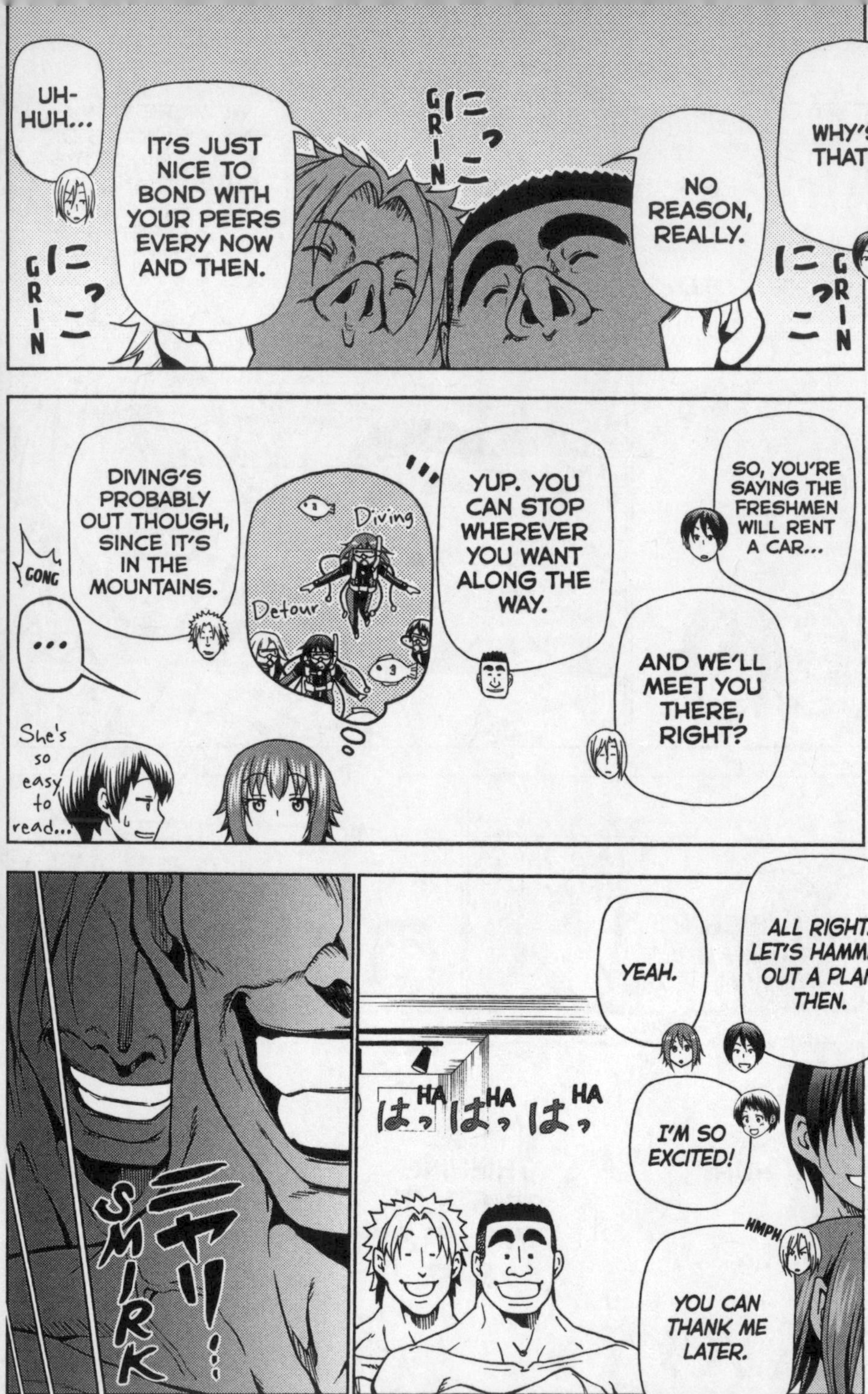

WHY'S THAT?
NO REASON, REALLY.
GRIN
GRIN
IT'S JUST NICE TO BOND WITH YOUR PEERS EVERY NOW AND THEN.
UH-HUH...
GRIN
SO, YOU'RE SAYING THE FRESHMEN WILL RENT A CAR...
YUP. YOU CAN STOP WHEREVER YOU WANT ALONG THE WAY.
AND WE'LL MEET YOU THERE, RIGHT?
Diving
Detour
DIVING'S PROBABLY OUT THOUGH, SINCE IT'S IN THE MOUNTAINS.
GONG
...
She's so easy to read...
ALL RIGHT. LET'S HAMMER OUT A PLAN, THEN.
YEAH.
I'M SO EXCITED!
HA HA HA
HMPH
YOU CAN THANK ME LATER.
SMIRK

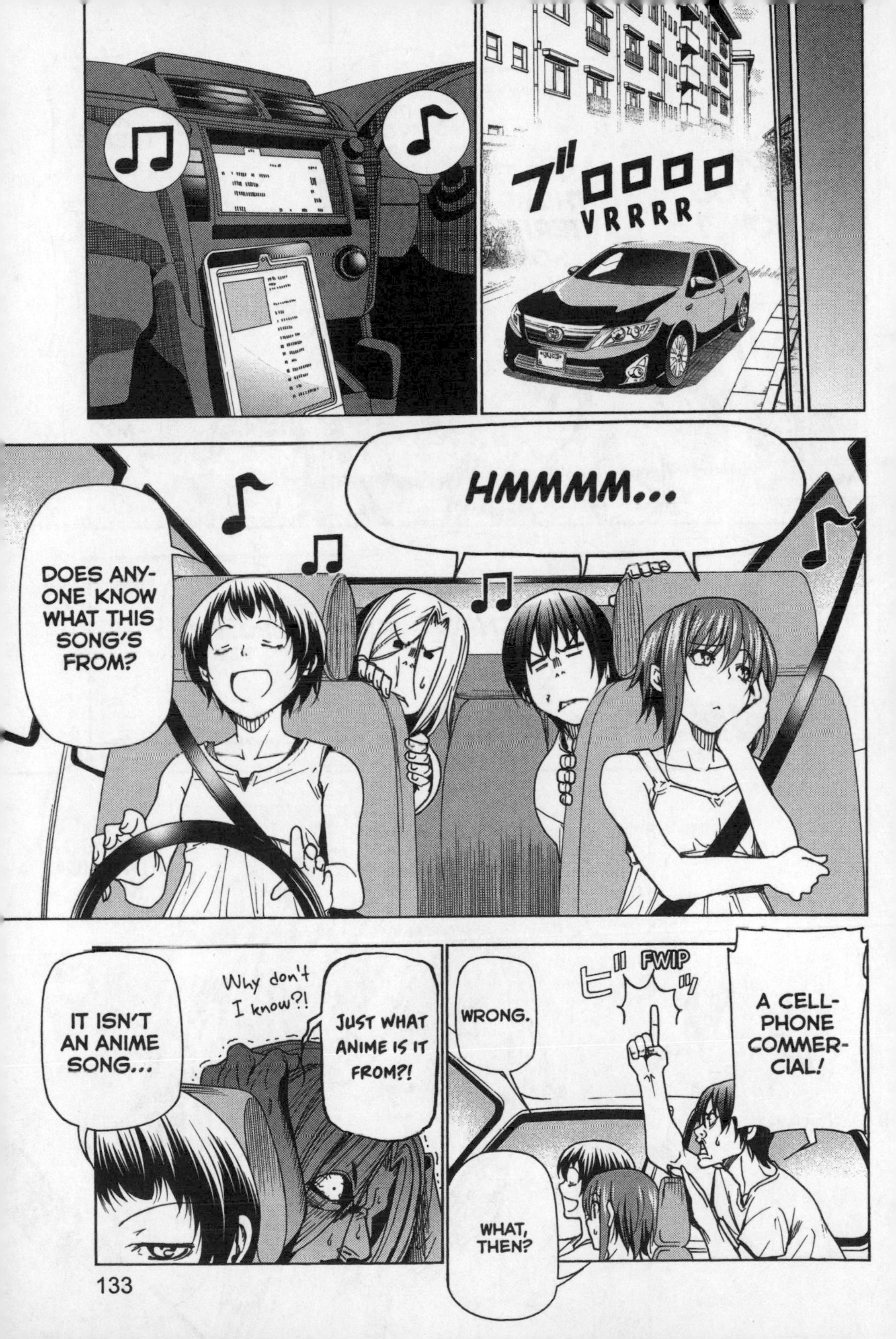
ブロロロロ
VRRRR
DOES ANY-ONE KNOW WHAT THIS SONG'S FROM?
HMMMM...
IT ISN'T AN ANIME SONG...
Why don't I know?!
JUST WHAT ANIME IS IT FROM?!
WRONG.
ビッ FWIP
WHAT, THEN?
A CELL-PHONE COMMER-CIAL!

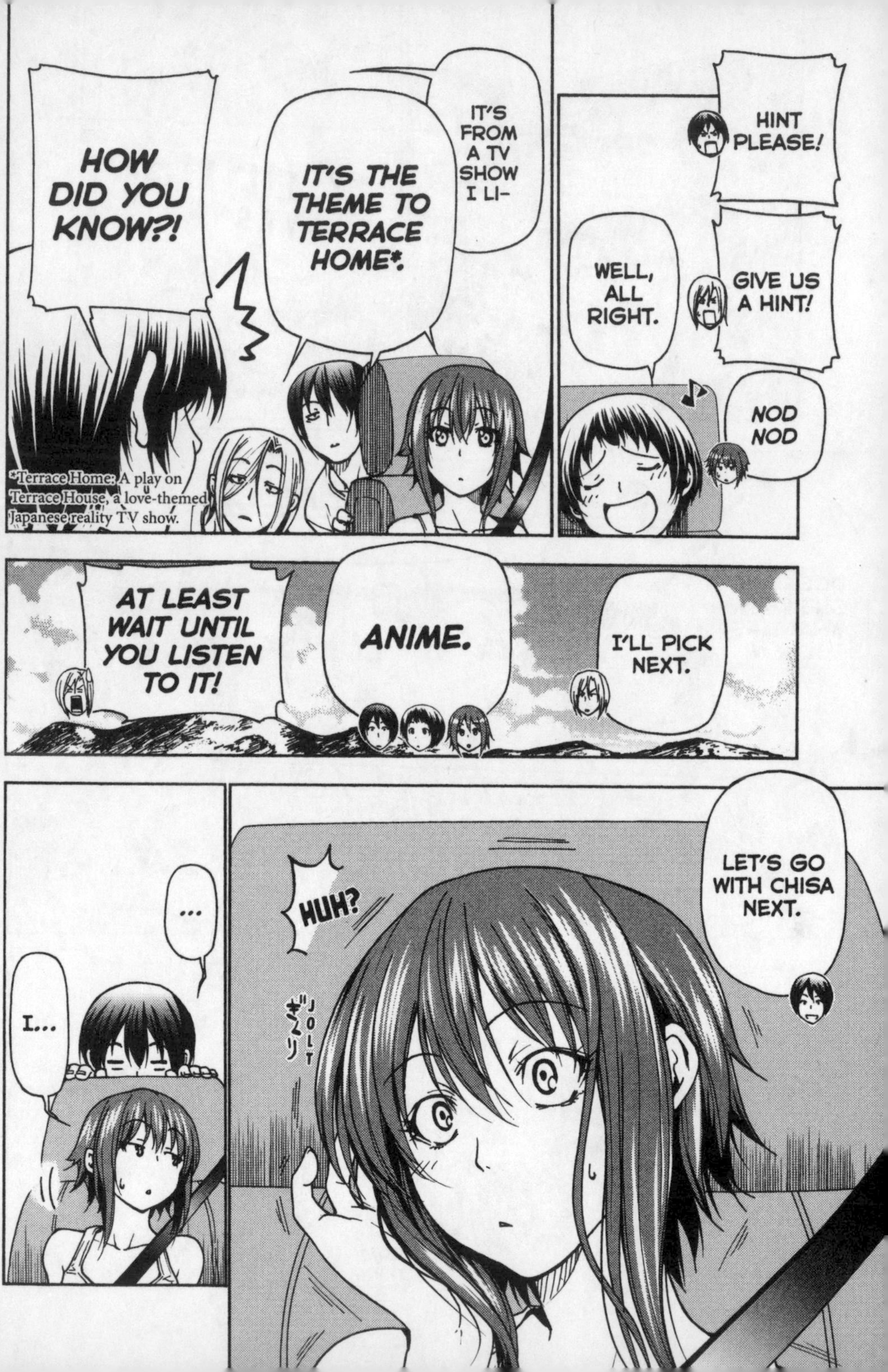
HINT PLEASE!
GIVE US A HINT!
WELL, ALL RIGHT.
NOD NOD
IT'S FROM A TV SHOW I LI-
IT'S THE THEME TO TERRACE HOME*.
HOW DID YOU KNOW?!
I'LL PICK NEXT.
ANIME.
AT LEAST WAIT UNTIL YOU LISTEN TO IT!
LET'S GO WITH CHISA NEXT.
HUH?
JOLT
...
I...
*Terrace Home: A play on Terrace House, a love-themed Japanese reality TV show.

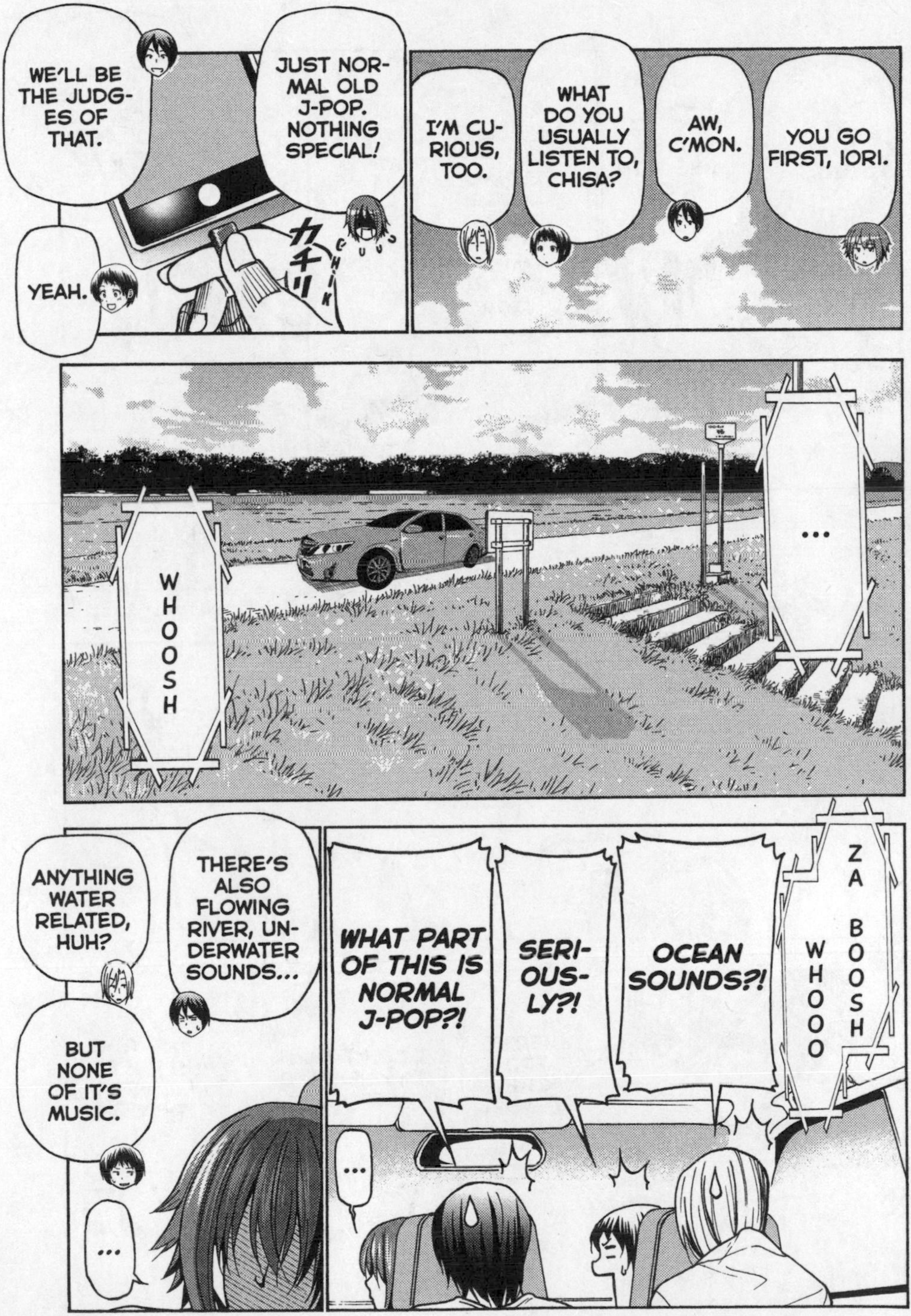
YOU GO FIRST, IORI.
AW, C'MON.
WHAT DO YOU USUALLY LISTEN TO, CHISA?
I'M CURIOUS, TOO.
JUST NORMAL OLD J-POP. NOTHING SPECIAL!
カチリ
CHIK
WE'LL BE THE JUDGES OF THAT.
YEAH.
...
WHOOSH
ZA BOOSH
WHOOO
OCEAN SOUNDS?!
SERIOUSLY?!
WHAT PART OF THIS IS NORMAL J-POP?!
...
THERE'S ALSO FLOWING RIVER, UNDERWATER SOUNDS...
ANYTHING WATER RELATED, HUH?
BUT NONE OF IT'S MUSIC.
...

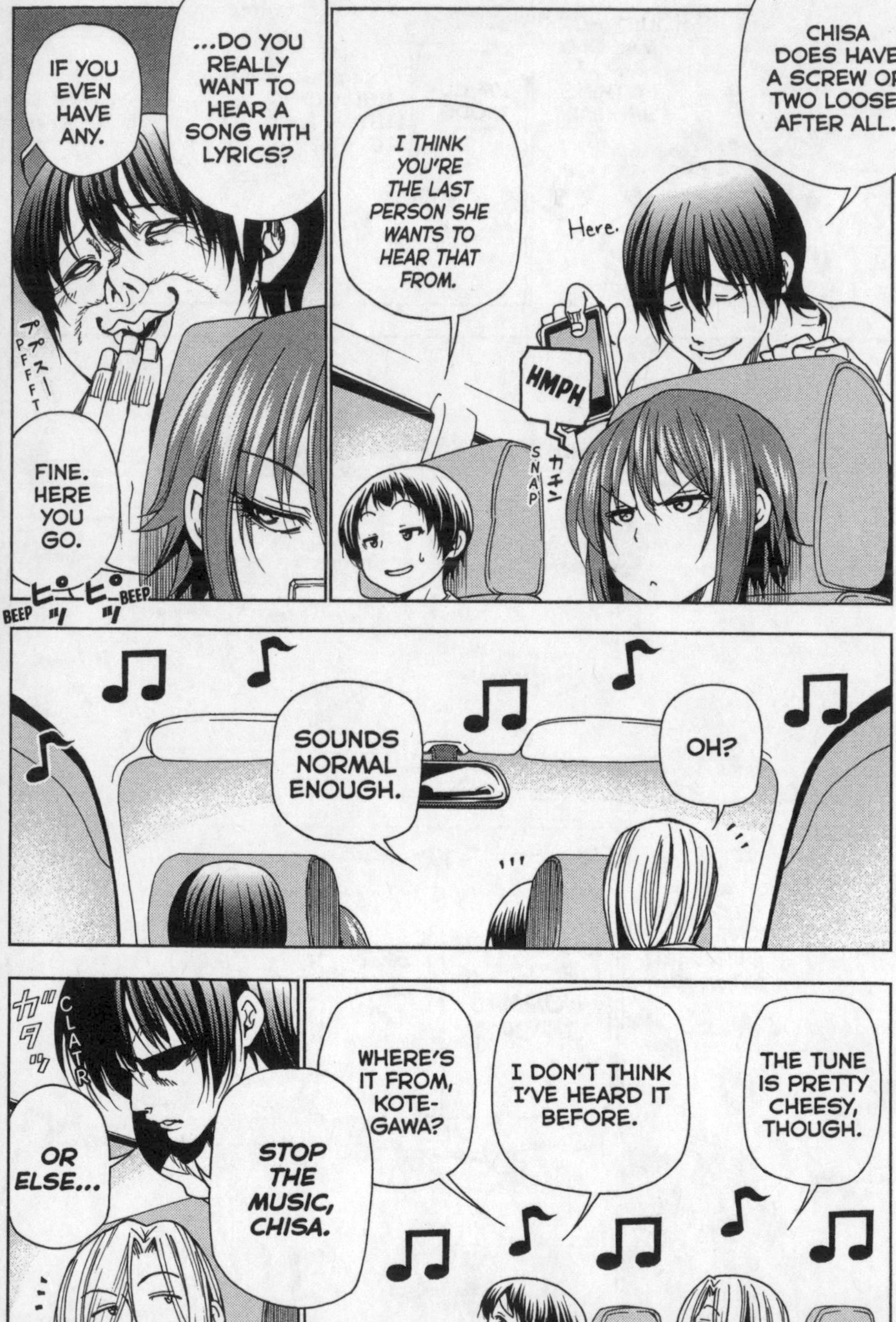

CHISA DOES HAVE A SCREW OR TWO LOOSE, AFTER ALL.
Here.
I THINK YOU'RE THE LAST PERSON SHE WANTS TO HEAR THAT FROM.
HMPH
カチン SNAP
...DO YOU REALLY WANT TO HEAR A SONG WITH LYRICS?
IF YOU EVEN HAVE ANY.
プスー PFFFT
FINE. HERE YOU GO.
ピッ BEEP ピッ BEEP
OH?
SOUNDS NORMAL ENOUGH.
THE TUNE IS PRETTY CHEESY, THOUGH.
I DON'T THINK I'VE HEARD IT BEFORE.
WHERE'S IT FROM, KOTE-GAWA?
ガタッ CLATR
STOP THE MUSIC, CHISA.
OR ELSE...

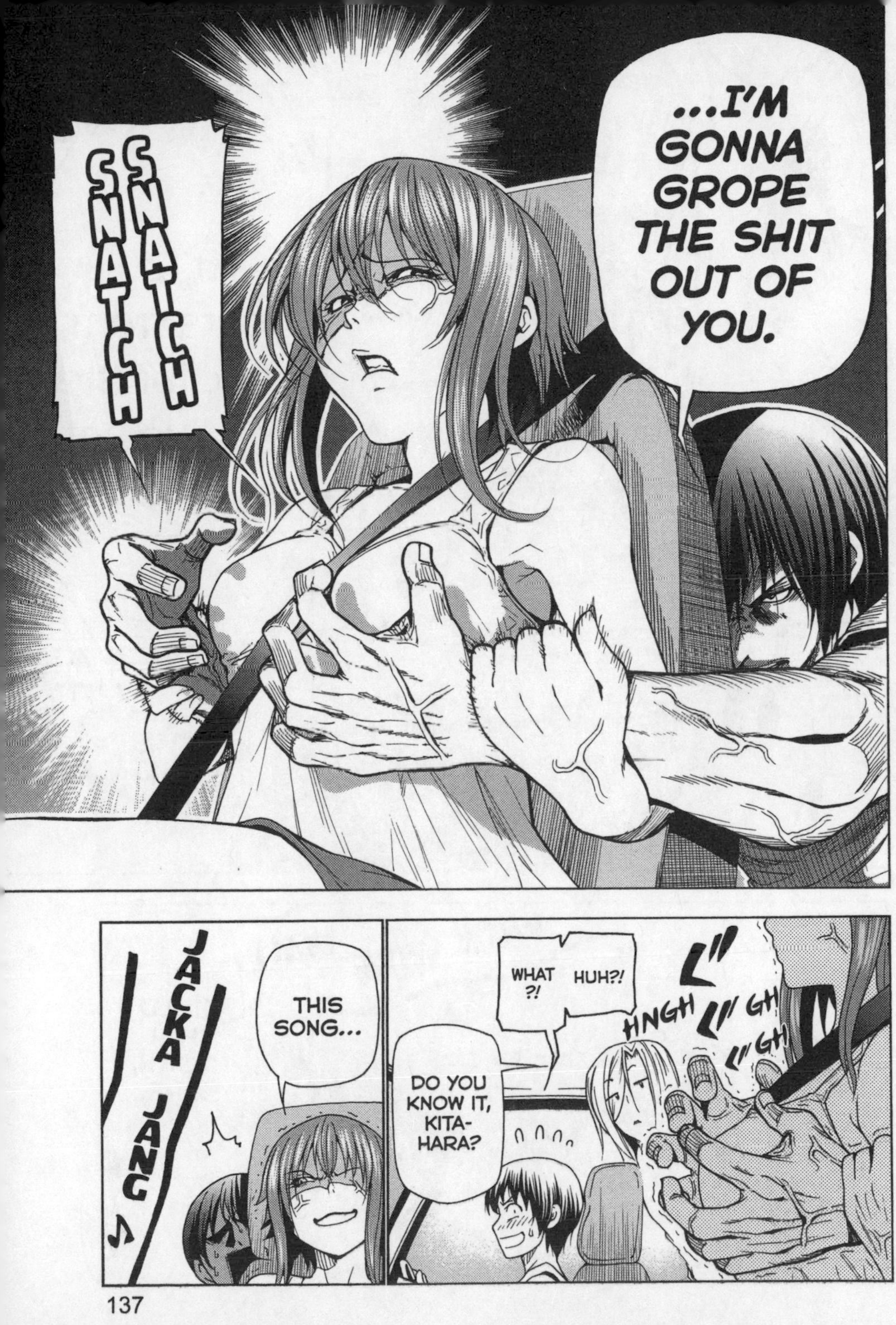
...I'M GONNA GROPE THE SHIT OUT OF YOU.
SNATCH SNATCH
HUH?!
WHAT ?!
HNGH
GH
GH
DO YOU KNOW IT, KITA-HARA?
THIS SONG...
JACKA JANG ♪

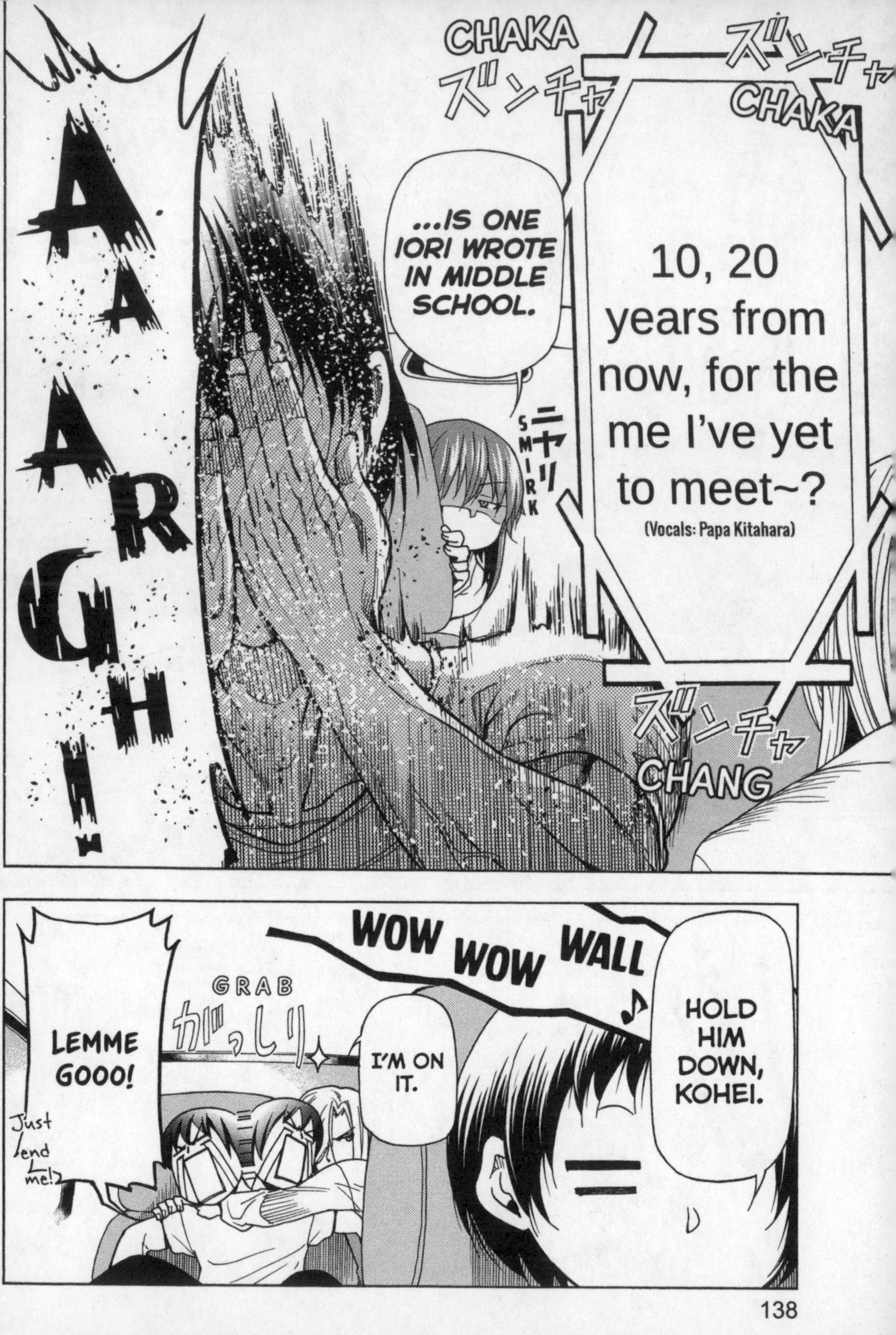
CHAKA
ズンチャ
ズンチャ
CHAKA
10, 20 years from now, for the me I've yet to meet~?
(Vocals: Papa Kitahara)
...IS ONE IORI WROTE IN MIDDLE SCHOOL.
SMIRK
ニヤリ
ズンチャ
CHANG
AAARGH!
WOW WOW WALL
HOLD HIM DOWN, KOHEI.
I'M ON IT.
GRAB
がっしり
LEMME GOOO!
Just end me!?

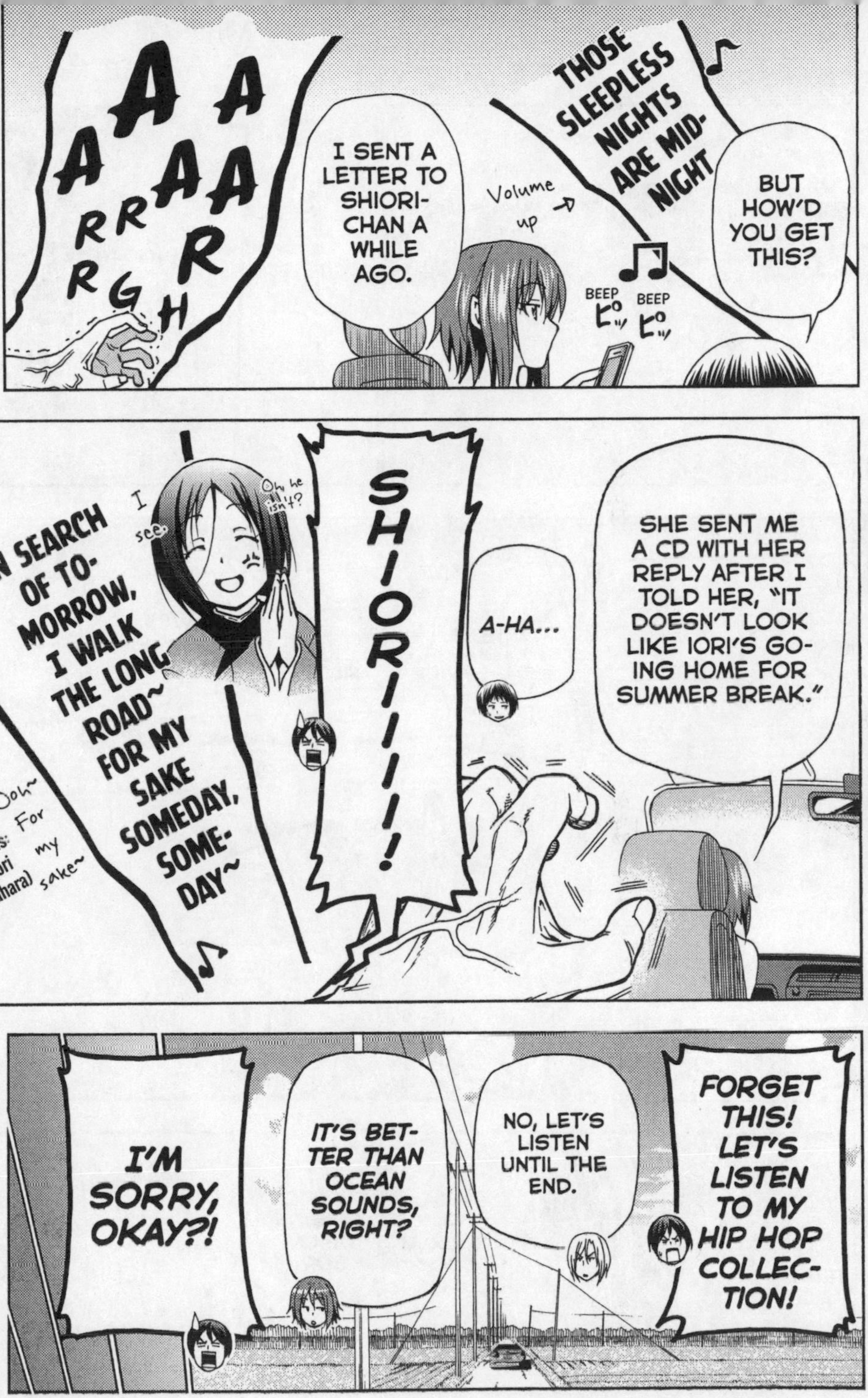
BUT HOW'D YOU GET THIS?
THOSE SLEEPLESS NIGHTS ARE MID-NIGHT
BEEP BEEP
Volume up
I SENT A LETTER TO SHIORI-CHAN A WHILE AGO.
AAAAARRRRGH
SHE SENT ME A CD WITH HER REPLY AFTER I TOLD HER, "IT DOESN'T LOOK LIKE IORI'S GO-ING HOME FOR SUMMER BREAK."
A-HA...
SHIORI!!!!!
Oh, he isn't?
I see.
IN SEARCH OF TO-MORROW, I WALK THE LONG ROAD~ FOR MY SAKE SOMEDAY, SOME-DAY~
Ooh~ For my sake~
(Chorus: Shiori Kitahara)
FORGET THIS! LET'S LISTEN TO MY HIP HOP COLLEC-TION!
NO, LET'S LISTEN UNTIL THE END.
IT'S BET-TER THAN OCEAN SOUNDS, RIGHT?
I'M SORRY, OKAY?!

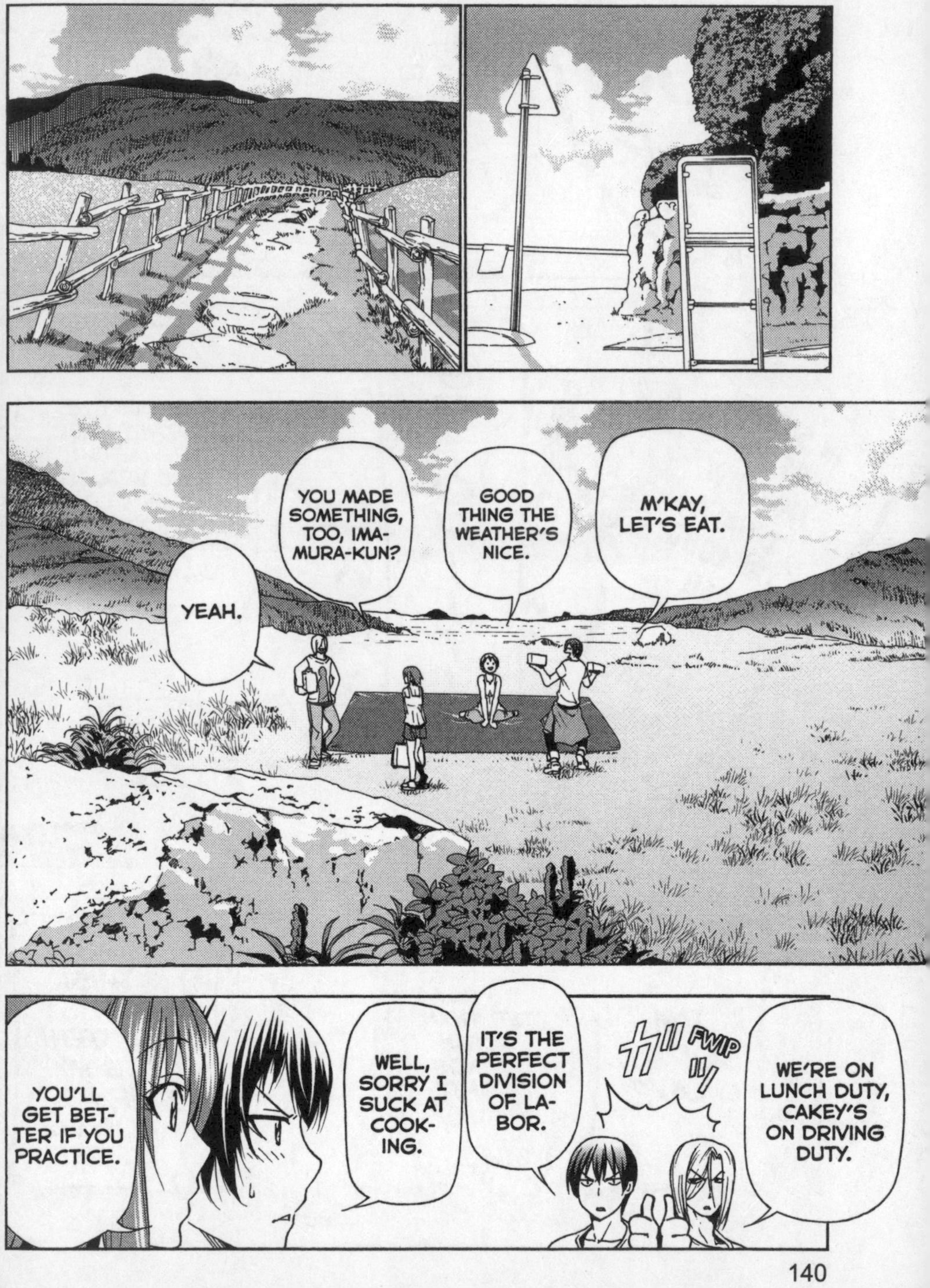
M'KAY, LET'S EAT.
GOOD THING THE WEATHER'S NICE.
YOU MADE SOMETHING, TOO, IMA-MURA-KUN?
YEAH.
WE'RE ON LUNCH DUTY, CAKEY'S ON DRIVING DUTY.
FWIP
IT'S THE PERFECT DIVISION OF LA-BOR.
WELL, SORRY I SUCK AT COOK-ING.
YOU'LL GET BET-TER IF YOU PRACTICE.

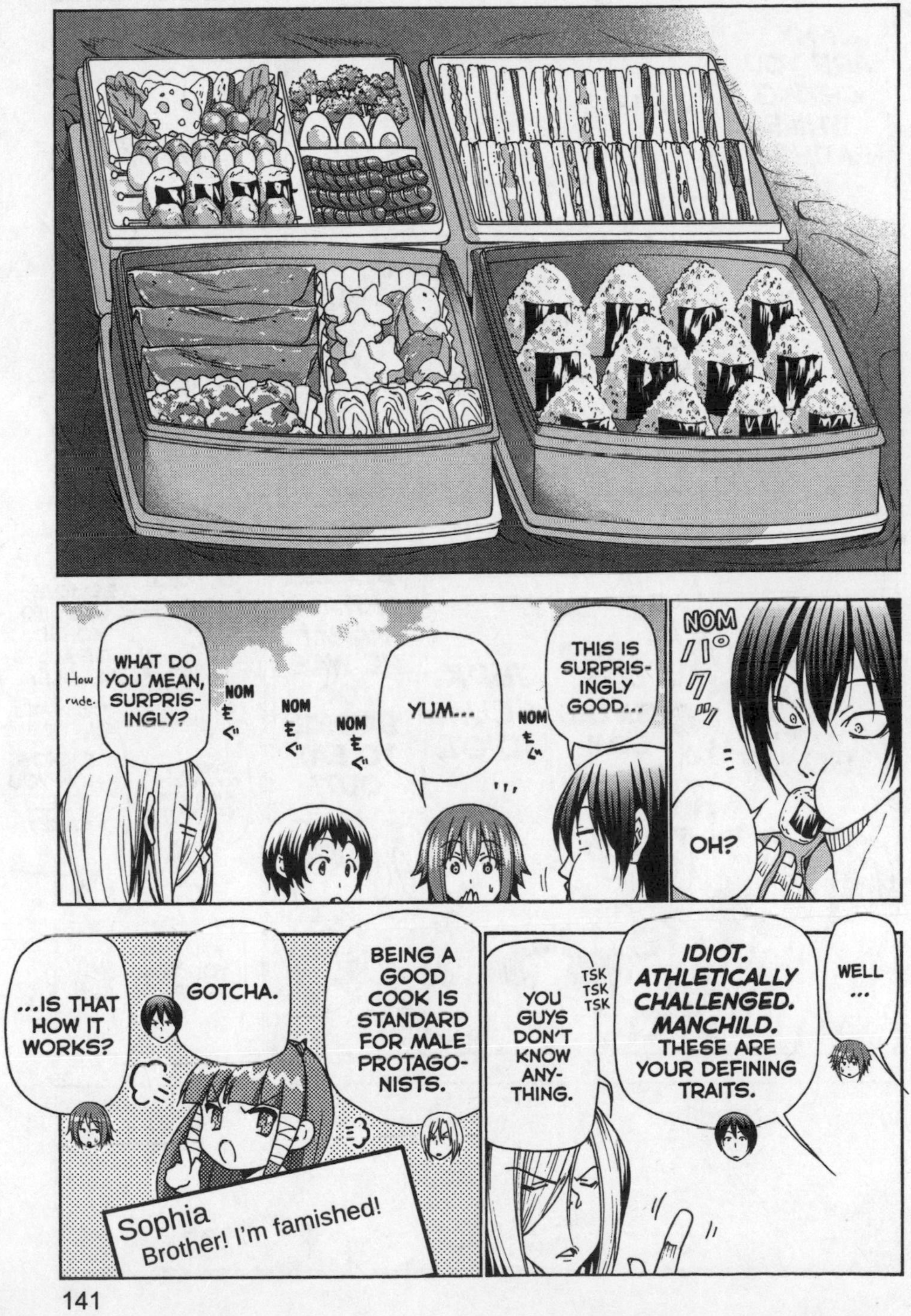
NOM
パクッ
OH?
THIS IS SURPRISINGLY GOOD...
NOM もぐ
YUM...
NOM もぐ
NOM もぐ
NOM もぐ
WHAT DO YOU MEAN, SURPRISINGLY?
How rude.
WELL ...
IDIOT. ATHLETICALLY CHALLENGED. MANCHILD. THESE ARE YOUR DEFINING TRAITS.
TSK TSK TSK
YOU GUYS DON'T KNOW ANYTHING.
BEING A GOOD COOK IS STANDARD FOR MALE PROTAGONISTS.
GOTCHA.
...IS THAT HOW IT WORKS?
Sophia
Brother! I'm famished!

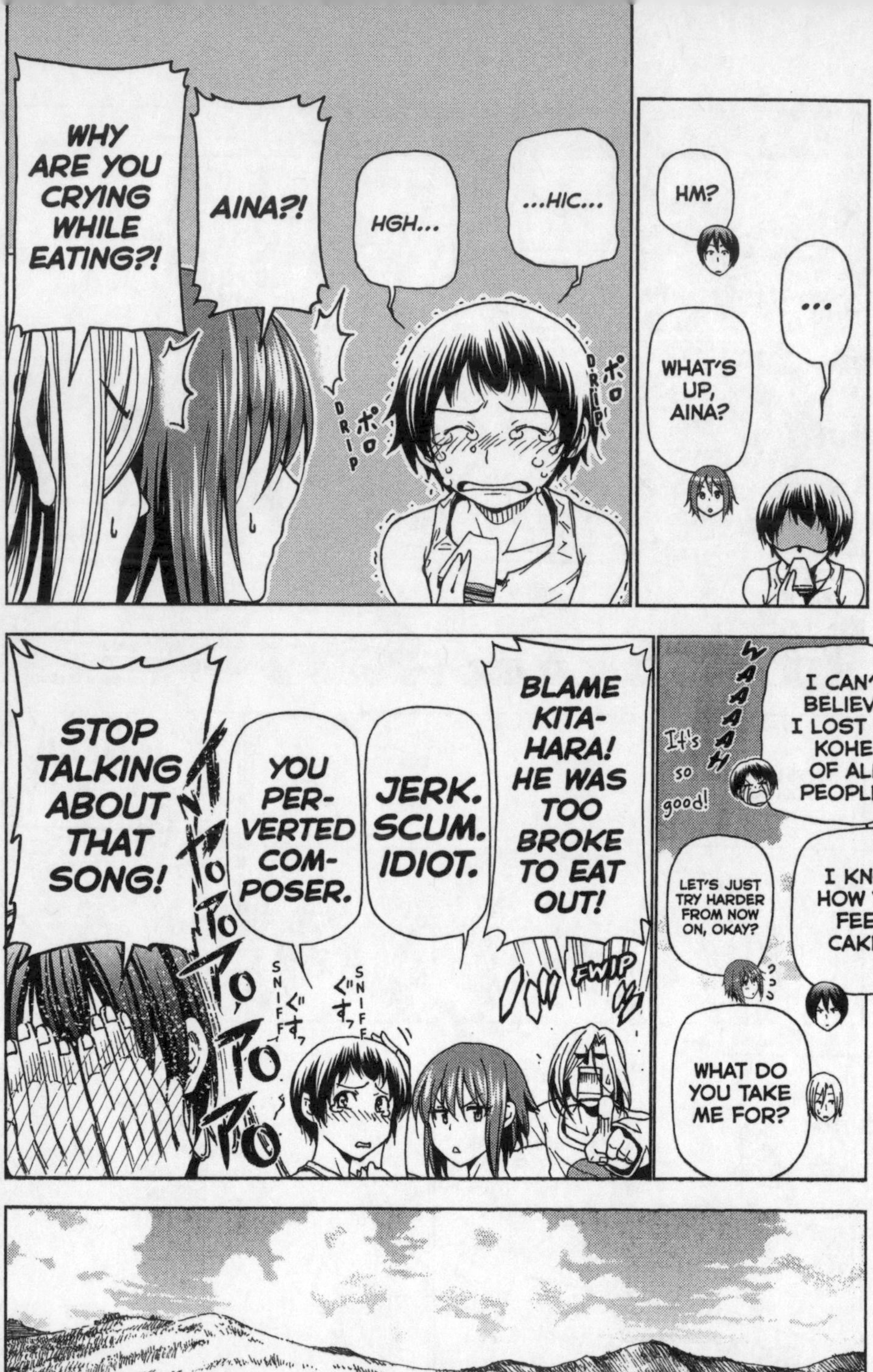
HM?
...
WHAT'S UP, AINA?
...HIC...
HGH...
ポロ DRIP
ポロ DRIP
AINA?!
WHY ARE YOU CRYING WHILE EATING?!
WAAAAAH
I CAN'T BELIEVE I LOST TO KOHEI OF ALL PEOPLE!
It's so good!
I KNOW HOW YOU FEEL, CAKEY.
LET'S JUST TRY HARDER FROM NOW ON, OKAY?
WHAT DO YOU TAKE ME FOR?
BLAME KITA-HARA! HE WAS TOO BROKE TO EAT OUT!
FWIP
JERK. SCUM. IDIOT.
ぐすっ SNIFF
YOU PER-VERTED COM-POSER.
ぐすっ SNIFF
STOP TALKING ABOUT THAT SONG!

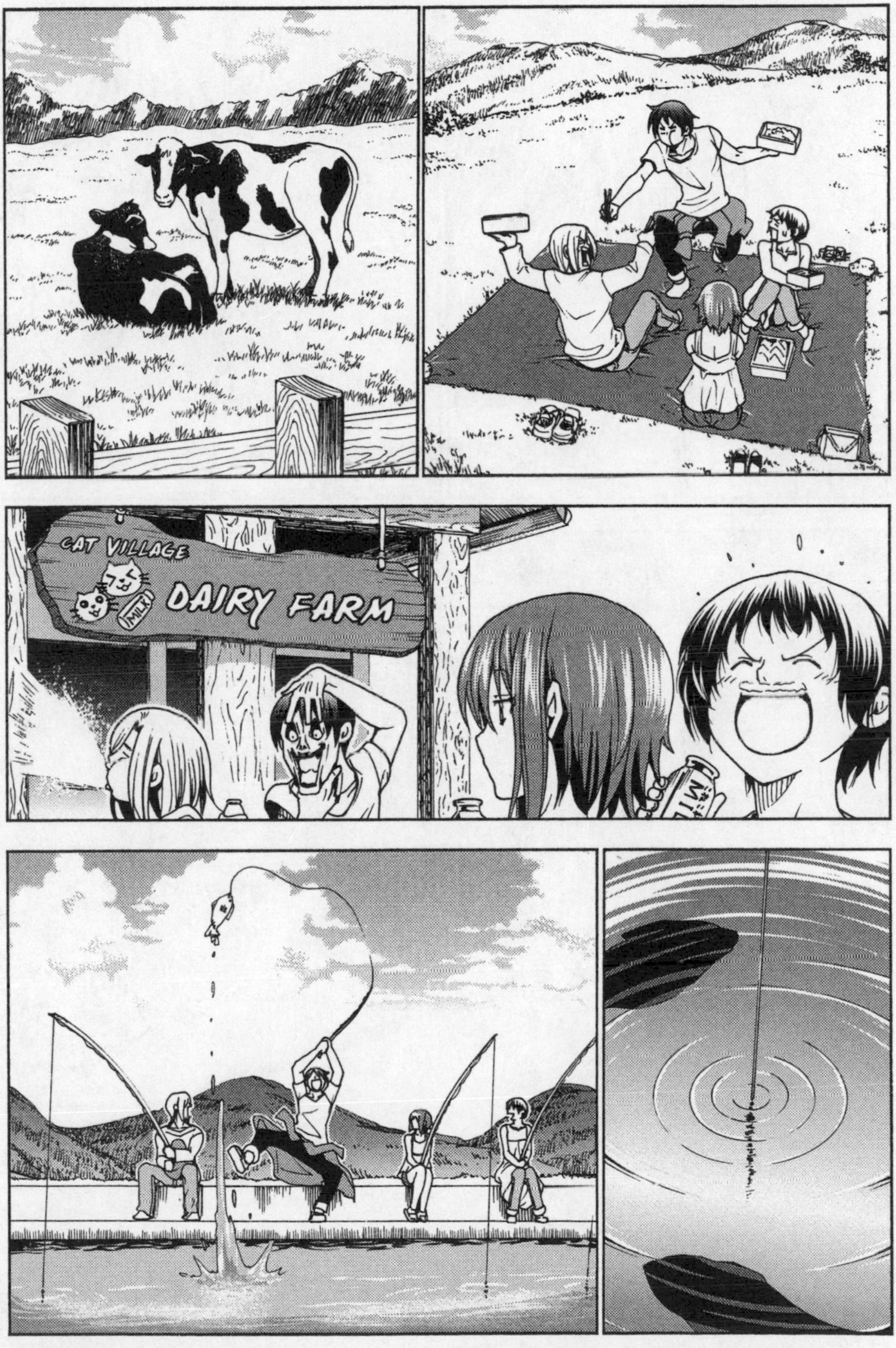
CAT VILLAGE
MILK
DAIRY FARM

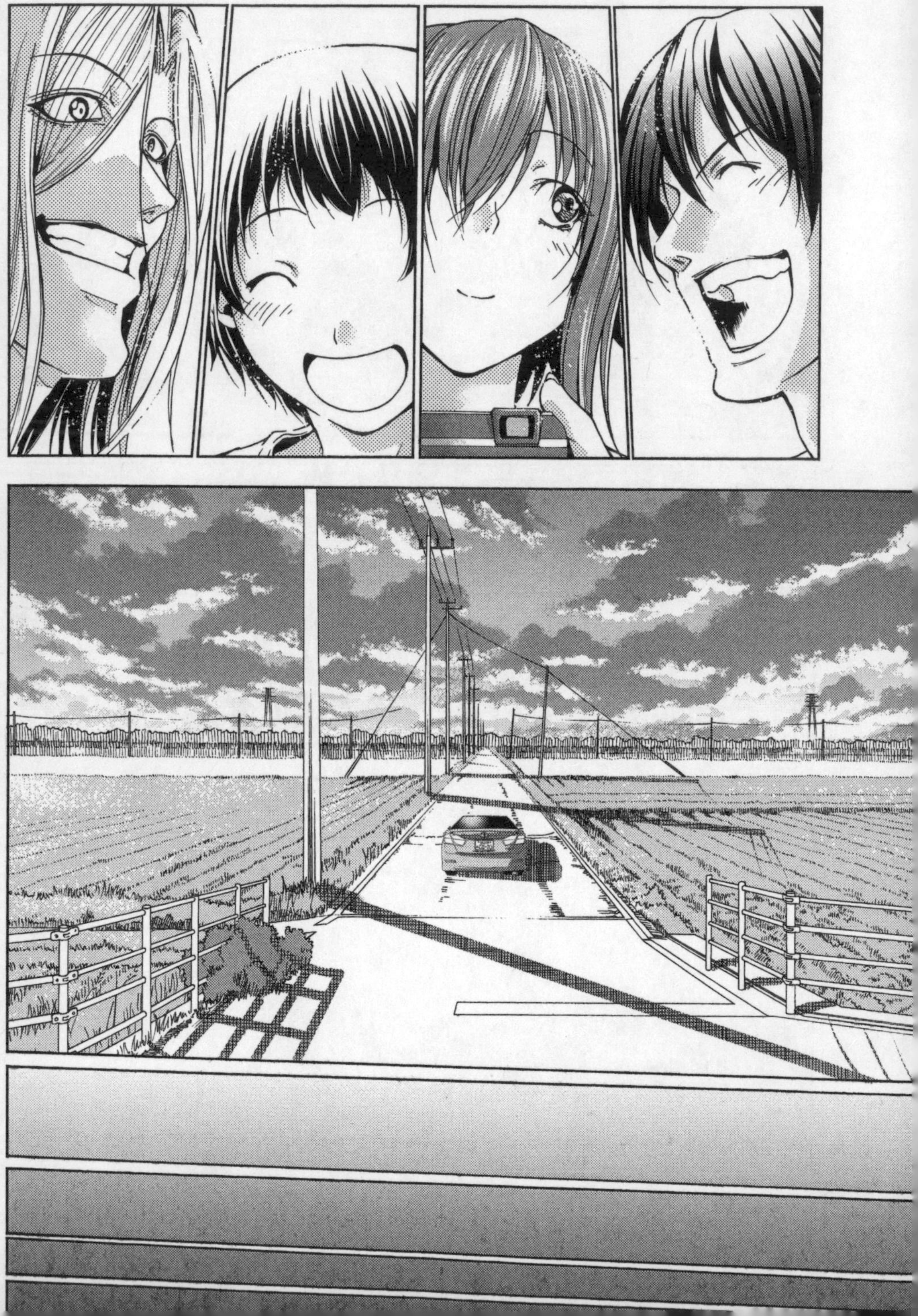

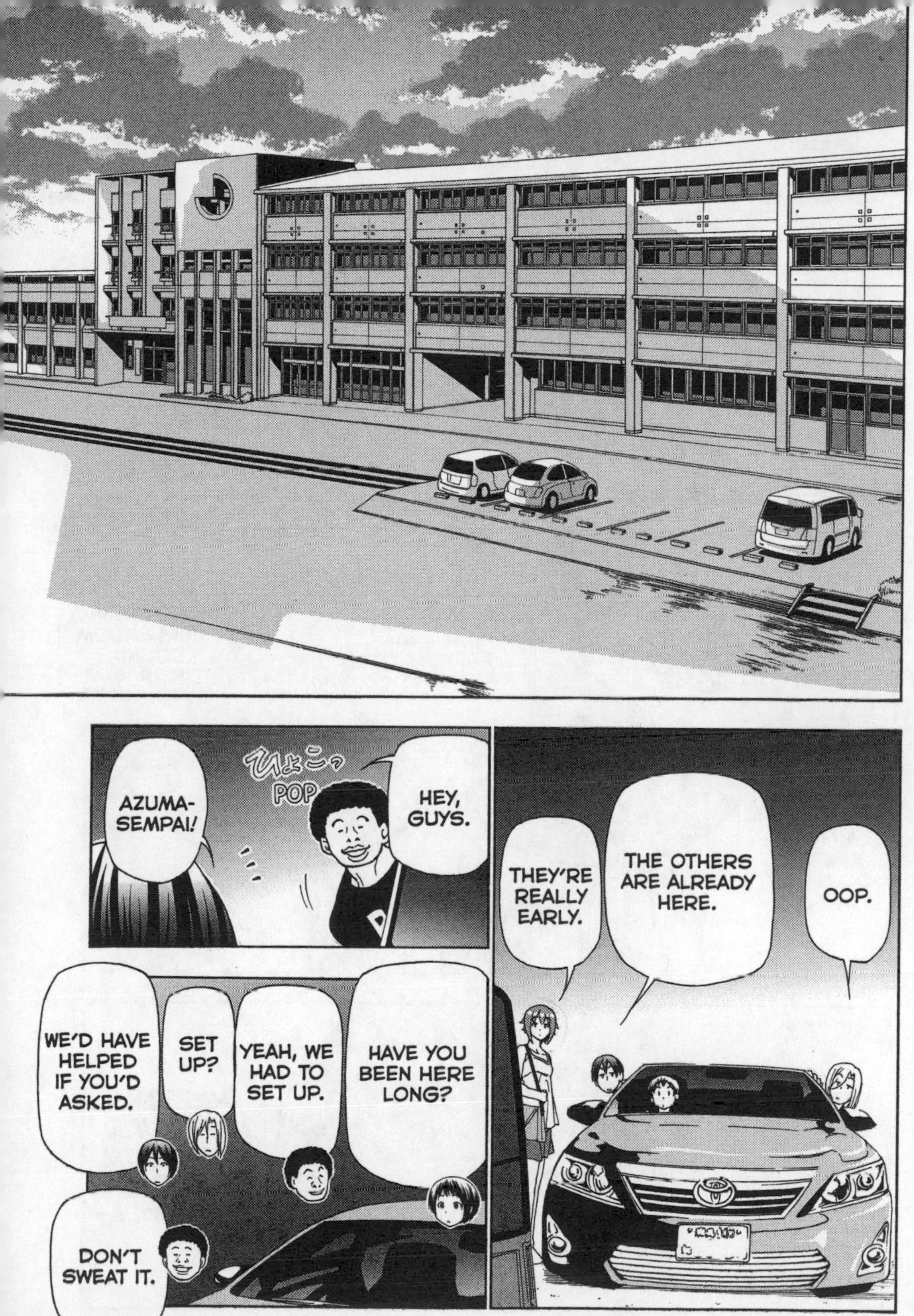
OOP.
THE OTHERS ARE ALREADY HERE.
THEY'RE REALLY EARLY.
ひょこっ POP
HEY, GUYS.
AZUMA-SEMPAI!
HAVE YOU BEEN HERE LONG?
YEAH, WE HAD TO SET UP.
SET UP?
WE'D HAVE HELPED IF YOU'D ASKED.
DON'T SWEAT IT.

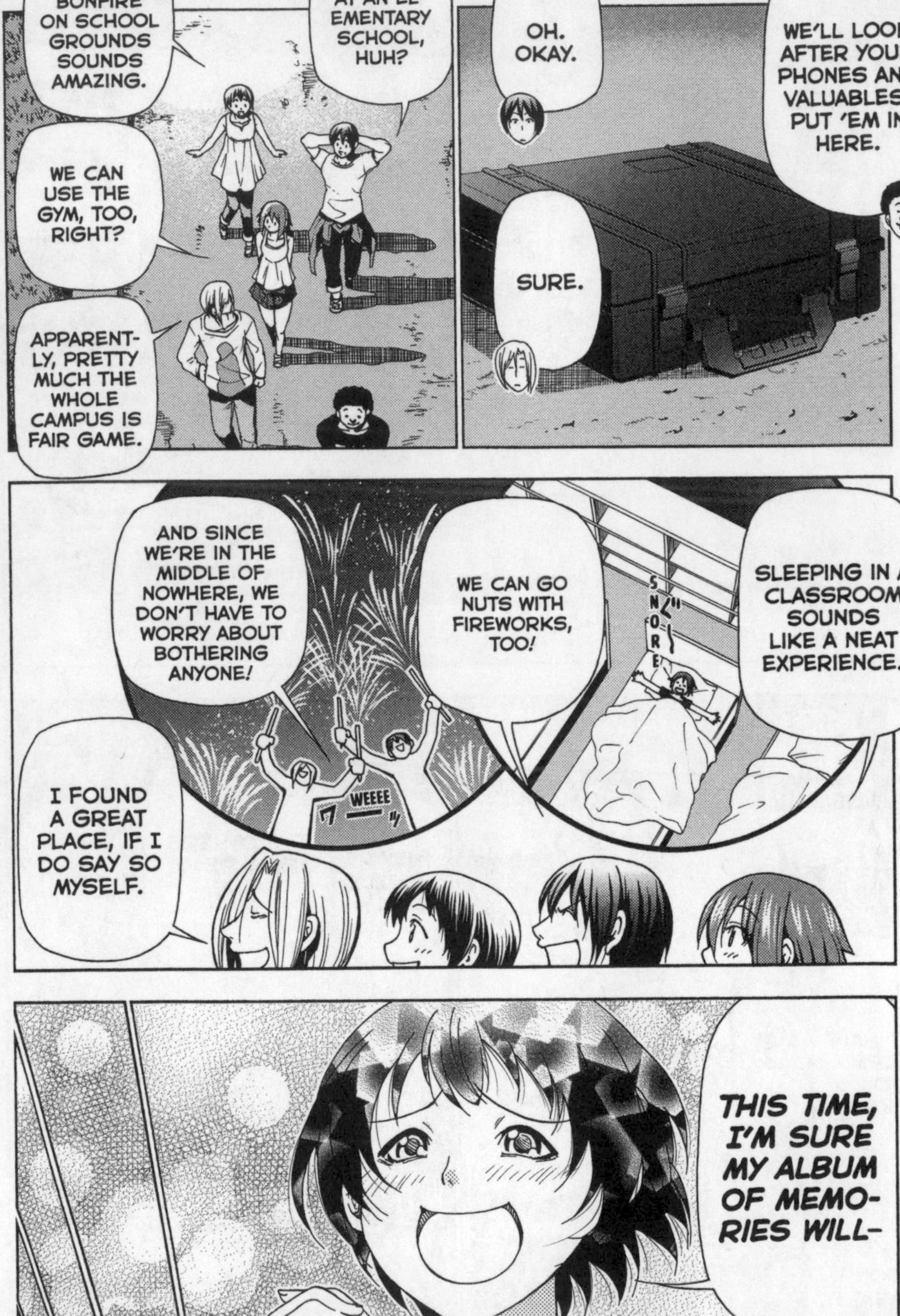
WE'LL LOOK AFTER YOUR PHONES AND VALUABLES. PUT 'EM IN HERE.
OH. OKAY.
SURE.
STAYING AT AN ELEMENTARY SCHOOL, HUH?
HAVING A BONFIRE ON SCHOOL GROUNDS SOUNDS AMAZING.
WE CAN USE THE GYM, TOO, RIGHT?
APPARENTLY, PRETTY MUCH THE WHOLE CAMPUS IS FAIR GAME.
SLEEPING IN A CLASSROOM SOUNDS LIKE A NEAT EXPERIENCE.
SNORE
WE CAN GO NUTS WITH FIREWORKS, TOO!
AND SINCE WE'RE IN THE MIDDLE OF NOWHERE, WE DON'T HAVE TO WORRY ABOUT BOTHERING ANYONE!
WEEEE
I FOUND A GREAT PLACE, IF I DO SAY SO MYSELF.
THIS TIME, I'M SURE MY ALBUM OF MEMORIES WILL-

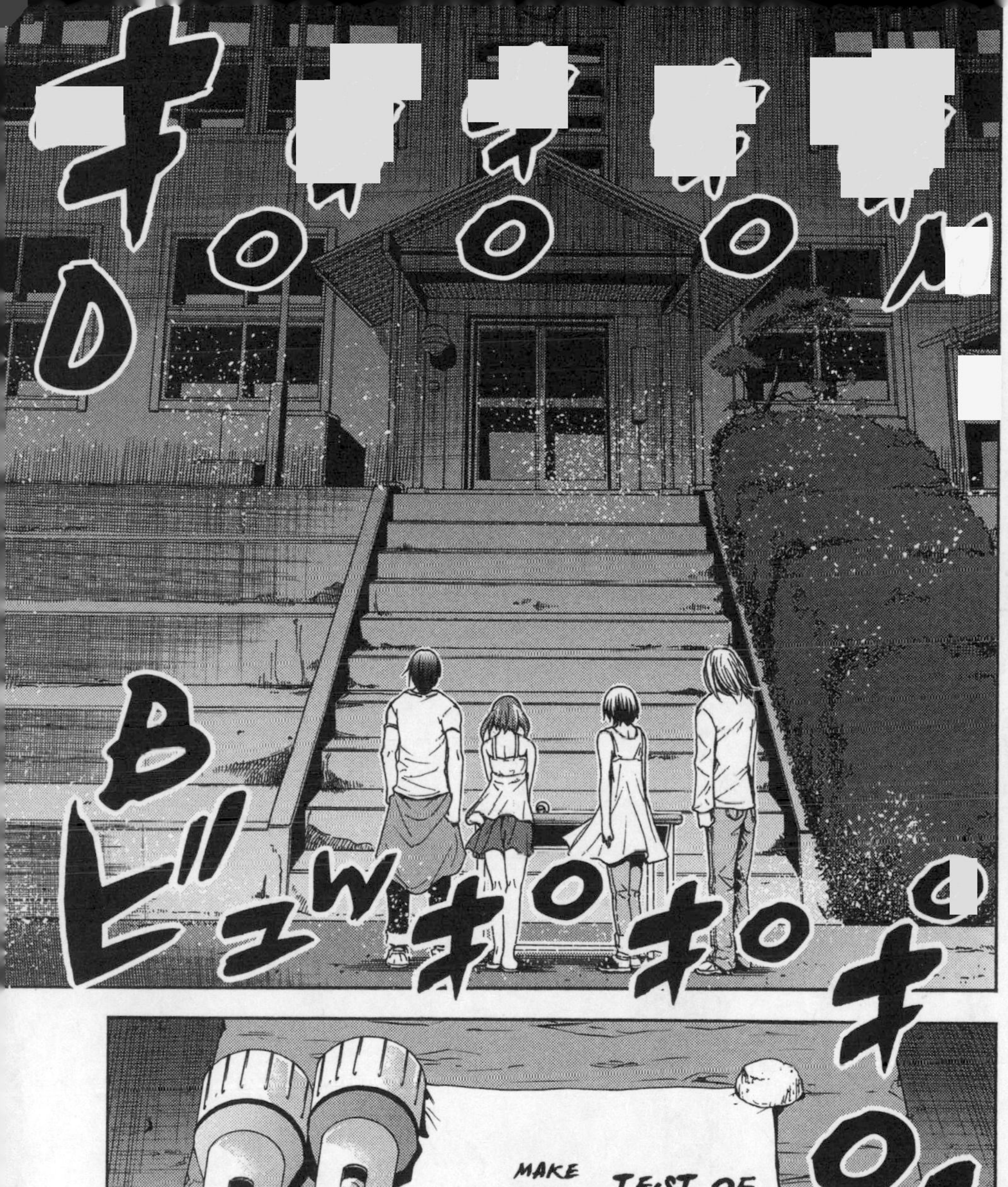

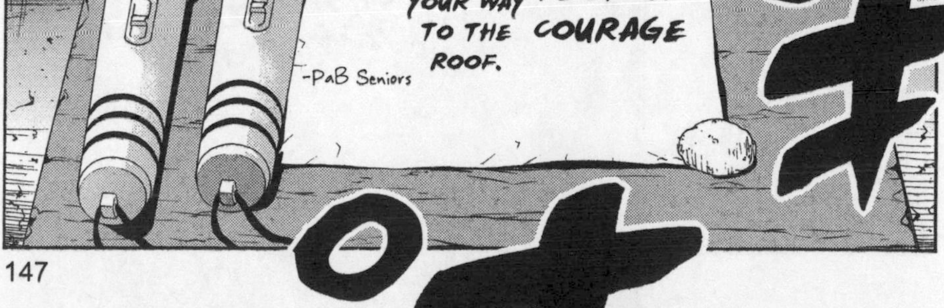
TEST OF COURAGE
MAKE YOUR WAY TO THE ROOF.
-PaB Seniors

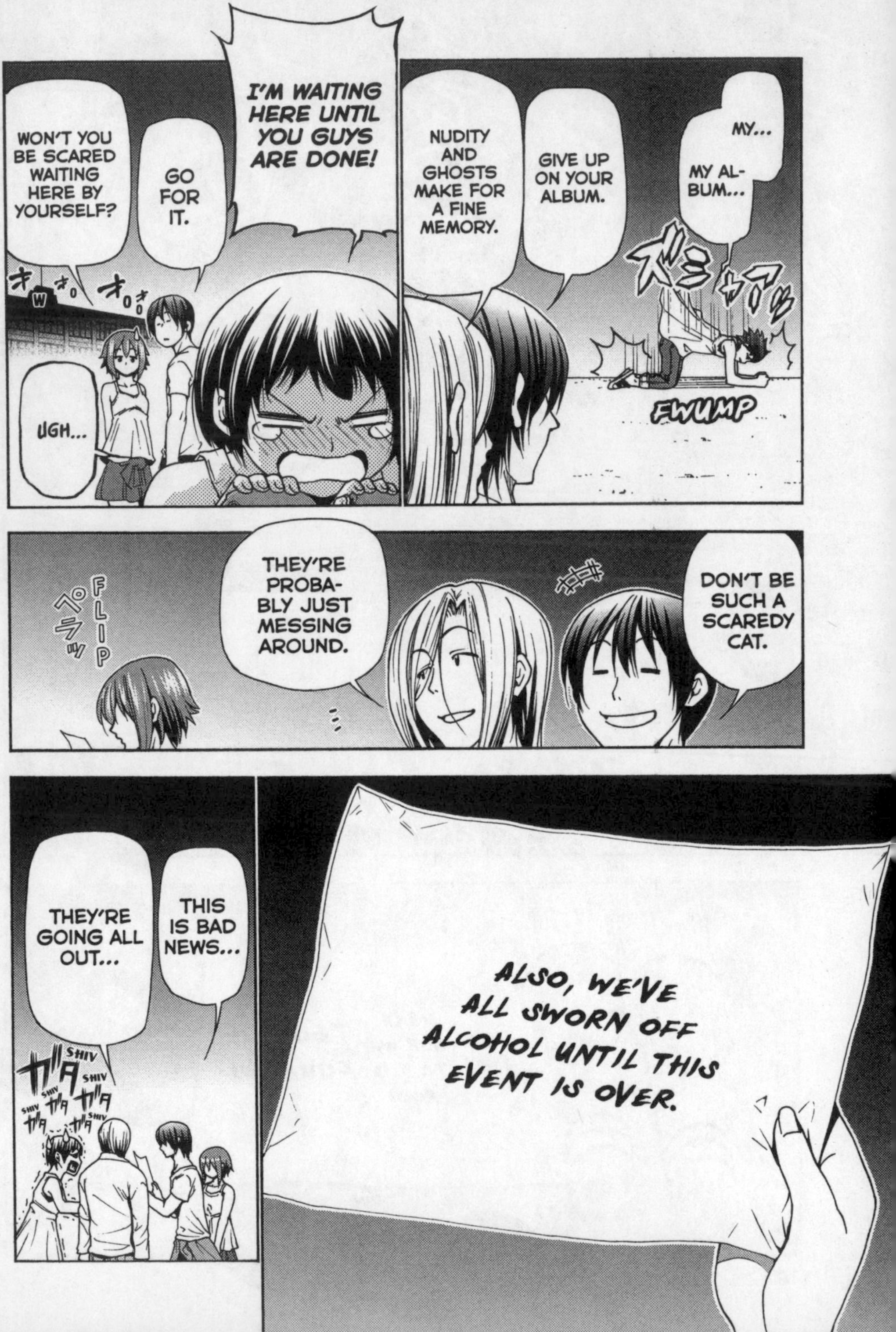
MY...
MY AL-BUM...
FWUMP
GIVE UP ON YOUR ALBUM.
NUDITY AND GHOSTS MAKE FOR A FINE MEMORY.
I'M WAITING HERE UNTIL YOU GUYS ARE DONE!
GO FOR IT.
WON'T YOU BE SCARED WAITING HERE BY YOURSELF?
UGH...
DON'T BE SUCH A SCAREDY CAT.
THEY'RE PROBA-BLY JUST MESSING AROUND.
FLIP
ALSO, WE'VE ALL SWORN OFF ALCOHOL UNTIL THIS EVENT IS OVER.
THIS IS BAD NEWS...
THEY'RE GOING ALL OUT...
SHIV SHIV SHIV SHIV SHIV

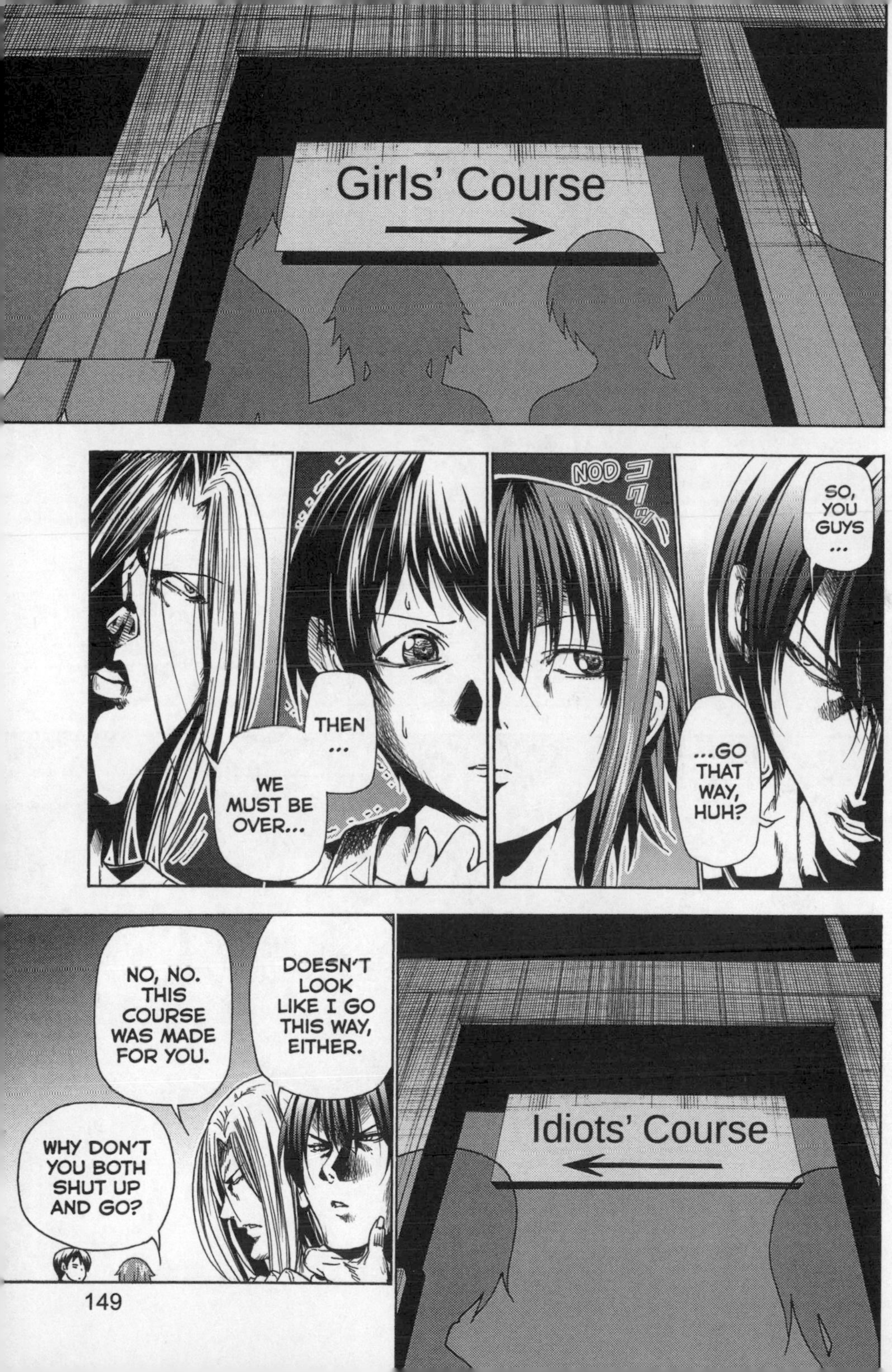
Girls' Course
SO, YOU GUYS...
...GO THAT WAY, HUH?
NOD
THEN...
WE MUST BE OVER...
Idiots' Course
DOESN'T LOOK LIKE I GO THIS WAY, EITHER.
NO, NO. THIS COURSE WAS MADE FOR YOU.
WHY DON'T YOU BOTH SHUT UP AND GO?

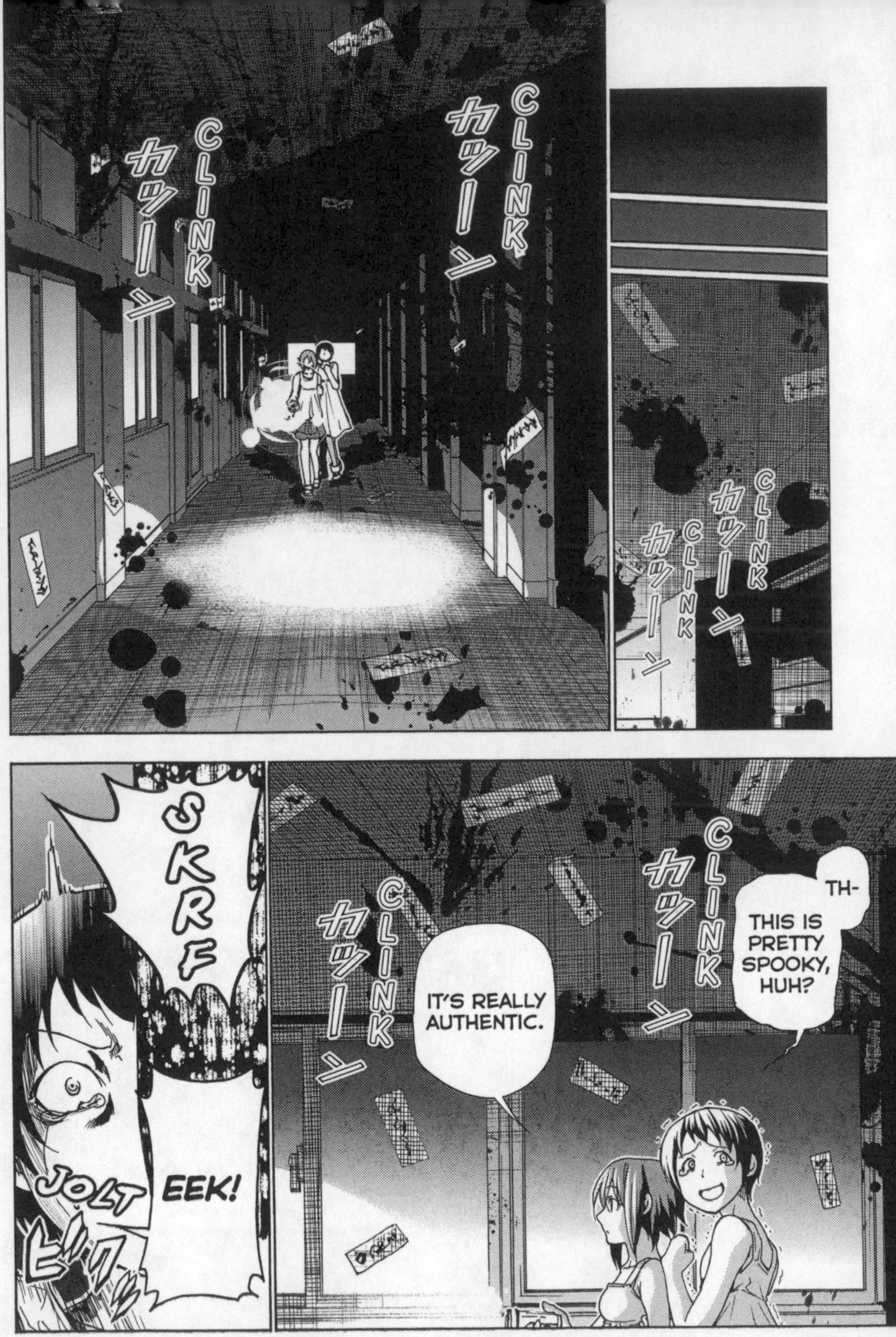
CLINK
カッーン
CLINK
カッーン
CLINK
カッーン
CLINK
カッーン
TH- THIS IS PRETTY SPOOKY, HUH?
CLINK
カッーン
IT'S REALLY AUTHENTIC.
CLINK
カッーン
SKRF
EEK!
JOLT

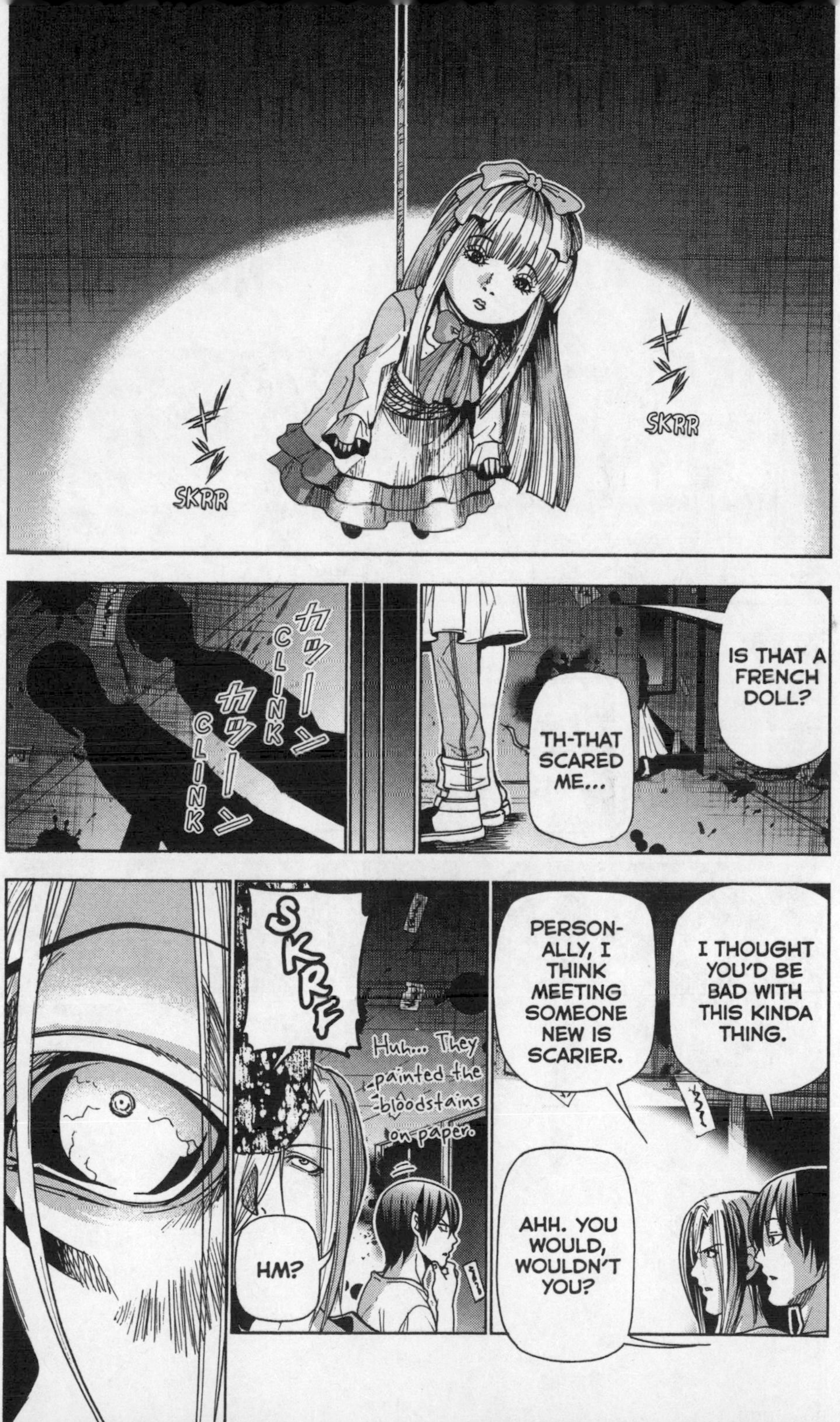
SKRR
SKRR
IS THAT A FRENCH DOLL?
TH-THAT SCARED ME...
カッーン CLINK
カッーン CLINK
I THOUGHT YOU'D BE BAD WITH THIS KINDA THING.
PERSON-ALLY, I THINK MEETING SOMEONE NEW IS SCARIER.
AHH. YOU WOULD, WOULDN'T YOU?
SKRY
Huh... They painted the bloodstains on paper.
HM?

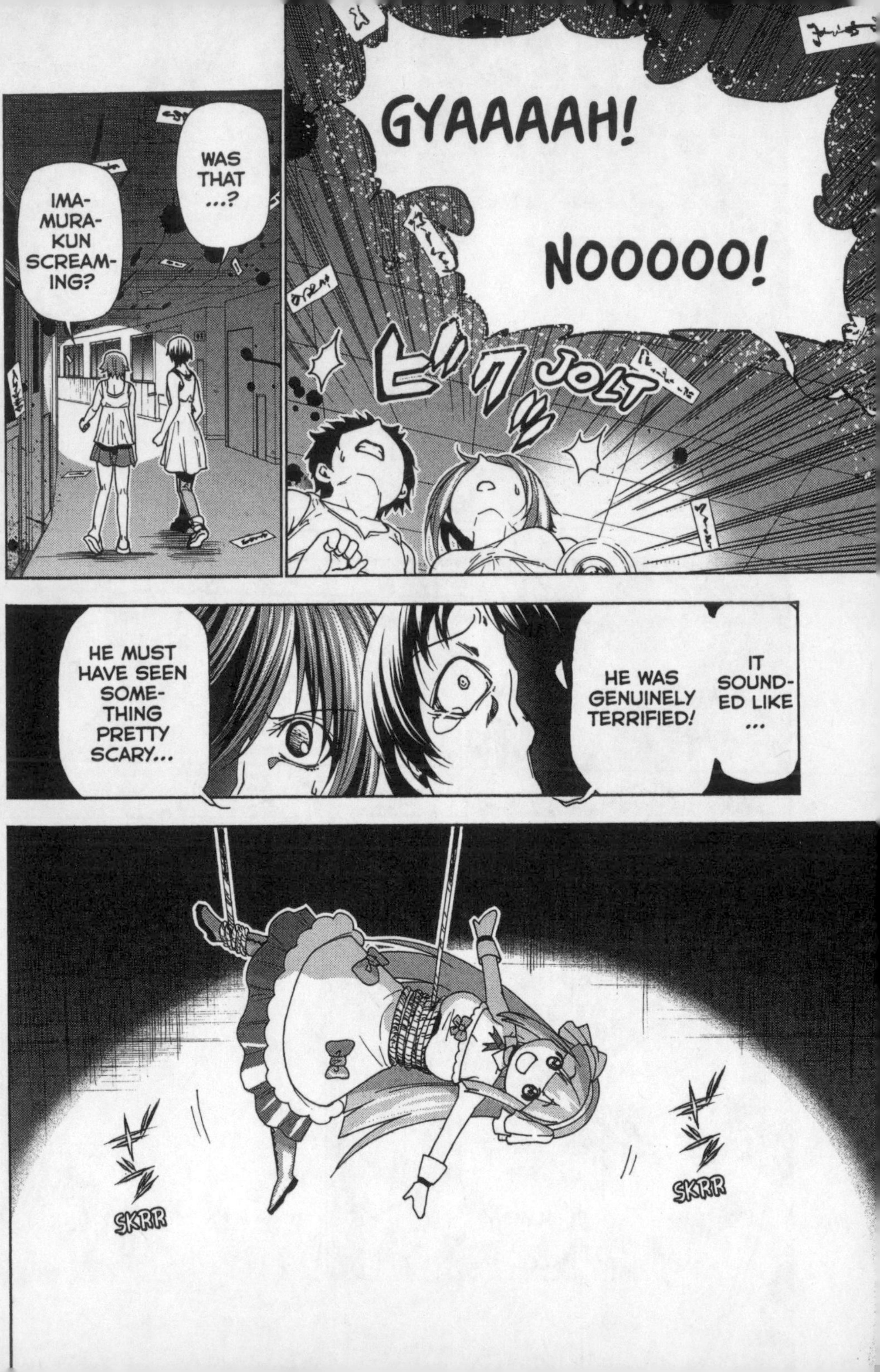
GYAAAAH!
NOOOOO!
JOLT
WAS THAT ...?
IMAMURA-KUN SCREAMING?
IT SOUNDED LIKE ...
HE WAS GENUINELY TERRIFIED!
HE MUST HAVE SEEN SOMETHING PRETTY SCARY...
SKRR
SKRR

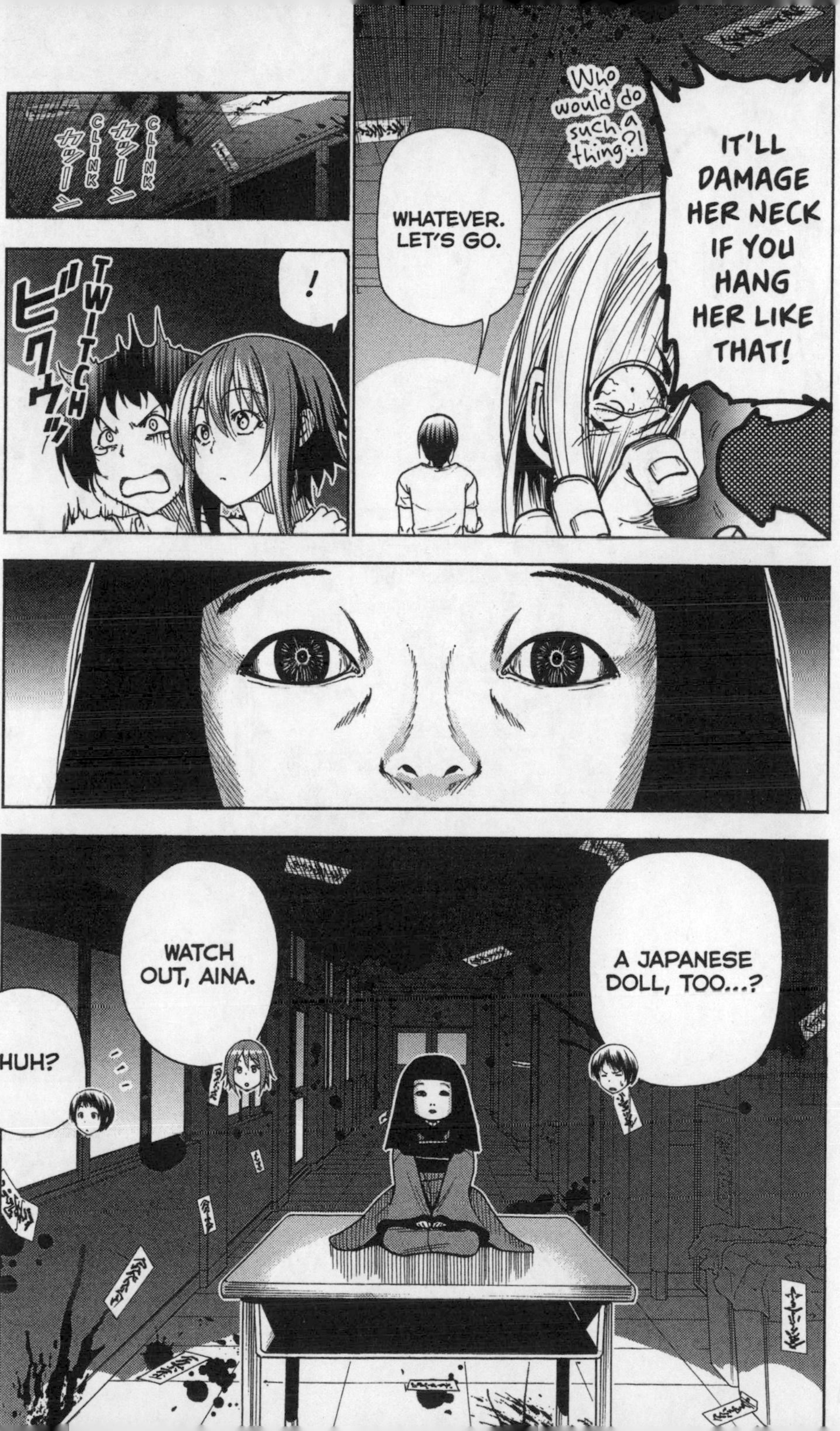
Who would do such a thing?!
IT'LL DAMAGE HER NECK IF YOU HANG HER LIKE THAT!
WHATEVER. LET'S GO.
CLINK CLINK
!
TWITCH
A JAPANESE DOLL, TOO...?
WATCH OUT, AINA.
HUH?

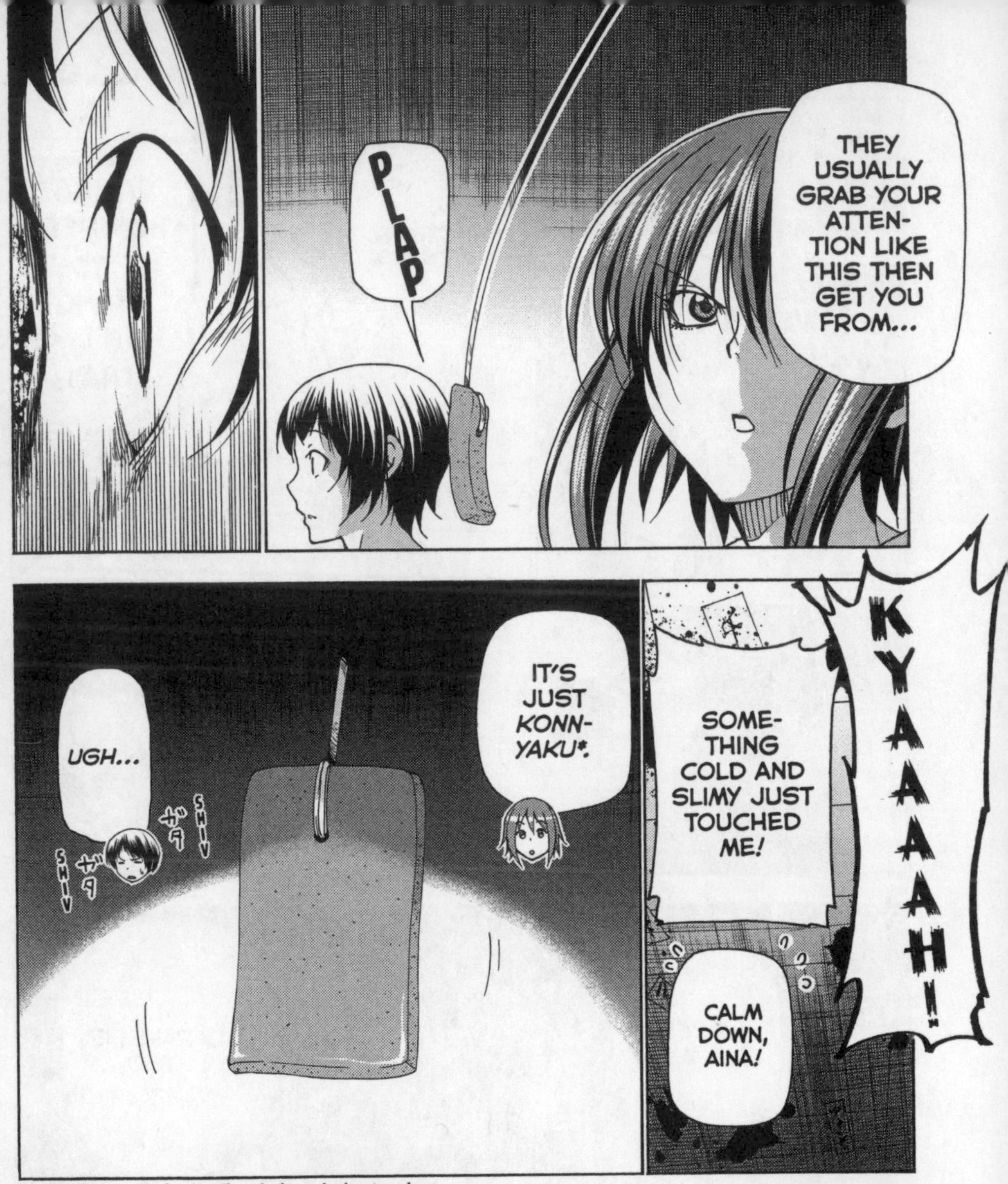
THEY USUALLY GRAB YOUR ATTEN-TION LIKE THIS THEN GET YOU FROM...
PLAP
KYAAAAH!!
SOME-THING COLD AND SLIMY JUST TOUCHED ME!
CALM DOWN, AINA!
IT'S JUST KONN-YAKU*.
UGH...
SHIV
SHIV

*Konnyaku: A jelly foodstuff made from the konjac plant.

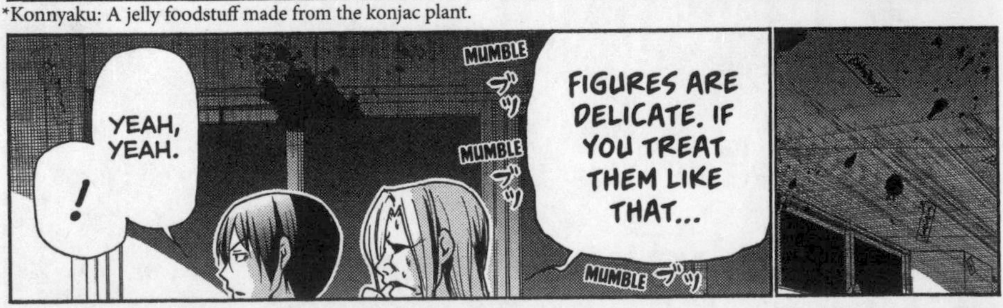
FIGURES ARE DELICATE. IF YOU TREAT THEM LIKE THAT...
MUMBLE
MUMBLE
MUMBLE
YEAH, YEAH.
!

PLAP

PLAP

YEAH, I KNOW. THEY'RE PROBABLY JUST TRYING TO—

WATCH OUT, KITA-HARA.

A JAP-ANESE DOLL?

THERE'S NOTHING SCARY ABOUT—

は, HA

HA は,

は, HA

AS IF THAT'S ENOUGH TO SPOOK US.

HA

は,

KONN-YAKU WARMED UP TO BODY TEMP, HUH?

PEEL ペーリッ

PEEL ペーリッ

I KNEW IT.

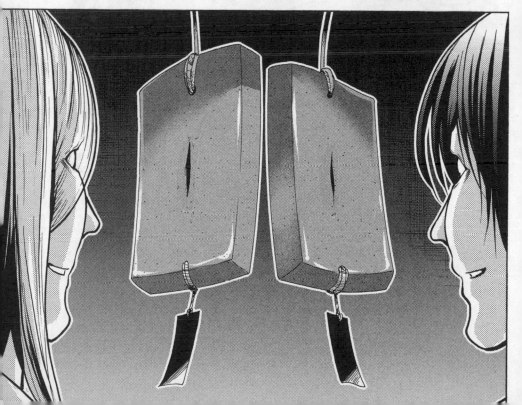

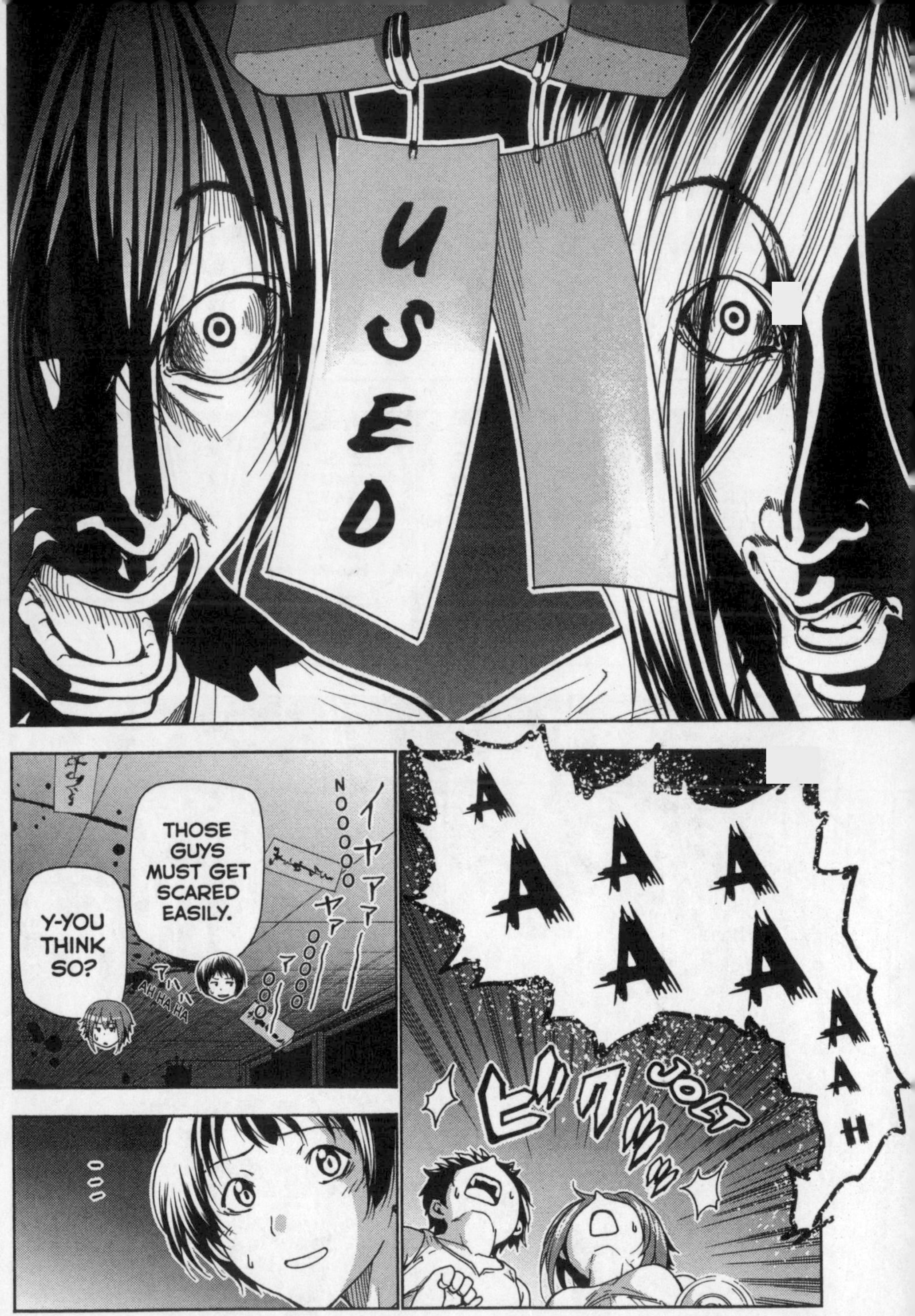
USED
AAAAAAAAAAH
ビクッ
JOLT
イヤァァー ヤァー
NOOOOOOOOOOOO
THOSE GUYS MUST GET SCARED EASILY.
アハハ
AH HA HA
Y-YOU THINK SO?
...

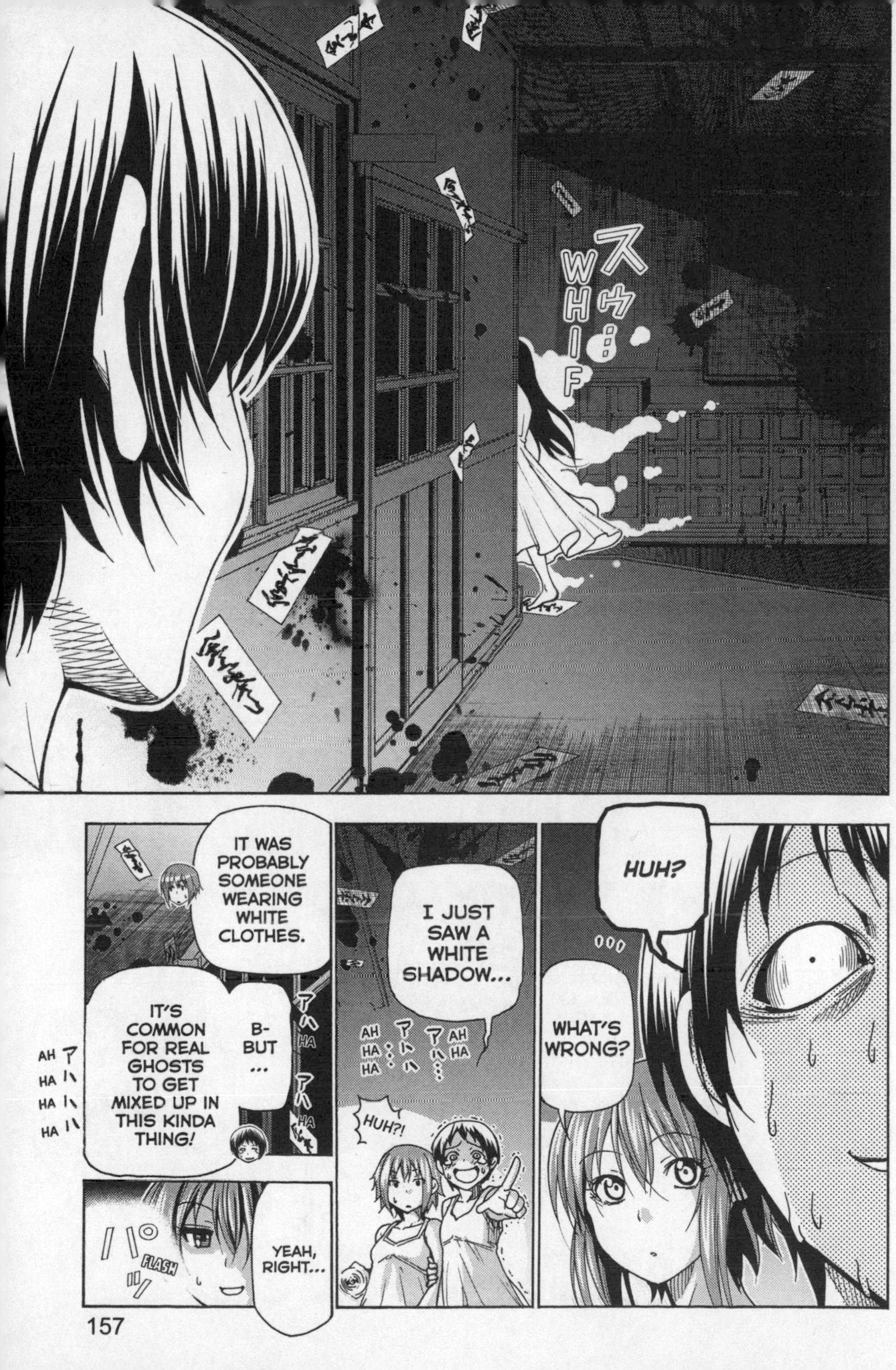
スゥ… WHIFF
HUH?
WHAT'S WRONG?
I JUST SAW A WHITE SHADOW...
AH HA アハ…
AH HA HA アハハ…
HUH?!
IT WAS PROBABLY SOMEONE WEARING WHITE CLOTHES.
B-BUT...
アハ HA アハ HA
IT'S COMMON FOR REAL GHOSTS TO GET MIXED UP IN THIS KINDA THING!
AH HA HA HA アハハハ
YEAH, RIGHT...
FLASH

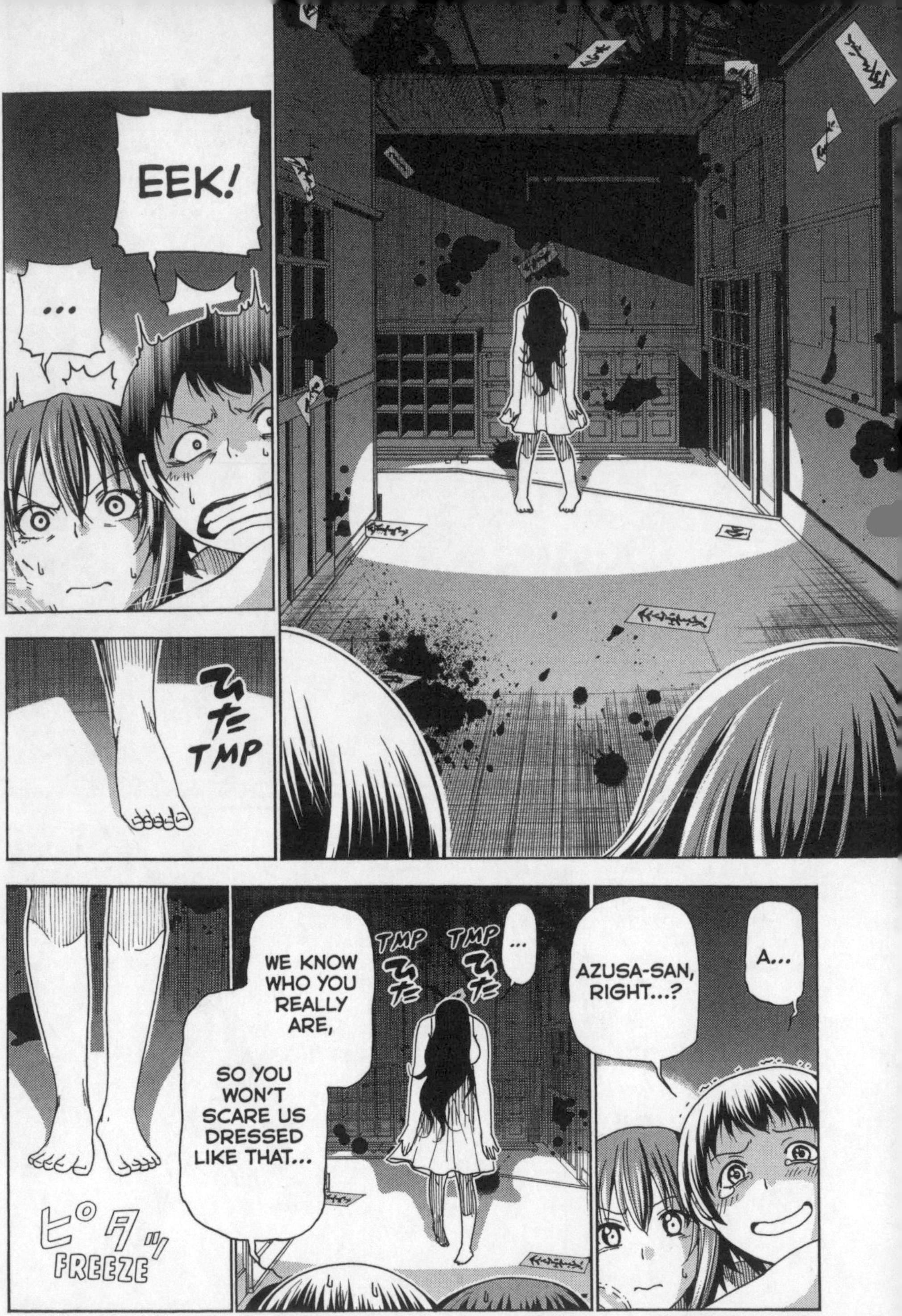
EEK!
...
ひた TMP
A...
AZUSA-SAN, RIGHT...?
...
TMP ひた
TMP ひた
WE KNOW WHO YOU REALLY ARE,
SO YOU WON'T SCARE US DRESSED LIKE THAT...
ピタッ FREEZE

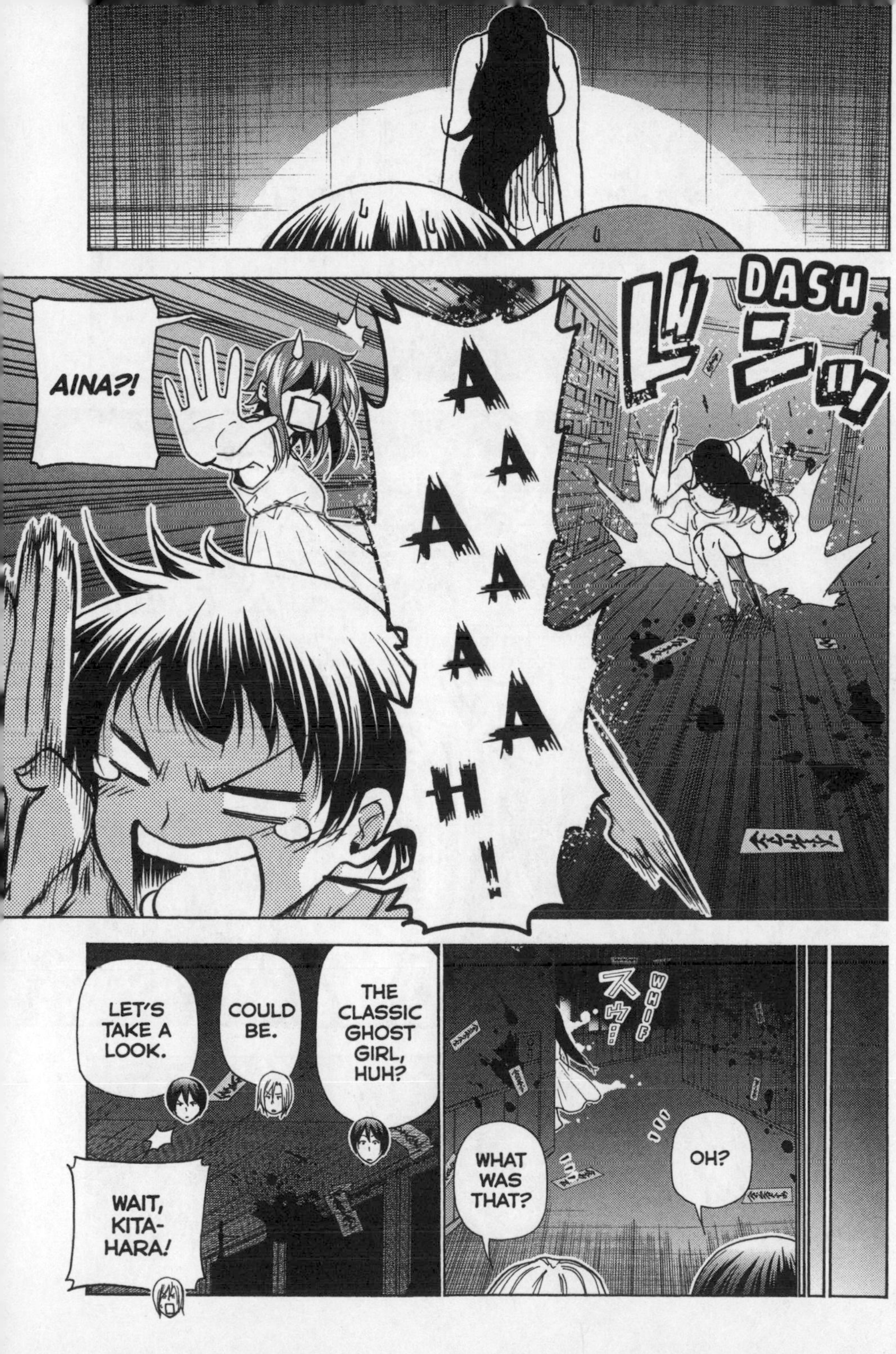
DASH
AAAAAAAH!!
AINA?!
WHIF
OH?
WHAT WAS THAT?
THE CLASSIC GHOST GIRL, HUH?
COULD BE.
LET'S TAKE A LOOK.
WAIT, KITA-HARA!

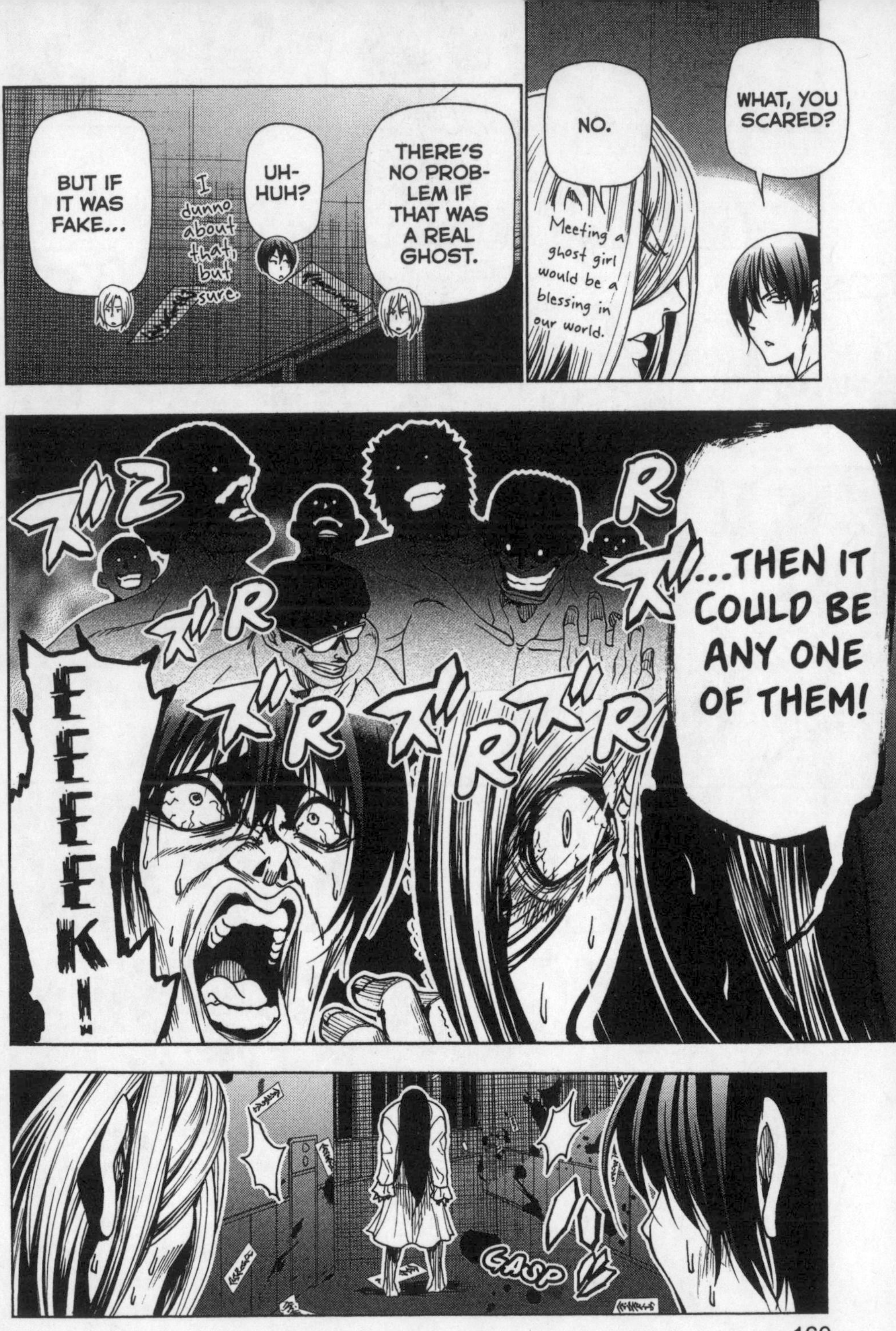

WHAT, YOU SCARED?
NO.
Meeting a ghost girl would be a blessing in our world.
THERE'S NO PROB-LEM IF THAT WAS A REAL GHOST.
UH-HUH?
I dunno about that, but sure.
BUT IF IT WAS FAKE...
...THEN IT COULD BE ANY ONE OF THEM!
EEEEEEK!!
GASP

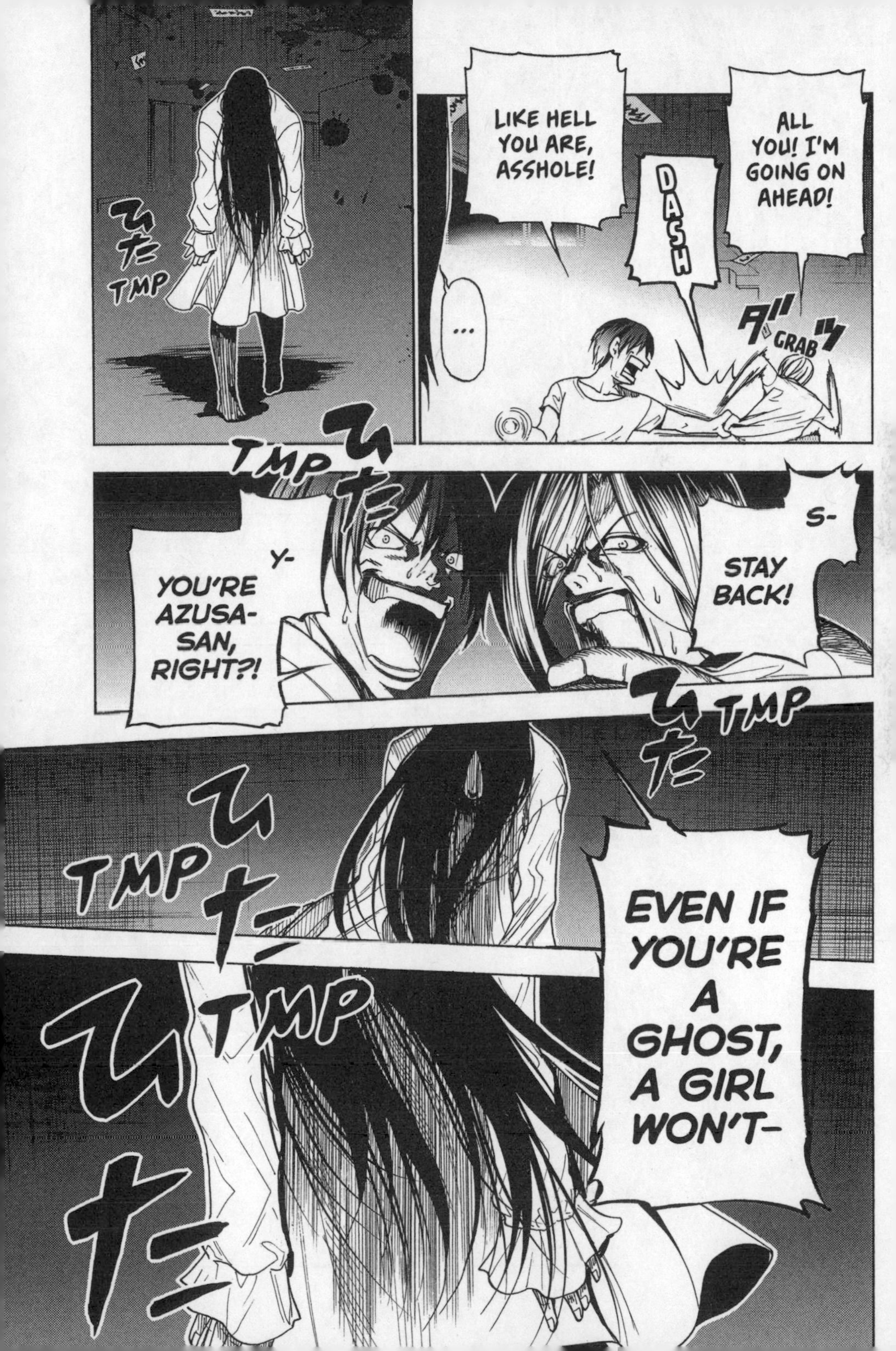
ALL YOU! I'M GOING ON AHEAD!
LIKE HELL YOU ARE, ASSHOLE!
DASH
...
GRAB
TMP
TMP
S-
STAY BACK!
Y-
YOU'RE AZUSA-SAN, RIGHT?!
TMP
EVEN IF YOU'RE A GHOST, A GIRL WON'T-
TMP
TMP

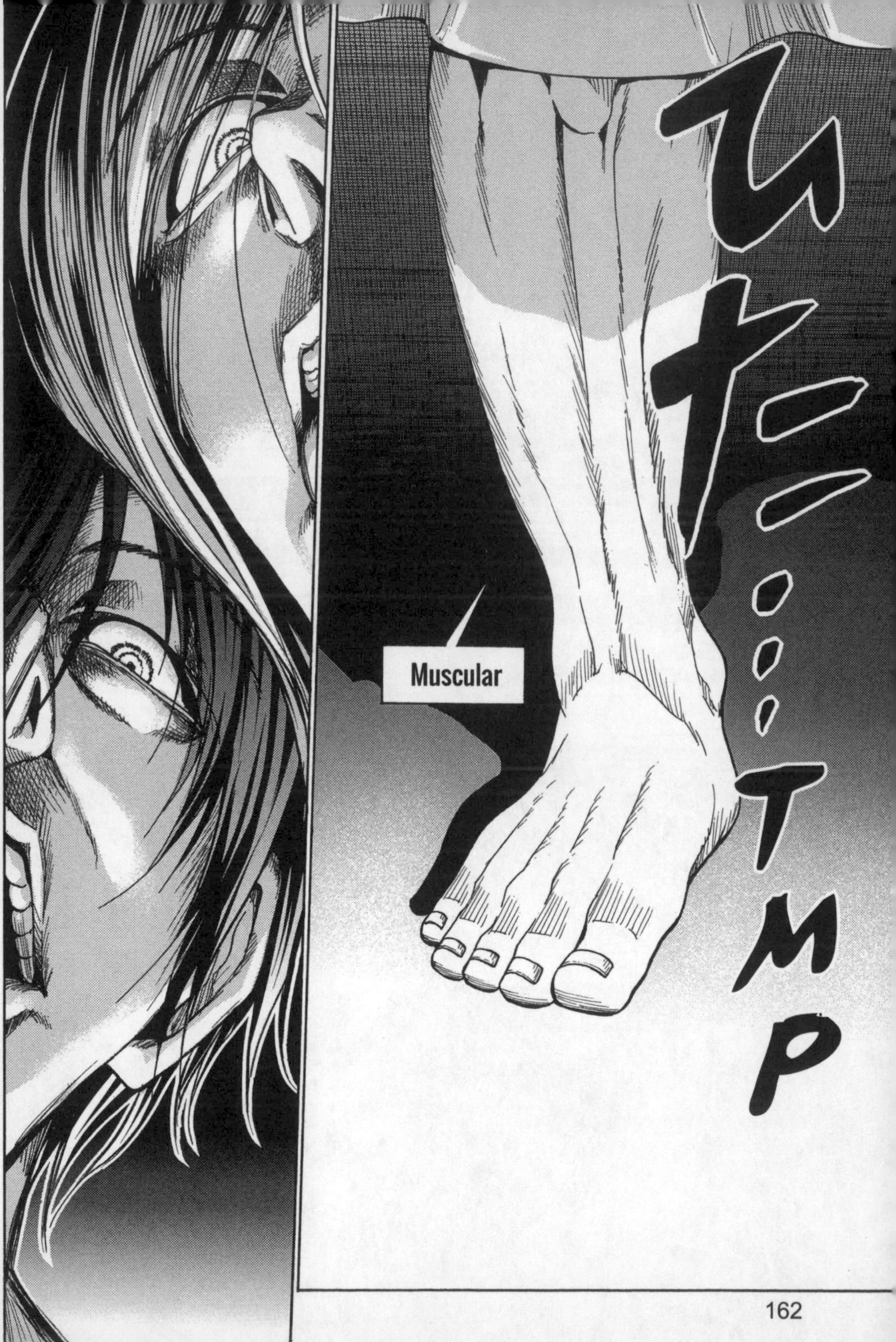
TMP
Muscular

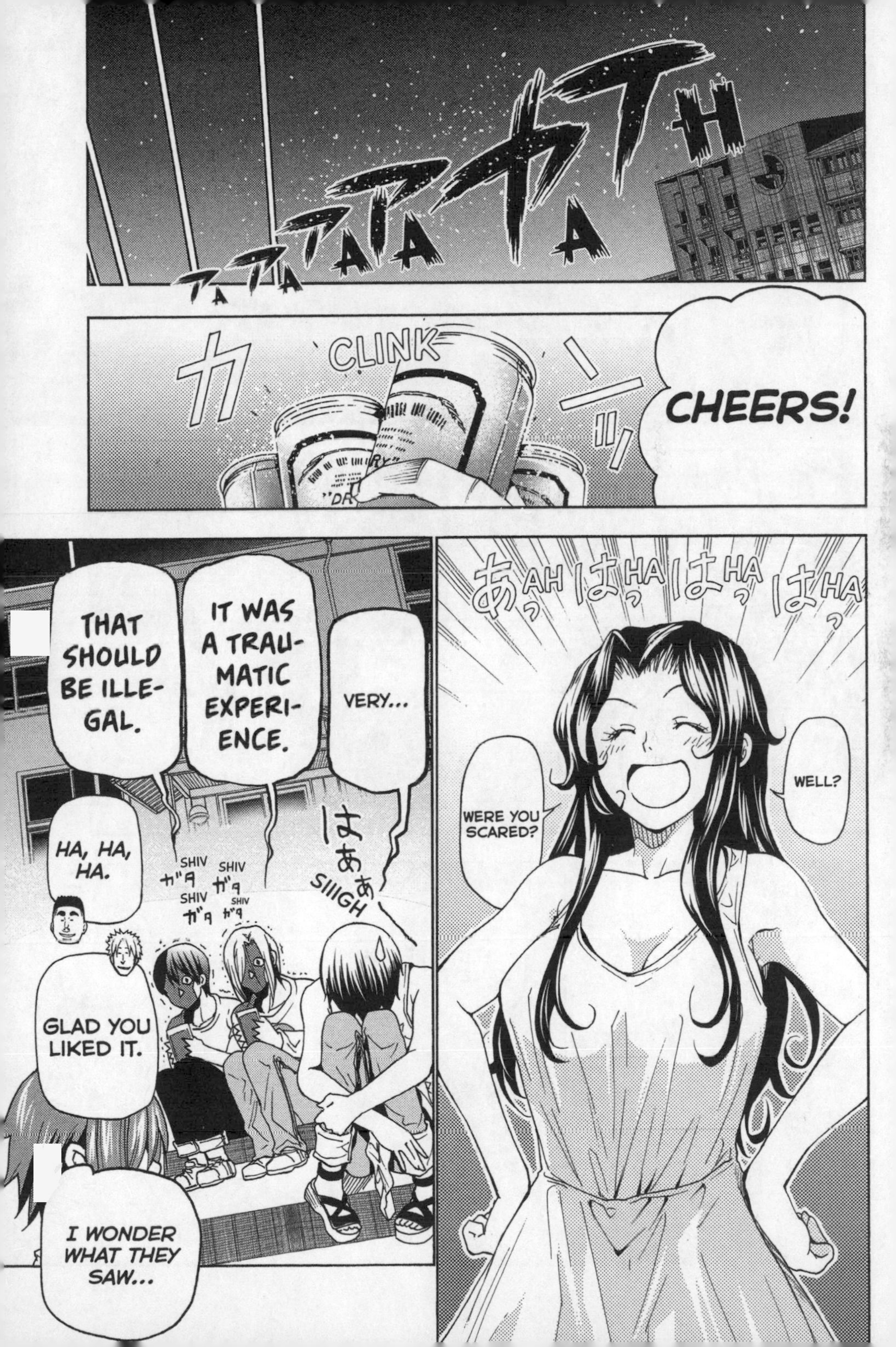
A A A A A TH
CHEERS!
CLINK
あっはっはっはっ AH HA HA HA
WELL?
WERE YOU SCARED?
VERY...
IT WAS A TRAU-MATIC EXPERI-ENCE.
THAT SHOULD BE ILLE-GAL.
はあぁ SIIIGH
ガタガタガタガタ SHIV SHIV SHIV SHIV
HA, HA, HA.
GLAD YOU LIKED IT.
I WONDER WHAT THEY SAW...

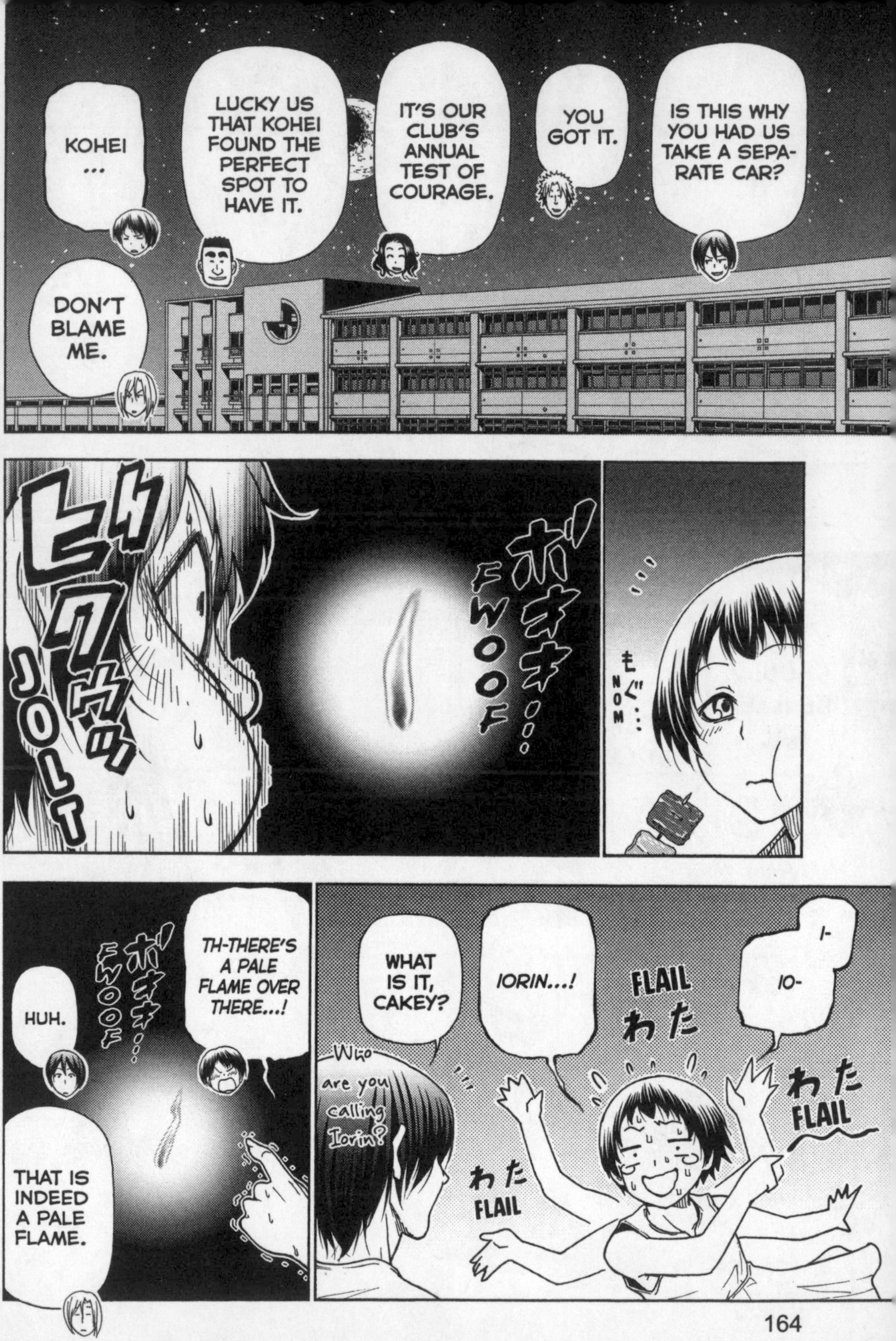
IS THIS WHY YOU HAD US TAKE A SEPA-RATE CAR?
YOU GOT IT.
IT'S OUR CLUB'S ANNUAL TEST OF COURAGE.
LUCKY US THAT KOHEI FOUND THE PERFECT SPOT TO HAVE IT.
KOHEI ...
DON'T BLAME ME.
...
もぐ... NOM
ボオオ... FWOOF
ビクゥッ JOLT
I- IO-
わた FLAIL
IORIN...!
WHAT IS IT, CAKEY?
Who are you calling Iorin?
わた FLAIL
わた FLAIL
TH-THERE'S A PALE FLAME OVER THERE...!
ボオオ... FWOOF
HUH.
THAT IS INDEED A PALE FLAME.

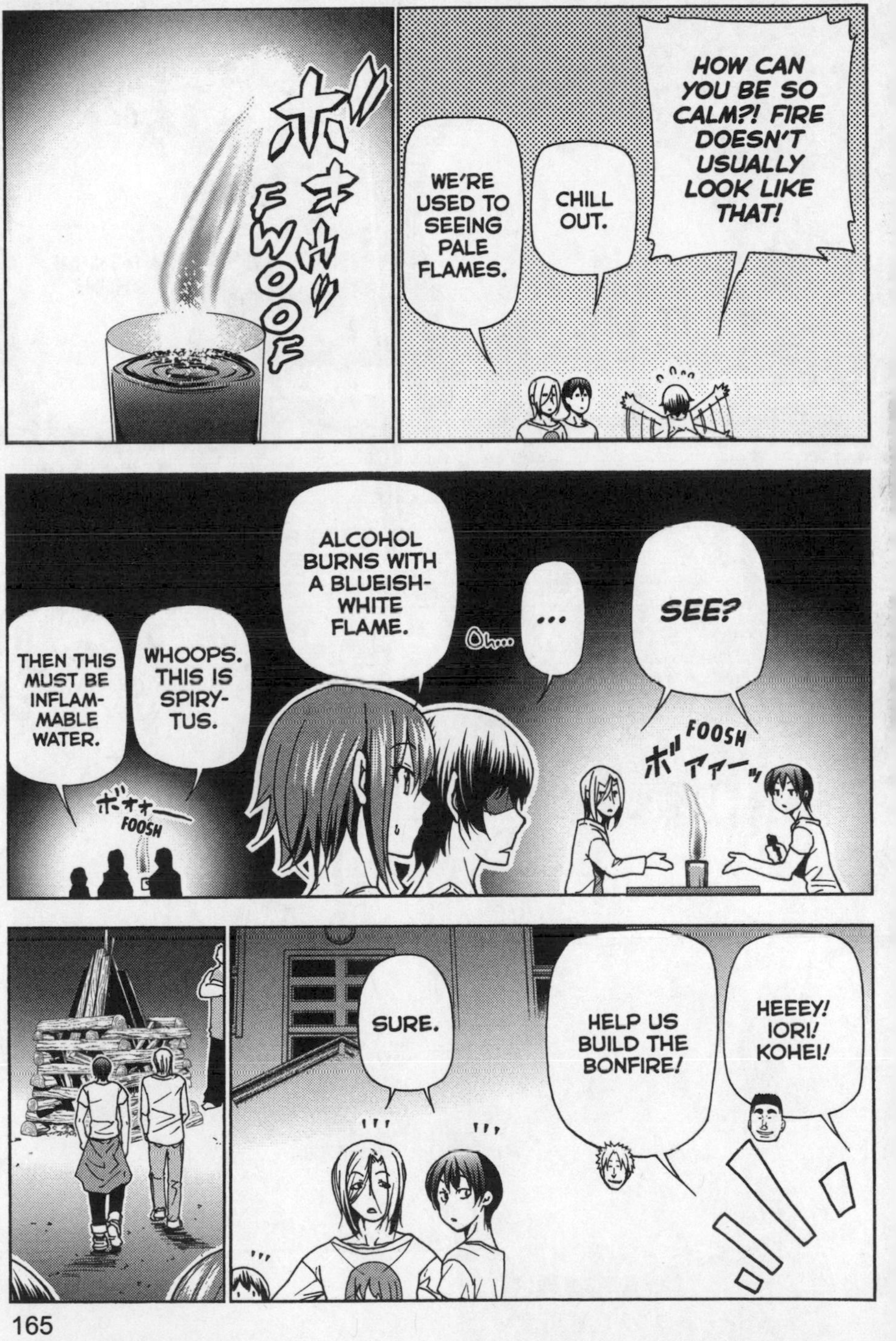
HOW CAN YOU BE SO CALM?! FIRE DOESN'T USUALLY LOOK LIKE THAT!
CHILL OUT.
WE'RE USED TO SEEING PALE FLAMES.
FWOOF
SEE?
...
Oh...
ALCOHOL BURNS WITH A BLUEISH-WHITE FLAME.
FOOSH
WHOOPS. THIS IS SPIRY-TUS.
THEN THIS MUST BE INFLAM-MABLE WATER.
FOOSH
HEEEY! IORI! KOHEI!
HELP US BUILD THE BONFIRE!
SURE.

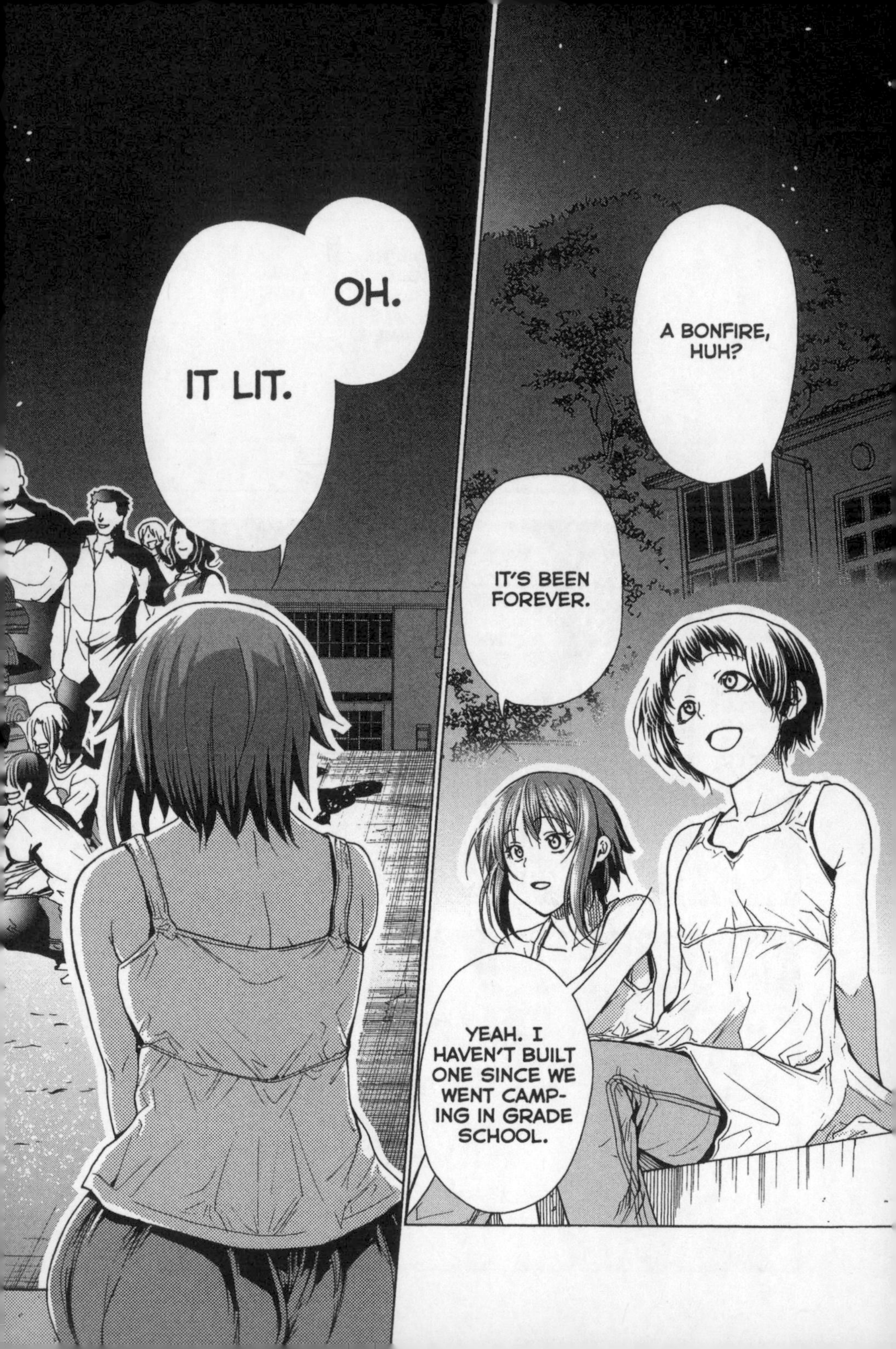
A BONFIRE, HUH?
IT'S BEEN FOREVER.
YEAH. I HAVEN'T BUILT ONE SINCE WE WENT CAMPING IN GRADE SCHOOL.
OH.
IT LIT.

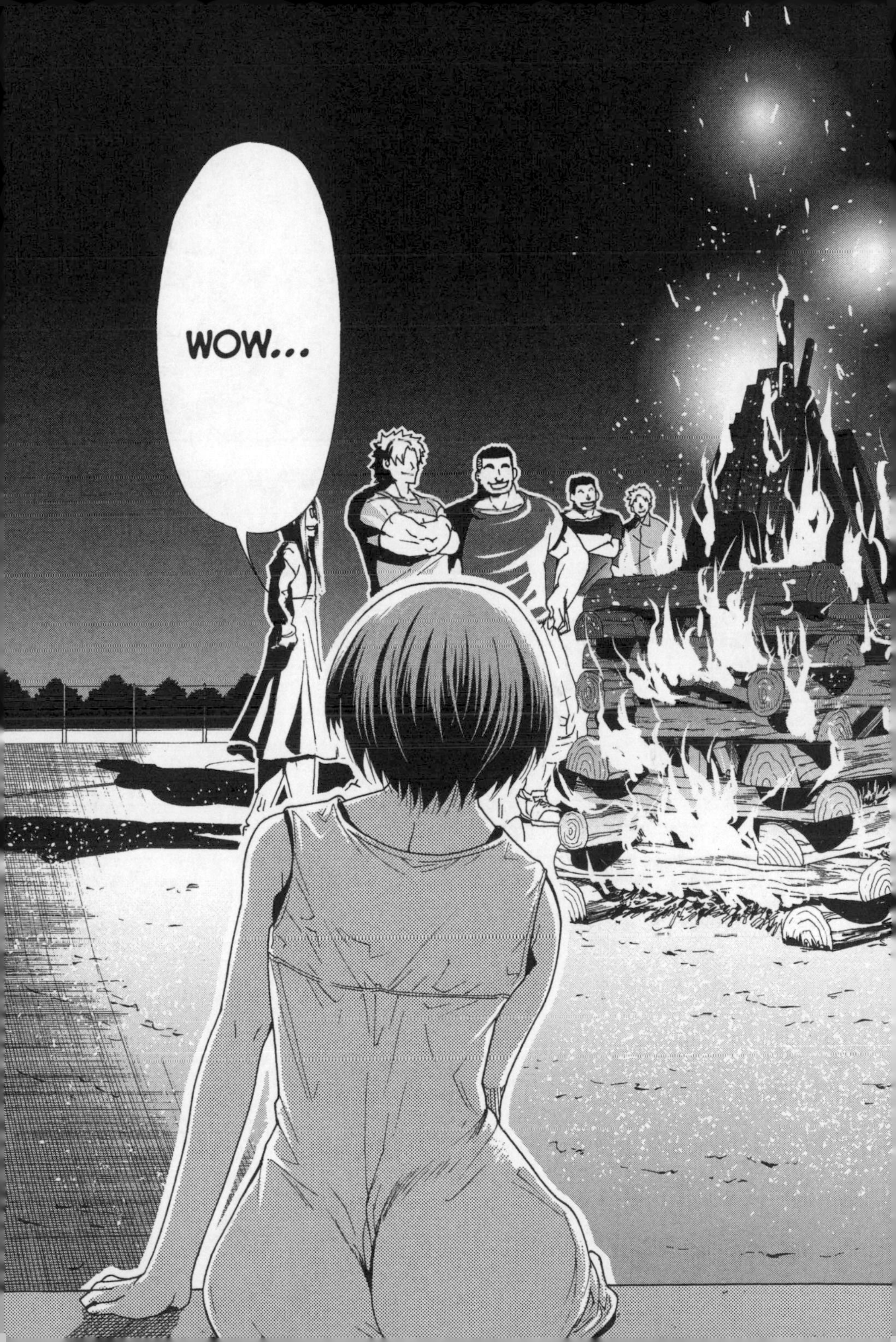
WOW...

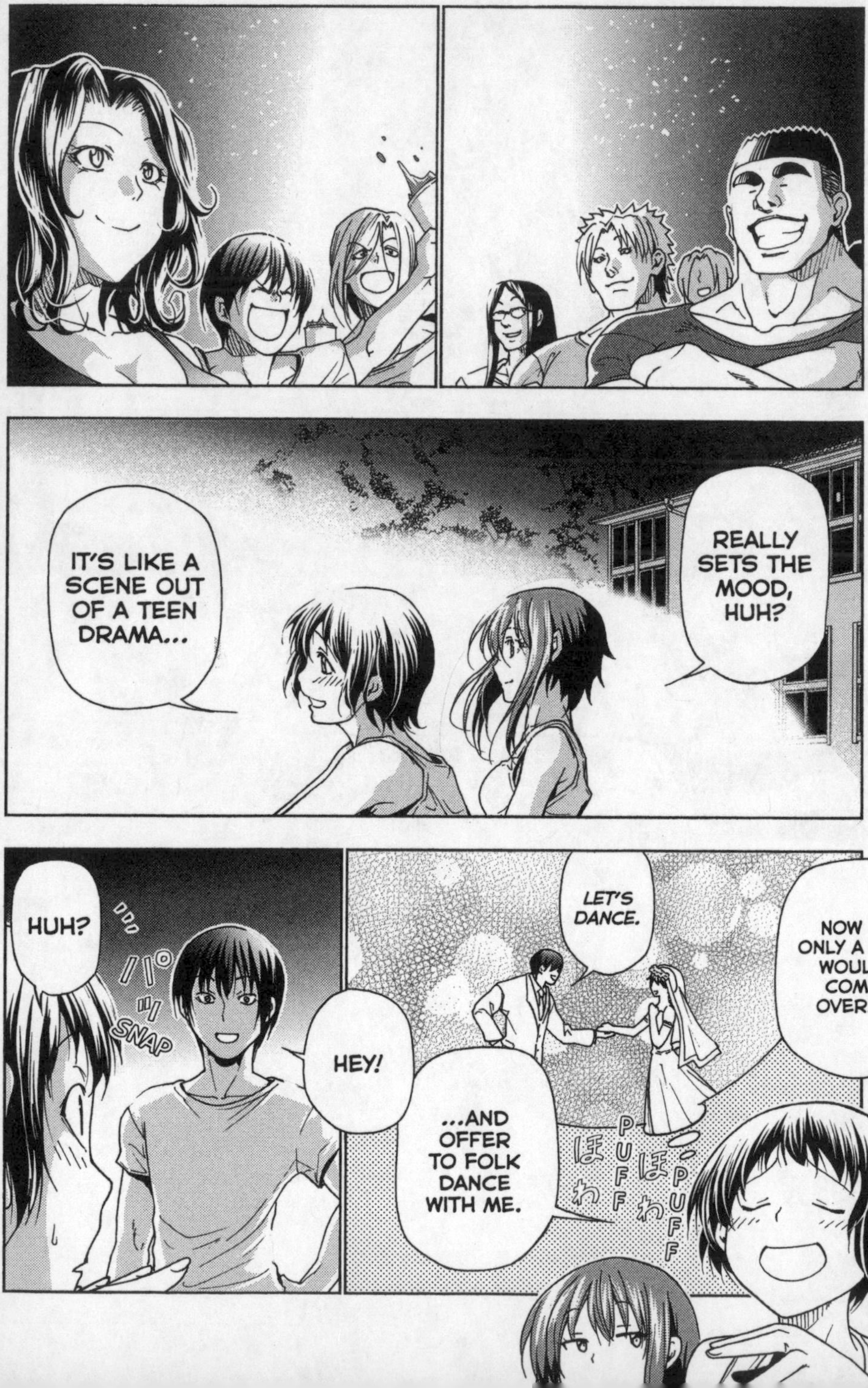
REALLY SETS THE MOOD, HUH?
IT'S LIKE A SCENE OUT OF A TEEN DRAMA...
NOW IF ONLY A BOY WOULD COME OVER...
LET'S DANCE.
...AND OFFER TO FOLK DANCE WITH ME.
ほわ PUFF
ほわ PUFF
HEY!
パッ SNAP
HUH?

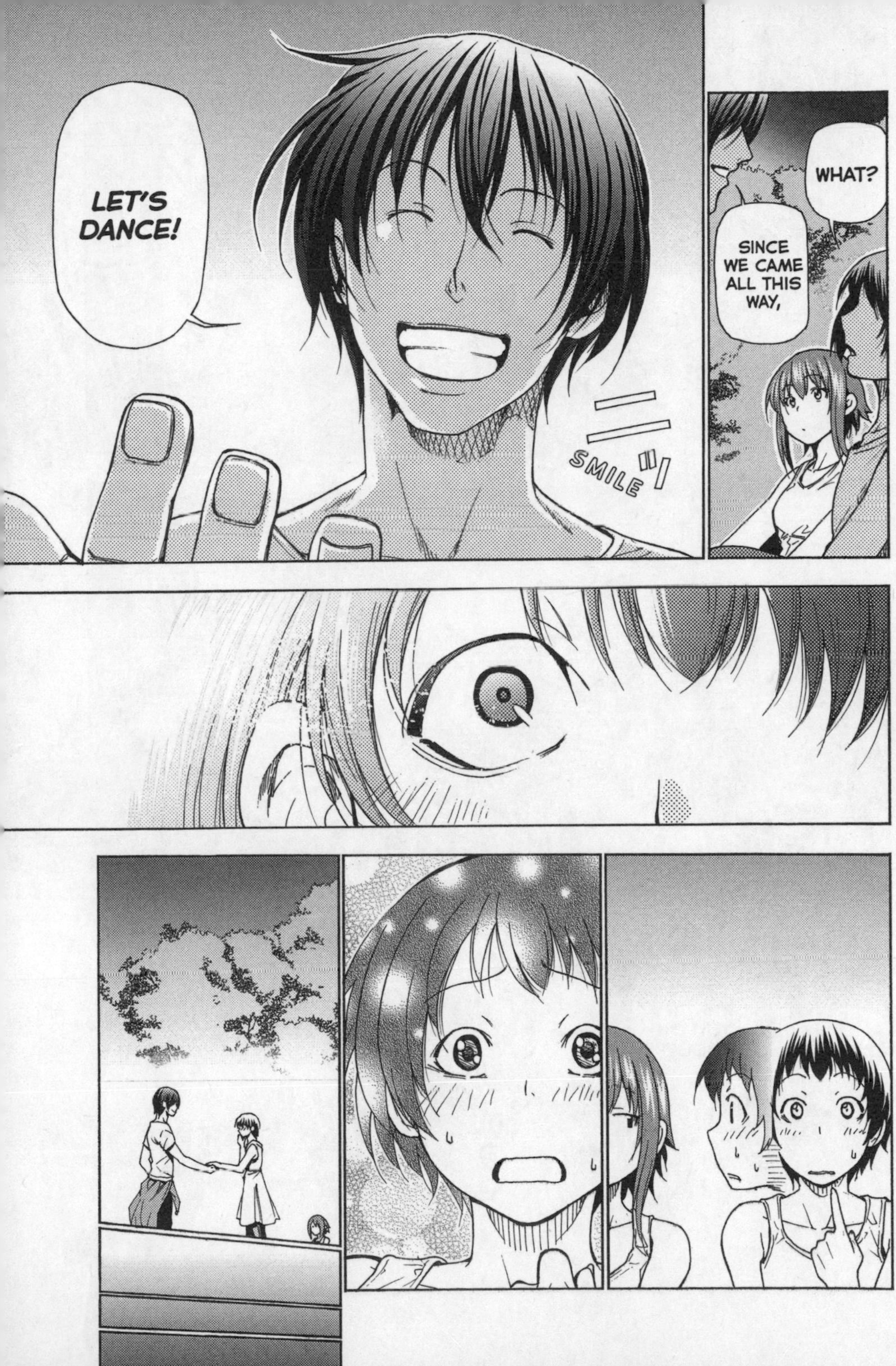
WHAT?
SINCE WE CAME ALL THIS WAY,
LET'S DANCE!
SMILE

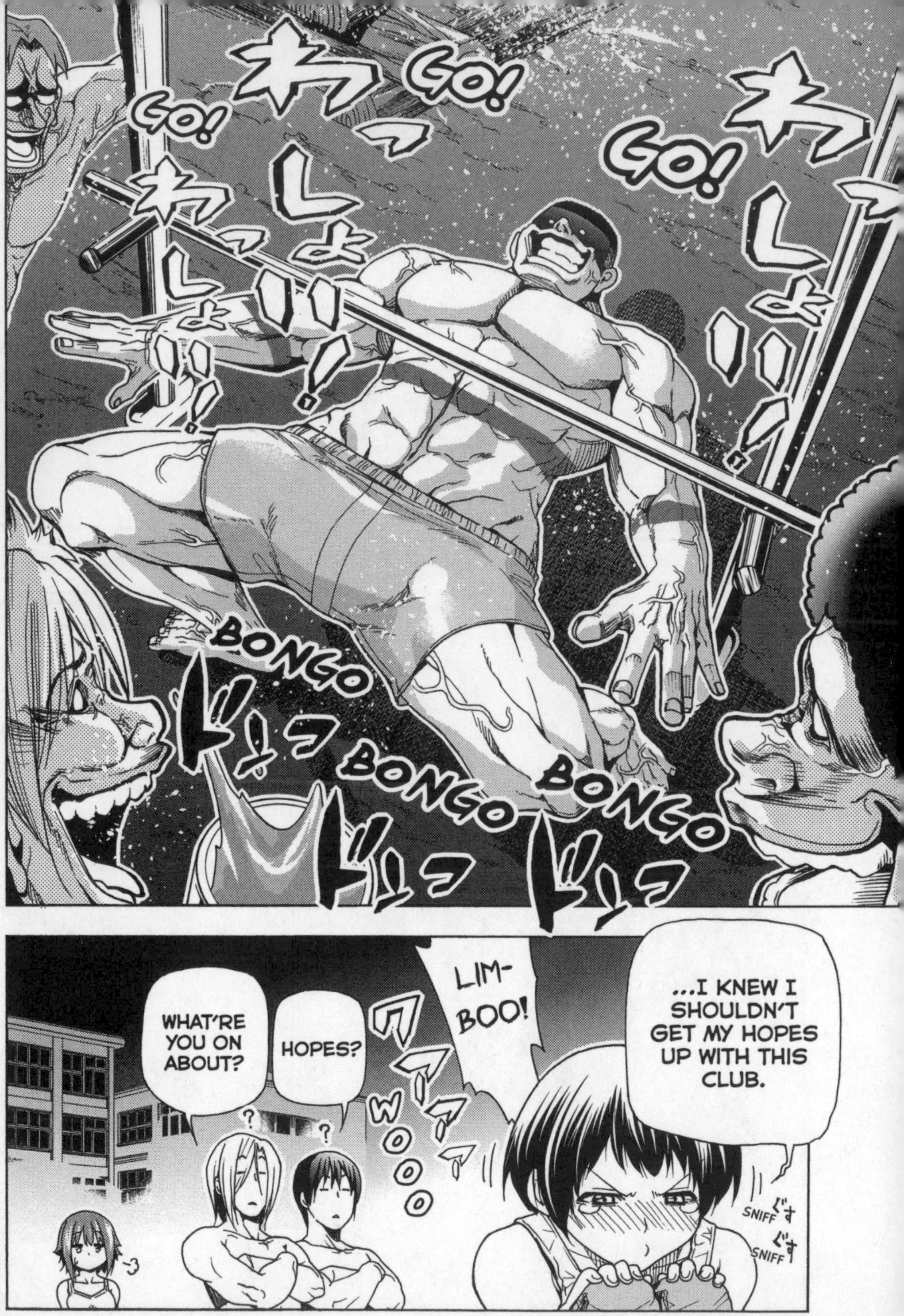
GO!
GO!
GO!
BONGO
BONGO
BONGO
...I KNEW I SHOULDN'T GET MY HOPES UP WITH THIS CLUB.
SNIFF
SNIFF
LIM-BOO!
WOOOO
HOPES?
WHAT'RE YOU ON ABOUT?

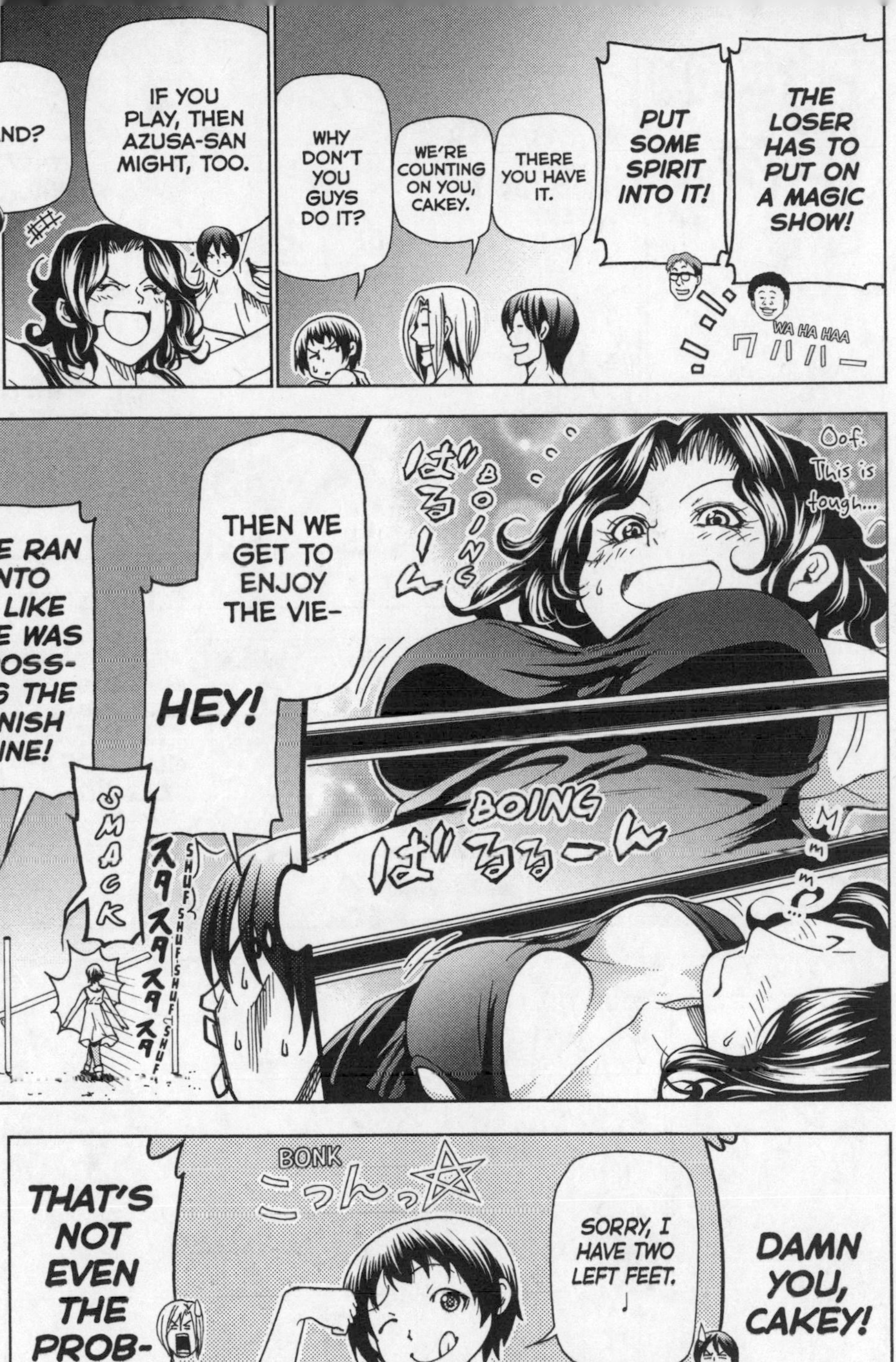
THE LOSER HAS TO PUT ON A MAGIC SHOW!
PUT SOME SPIRIT INTO IT!
WA HA HAA
ワハハー
THERE YOU HAVE IT.
WE'RE COUNTING ON YOU, CAKEY.
WHY DON'T YOU GUYS DO IT?
IF YOU PLAY, THEN AZUSA-SAN MIGHT, TOO.
AND?
Oof. This is tough...
BOING
ばるるーん
BOING
ばるるーん
Mmm...
THEN WE GET TO ENJOY THE VIE-
HEY!
SHE RAN INTO IT LIKE SHE WAS CROSSING THE FINISH LINE!
SMACK
SHUF SHUF SHUF SHUF
スタスタスタスタ
DAMN YOU, CAKEY!
SORRY, I HAVE TWO LEFT FEET.
BONK
こつんっ
THAT'S NOT EVEN THE PROBLEM!

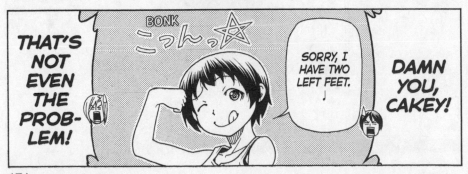

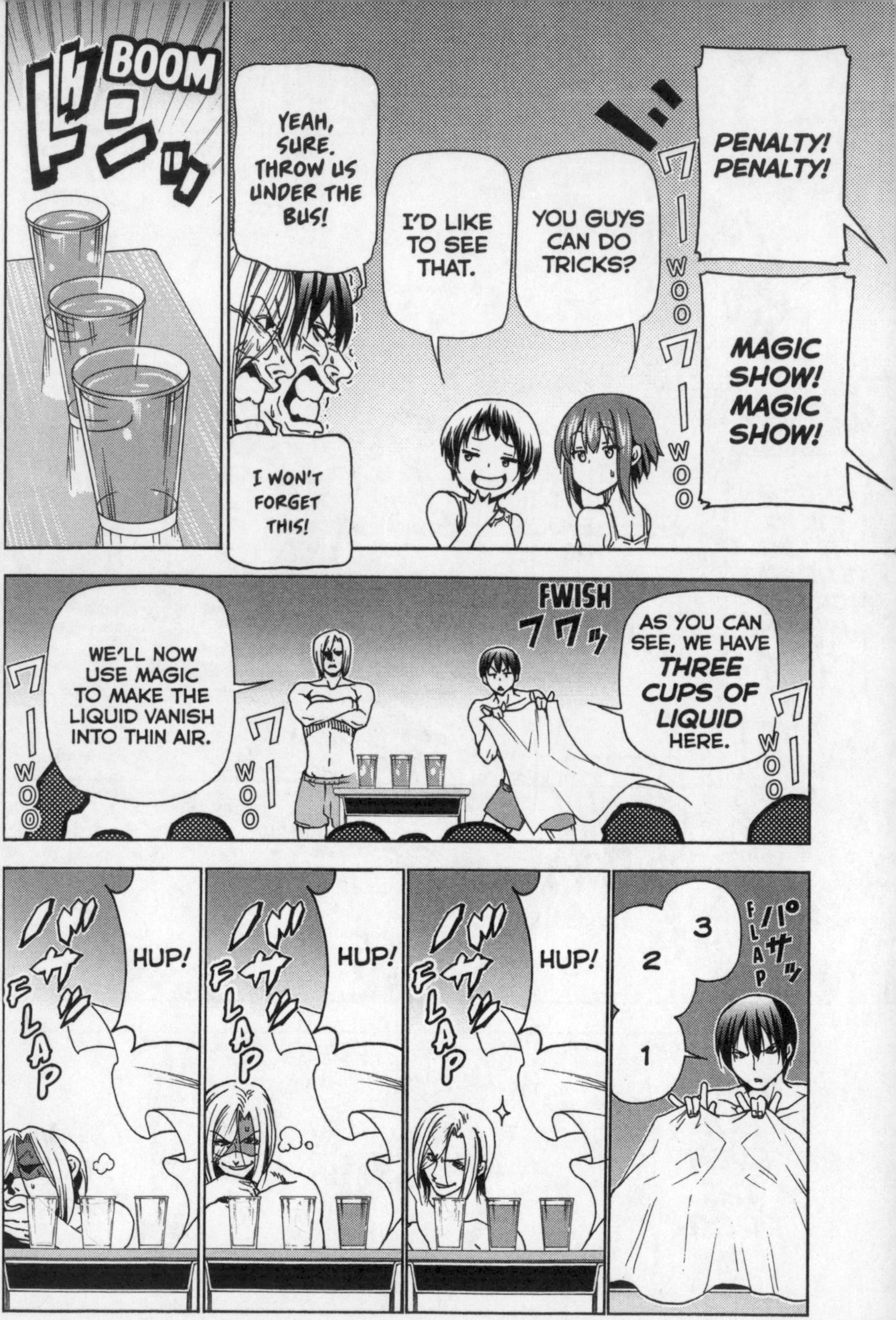
PENALTY! PENALTY!
MAGIC SHOW! MAGIC SHOW!
WOO
WOO
YOU GUYS CAN DO TRICKS?
I'D LIKE TO SEE THAT.
YEAH, SURE. THROW US UNDER THE BUS!
I WON'T FORGET THIS!
BOOM
FWISH
AS YOU CAN SEE, WE HAVE *THREE CUPS OF LIQUID* HERE.
WOO
WOO
WE'LL NOW USE MAGIC TO MAKE THE LIQUID VANISH INTO THIN AIR.
WOO
FLAP
3
2
1
HUP!
FLAP
HUP!
FLAP
HUP!
FLAP

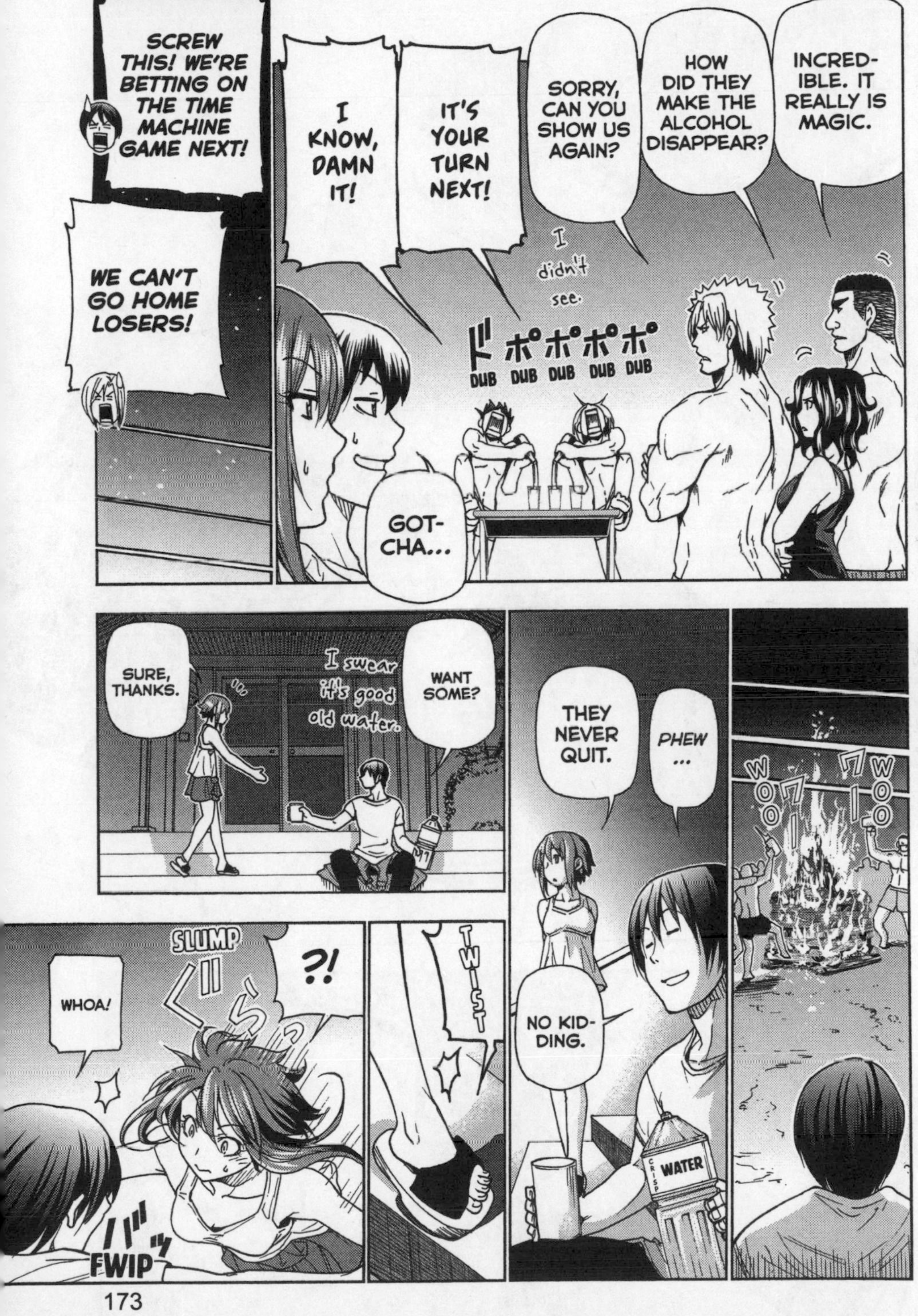
INCRED-IBLE. IT REALLY IS MAGIC.
HOW DID THEY MAKE THE ALCOHOL DISAPPEAR?
SORRY, CAN YOU SHOW US AGAIN?
I didn't see.
IT'S YOUR TURN NEXT!
I KNOW, DAMN IT!
ドポポポポ
DUB DUB DUB DUB DUB
GOT-CHA...
SCREW THIS! WE'RE BETTING ON THE TIME MACHINE GAME NEXT!
WE CAN'T GO HOME LOSERS!
WOO ワー WOO
PHEW...
THEY NEVER QUIT.
NO KID-DING.
WANT SOME?
I swear it's good old water.
SURE, THANKS.
WATER
CRISP
TWIST
SLUMP
くら
?!
WHOA!
バッ
FWIP

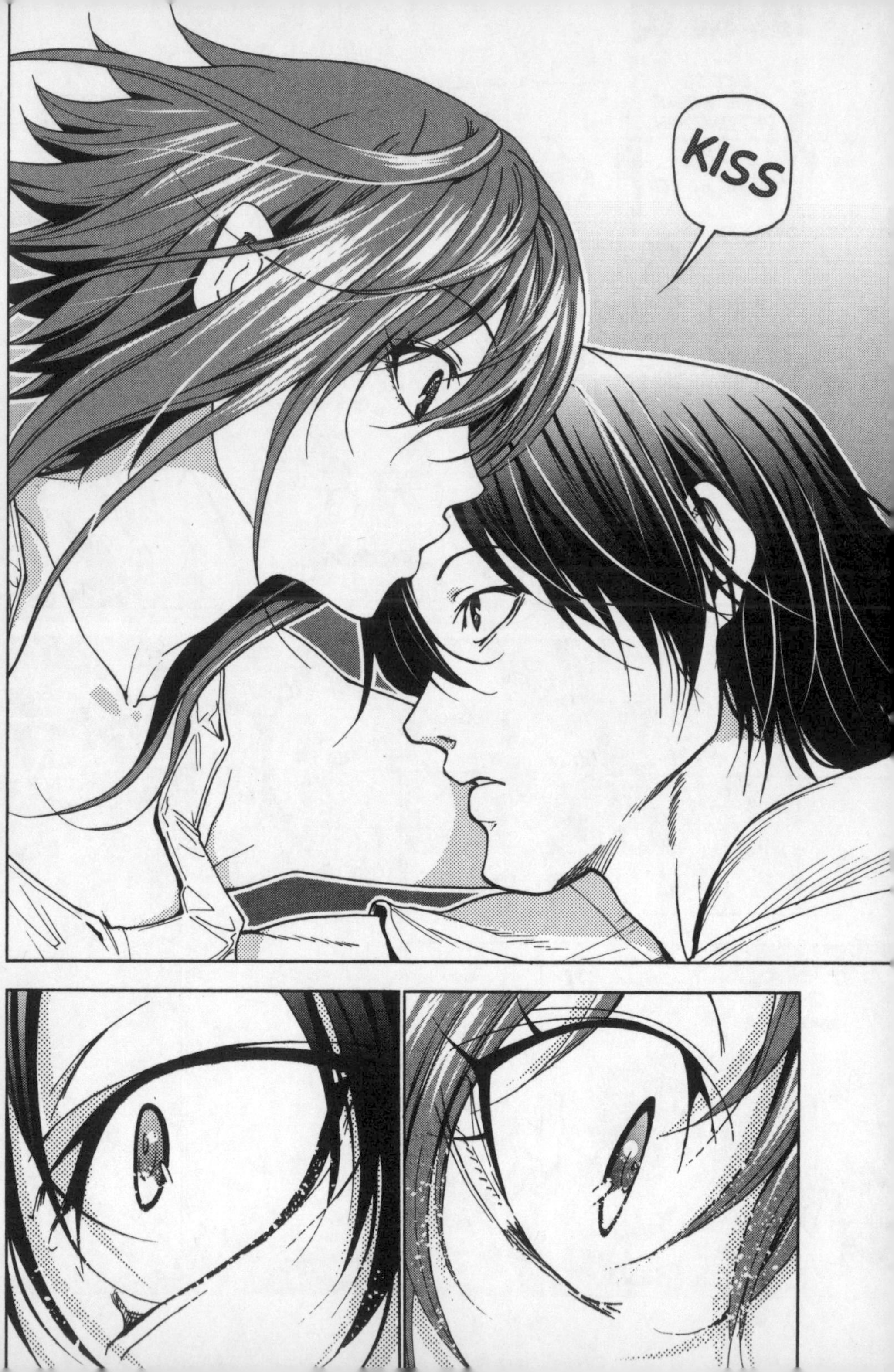
KISS

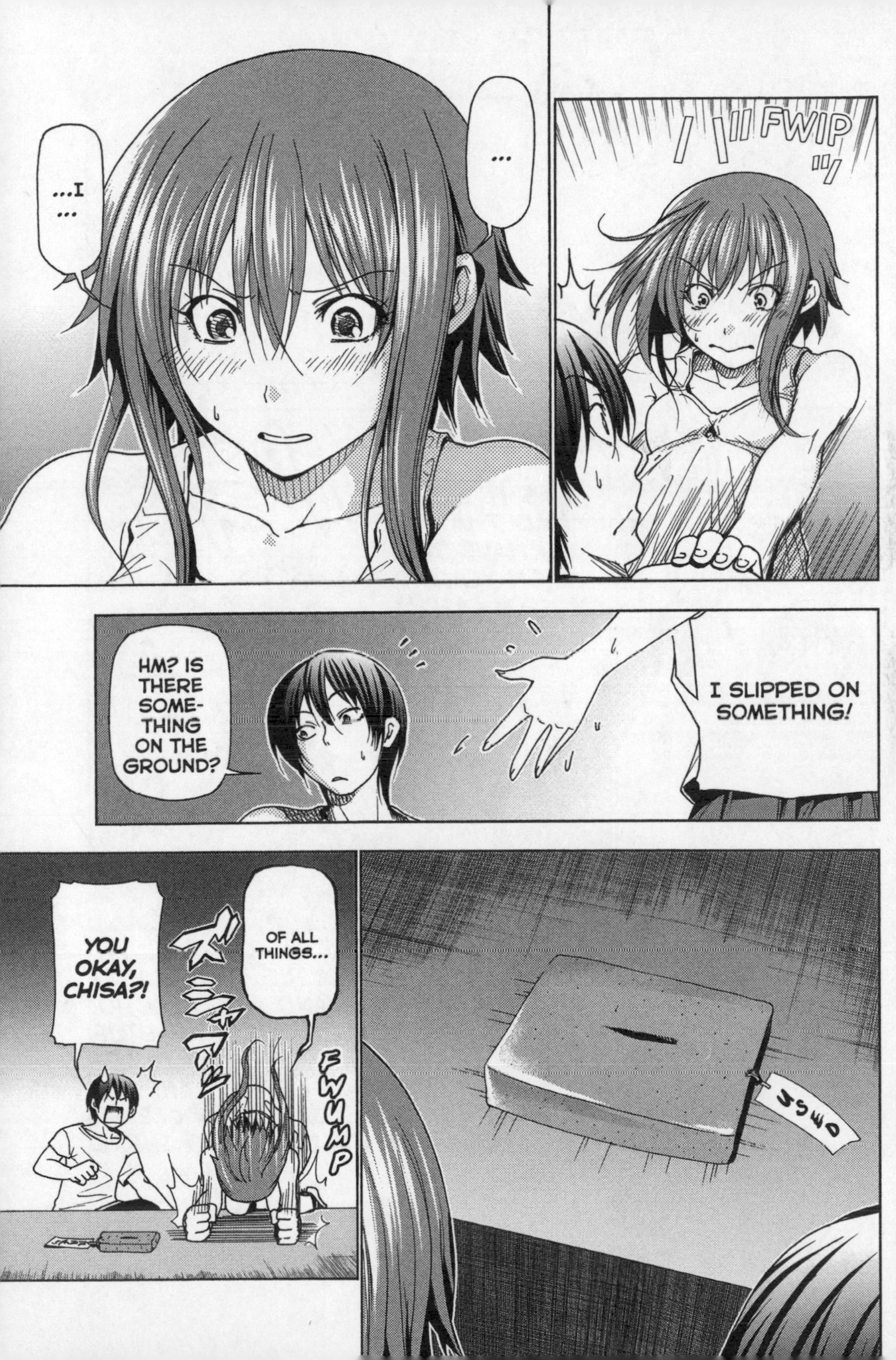
FWIP
...
...I ...
I SLIPPED ON SOMETHING!
HM? IS THERE SOMETHING ON THE GROUND?
OF ALL THINGS...
FWUMP
YOU OKAY, CHISA?!

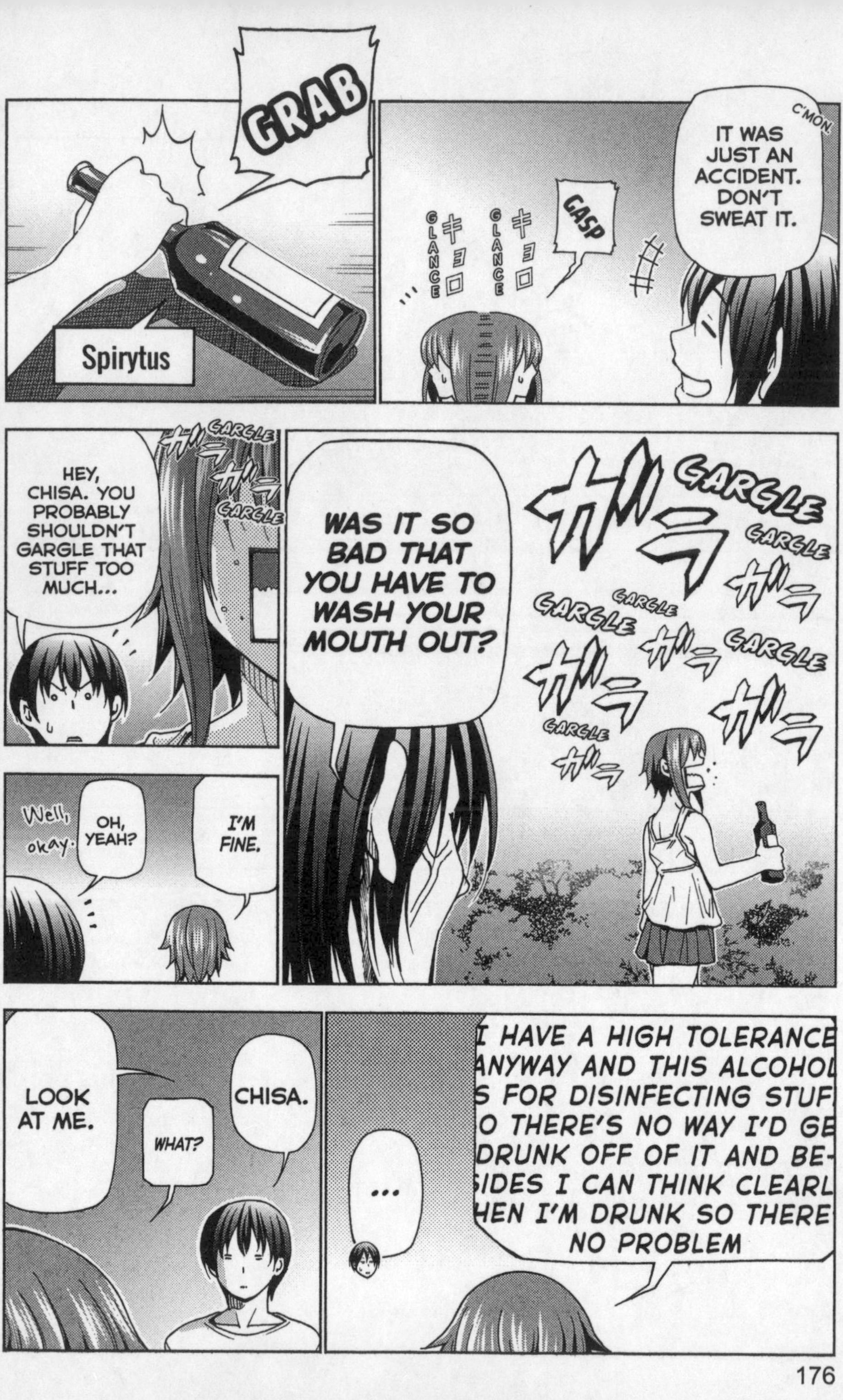
C'MON.
IT WAS JUST AN ACCIDENT. DON'T SWEAT IT.
GASP
キョロ GLANCE
キョロ GLANCE
GRAB
Spirytus
ガラ GARGLE
ガラ GARGLE
ガラ GARGLE
ガラ GARGLE
ガラ GARGLE
ガラ GARGLE
WAS IT SO BAD THAT YOU HAVE TO WASH YOUR MOUTH OUT?
ガラ GARGLE
ガラ GARGLE
HEY, CHISA. YOU PROBABLY SHOULDN'T GARGLE THAT STUFF TOO MUCH...
I'M FINE.
OH, YEAH?
Well, okay.
I HAVE A HIGH TOLERANCE ANYWAY AND THIS ALCOHOL S FOR DISINFECTING STUF O THERE'S NO WAY I'D GE DRUNK OFF OF IT AND BE-SIDES I CAN THINK CLEARL HEN I'M DRUNK SO THERE NO PROBLEM
...
CHISA.
WHAT?
LOOK AT ME.

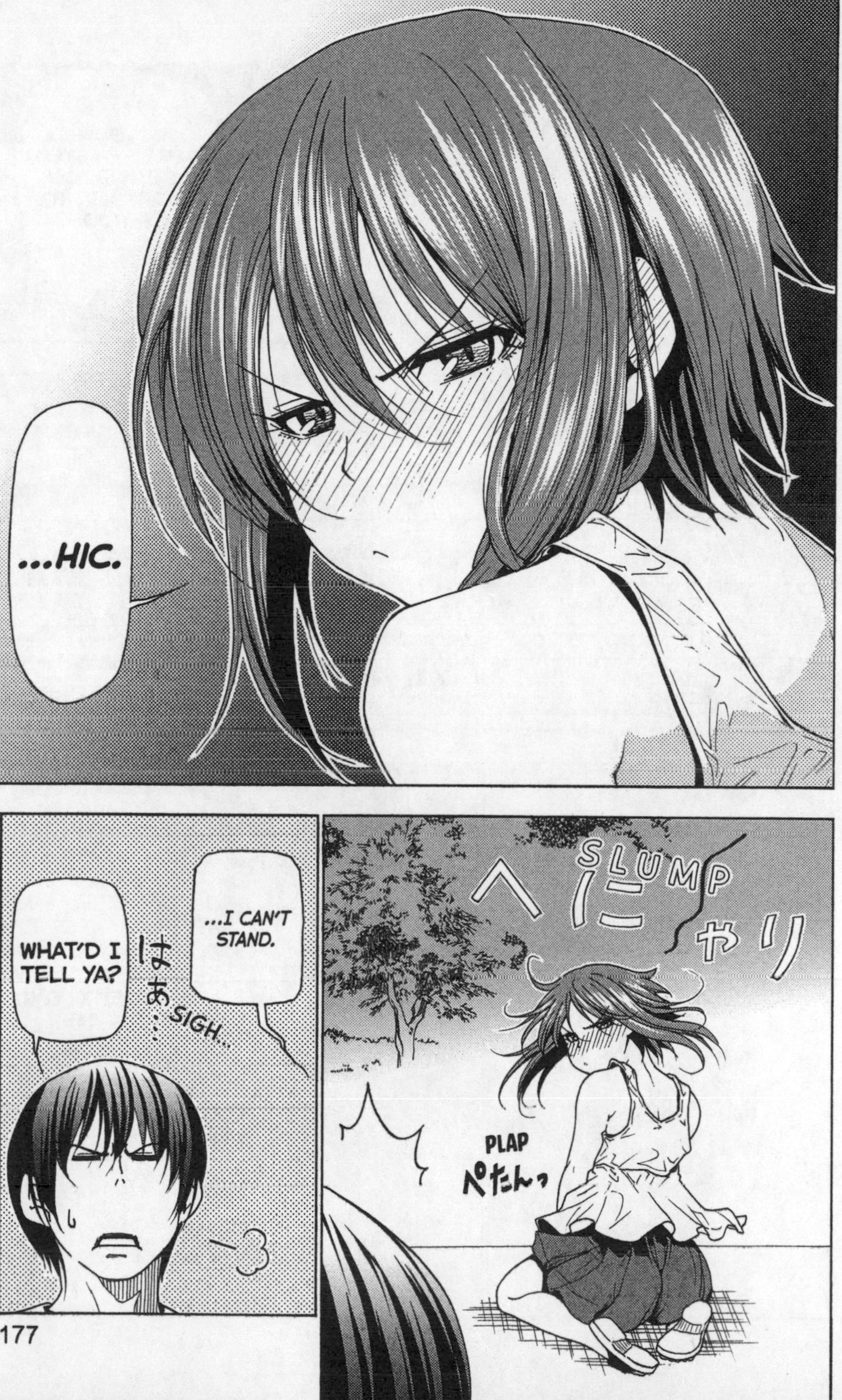
...HIC.
へにゃり
SLUMP
PLAP
ぺたんっ
...I CAN'T STAND.
はぁ…
SIGH...
WHAT'D I TELL YA?

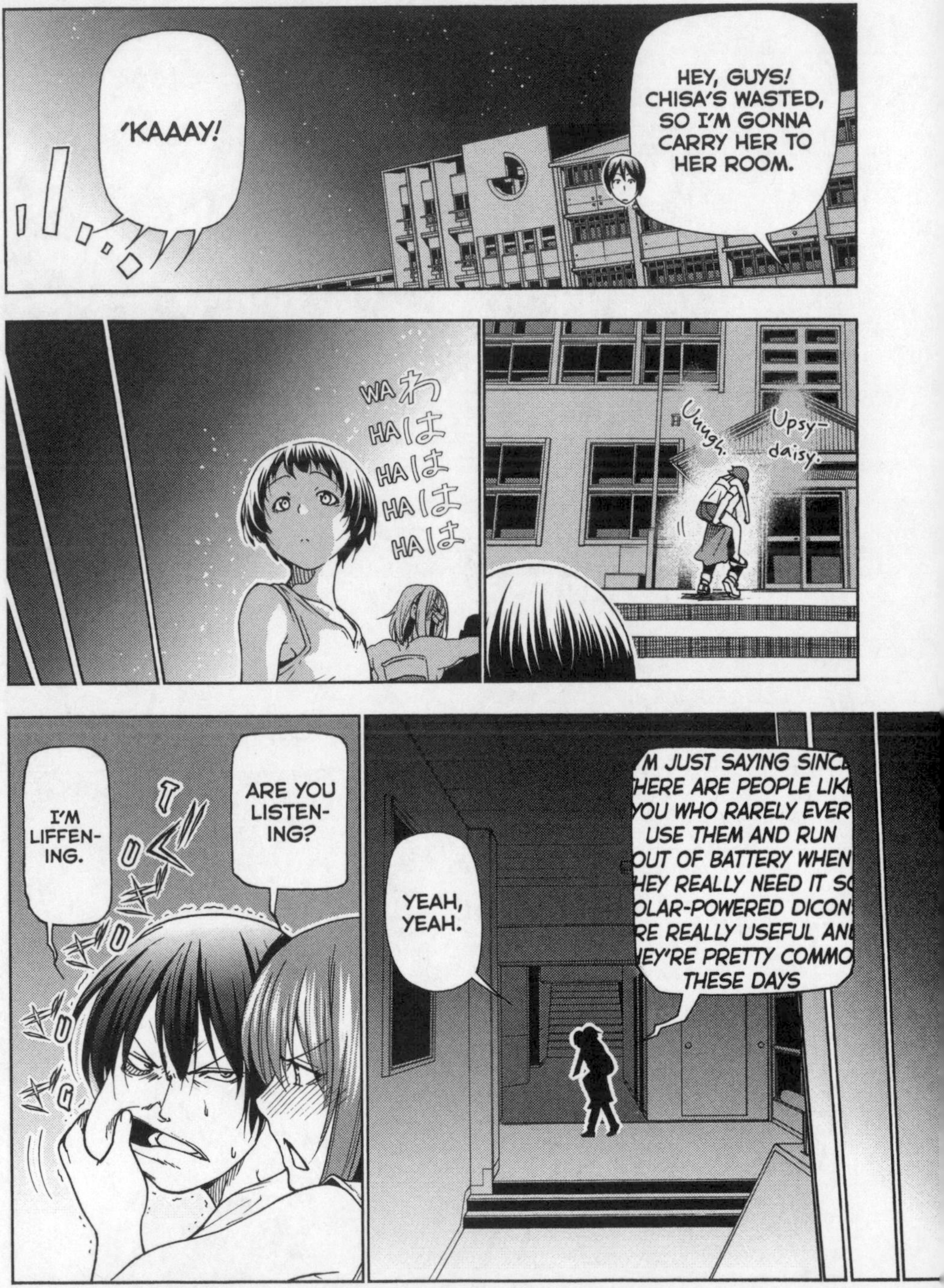
HEY, GUYS! CHISA'S WASTED, SO I'M GONNA CARRY HER TO HER ROOM.
'KAAAY!
Upsy-daisy.
Uuugh.
WA わ HA は HA は HA は HA は
M JUST SAYING SINC HERE ARE PEOPLE LIK YOU WHO RARELY EVER USE THEM AND RUN OUT OF BATTERY WHEN HEY REALLY NEED IT S OLAR-POWERED DICON RE REALLY USEFUL AN HEY'RE PRETTY COMMO THESE DAYS
YEAH, YEAH.
ARE YOU LISTEN-ING?
I'M LIFFEN-ING.

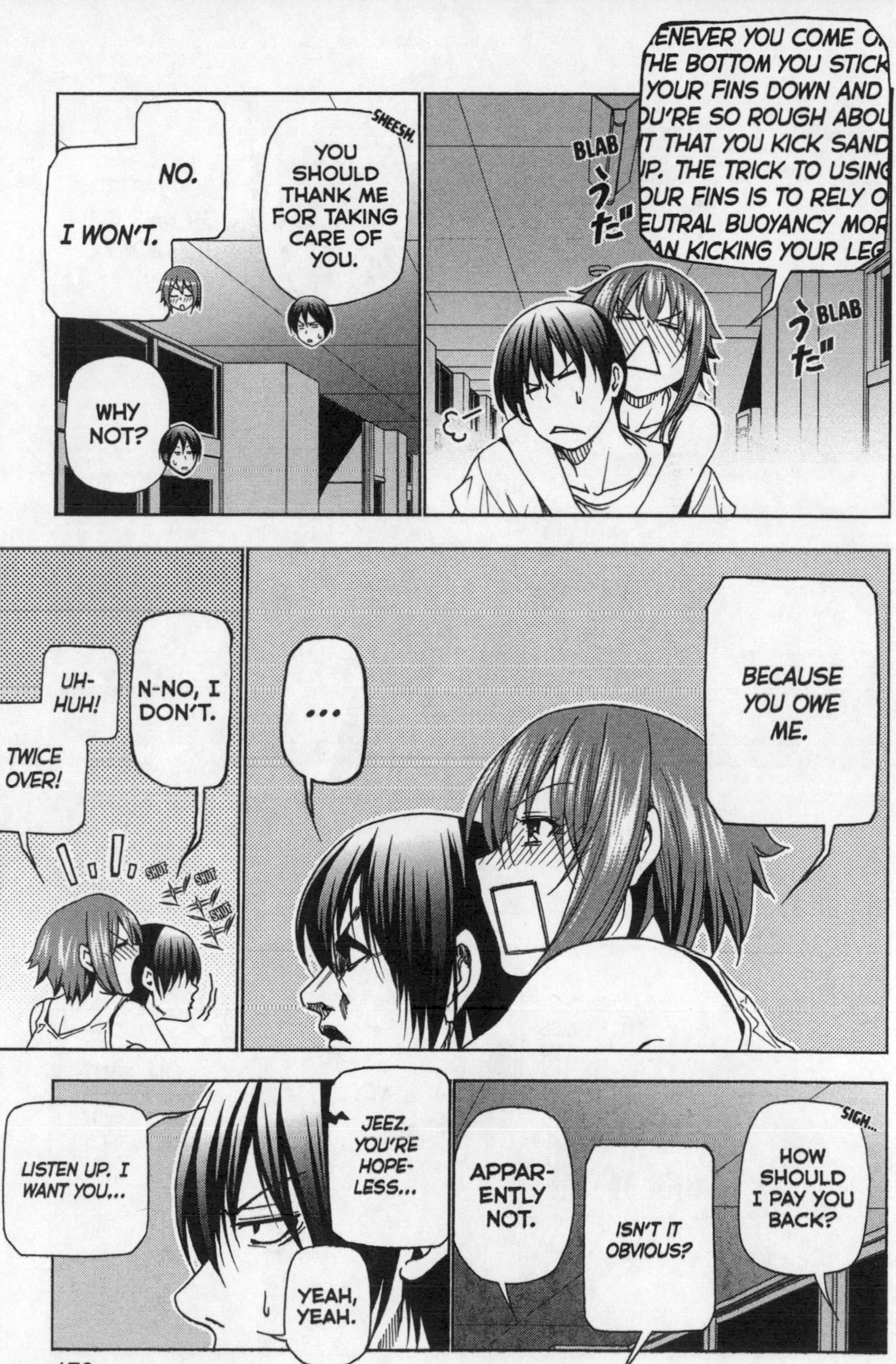
ENEVER YOU COME O
HE BOTTOM YOU STICK
YOUR FINS DOWN AND
OU'RE SO ROUGH ABOU
T THAT YOU KICK SAND
P. THE TRICK TO USING
OUR FINS IS TO RELY O
EUTRAL BUOYANCY MOR
AN KICKING YOUR LEG
BLAB うだ
BLAB うだ
SHEESH.
YOU SHOULD THANK ME FOR TAKING CARE OF YOU.
NO. I WON'T.
WHY NOT?
BECAUSE YOU OWE ME.
...
N-NO, I DON'T.
UH-HUH! TWICE OVER!
SHUT
SHUT
SHUT
SIGH...
HOW SHOULD I PAY YOU BACK?
ISN'T IT OBVIOUS?
APPARENTLY NOT.
JEEZ. YOU'RE HOPELESS...
LISTEN UP. I WANT YOU...
YEAH, YEAH.

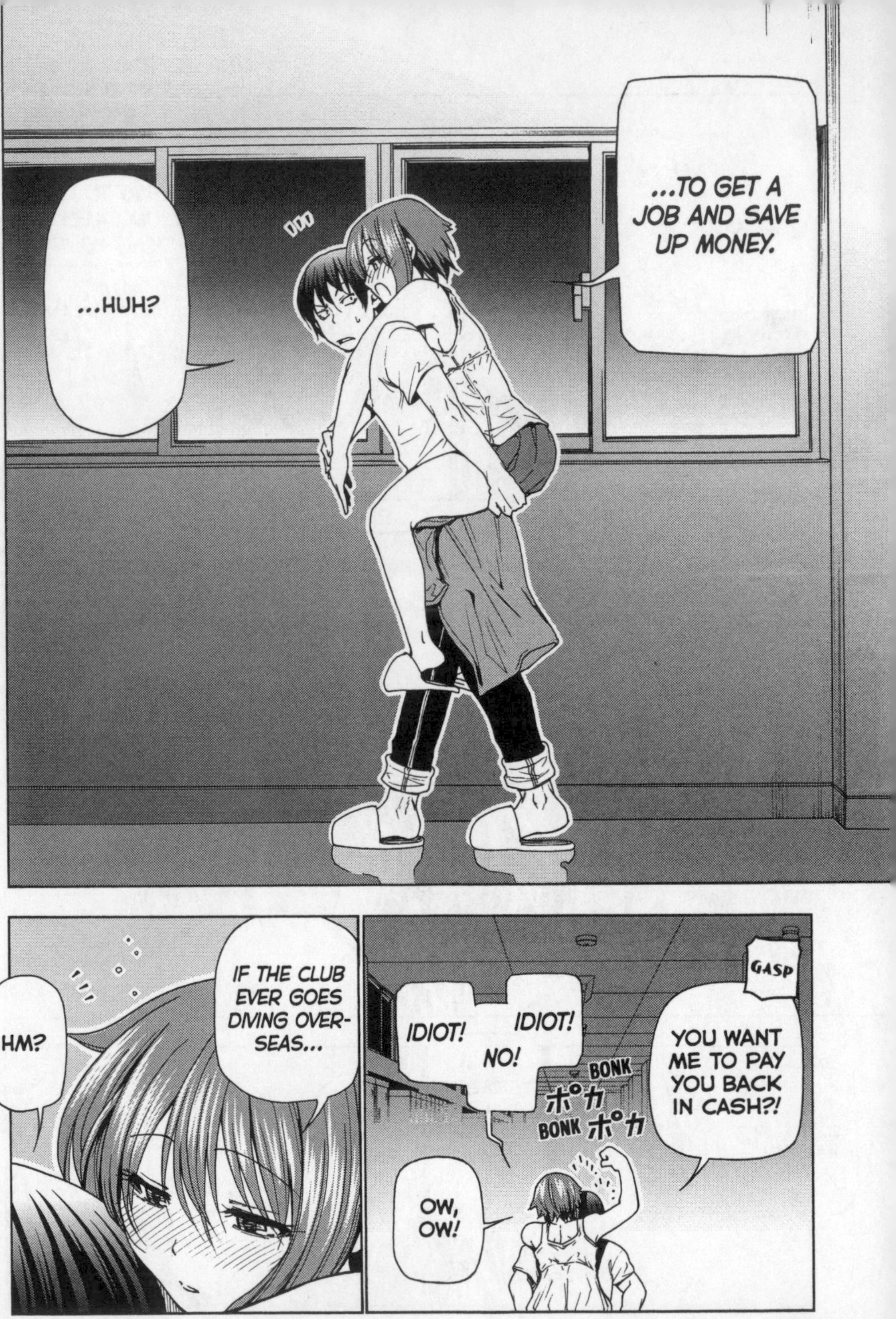
...TO GET A JOB AND SAVE UP MONEY.
...HUH?
GASP
YOU WANT ME TO PAY YOU BACK IN CASH?!
IDIOT!
NO!
IDIOT!
BONK ポカ
BONK ポカ
OW, OW!
IF THE CLUB EVER GOES DIVING OVER-SEAS...
HM?

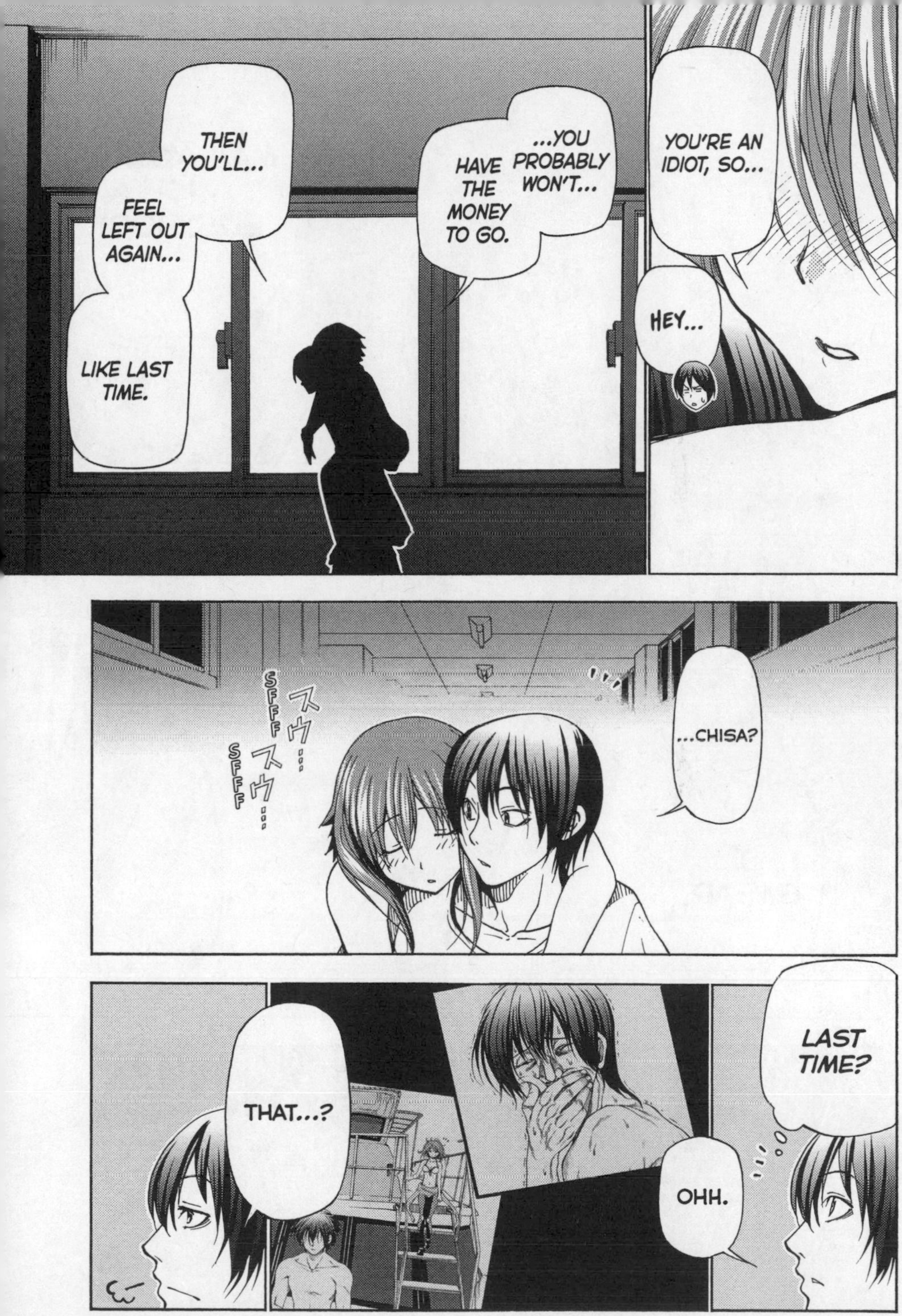
YOU'RE AN IDIOT, SO...
HEY...
...YOU PROBABLY WON'T...
HAVE THE MONEY TO GO.
THEN YOU'LL...
FEEL LEFT OUT AGAIN...
LIKE LAST TIME.
...CHISA?
スゥ... SFFF
スゥ... SFFF
LAST TIME?
OHH.
THAT...?

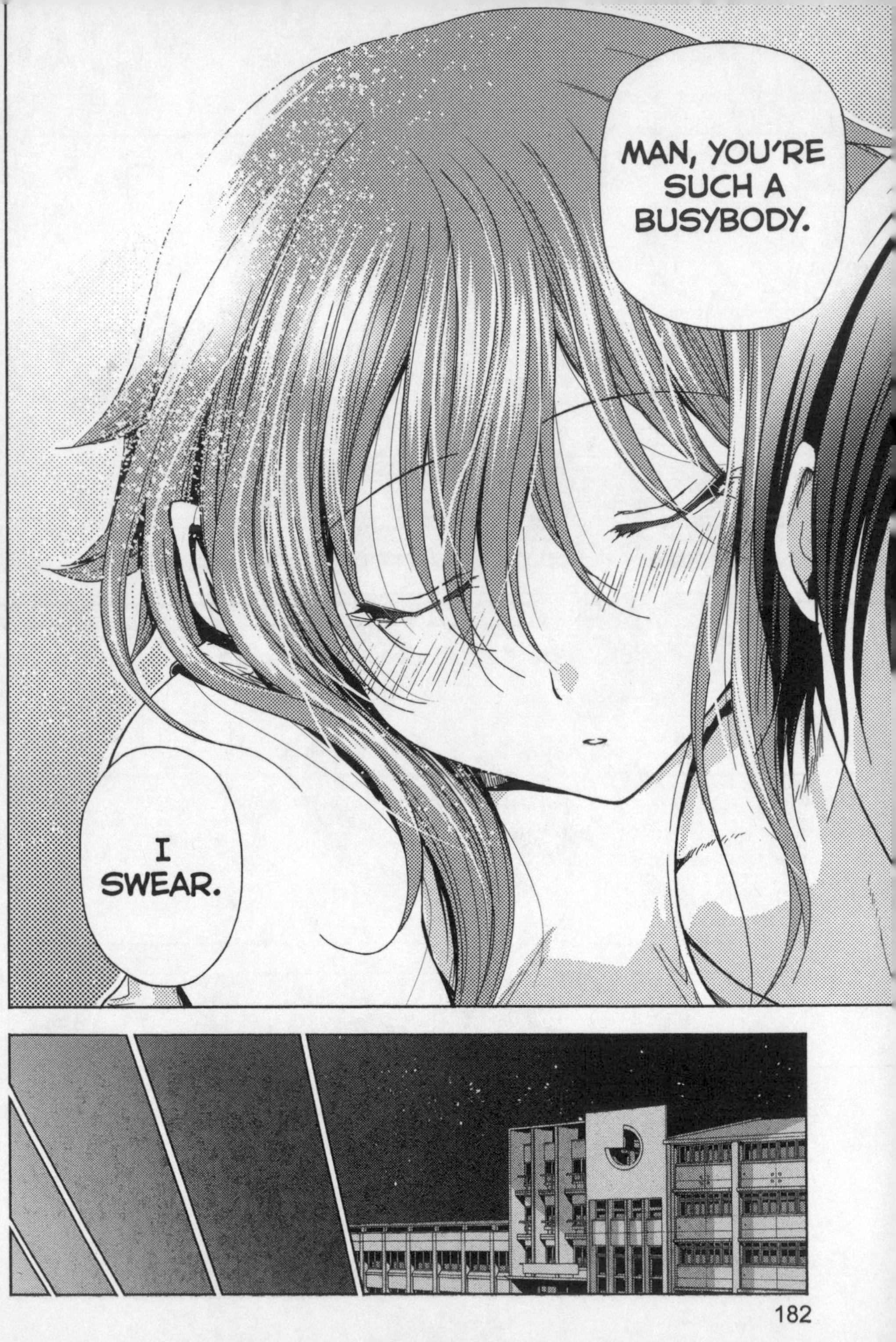
MAN, YOU'RE SUCH A BUSYBODY.
I SWEAR.

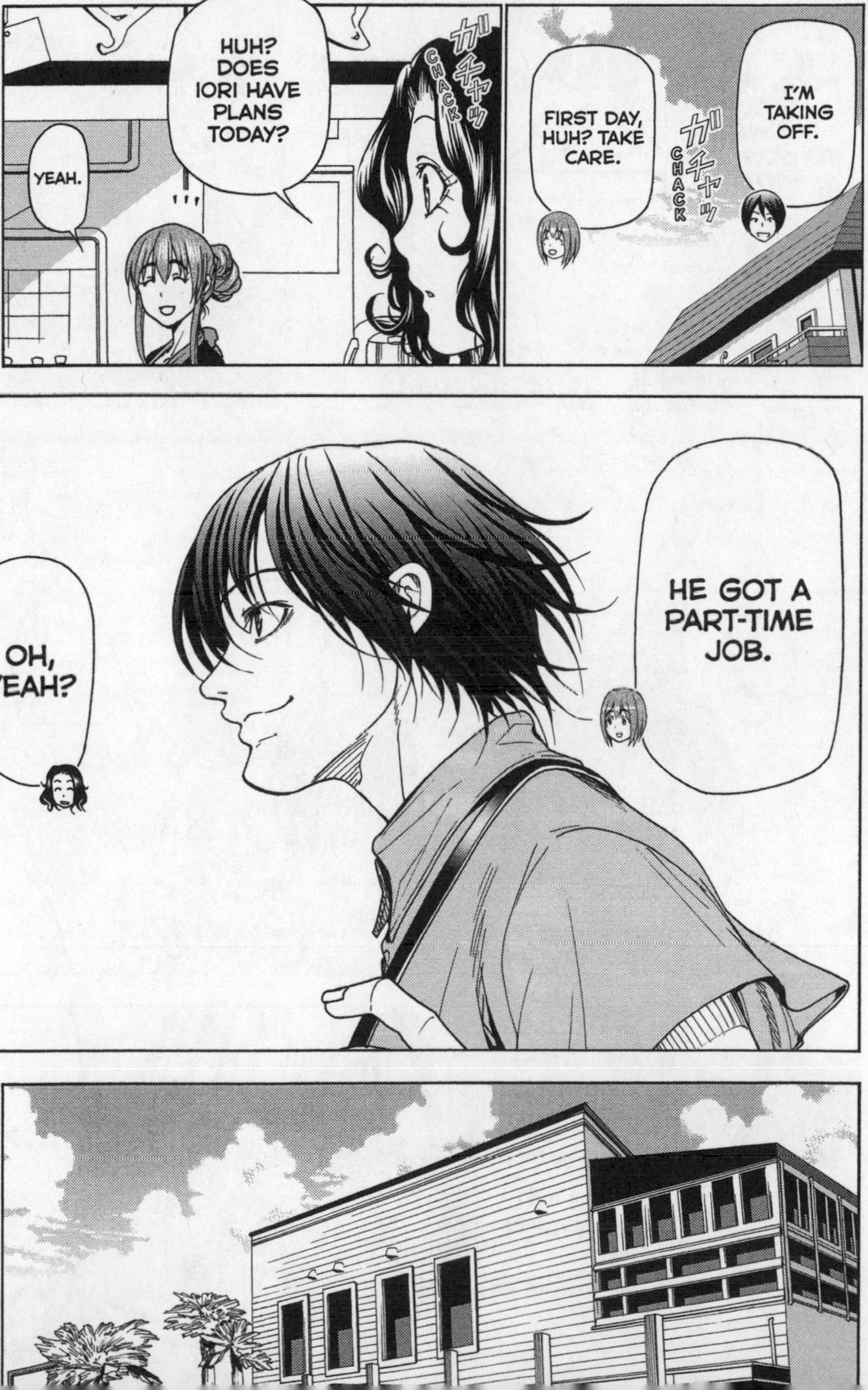
I'M TAKING OFF.
ガチャッ CHACK
FIRST DAY, HUH? TAKE CARE.
ガチャッ CHACK
HUH? DOES IORI HAVE PLANS TODAY?
YEAH.
HE GOT A PART-TIME JOB.
OH, YEAH?

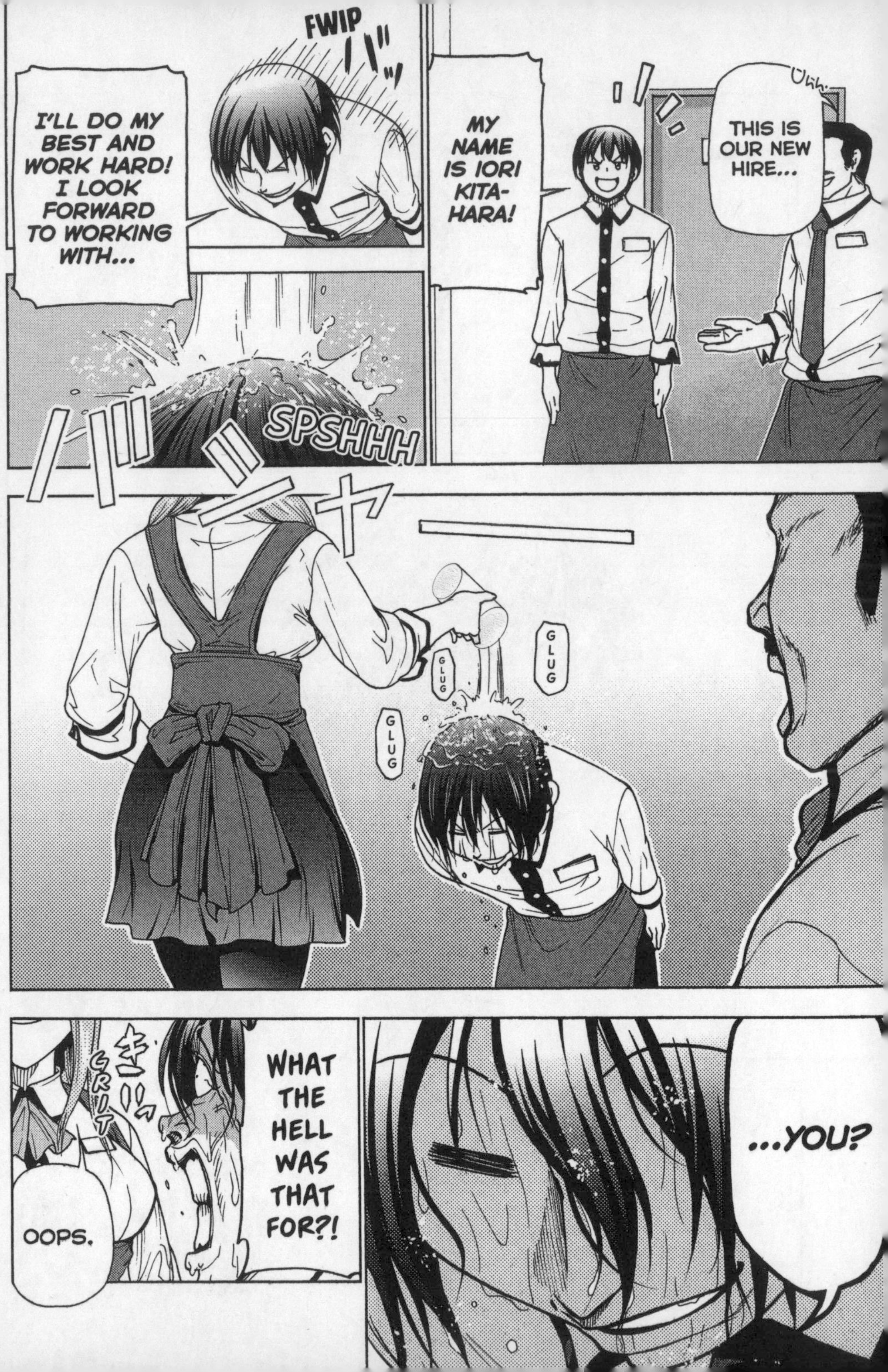

Uhh.
THIS IS OUR NEW HIRE...
MY NAME IS IORI KITA-HARA!
FWIP
I'LL DO MY BEST AND WORK HARD! I LOOK FORWARD TO WORKING WITH...
SPSHHH
GLUG
GLUG
GLUG
...YOU?
WHAT THE HELL WAS THAT FOR?!
GRIT
OOPS.

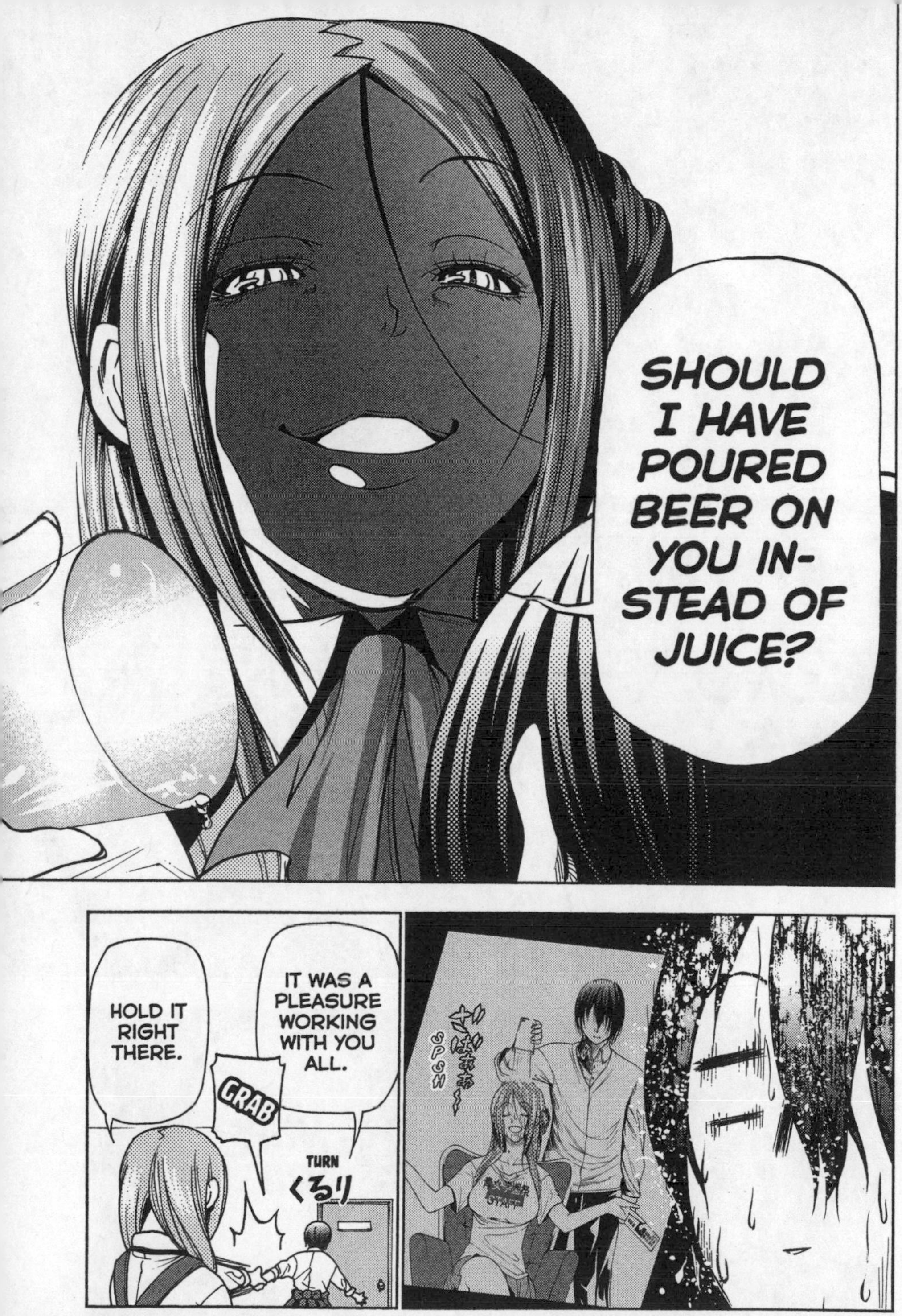
SHOULD I HAVE POURED BEER ON YOU IN-STEAD OF JUICE?
SPSH
ざばぁぁ～
IT WAS A PLEASURE WORKING WITH YOU ALL.
HOLD IT RIGHT THERE.
GRAB
TURN
くるり

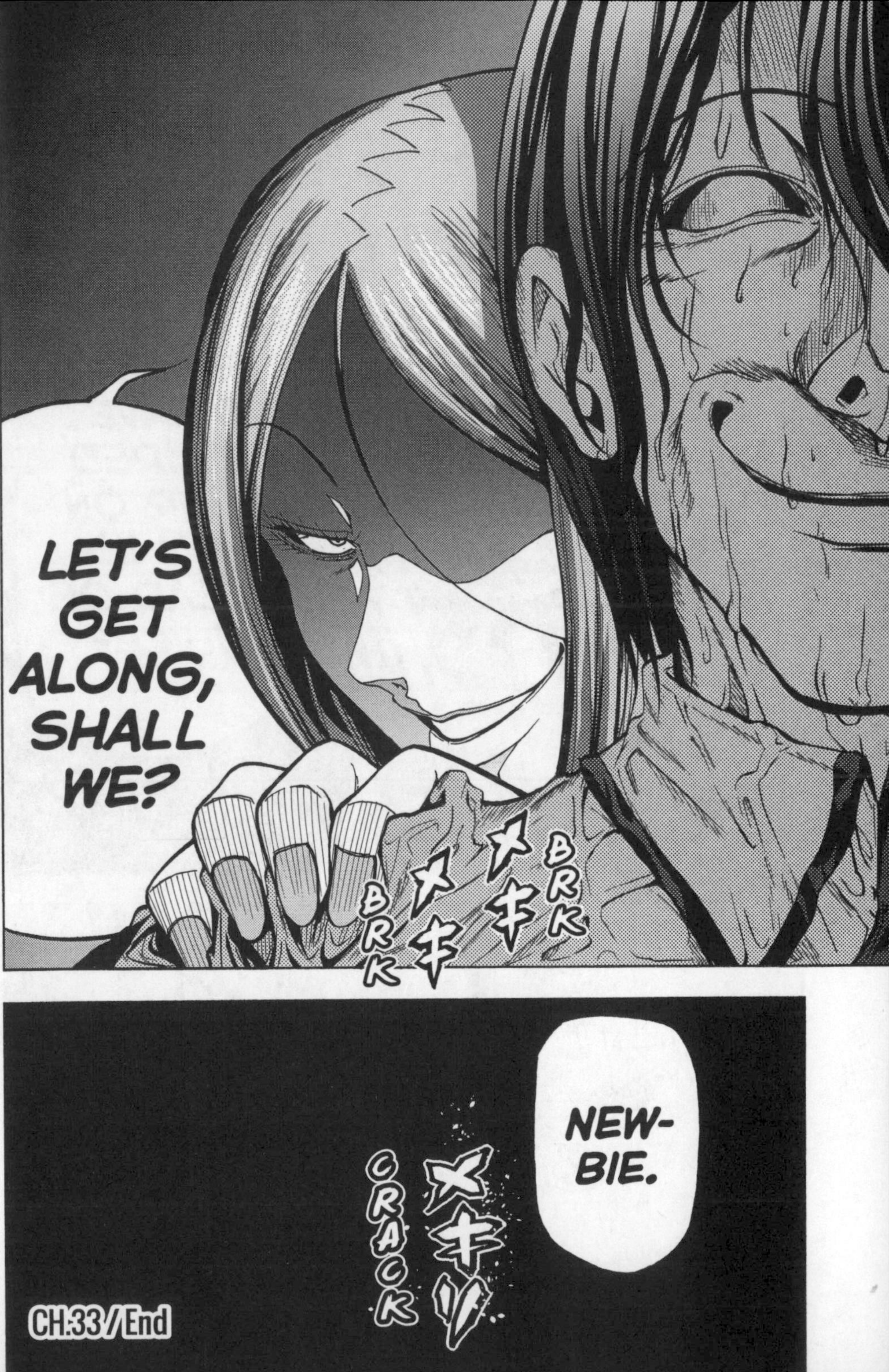

LET'S GET ALONG, SHALL WE?
BRK BRK
NEW-BIE.
CRACK
CH:33/End

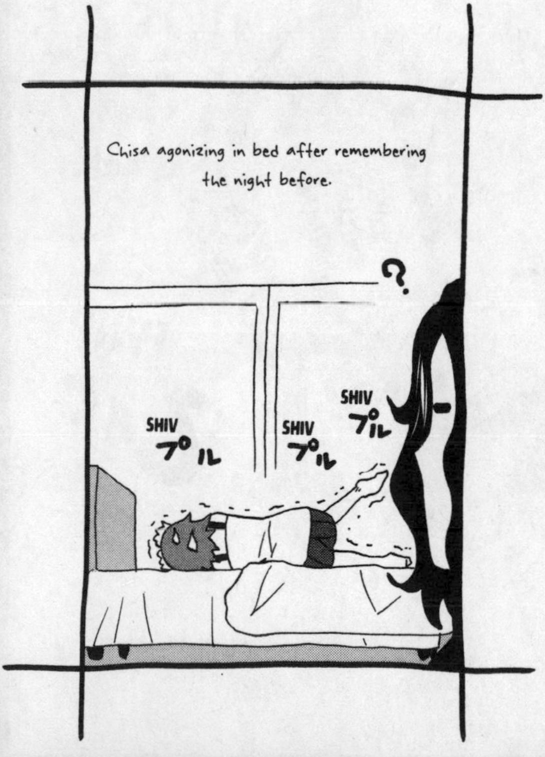
Chisa agonizing in bed after remembering the night before.
?
SHIV
プル
SHIV
プル
SHIV
プル

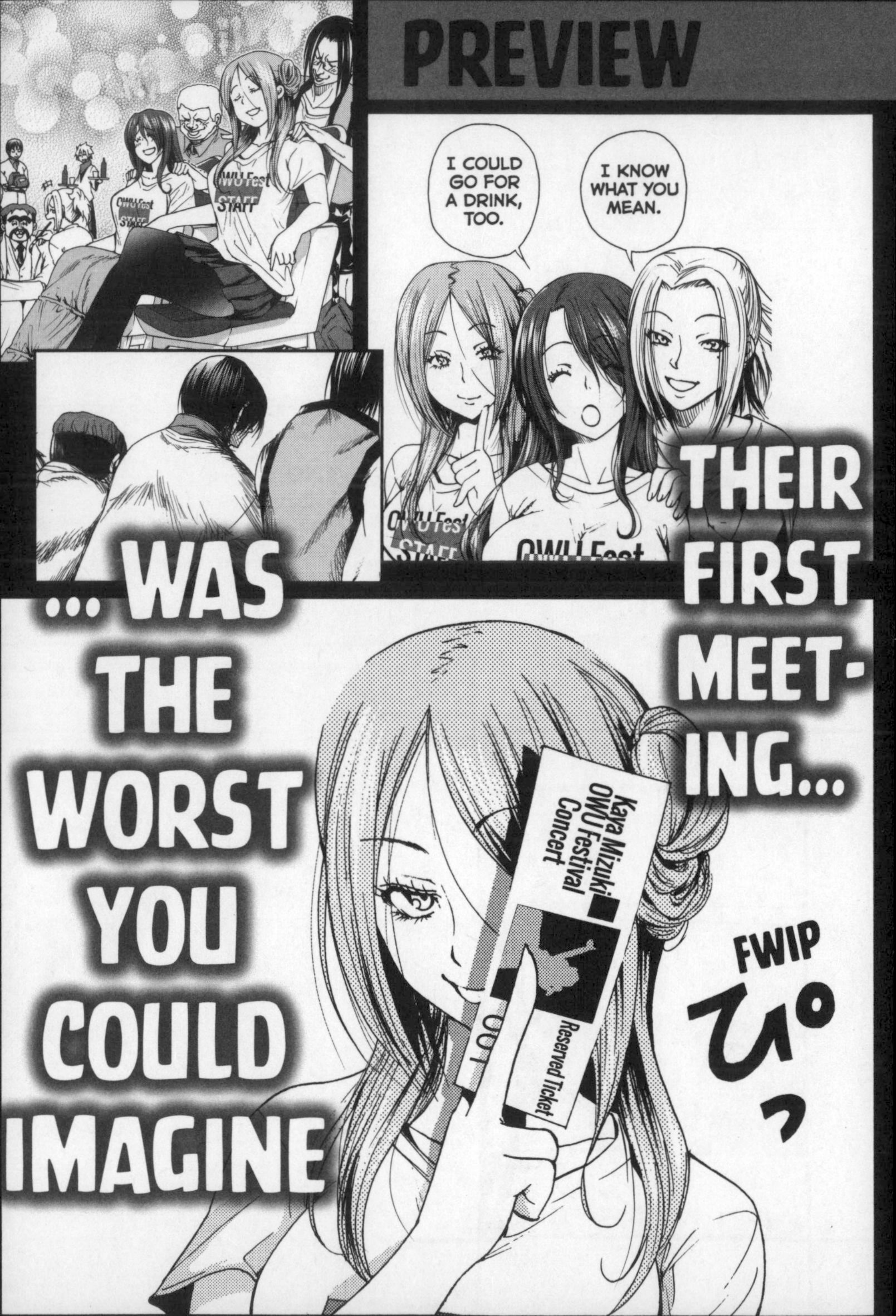
PREVIEW
OWU Fest
STAFF
I KNOW WHAT YOU MEAN.
I COULD GO FOR A DRINK, TOO.
THEIR FIRST MEET-ING...
...WAS THE WORST YOU COULD IMAGINE
Kaya Mizuki OWU Festival Concert
Reserved Ticket
001
FWIP
ぴっ

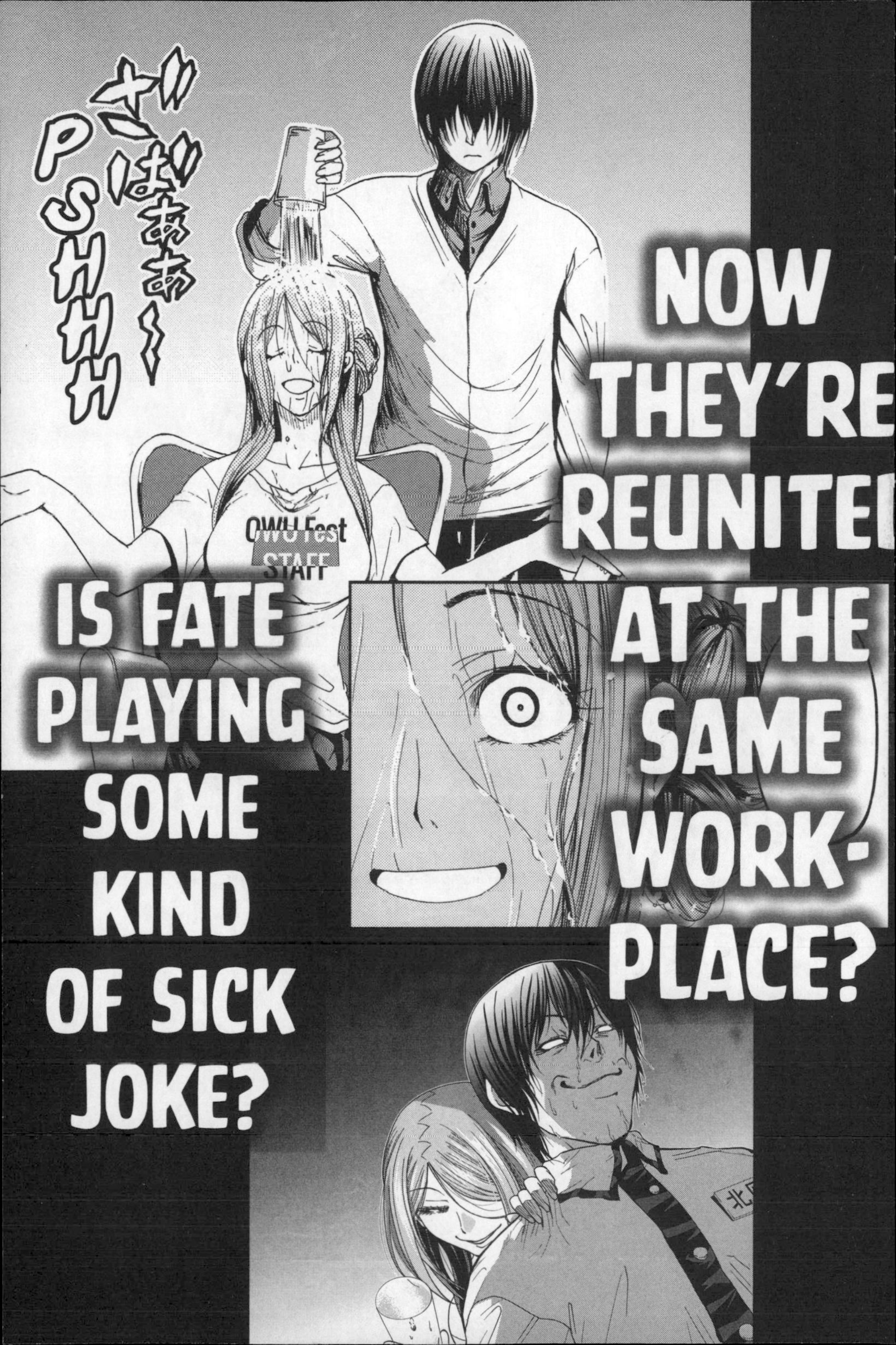
ざばああ〜
PSHHHH
OWU Fest
STAFF
NOW THEY'RE REUNITED AT THE SAME WORK-PLACE?
IS FATE PLAYING SOME KIND OF SICK JOKE?

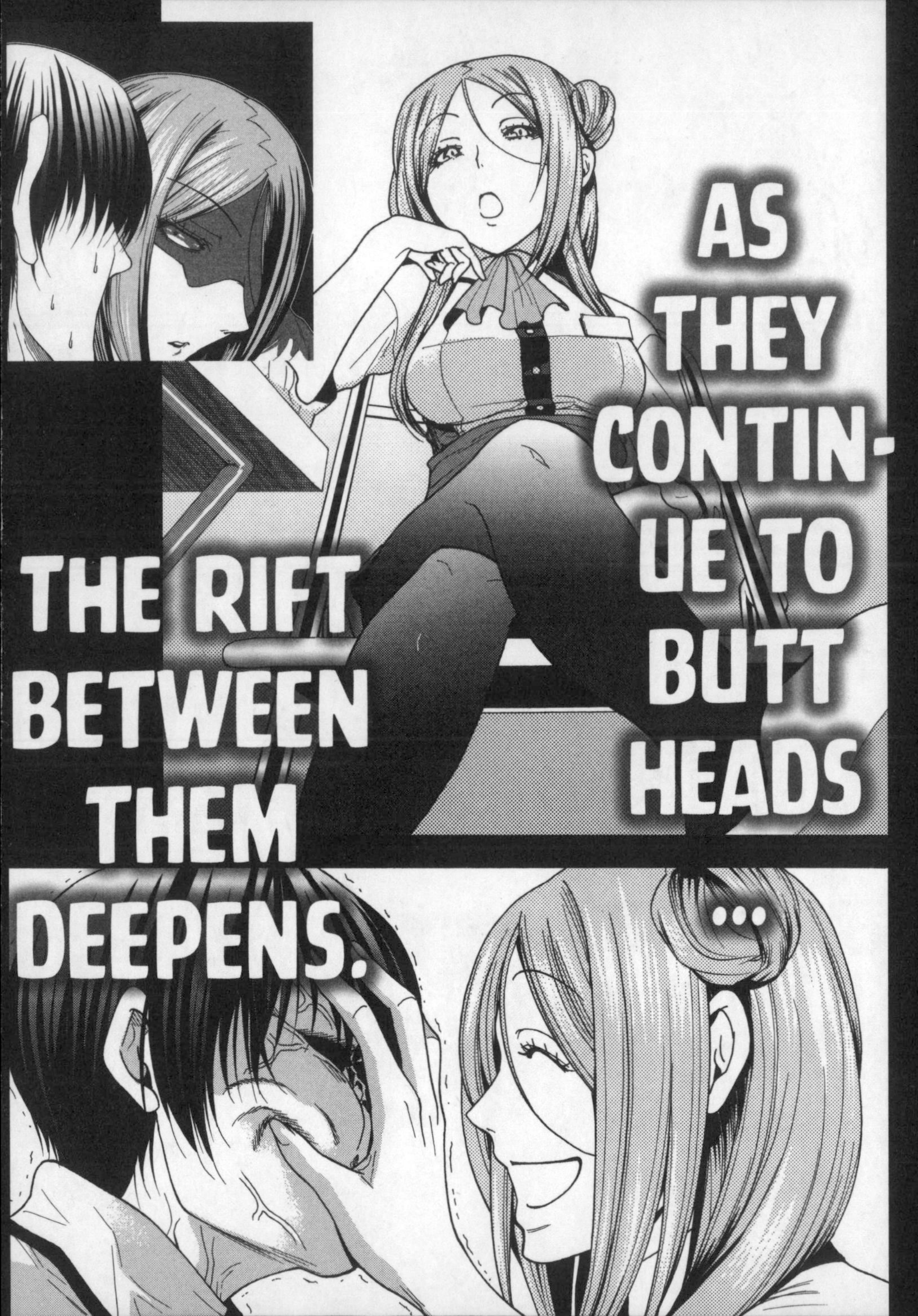
AS THEY CONTIN-UE TO BUTT HEADS
THE RIFT BETWEEN THEM DEEPENS.
...

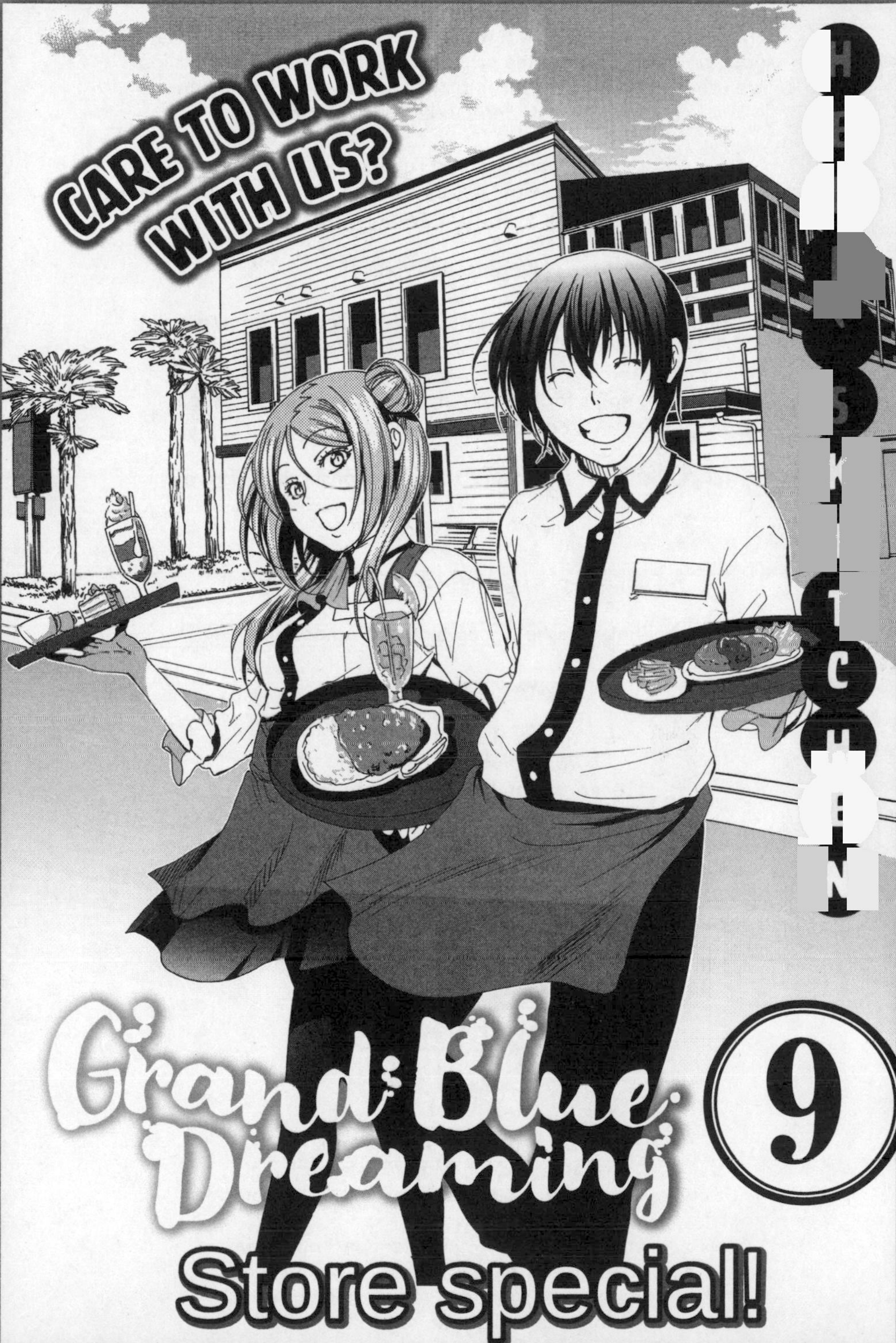
CARE TO WORK WITH US?
Grand Blue Dreaming
9
Store special!

A Kodansha Comics Trade Paperback Original
*Grand Blue Dreaming 8* copyright © 2017 Kenji Inoue/Kimitake Yoshioka
English translation copyright © 2019 Kenji Inoue/Kimitake Yoshioka

All rights reserved.

Published in the United States by Kodansha Comics, an imprint of Kodansha USA Publishing, LLC, New York.

Publication rights for this English edition arranged through Kodansha Ltd., Tokyo.

First published in Japan in 2017 by Kodansha Ltd., Tokyo.

ISBN 978-1-63236-837-9

Original cover design by YUKI YOSHIDA (futaba)

Printed in the United States of America.

www.kodansha.us

9 8 7 6 5 4 3
Translation: Adam Hirsch
Lettering: Jan Lan Ivan Concepcion
Editing: Sarah Tilson and David Yoo
Editorial Assistance: YKS Services LLC/SKY Japan, INC.
Kodansha Comics edition cover design by Phil Balsman

Publisher: Kiichiro Sugawara
Managing editor: Maya Rosewood
Vice president of marketing & publicity: Naho Yamada

Director of publishing services: Ben Applegate
Associate director of operations: Stephen Pakula
Publishing services managing editor: Noelle Webster
Assistant production manager: Emi Lotto